Organisational Change

Organisational Change

Harsh Pathak

Visiting Faculty
Jawaharlal Nehru
University and Amity
University

PEARSON

Senior Acquisitions Editor: Praveen Tiwari
Assistant Production Editor: Amrita Naskar
Composition: Tej Composers

ISBN 978-81-775-8431-8

First Impression, 2011

Published by Pearson India Education Services Pvt.Ltd,CIN:U72200TN2005PTC057128.
Formerly known as TutorVista Global Pvt Ltd, licensees of Pearson Education in South Asia

Head Office: 7th Floor, knowledge Boulevard, A-8(A) Sector-62, Noida (U.P) 201309, India

Registered Office: Module G4, Ground Floor, Elnet Software City, TS -140,Block 2 & 9
Rajiv Gandhi Salai, Taramani, Chennai, Tamil Nadu 600113.,Fax: 080-30461003,
Phone: 080-30461060, www.pearson.co.in email id: companysecretary.india@pearson.com

Digitally Printed in India by Repro India Ltd. in the year of 2016.

Dedicated to

Lord Krishna

Parents

My source of inspiration and courage

Contents

Foreword

From the time we get up to the dreams we see, the only thing constant in our life is change. Change is often seen as a temporary phase disrupting our well-charted routine of life. Change is intimidating to most because it initiates a different mode of action from what we have been used to earlier. It invites the challenge of behaving in a different manner and, sometimes, even a different way of thinking.

Change must be evaluated. All progress is change; but all change is not progress. Once evaluated on the grounds of rationality, we must face it and deal with it. In not doing so, we fail to realize that change actually triggers an opportunity for the manifestation of higher goals and a break from the rigmarole mechanistic way of living. Change gears us to catch up the pace of time to reach destinations effectively. The journey to achievement has personal and environmental constraints. Change acts as a tool to overcome the hurdle of volatility of environment.

We tend not to appreciate the potential value of our existing capabilities and strengths because they have become commonplace. When we take them for granted, they become invisible and hence redundant. So, we need new perspectives and vision to speed up growth.

This book is about you. It is about the challenges you face in the epicenter of unpredictability. It is about keeping your foothold on the slippery mud. It is about learning techniques to manage businesses and lives better.

The choice is yours – either rein change or be reined forever!

Organisation Change will give you insights and tools to be better able to deal successfully with permanent whitewater. I'm excited by this book and by the potential it creates for thousands of readers.

God Bless!

Shiv Khera

Preface

The concept of the "survival of the fittest" proposed by Charles Darwin is the real mantra of success in business. Survival and growth are the two major objectives of any organisation and every organisation is compelled to establish a perfect balance between both.

One cannot survive and grow in isolation. It has to *change* to be able to sustain itself, and no business organisation is an exception to this principle. Introducing *change* in the organisation is not a simple task, for an effective introduction of *change*, understanding of certain concepts and skills is essential.

Certain questions commonly asked by business organisations are:

- Is *change* management necessary?
- Whether we did what we had to do to survive, sustain or grow?
- Is *change* acceptable in my organisation?
- Were our past business practices faulty?

The management seems to be spending more time worrying about these questions and how people in the organisation feel about *change*, instead of working on how to implement a *change*. At present, all business organisations are going through the phase of transformation and learning. This requires all managers to be more informed and also to be experts in understanding the following points about management of *change*.

- Managing *change* is not about "soft" skills. It is about developing specific management competencies around effective *change* leadership. These new management competencies are essential in today's workplace.
- Management of *change* is necessary to manage business risks during *change* process, including avoiding the loss of valued employees, minimising productivity drops, avoiding negative impacts on the customers and enabling the *change* to be implemented on schedule and on budget.
- Managing *change* benefits employees by keeping them involved and informed throughout the *change* process. This enables the employees to make informed choices about how they will make transition through the *change* rather than react on the basis of fear.
- Management of *change* provides the tools to proactively manage resistance to *change* and to deal decisively with resistance to *change*, that is persistent and threatening to the organisation. Without these tools, *changes* can become mired in workplace politics and ultimately fail.

The workplace is far more different today than what it was 10 years ago. Now, *change* is the norm. Employees view their career and role in the company with new paradigm. In response, employer or top management must also adapt and develop *change* management skills to build the organisation as a learning organisation.

Nowadays, management scholars and professionals tend to study the management of *change* in their management curriculum. At present, no comprehensive book on this topic is available to them. The unavailability of the sequential subject matter on managing *change* renders them less competent in mastering this strategic area. Therefore, this book, which comprises 11 chapters and 20 case studies, focuses specifically on this area. This book covers all the relevant information and text related to the effective management of an organisation through the management of *change*.

The book is dedicated to this understanding that ultimate objective of management of *change* is to make an organisation a "learning organisation" so as to survive and sustain its growth.

I am confident about the usefulness of this book for management faculties, scholars and professionals in understanding the concept and practices of *change* in a business organisation striving for excellence.

Acknowledgement

I strongly believe that creativity is only possible when Almighty's grace and elders' blessings are bestowed. This work would not have been possible without the support and consistent encouragement of my father, the late Dr Rajendra Pathak; mother Mrs. Maya Pathak; my siblings, Dr Jaishree Pradeep Shukla, Dr Sangita Rajiv Dwivedi, and Dr Seema Somnath Majumder; my daughter Shambhvi and especially my wife Shweta, who happened to be a counselor and constant critic at the same time, to bring the best out of this adventure of writing something on *change*.

The words of acknowledgement seem inadequate while extending my gratitude to my *vocational mentor*, Senior Advocate Vivek K. Tankha (Additional Solicitor General for India), *conceptual mentor*, Shiv Khera (internationally acclaimed management guru) and *academic mentor*, Professor Pradeep Joshi (Chairman Madhya Pradesh Public Service Commission). I hereby further acknowledge the work of all other authors, writers or speakers who have worked on this subject and their hard work directly or indirectly influenced my thoughts or writing.

I sincerely thank Raza Khan, Shadan Perveen, and Praveen Tiwari of Pearson for giving me this opportunity, and extending their advice, support and trust for writing this book. Their confidence is the real motivator for me to strive for excellence in this book.

I also wish to thank my friends, who contributed in making this book exclusive and interesting for readers. During my association with them, I felt the power of teamwork and pleasure of having genuine friends.

Finally, I would like to extend my heartfelt gratitude to God for bestowing me with such people in my life, whom I have acknowledged here, and my parents for making me a responsible individual of the society.

With this, I humbly submit this book to my readers for reading. Their words of appreciation and suggestion will be the actual acknowledgement of this book. Thank you.

Happy Reading!

Harsh Pathak

About the Author

Dr Harsh Pathak, MBA, LLB, Ph.D. (Strategic Management and International Laws) is a practising advocate at the Supreme Court of India.

Dr Pathak is associated with various national and international organisations as a lawyer and consultant. He is a regular speaker on change environment at global conferences and seminars. He is also associated with global universities as a visiting faculty. Dr Pathak is a strong votary of educational, organisational and judicial reforms and he strongly believes that the organisational adaptability for change is the precursor to reform.

The experience gained by him over the years during his travels and interactions with people across the world is churned out in the form of this book, which deals with managing change in an organisation.

Chapter 1

Business Organisation: The Domain of Change

Chapter Outline

- Introduction: Meaning of Business As a Domain of Change
- Organisation: The Key Area for Change
- Organisational Structure
- Forms of Business Organisation
- Tool for Designing Sound Business Organisation
- Organisation and Environment
- Environmental Factors Leading to Change
- Dimensions of Environment
- Nature of Organisation-Environment Interface for Change
- Role of Three Basic Circles for Organisational Change
- Summary
- Case Study
- Review Questions
- Exercises

> "Up to a point man's life is shaped by environment, heredity, and movements and changes in the world about him. Then there comes a time when it lies in his grasp to shape clay of his life into the sort of thing he wishes to be. Only the weak blame parents, their race, their times, lack of good fortune, or the quirks of fate. Everyone has it within his power to say, " This I am today; that I will be tomorrow."
>
> — Louis L' Amour

1.1 INTRODUCTION: MEANING OF BUSINESS AS A DOMAIN FOR CHANGE

In common parlance, the word "business" means to keep a man busy in some work. Generally, a man may remain busy either for earning the money or for providing some services free of cost as they are included in social services, and if they are for money making, they are included in business and commerce.

Literally, "business" means what keeps one basify or occupied. But every engagement or occupation will not constitute "business." Only those human activities directed towards earning money or creating profit would come within the purview of the term 'business.' An activity in order to become a business should satisfy the following conditions (Fig. 1.1).

1. It should be regular.
2. It should result in sale.
3. It should aim at profit.
4. It should contain some element of risk.

Fig. 1.1 Essential features of business

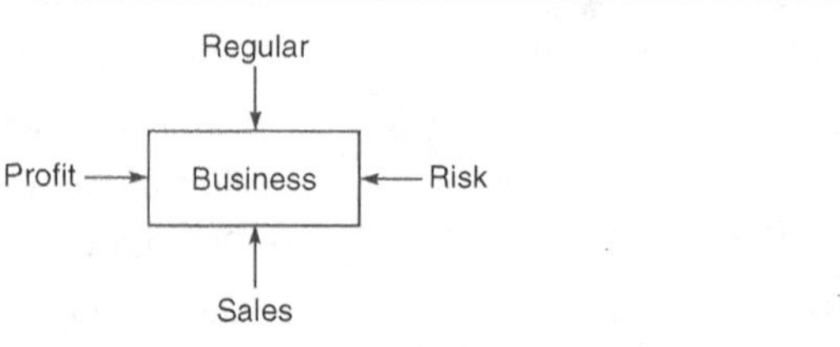

Previously, the sole objective of business was profit maximisation at any cost. Business was regarded as an end in itself. But now the concept of business has been changed. It does not live in a vacuum. Business is not an end but a valuable means to achieve an end, namely, human welfare and public good.

Business means the field of trade, commerce and industry and a network of ancillary services which help and interpenetrate the world of business as a whole. In short, business is a combination of the different factors of production (land, labour, capital, materials, enterprise, organisation and management) which are to be utilised effectively for profit through service.

Definitions

Some comprehensive definitions of business are as follows.

- "An institution organised and operated to provide goods and services to the society under the incentive of private gain."

  Wheeler

- "Business may be defined as an activity in which different persons exchange something of value, whether goods or services, for mutual gain or profit."

  Peterson & Plowman

1.2 ORGANISATION: THE KEY AREA FOR CHANGE

Organisation is a mechanism or a basic framework enabling persons to work together effectively and achieve the set goals, through integrated group efforts. The word "organisation" has been derived from the word "organ" which means various limbs or parts of a body. The human body is a combination of various limbs and if any one of the limbs stops functioning properly, then some defects develop in the human body. Similarly, no business activity can be undertaken without the five factors of production, namely, land, labour, capital, enterprise and organisation. The four factors may prove ineffective in the absence of the fifth—the organisation. The meaning of organisation lies in its functions. The function of organisation is to arrange, guide, coordinate and direct the activities of the other factors of production so as to accomplish the objective of the enterprise.

1.3 ORGANISATIONAL STRUCTURE

Organisation is a structural framework for carrying out the functions of planning, decision making, control, communication, motivation and so on. People or human resource is the most important element of any organisation. These individuals are specialised in their field and unique in themselves. Thus, these diversity of skills tends to form various groups which, in turn, comprise the whole organisation. The various groups formed are responsible for certain sub-objectives of the organisation. Each group in itself needs to be bound by formalised work division amongst members, coordination of their activities, well-defined rules and procedures governing their working relationships and communication modes.

Drawing an analogy with the human body, the structure represents the anatomy while the processes represent the physiology of an organisation. The structural aspects include job design, work levels, authority relationships and work methods. The processes include the nature of information flow and communication in the organisation, control and coordination functions. The behavioural aspects of organisation, which are related to the skin of the human behaviour, include factors such as motivation, leadership, job satisfaction and so on.

Thus, structure provides an organisation capabilities to perform all tasks which are essential for an organisation to sustain itself. It provides the organisation a mechanism to generate the large variety of responses required to meet the challenges posed by the environment.

1.3.1 Types of Organisational Structure

An organisational structure defines how job tasks are formally divided, grouped and coordinated. The common organisational designs, which are found in organisations, are shown in Fig. 1.2.

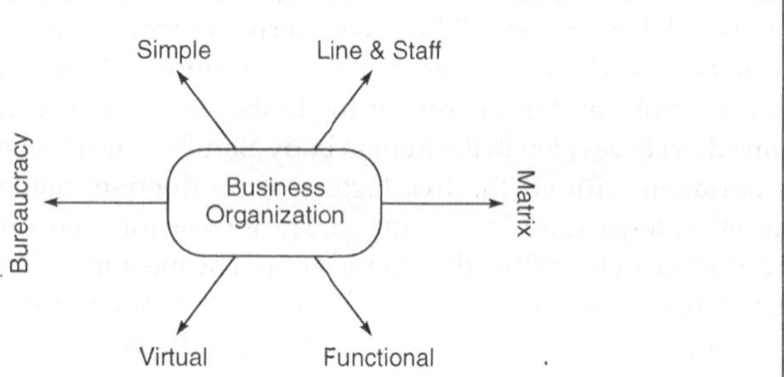

Fig. 1.2 Types of organisational structure

The Simple Structure

It has a low degree of departmentalisation, wide span of control, authority centralised in a single person and little formalisa-tion. The simple structure is a "flat" organisation, it usually has only two or three vertical levels, a loose body of employees and one individual in whom the decision-making authority is centralised. The strength of simple structure lies in its simplicity.

Line and Staff Organisation

This is a formal type of organisation. Line authority is defined as the right of a supervisor or require certain kinds of performance from subordinates. In contrast, staff authority has the right to advise, but not to give orders.

The Bureaucracy

The bureaucracy is characterised by highly routine operating tasks achieved through specialisation, very formalised rules and regulations, tasks are grouped into functional departments, centralised authority, narrow spans of control and decision-making that follows the chain of command. The primary strength of the bureaucracy lies in its ability to perform standardised activities in a highly efficient manner.

Matrix Structure

The matrix combines two forms of departmentalisa-tion; functional and product. The strength of functionalal departmentalisation lies in putting like specialists together, which minimises the number necessary, while it allows the pooling and sharing of specialised resources across product. Thus, a matrix structure has a dual chain of command.

The Virtual Structure

It is highly centralised with little or no depart-mentalisation. A virtual structure is highly flexible. This organisation stands in sharp contrast to the typical bureaucracy that has many vertical levels of management and where control is sought through ownership. The core of this organisation is a small group of executives.

The Functional Structure

It is the basic building block of an organisation. It is the module from which other forms are built. Here, activities are grouped together by a common function. It is commonly described as "organising work into related bundles of skills." Each functional unit has a dissimilar set of duties and responsibilities.

These are some of the common applied organisational structures to understand and incorporate the mechanism of change.

1.4 FORMS OF BUSINESS ORGANISATION

We are now clear with the terms "business" and "organisation." As far as the term 'form' is concerned, it refers to the structure of any business enterprise from the standpoint of (i) ownership (ii) size and (iii) law. Form defines the ownership of the organisation, its size (small, medium or big) and scope of its authority and limitations under the law.

In the present day, business organisation has been accepted as a profession because of the complexities of modern business. So more and more qualified and trained people are needed to solve the complexities of business. Business can be run on different setups of organisation. For instance, it can be run by a single person, with limited capital and resources. It can be run jointly by two or more persons who will contribute a larger capital and larger resources. It can also be carried on a co-operative basis, where helping each other is the basic norm. All the above organisations are different from one another. This distinction may be visible in the ownership, management technique, control of the set-up or in the total earnings and its sharing.

Business organisation is an institutional arrangement to carry on any business activity. Modern business is carried on by the following forms of business organisations (Fig. 1.3).

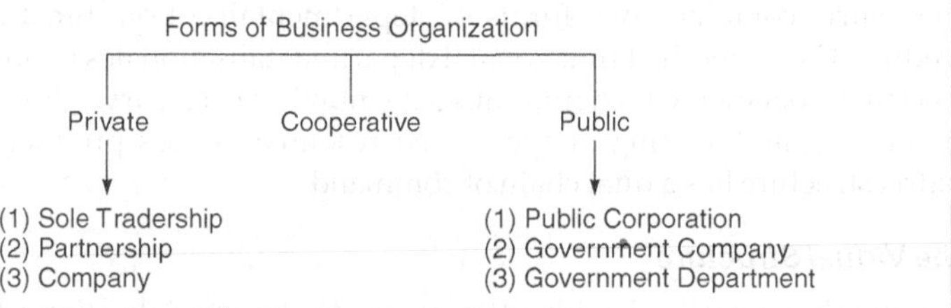

Fig. 1.3 Forms of business organisation due to ownership pattern

1.4.1 Private Sector Business Organisations

Sole Tradership

In a sole proprietary business, also known as "one-man business," one person is solely responsible for providing the capital, for bearing the risk of the undertaking and for the management of the business.

Partnership

This is an association of two or more persons to carry on as co-owners of a business and to share its profit and losses.

Company Organisation

(i) ***Private company*** It can be formed according to the provisions of the Indian Company Law.

(ii) ***Public company*** Any company which is not a private company, is a public company. It is recognised by law as an artificial person having separate legal existence.

1.4.2 Public Sector Business Organisations

Public Corporation

It is established under a Special Act of the legislature (of the state government). It enjoys a separate legal existence and its working is not affected by government rules and regulations. RBI and Damodar Valley Corporation are a few examples of it.

Government Company

It is set-up under the Companies Act, 1956, with the government contributing either its entire share capital or majority of the shares (at least 51per cent). Government companies are registered both as public limited and private limited companies. The Coal Mines Authority Ltd., Steel Authority of India Ltd. are examples of government companies.

Government Department

In a departmental organisation, the enterprise works as a part of government department and is headed by a minister. In India, railways, post and telegraph, radio and television function as government departments.

1.4.3 Co-operative Sectors Business Organisation

Co-operative sector are also known as non-capitalist organisations. In such organisations, we see co-operation in place of competition and service in place of profit-making. "Each for all and all for each" is the principle of such organisations. Co-operative organisations represent united and collective action for the general benefit of all members in any branch of economic activity. These again may be sub-divided into co-operative societies or cooperative stores.

1.5 TOOLS FOR DESIGNING SOUND BUSINESS ORGANISATION

A sound organisational structure can be established for the purpose of effective change management on the basis of the following points (Fig. 1.4).

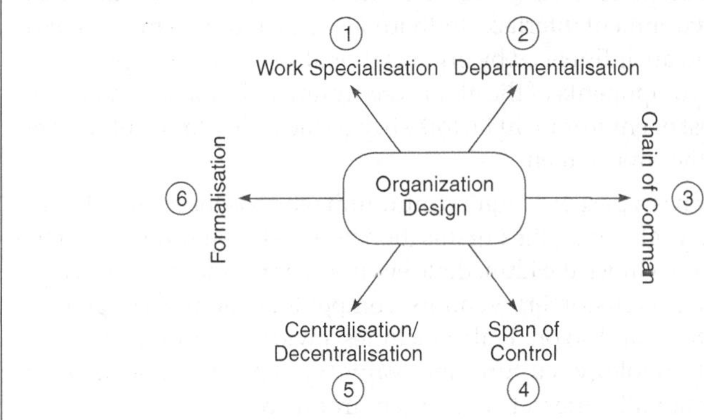

Fig. 1.4 Process of organisational design

Work Specialisation

The organisation should be set up in such a way that every individual should be assigned a duty according to his skills, education and qualification. The person should continue work so that he specialises in it.

Departmentalisation

In the absence of co-ordination, there is a possibility of setting up different goals by different departments. So, there should be some agency to co-ordinate the activities of various departments.

Chains of Command

Authority flows downward in the line. Every individual is given authority to get work done. Although authority can be delegated, ultimate responsibility lies with the individual who has been assigned the work.

Span of Control

Span of control indicates the number of subordinates who can be supervised by a supervisor.

Centralisation/Decentralisation

This means assignment of work should be such that every person should be given only that work which he can perform well.

Formalisation

The organisation should provide for the distribution of work in such a manner that uniformity is maintained.

1.6 ORGANISATION AND ENVIRONMENT

Wheel within a wheel, within a wheel; that is how we describe the individual-organisation-environment interface. Individuals as members of the organisation influence and are influenced by organisational structures and processes. Organisation as components of the global environment influence and are influenced by a host of environment factors such as the technology, culture and value system of the environment.

An organisation is a part of a larger continuum which is the society. Everything in the society other than the organisation itself, is the environment of the organisation. This includes the immediate environment or the "task" environment which covers its customers, vendors, competitors, regulatory agencies, financial institutions and so on. It also includes a wider environment which comprises the technology, culture and value system of the society. An organisation continually interacts with its environment.

A business organisation is an open system as it influences and is also influenced by its environment continuously. It is an adaptive, open system. It receives inputs from the society in the form of raw materials, labour, capital and information. These resources are combined and transformed by management of the business organisation into desirable outputs of goods and services required by consumers. Changing conditions in the environment can influence the operations and plans of the firm.

Business organisation must adapt itself constantly with changing conditions in its environment. Every organisation must be aware of environmental elements. They are numerous and changing. Some are important to the success or failure of a business. Some are internal, while others are external. A healthy organisation realistically deals with them. It adapts and helps to shape its environment so that it can become and remain viable. It must establish a healthy interrelationship with its changing environment. It is for the natural advantage of both organisation and its environment.

Environment factors combines external environment, operating environment and internal environment. This can be explained with the help of Fig. 1.5.

Fig. 1.5 Types of business environment

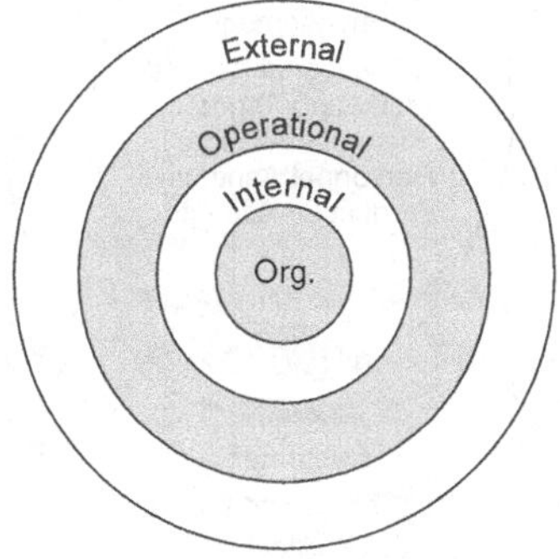

1.7 ENVIRONMENTAL FACTORS LEADING TO CHANGE

Environmental factors are numerous and complex. Some of these factors are static while others are dynamic. One of the most critical challenges is to cope with the environmental dynamics of change which many a time assumes the nature of turbulence.

Just as the life and success of an individual depend on his innate capabilities, including physiological factors, traits and skills and ability to cope with the environment, the survival and success of a business firm depends on its innate strength—resources at its command, including physical resources, financial resources, skills and organisation—and its adaptability to the environment.

Every business enterprise, thus, consists of a set of internal factors and is confronted with a set of external factors (Fig. 1.6). The internal factors are generally regarded as controllable factors because the company has control over these factors; it can alter or modify such factors as its personnel, physical facilities, organisation and functional means, to suit the environment.

As the environmental factors (external) are beyond the control of a firm, its success will depend to a very large extent on its adaptability to the environment that is, its ability to properly design and adjust the internal (the controllable) variables to take advantage of the opportunities and to combat the threats in the environment.

Fig. 1.6 Business environment and its factors

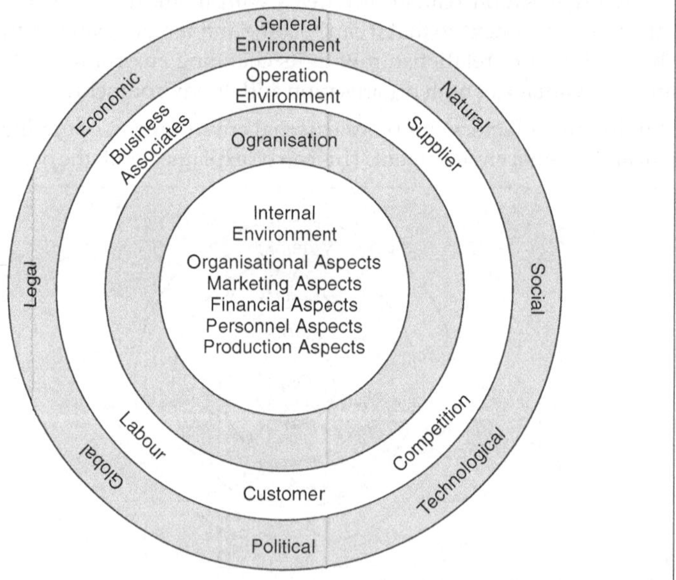

1.7.1 External Forces of Change

Change is a way of life. External forces of change are classified under five broad categories.

a. Economic environment
b. Technological environment
c. Political and government environment
d. Socio-cultural environment
e. Operating or task environment

Economic Environment

Economic conditions, economic policies and the economic system are the important external factors that constitute the economic environment of a business.

The economic conditions of a country, for example, the nature of the economy, the stage of development of the economy, economic resources, the level of income, the distribution of income and assets are among the very important determinants of business strategies.

Nature of the Indian Economy Economy is the study of available resources of a nation and their awareness and feasible utilisation in consolidation with nation's wealth. In India, we have mixed economic system. A mixed economy is one in which the private and the public sector actively function side by side. The mixed economy is a popular form of organisation today world. It is an economic system which has the advantages of flexibility and stability if it is operated sincerely by farsighted politicians.

There are three distinct economic philosophies, namely, capitalism, socialism and communism. The state has to play different types of roles in a capitalist, socialist and mixed economy. But the economic functions of these economies are the same because all of them are faced with the same economic problem—the problem of scarcity of resources. The difference between the role of the state in these economies arises from the way the economics problem is solved.

A *capitalist* economy is also called a free enterprise economy because the government restrictions on production and distribution are least possible in such an economy. A capitalist economy is also called a free market economy because supply and demand forces are allowed a free play in the market for factors as well as for products. This type of economy is also known as least intervention economy because the government in this economy is supposed to intervene into the functioning of an economy only when it is a absolutely necessary.

A *socialist* economy is a fully planned economy in which the natural resources of the country are socially owned and managed according to socially decided priorities. Price mechanism does not play an active role in the allocation of economic resources. There is, in fact, hardly a private enterprise in a socialist economy. Under socialism, the tools of production are organised, managed and owned by the government, with the benefits accruing to the public. It believes in providing employment to all and emphasises suitable rewards to the efforts put in by every worker.

The state has to play a very tactful role in a *mixed developing economy* like India. In such an economy, there is a public sector which is under the control and direction of the government and there is a private sector where price mechanism is allowed a free play. Depending upon the economic conditions in the economy, the state has to strive to keep a balance and cooperative exchange between the two sectors. The mixed economy is a popular form of organisation of the economy in the world today.

Ours is a mixed economy in which both public and private enterprises would work side by side. In a mixed economy, private, public, joint sectors and the like, all have some say in the major decisions that influence the functioning of an economy.

A mixed economy is necessarily a planned economy. This type of economy does not merely call for co-existence of the two sectors, private and public, but also suggest interpenetrating. It is argued that private because of the massive public money invested through the public financial institutions.

In terms of *economic change*, it implies upliftment of economic status of the common man who has been surviving in a state of deprivation and impoverishment. In terms of five year plans, India aims at efficiency, justice, stability and growth. In order to promote a higher rate of growth, large investments are undertaken. Such investments increase the flow of money faster than the flow of output and, as a result, *inflation* starts. Thus, price stability comes in conflict with economic growth. Economic change, in short, implies the change which seeks to improve the economic life of people and society. This relates to the progress made in interrelated dimensions which may be described as (i) output and incomes; (ii) Conditions of production; (iii) levels of living including nutrition, housing, health and education; (iv) attitude to work (v) institutions; and (vi) policies.

Technological Environment

Changing technology has been a reality from time immemorial. However, the rate of change which perhaps one should consider to be a slow one in the past, is taking place today at a tremendous speed. Changing technology growth has repercussions on individuals engaged in an industrial organisation whose main aim is survival and growth; hence change and innovation.

The rapid rate of change in the environment would seem to indicate a short term flexible response, but inflexibility of their major tool, technology, requires long term decisions. Technology also has to keep pace with the needs of domestic demand, the competitiveness within and without national boundaries, the effect on employment, the needs of capital and the local availability of the components of such technology. *Technological change* occurs when the technological capacity is matched with a need of society, be it for the individual as consumer (products and services), the organisation as an operation (equipment and processes) or society as a whole (environmental protection, defence, health) through the causal linkages. Technological factors sometimes pose problems. A firm which is unable to cope with the technological changes may not survive. Further, the differing technological environment of different markets or countries may call for product modifications.

Technology Transfer In any society, growth would be possible only through the introduction of improved technical inputs into the process of economic transformation. In the last few decades, it has become quite clear that no economic development would be possible without higher technological input available in the society. Though our planners have pointed out that a fund must be created and selective capital be invested in growth for development of the economy if the country wants to achieve desired rate of growth. The importance of capital cannot be derived, but capital by itself will not be able to bring about the change which we are looking for. Capital can only be a means for facilitating input of technology. Hence, capital and money alone cannot make us move faster towards our desired goal, but it is the application of latest technology which may help.

Technology gives its owner temporary advantage over his competitors. That is why the owner of technology tries to keep his technique away from use by others through registration as patent and charges price from those who want to use it. The acquisition of technology from external sources is known as *technology transfer*.

Technology may be considered as improving something already being done, satisfying a need long recognised and creating the possibility of a new need. There may be invention or innovation in this process. Technical change in a country in its early stage of development is mainly the result of advanced technology imported from industrially and technologically advanced countries.

An appropriate technology that will maximise employment and at the same time provide consumer's products at reasonable prices has yet to be evolved. Sometimes it is argued that developed countries, while entering the developing countries, must evolve an appropriate technology suitable to their environment and should not transfer their highly sophisticated technologies.

Changes in technology are occurring at a very fast rate. It has its impact on the organisation. Even the computer technology, with all its impact and influence, has been a major force to effect organisational change. A technological change, which we see around us nowadays, is automation which is done in various organisations. For example, ATMs have now been introduced in various banks, which has facilitated the services of consumers. To survive, the organisation has to change to adjust with new technology, otherwise it will fail to compete with other competitors.

Change of technology will, however, depend on a number of factors. They are:

(i) The government's policy to import that technology from outside if it is not available locally
(ii) Cost at which it is available
(iii) Approval of social forces including labour unions and other organisations.

Before allowing imports of machines and know-how, the government will have to be very clear about the impact on its resources, terms and conditions of the suppliers and overall effect on the socio-economic development of the country. Similarly, an organisation interested in installation of such technology has to calculate its cost in terms of profit-sharing or employment.

Once it is decided to replace the labour intensive technology by the capital-intensive technology, it will create surplus of manpower within the organisation. The technique of computerisation and robotisation will force managers to create alternate jobs for the surplus manpower as all cannot be fired from the organisation. New ventures and new jobs shall have to be created in this process of change.

Political and Government Environment

Political and government environment has a close relationship with the economic system and economic policy. Political stability of the country is another factor which affects business activity. Business thrives where there is political stability. The government of every country formulates and executes a set of policies that are executed through legislation. These legislations and enactments, rules and plans, statements and announcements, directives and guidelines by the government constitute the politico-legal environment.

With a view to protecting consumer interests, regulations have become stronger in many countries. Regulations to protect the purity of the environment and pressure the ecological balance have assumed great importance in many countries. Many countries today have laws to regulate competition in public interest. Elimination of unfair competition and dilution of monopoly power are the important objectives of these regulations. The MRTP Act controls monopolistic, restrictive and unfair trade practices which are prejudicial to public interest.

Certain changes in government policies such as the industrial policy, monetary policy, fiscal policy and trade policy may have profound impact on business. Some policy developments create opportunities as well as threats. In other words, a development which brightens the prospects of some enterprises may pose a threat to some others. The industrial policy lays down the nature of industrial activity which could be taken up by the private enterprises. If the policy puts restrictions on the span of activity of the private sector, it will have to change. It may have to switch over to other production activity which is allowed in the industrial policy. Similarly, the method of production and the technology to be used are also determined by the government's policy. Any method or technology not approved by the government will have to be changed by the organisation if it wants to remain in production line.

Monetary policy relates to money and credit supply. Organisation policy and program will have to correspond to the nature of policy pursued by the government. A liberal or restrictive policy makes all the difference.

Fiscal policy in the form of tax policy and tax incentives forces the managers to bring about even structural changes in an organisation's structure and design. Product diversification, product mix, locational pattern and even the compensation plan and policy shall be determined by the fiscal policy of the government. It is the fiscal policy which encourages or discourages the policy of modernisation to be adopted by management.

Trade policy, determining the direction and pattern of trade—both domestic and foreign—and the incentive package for encouraging exports and restrictions imposed to curb imports may also require the managers to effect needed changes in their production, export and import programmes. With changes in the production, the organisational structure shall have to be changed. If the organisation switches over from buying to manufacturing or vice versa, the whole organisational design and structure shall undergo a change. In the same manner, if the government allows imports of certain goods or reduces the component of protection, these changes in trade policy will force the organisations to adapt accordingly.

Political change does not necessarily mean the change in the government but in the political apparatus which seeks to ensure participation of people in all political matters at different levels. Political factors in the form of change of government, internal crises in the form of riots or civil war or external hostility force management to change. Change of government implies change of ideology and thus change in the government's policy. In times of war, certain changes may become imminent. Some enterprises may resort to mergers or other forms of combinations. Similarly, conditions of internal strife may result in a change in structure, place of work or even the product mix.

To bring about political change in the country it becomes imperative to enforce effective participation of people and institutions in the governance and regulating the political apparatus of the country. It requires participation of people from the grassroot to the highest level and the commitment of political forces to bring about the desired change.

Socio-cultural Environment

The socio-cultural fabric is an important environmental factor that should be analysed while formulating business strategies. The buying and consumption habits of the people, their language, beliefs and values, customs and traditions, tastes and preferences, education are all factors that affect business. For a business to be successful, its strategy should be the one that is appropriate in the socio-cultural environment.

The key to social change is the inventions which seek to transform the existing elements into a new form according to needs of society. Innovations in material objects such as science and technology and non-material objects such as social institutions, culture, philosophy and fine arts tend to accumulate to change the old value system and the components of culture to suit modern requirements.

Behaviour is the function of man and his environment. His attitude, value system and perception duly insulated with social beliefs and customs are reflected in his personality. Social ethics and components of culture in the form of social beliefs, customs, values and so on should not be perceived as barriers but pave the way for better organisational structure. A number of research studies suggest that socio-cultural environments and beliefs has a profound influence on an organisation.

Persons with different socio-cultural backgrounds will require commensurate organisational set-up because the attributes of socio-cultural environments develop the traits of independence, aggression, competitiveness and cooperation.

Culture becomes social ethos through the writ of the family and society in which he lives. It is known as the process of socialisation. This socialisation process, indoctrinates the individual with cultural dynamics which, in turn dictates the pattern of behaviour. The family, social groups and other social forces – all contribute to socialisation of culture; it gives direction to behaviour as individual and in-group. Even values and beliefs associated with colour vary significantly between different cultures. Blue, considered feminine and warm in Holland, is regarded as masculine and cold in Sweden, Green is a favourite colour in the Muslim world, but is associated with illness in Malaysia. White indicates death and mourning in China and Korea, but in some countries, it expresses happiness and is the colour of the wedding dress of the bride. Thus, a sharp difference is noticeable in the behaviour patterns of people living in different socio-cultural environments.

The organisational structure in terms of authority relations, span of control, levels of centralisation and decentralisation will have to be changed to suit the requirements of people joining the organisation. Instead of behaviour modification, it is appropriate if the organisation is changed which is comparatively easier and simpler. The organisation should also take note of other social forces operating outside the organisation. The emergence of trade unionism forces the organisation to resort to participative management, job enrichment, distribution of jobs, changed methods of job evaluation and performance analysis also require the organisations to change to concede to demands of the social forces, which were hitherto absent from the social scene of the organisation.

Operating or Task Environment

It consists of direct action elements in the environment such as shareholders, suppliers of raw materials, labour organisations, customers, regulating agencies, competitors and business associates. These are the immediate external forces, which have direct influence over the organisation and its management.

Supplier The suppliers include those groups which provide capital and material to the organisation. The shareholders, debenture holders, banks and other financial institutions influence the business policies and strategies to a great extent.

Labour In big organisations where hundreds of workers are employed, the labour force is organised in the form of trade unions. The trade unions interact with the management for higher wages and bonus, better service conditions, health facilities and so on.

Customers Customer satisfaction is the ultimate aim of all economic activity. This involves more than the offer of products at the lowest possible price. Consumers' organisation keep a watch on the activities of business enterprises and raise their voice against enterprises indulging in unfair practices.

Regulating Agencies The regulators include government departments and other organisations, which monitor the activities of business.

Competitors The policies and practices of competitors have direct influence on a business unit. If the competitors reduce the price of a product, or improve its quality, the business unit has to respond by bringing the due amendment in its business process.

Business Associates The existence of business allies offers strength to a business enterprise. It is easier to borrow capital from business associates during a period of emergency. Similarly, arrangements with business associates could be entered into for the supply of raw materials or for the sale of finished products.

1.7.2 Internal Forces for Change

A number of factors existing within the organisation may also force managers to change. They are basically related to marketing, finance, research and development. Human resource development related operations in the organisation may be summarised as follows:

Organisational Objective

With a change in organisational objectives, organisational structure too needs to be changed. If the organisation decides to switch over from the objective of manufacturing of goods to buying of goods in the market for purposes of selling under its name, the entire structure will change.

Machinery and Equipment Management

Organisational design, its structure and its overall operationality are influenced by the machinery and equipment. Modern machinery, though dispensed with man on machine consequent to automation and remote control devices, has shifted to research of development and such critical areas which have a vital bearing on the system of organisation. This has brought about structural changes in the organisation's design and structure process.

Methods and Procedures of Work

With the changes in organisational structure, the mechanics of work and the use of modern machines and equipment, the methods and procedures of work have undergone complete transformation.

Work Standards, Personnel and Organisational Adjustment

With new procedure and methods, the standards of work performance have charged with a new sense of expectations both on the part of the individual and the organisation. Consequently, the spectrum of the organisation's expectations is apt to keep pace with new developments. Such a state of change warrants a pattern of readjustment both on the part of the workers as well as the organisation.

Inter and Intra Personal Relationship

When the organisational structure and design change, it will evolve a new set of relationships among individual and groups operating at different levels in the organisation. These patterns of authority and responsibility will change with the introduction of greater decentralisation and departmentation within the organisation. There is a clear-cut distribution of authority and responsibility (keeping in view the span of control, the authority expectations of responsibility and the principle of optimal use of manpower by avoiding overlapping or duplication of authority.) Due to internal conflicts new departments or units may be created to accommodate certain kinds of personalities or some other organisational change may be devised to establish harmony in interpersonal relationship.

Insufficiency of Executives

An expanding organisation requires a constant supply of trained executives to take up various new jobs. Training of managers technically known as management development, is a very difficult task in most organisations. In the absence of adequate availability of trained and efficient managers, some structural changes in the organisation will be needed to utilise optimally the services of the existing managers.

External factors are beyond the control of individual, industrial enterprises and their management. The environment pose a threat to a firm or offer immense opportunities for exploitation. It is important that the firm should be aware of the existing environment, task and internal environment.

1.8 DIMENSIONS OF ENVIRONMENT

1.8.1 Multidimensional Environment

The environment of the organisations are multi-dimensional as explained below:

a. Complexity

The external environment may range from simple to complex. When there are a few forces and their influence is predictable, they denote a simple environment. When a number of forces operate together and each wields a considerable influence, the environment is termed as complex.

b. Volatility

When the rate of change in environment is insignificiant, it is termed as a stable or static environment. But the environment of modern organisations is dynamic because of an increased rate of change. The nature and degree of change is not predictable.

c. Capacity

The capacity of an environment refers to the degree to which it can support growth. A rich and growing environment can generate excess resources which can work as a buffer for the organisation in times of relative scarcity.

1.8.2 Stable, Changing and Turbulent Environment

Toss A. Webber has identified three types of environments which are discussed below:

(a) Stable Environment

A stable environment is one with little or no unexpected or sudden change. However, it is difficult to find stable environment because of changes in technology, society and other spheres.

(b) Changing Environment

In a changing environment, innovation may occur in product, market, law, or technology. Such changes are, however, unlikely to take the top managers of the organisation completely by surprise.

(c) Turbulent Environment

When competitors launch new, unexpected products, when laws are passed without appreciable warning and when technological breakthroughs suddenly revolutionise product design or product promotions, then the organisation is said to be in a turbulent environment.

1.9 NATURE OF ORGANISATION-ENVIRONMENT INTERFACE FOR CHANGE

An organisation interacts with the external environment, exchanges resources with it, influences it, and in turn is influenced by the various variables therein. Different elements of the environment interact with the various subsystems of the organisation in different ways and to different degrees (Fig. 1.7).

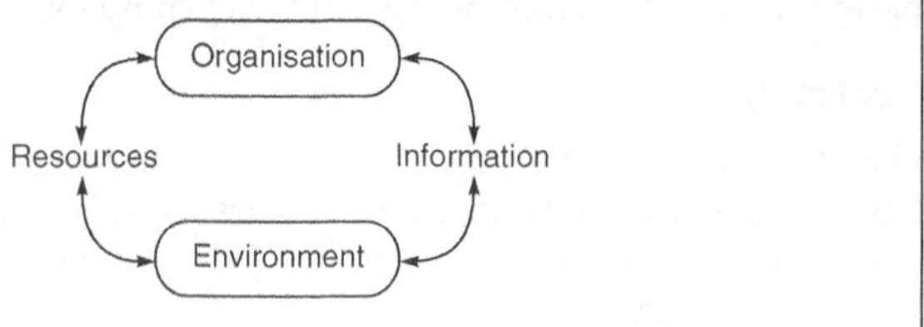

Fig. 1.7 Organisation environment interface for change

Exchange of Information

Since an organisation is a part of its environment, it must exchange information with the environment. The organisation as a system, with information processing sub-systems, operates in such a manner as to keep itself fully informed of its environment. It scans the environmental forces and their behaviour and collects important information to be used for decision-making and control purposes.

Exchange of Resources

An organisation in an open system who gets inputs from the environment and in turn supplies its output to the environment. The organisation receives inputs in the form of finance, materials, labour, equipment and so on from the external environment through contractual and other arrangements.

The organisation is dependent on the external environment for the disposal of its output. This is also an interaction process—perceiving the needs of the external environment and catering to them, that is, satisfying the needs and expectations of the customers. Besides customers, the management has to meet the demands of other groups such as shareholders, creditors, workers, suppliers of materials, general public and so on.

Exchange of Influence

The external environment holds considerable power over the organisation both by virtue of its being more global and inclusive and also by virtue of its being more global and inclusive and also by virtue of its command over information and other inputs. It offers a range of opportunities, incentives and rewards, on the one hand, and a set of constraints, threats and restrictions, on the other.

The influence of environment on the organisation is universal as it depends on the environment not only for procurement of inputs, but also for sale of its output.

Sometimes, the organisation may also be in a position to wield considerable power over some of the elements of the external environment by virtue of its command over resources and information.

The dependence and influence between the organisation and the external environment is reciprocal to a large extent. Organisational dependence on the environment means environmental power and control over the organisation.

1.10 ROLE OF THREE BASIC CIRCLES FOR ORGANISATIONAL CHANGE

Our decisions are influenced by three basic things which are called the three basic circles (Fig. 1.8). The first or the outer circle is the circle of concern. It encompasses everything we are concerned about or everything which is present in our surrounding and which revolves around us. Like we are usually concerned with our health, family, friends, investments, meeting with a boss, a family outing, neighbour's new purchase, new policies of government, the thread of nuclear war and so on.

Fig. 1.8 Three basic circles

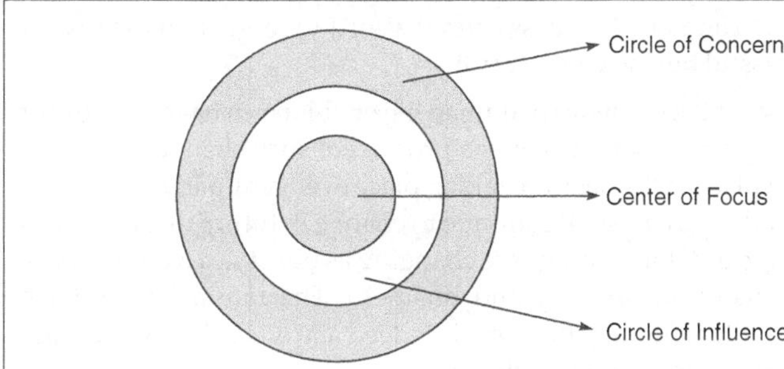

The second circle that usually falls within this circle of concern is called the circle of influence. This circle defines the area of concern where we can actually make a difference. In the above case, we may not be able to influence the policies of government and the threat of nuclear war, but we can do something about our health, family and investments.

But the most effective use of our time and energy is generally in the third circle—the centre of focus. In this circle there are things we are concerned about, that are within our ability to influence, that are aligned with our mission and are timely.

When we operate in our circle of concern, we basically waste effort on things we have no ability to control or affect. When we operate within our *circle of influence*, we do some good, but what we do may be at the expense of something better. In the centre of focus, we maximise the use of our time and effort.

It is the same with an organisation and a business. A business should put its time and effort in the centre of focus which is under its control and influence, that is, on factors which are controlled by a business, usually internal factors and somewhat to the circle of influence which includes the factors in the operating environment. A business should not waste time and efforts working in the circle of concern which is analogous here to the external environment. However, today this is no longer true. Organisations are continuously influenced by external variables. Reality deletes that organisations do not exist in a vacuum but are continuously affected in numerous ways by changes in the society.

Today, a business is operating in a dynamic environment where everything is changing and changing fast. A successful business is one which not only recognises this fact and prepares to face the challenges posed by the change but influences the speed and directionality of change to make the conditions more conducive for its survival and growth.

While business enterprises in developing countries have a large scope for growth and development, it is essential that under their present conditions, efforts are not merely directed towards creating products and developing markets but towards acting as agents of change for the happiness of the masses. In this changing environment, business cannot afford to forget that man is the core of any successful business enterprise.

The 50,000 years of the existence of human life on this earth have been full of changes and today's civilisation is only a product of such changes. Changes have, thus, taken place in the past, are taking place even now and the environment (internal and external) shall continue to change in future too. Our ways of seeing, thinking and doing things are changing as our styles, values, goals, religion, government, technology and business. The rate at which such changes are encountered by any business is indeed alarming. Today, the main business of a business is to manage change.

SUMMARY

- Business means what keeps a man busy. Any activity, which has regularity, profit motive, element of risk and followed by sales, is known as business. Nowadays, the prime objective of business is not only to earn profit but to get maximum customer satisfaction.
- Organisation is mechanism or a basic framework enabling persons to work together effectively and achieve the set goals through integrated group efforts. There is great importance of individual objectives in the organisation. There is a reciprocal relationship in the organisation between the individual needs and the organisational performance.
- Organisational structure is the formal framework of the organisational operations. The common designs are: simple, bureaucratic, matrix, virtual, line and staff and functional. On the basis of the ownership, business is classified into private, public and cooperative organisations.

  Organisational design is the basic process by which the organisational structure is determined. These are (i) work specification, (ii) departments, (iii) chain of command, (iv) span of control, (v) centralisation and decentralisaton and (vi) formalisation.
- Organisational environment is a factor of those systems that surround the organisation. Those factors which are not within the control of organisation are called external environment factors. They are natural, socio-cultural, economic, politico-legal, technological, and global in nature.
- Those factors which are partly in the control of the organisation are called operational or task environmental factors. They are suppliers, labour, distributors, customers, competitors and business associates.
- Those factors which are within the control of the organisation are known as internal environment factors such as the production, marketing, finance, human resource, research and development functions.
- The environment of the organisation is multi-dimensional. These dimensions are: complex, volatile, capacity, stable, changing and turbulent in nature.
- The due exchange of information and resources between the organisation and the environment influences their relationship.
- Finally, the overall relationship between the business organisation and it's environment is illustrated with the help of the three cycles—circle of concern, circle of influence and centre of focus. It explains that a mutual fit between the organisation and the environment is required.
- Since the environment is dynamic, it is important for the organisation to change itself to make it compatible. This is the only way to achieve the sustainable development.

Case Study: A Container Leasing Company

History

A major company in the container leasing arena needed to succeed in this extremely complex global industry, with narrow margins in a highly competitive environment. The company decided on a comprehensive initiative to upgrade its management practices, develop its organisational infrastructure to better support its business goals, and move to a more mature phase of development.

Task

A change agent was engaged on a long-term basis through one of its strategic partners to help the company develop and implement a comprehensive programme of consulting and training projects in support of the overall initiative.

Intervention

The change agent developed and implemented an extensive modular series of training, organisational development, and coaching projects for the company.

Training projects A training needs assessment, delivery of a management development program to all managers at headquarters and in the European regional offices, development and delivery of a performance appraisal training programme, a leadership development programme for vice-presidents, a coaching programme on effective communication, meeting management training, and training sessions for executives and senior managers on strategic planning and organisational development.

Organisational development projects Improving decision-making, defining the HR/OD function and strategy for the company, developing a performance management system, developing a distance learning capacity for the company, facilitating an executive retreat and leadership trek, and consultation on internal communications, strategic planning, and organisational communication.

Coaching projects Communication coaching for small groups, coaching and mentoring of individual managers, and ongoing advice and consultation with the company's senior executives.

Result

Over a period of 18 months, a significant organisational transformation took place from a culture and processes appropriate to a start-up company to practices and structures capable of sustaining a large and mature company.

Key Disciplines

Business Organisation, Change Management, Organisation Development, Strategic Planning, Organisational Culture, Human Resource Strategy, Training Needs Assessment, Management Training, Performance Management, Executive Coaching, Leadership Development, Retreat Facilitation, Team Building, E-training Solutions.

REVIEW QUESTIONS

1. Define the term business as a concept.

2. What are the different types of organisational structure and, how is a sound organisational structure designed?
3. Explain environment of a business? Take a hypothetical example of any business unit to substantiate your answer.
4. What are external, operational and internal environmental factors?
5. What are the different relationships that exist between the organisation and the environment?
6. Write brief notes on:
   (i) Three basic circles of business environment.
   (ii) Dimensions of environment.

EXERCISE 1

This exercise is very flexible, and will help teams and leaders to develop understanding of team and organisational structures, dynamics, politics, communications, responsibilities, perceptions, relationships, and so on to understand the functioning of the business organisation.

The exercise is for groups of any size, subject to creating syndicate teams of three to eight people at the most. (Large syndicate teams make it more difficult to ensure full participation by all team members.) Issue each team with a large sheet of paper (for teams of four or more, join two sheets of flip-chart paper together to create a big workspace) and some coloured marker pens.

The aim of the exercise is for each team to create a representation or metaphor of a particular work team, or department, or organisation as if it were an "animal kingdom" or animal society of some sort. The team(s) can use any living creature, for example, insects, birds, fish, dinosaurs to create their metaphor.

The facilitator should stipulate the part of the organisation that is to be represented, that is, translated into a metaphorical society of animals and living creatures. The team(s) can choose any form of representation and layout to create their animal kingdom metaphors—for example, names of animals in a hierarchical structure, or drawings of animals, such as a plan view of a jungle, a section view of a beehive, or ants' nest.

The teams then present their metaphors to the group, and discuss the meanings and feelings about the animal kingdom they have created, which will obviously reflect feelings and attitudes about the real work situation that the metaphor represents. The situation to be represented can also be extended to include customers and suppliers.

This exercise will be helpful for interconnected teams to develop mutual understanding, and will also reveal to facilitators and managers the attitudes and opportunities for improving and clarifying relationships, expectations, responsibilities, politics, and organisational culture. Using metaphors, especially those which enable the expression of strong characteristics (such as animals and wildlife), is an excellent way for people to consider, express, and discuss views about structure, relationships, behaviours, and so on, which otherwise tend not to surface.

EXERCISE 2

This exercise can be carried out in pairs, with several pairs playing the game at the same time, or one pair playing the game while the rest of the group watches. Two people sit back to back. Each has a piece of paper (a rectangular - not square sheet of paper; a large sheet of newspaper works well particular if the activity is being observed).

One player (the instructor) folds and tears his sheet of paper while reading out instructions to the other person (the student) on how the latter must fold and tear/cut his sheet of paper. For added interest, issue each pair with a hole-punch and a pair of scissors (smaller sheets of paper are more likely to require scissors). Other than giving the instructions, the players cannot discuss or explain anything else. Instructions must be read out exactly as they appear on the instructions sheet, which is created and supplied by the facilitator. Neither player must be able to see what the other is doing while the exercise is under way.

After the instructions have been completed, the team members turn and face each other, unfold their sheets, and compare their paper dolls, which will look quite different, even though each has been made from the same instructions. Here are examples of instructions for the instruction sheet. You can create your own variations or use these, or reduce them for a quicker, simpler exercise. Do not include the bracketed points; those are the facilitator's notes and meant to help with the review.

a. Fold the paper in half horizontally (this depends on what way the sheet is held and could be interpreted to be folded along the length or breadth).
b. Fold in half again diagonally (again, this is open to interpretation—normally an asymmetrical corner-to-corner fold).
c. Fold in half again vertically (open to interpretation).
d. Fold the top right corner so that the point is at the centre of the folded sheet (the folded corner could be one of four).
e. Fold the longest point to the corner farthest from it (open to interpretation).
f. Fold in half again or as close to two halves as possible (it may not possible to fold exactly into two symmetrical or even asymmetrical halves).
g. Tear or cut off 2 cm of the sharpest corner with a straight cut or tear.
h. Tear or cut off 1 cm of the opposite or farthest corner to the above corner with a curved cut or tear (curved in what way? — open to interpretation).
i. Punch three holes along the longest edge (where exactly along the edge is open to interpretation).
j. Punch two holes in the next-to-longest edge (where exactly along the edge is open to interpretation).
k. Cut a 0.5 cm sharp "V" two-thirds into the shortest edge (open to interpretation).
l. Unfold the paper and compare your paper doll with your partner's.

Points for the Debrief and Review Discussion

How many of you ended up with paper projects exactly the same? Why were you unable to end with exactly the same dolls? What instructions were the least helpful and why? How could these instructions have been made clearer? What clarifying questions would you have asked if permitted? What additional tools or devices would help the reliability of the instructions and fullness of understanding—the obvious ones are a ruler and a diagram for each stage.

The point here is that complex instructions often need tools, references, examples, or other devices to enable clarity and accuracy, and the responsibility is with the writer to take the initiative to use and include these aspects if required. Do not assume that words alone are sufficient, because they rarely are.

As an extension of the exercise ask everyone (in pairs, a group discussion, or brainstorming exercise) to rewrite the instructions to guarantee producing two identical dolls.

Note

If you are facilitating this exercise, try out your instructions before using them in the activity.

Chapter 2

Organisational Culture and Change

Chapter Outline

- Introduction
- Sources of Culture
- Types of Culture
- Significance of Culture during Change
- Concept of Global Organisational Culture
- Organisational Climate
- Functionalities and Dysfunctionalities of Cultures
- Strengths and Weaknesses of Indian Culture
- Top Management and Organisational Culture
- A Proactive Approach to Culture and Change
- Summary
- Case Studies
- Review Questions
- Exercise

> "If first priority is given to preservation of traditional culture and second to earning wealth, it is like spending on the sweet dish first and being left with no money for the dinner."
>
> — Anonymous

2.1 INTRODUCTION

Culture can be considered as the learning imbibed through our interactions with the environment during our development and growth years. This learning includes values, ideas, perceptions, preferences, concept of morality, code of conduct, and so on that come to us from our family and society. The culture of an individual determines many of his responses to a given situation.

Organisational culture is a system of shared beliefs and attitudes that develop within an organisation and guides the behaviour of its member. It is also known as "corporate culture," and has a major impact on the performance of the organisation and specially on the quality of work life of all levels of employees.

Corporate culture "consists of the forms, values and unwritten rules of conduct of an organisation as well as management styles, priorities, beliefs and inter-personal behaviours that prevail. Together they create a climate that influences how well people communicate, plan and make decisions." Strong corporate values let people know what is expected of them. There are clear guidelines for employee behaviour within the organisation and their expected code of conduct outside the organisation. When employees understand the basic philosophy of the organisation, they are more likely to make decisions that will support the standards set by the organisation and reinforce corporate values.

The word "culture" has been derived metaphorically from the idea of "cultivation." When we talk about culture, we are typically referring to the pattern of development reflected in a society's system of knowledge, ideology, values, laws, social norms, and day-to-day rituals. Since the pattern of development differs from society to society, so does the culture vary according to a given society's stage of development. Culture variation among societies requires a study of cross-national and cross-cultural phenomenon within organisations. For example, the Japanese work culture is very different from the American work culture. In America, the ethics of competitive individualism shapes the organisational management and operational performance. The industrial and economic performance in America is taken as a kind of game in which each individual desires to be a "winner" in order to receive a reward for successful behaviour. This work culture is a continuation of the general culture and family upbringing where children are encouraged to "think for themselves," and show a sense of assertion and independence.

Japanese culture, on the other hand, encourages individuals to work as a part of the team, thus encouraging interdependence, shared concerns, and mutual help. The organisation is viewed as a family to which workers frequently make lifelong commitments, workers see the organisation as an extension of their own families. The authority relations are often paternalistic in nature and strong links exist among the welfare of the individual, the corporation, and the nation.

2.2 SOURCES OF CULTURE

The organisation's culture is affected by three general factors: broad external influences, societal values, and natural culture and organisation-specific factors (Fig. 2.1).

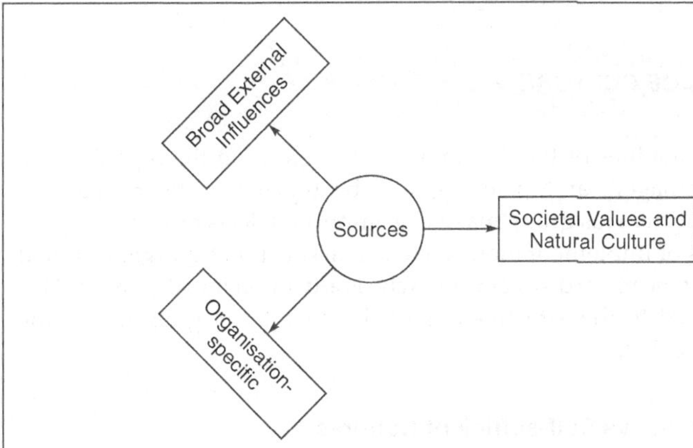

Fig. 2.1 Factors affecting an organisation's culture

(a) Broad external influences are factors over which the organisation has little or no control, such as the natural environment and historical events which have shaped the society.

(b) Societal values and natural culture are generally the dominant beliefs and values of the broader society—values such as individual freedom, beliefs about the goodness of humanity, orientation towards action, power distance norms, and so forth. For example, societies differ in time orientation. It was found that Japan has the strongest time consciousness, the United States second, and Indonesia last. Difference in time orientation within the broad society will be reflected in the cultures of organisations. In southern Europe, for example, the workday does not begin until 8.30 or 9.00 a.m., and it usually ends well after 6.00 p.m. This is very different from the workday in United States which stretches from 8.00 a.m. to 5.00 p.m.

(c) Organisation-specific factors too affect organisational culture. We have already discussed how the volatility of the technological environment will affect the organisation's skill requirements. This could have a number of different effects on the organisation's culture. In more volatile contexts, it is likely that there will be more educated employees who come with strong professional values developed through occupational socialisation. This could create fragmented occupational subcultures, such as groups with different ideologies and values which may make it quite difficult to develop a strong, single culture. Environmental volatility will also affect the organisation's power structure. Groups that interact with the more volatile environment will have more power and, therefore, become the dominant coalition whose values will drive the organisational culture.

Another organisation-specific factor is the nature of the industry. Firms in the same industry share the same competitive environment, customer requirements, and legal and social expectations.

2.3 TYPES OF CULTURE

The nodal personalities of the dominant power group in the organisation, usually key managers at top levels, will be the major determinant of organisation culture. This group makes the important decisions about strategies and modes of implementation, such as market strategy, organisational design, nature of the reward system, and who is advanced into the group. This is directly related to the effectiveness of the change programmes in the organisation (Fig. 2.2).

2.3.1 Charismatic vs Self-sufficient Cultures

A charismatic organisational culture is associated with a dramatic managerial personality. Dramatic mangers have feelings of grandness, a strong need for attention from others, and act in ways to draw attention to themselves. They tend to be exhibitionists, seeking excitement and stimulation. However, they often lack self-discipline, cannot focus their attention for long periods of time, and tend to be charming but superficial. They frequently exploit others and often attract subordinates with high dependency needs.

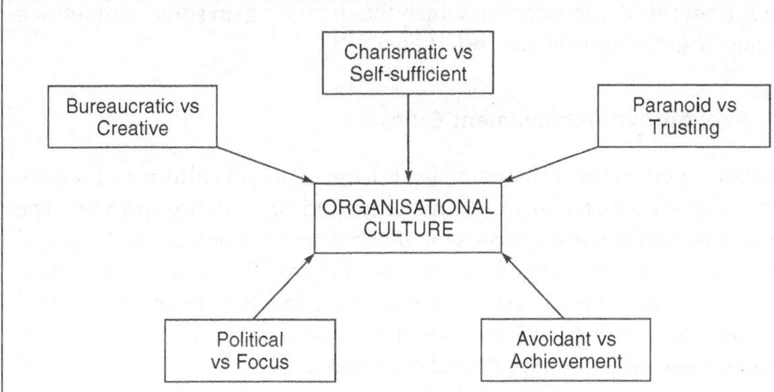

Fig. 2.2 Type of organisational cultures

Decision-making is based on intuition, guesswork, and hunches, without careful analysis of the environment or the capabilities of the organisation. Often the organisational structure and human resources are inadequate to handle the desired growth. Power is concentrated at the top of the organisation.

Firms with a self-sufficient culture emphasise independence, individual initiative, and achievement. Members believe that the success of the firm depends on how well individuals succeed as individuals. In these firms, managers have opportunities to develop and advance at their own rates. Achievement and self-discipline are recognised and rewarded.

2.3.2 Paranoid vs Trusting Culture

The paranoid culture results from a style based on suspicion. The suspicious manager feels persecuted by others and does not trust many people. The manager's behaviour is, therefore, guarded and secretive, believing that subordinates are lazy, incompetent, and secretly wish to "get" him. He feels hostile towards others, particularly peers and subordinates, and acts aggressively towards them.

In paranoid cultures, there is a strong sense of distrust and suspicion. The top managers in paranoid firms are not proactive. Members of such a culture do not easily share important information with others for fear that it would be to their cost. In paranoid cultures, the members tend to act passively and do not actively participate in important organisation matters. This results in either paralysis of the organisation or directive action by the top management in order to initiate events.

In a trusting culture this unrealistic fear is not present. There is a sense of trust, fairness, and openness towards others. Managers are self-confident, and they believe that other managers, professionals, and workers in the firm have the competence and motivation to succeed. This could result in an active search for new strategic niches in which the firm can gain some competitive advantage if such ventures are undertaken.

2.3.3 Avoidant vs Achievement Cultures

A depressive personality orientation leads to an avoidant culture. Depressive tendencies arise out of feelings of helplessness and dependence on others. The depressive person has strong needs for affection and support from others and feels unable to act and change is the course of events. These feelings of inadequacy are related to very passive behaviour and inaction. Depressives often seek justification of their actions from other significant actors; in the case of managers, these might be experts and consultants.

A feature of organisations with avoidant cultures is that the dominant coalition seeks to avoid change. They are passive and purposeless. Managers avoid making decisions. Change is resisted because it may threaten the current organisation values and power structure; appropriate action is avoided. The relatively low level of external changes and the desire of the management to retain control result in little activity, low self-confidence, high anxiety, and an extremely conservative culture.

In an achievement culture, members of the top executive group value logical analyses and rational processes. They seek to understand the strengths and weaknesses of the firm relative to its competitors. The managers recognise a need to change and feel confident that changes can be made. With information about the availability of opportunities, managers are willing to make a decision and take action to take advantage of the opportunities.

2.3.4 Politicised vs Focused Cultures

Politicised cultures are present in orga-nisations when the nodal organisational personality has a detached orientation. Those with this orientation have a strong sense of detachment from others and of not being connected with the environment. They believe that interaction with others will be harmful and avoid emotional relationships because they fear they will be demeaned by others. Aloofness and coldness characterise their relationships. They are socially and psychologically isolated and do not care about it.

In a politicised organisation culture there is no clear direction. The chief executive is not strong being detached from the organisation. Lacking leadership, managers at lower levels try to influence the direction of the firm. There are often several coalitions competing for power because of lack of leadership. Managers are involved in these divisive power struggles to enhance their own position and status, and there is minimal concern with the success of the organisation.

In a focused culture, members share similar perspectives about the organisation's sense of direction. This flows from the clear direction set by the top executives, and there is member commitment and enthusiasm towards these objectives.

2.3.5 Bureaucratic vs Creative Culture

A bureaucratic culture is a result of a compulsive nodal organisational personality. Compulsive people have a very strong need to control the environment. Such people view things in terms of domination and submission. They behave in a meticulous way and focus on very specific but often trivial details. Compulsive managers are devoted to their work and tend to show deference to those above them and act in autocratic ways towards subordinates. They have strong preferences for well-ordered systems and processes.

In the bureaucratic culture, the concern has more to do with how things look rather than with how things work. Managers focus more on the rules of working together than on the purpose of those rules—achieving good organisational performance. There are specific, detailed, formalised control systems, and they are used to monitor the behaviour of the members.

In a creative culture, members are more self-disciplined. They can work together as a team without excessive reliance on rules and procedures. They are knowledgeable about the work of others and about task interdependencies. Co-ordination among members is a somewhat intuitive process that develops from experiences of working together and being successful. The members know that co-operation is the basis for success.

These are some of the basic types of cultures on which the effectiveness of change management depends. If the organisation is self-sufficient, trusting, achievement-oriented, focused, and creative then the resistance to change is minimum and change can be introduced successfully with minimum effort.

2.4 SIGNIFICANCE OF CULTURE DURING CHANGE

The possible implication that all current Indian values are wrong and should be changed is not intended. Certainly, there are values currently operative which should be preserved, which will continue to serve the needs of individuals and of society. The impatient reformer may want to change the entire society overnight. He may see only the negative aspects of the traditional ways and feel that the perpetuation of the present way of life serves no purpose. There is little he can do to realise his desire, for social change is by nature very slow. It can only be made less slow. Such a pessimistic view of the current culture can work against his best efforts, for it may cause him to overlook ways in which the present cultural system serves a constructive purpose during a period of change, and to ignore customs and values, which can definitely aid the introduction of innovations.

In the first place, a reasonable degree of stability is required as a setting for planned change. Organised programmes for development cannot function amid extreme social turmoil or political instability. Systematic planning of projects requires predictable patterns of activity and routine organisations through which to work, faulty though they may be. There must be an ongoing, structured way of life within which to initiate change. The responsibilities of various individuals must be known; the methods of decision-making must be subject to analysis; the multiplicity of factors which give a society its cultural character must be amendable to consistent identification. These factors make it possible for the planner and the agent of change to do their work with some assurance that their plans and procedures will be dependable. In the absence of organisation that traditional practices and values give a society, a planned approach to change would be very difficult.

In the second place, the continuity of ways of living provided by tradition gives a needed psychological security to individuals caught up in changing times. Human beings need something dependable and familiar on which to lean while wrestling with new concepts and practices. They need to maintain a certain feeling of integrity, position, worthiness, self-respect, and dignity. Where the threat to the individual's way of life is great, he tends to develop traits of insecurity—aggression, defensiveness, retaliation, and over-justification for the present situation and his personal behaviour; or he may become a misfit.

In the third place, traditional institutions, and individual practices and values often serve to facilitate change. For instance, the psychological and material security provided by the joint family system to young people who want to study abroad, set up an independent business, or move to the city to take up professional work. This assumes, of course, that the new endeavour of the young person does not force a complete break with his family. Continuing family ties also make it possible for such ventures where young people are able to influence other members of the family. All societies have ways of identifying certain persons as informal leaders, persons to whom groups or communities look for guidance, to set a pattern, or to say "yes" or "no" to new ideas. The existence of such patterns of leadership often makes it possible for a new idea or practice to get a hearing, to be given a trial assuming that the leader can be convinced of the merit of the innovation or is willing to experiment with it. Without the role of traditional leadership, it would be necessary to convince each and every individual separately that the innovation is worth a try.

Traditional culture may possess qualities which should be and will be preserved. What these qualities are will vary from society to society. These changes, taking place in related aspects of the culture, or lead traditional values may need to be revived and revitalised.

In short, traditional values, customs, and institutions, while subject to necessary change, provide for order and predictability without which planned change would be impossible; they give desired psychological security to persons threatened by change, and they provide the vehicle for change even while they themselves are undergoing alteration.

Traditional values, and their associated institutions and practices, are perpetuated because of their functional worth to the people of a society. It follows that change must prove its worth if it is to become an accepted part of life. In other words, the features of a culture are what the majority of people, or large groups within the whole, have accepted as meaningful for their lives. It follows, therefore, that changes in culture can be brought about only to the extent that people initiate or accept the change and make it a part of their life; lasting change must be meaningful and rewarding.

Motivation for change may come from many sources—the emergence of new problems which urgently need solution, or development of a new consciousness of old problems; contact with other ways of life; informative and educational programmes designed by agents of change to promote particular projects; the recommendations of respected leaders and scholars; innovations already accepted, which encourage or make necessary additional changes; demonstration of new devices, tools, or ways of working which seem to be an improvement on those currently in use; major changes in the environment such as the opening of a new canal; and pressure from government through legislation or administrative regulations, which enforce new requirements or procedures, or promote new programmes. Whatever the motivation for change, significant and lasting change will result only when a new idea, method, or practice is accepted by the people as a meaningful addition or substitution. Culture cannot be changed by decisions at the top levels of management alone. Management action may be one of the influences on the acceptance of innovations, but it does not constitute change in and of itself. Involvement in and acceptance of change must have a broad base in the organisation.

Furthermore, the accepting of a new idea depends on its functional utility in a variety of senses. People cling to traditional ways because they provide emotional satisfaction as well as meet practical needs, they lend integrity to personality, provide for acceptance and identification for the individual, and a feeling of psychological safety. New ideas may be rejected if they threaten the psychological, functional, cultural factors even though they may be preferable for practical reasons. For instance, good teachers in India are identified and rewarded by society in terms of the percentage of their students who pass the external examination. They hesitate to accept new methods and purposes of teaching, despite the recognition of the validity of the new methods, because they pose a threat to the results that give the teachers emotional and psychological satisfaction.

Moreover, an old way of doing something may be valued not so much for its obvious purpose but because it serves a number of secondary purposes. The new method may appear to serve the obvious function more adequately but it may not contribute at all to the other purposes that are perceived to be important. As a result, the new idea is rejected. For instance, villagers in several countries have hesitated to use piped water systems, not because the new system does not provide a more adequate and more healthy water supply, but because the open well fulfills a social function for the women who carry the water. The piped water supply does not serve this secondary purpose and hence found difficulty in being accepted.

Change should be viewed more as development from within the tradition than as a "break with the past." Careful planning for change, therefore, requires a thorough analysis and understanding of the traditional culture and of the proposed innovations, and of predictable interaction between the two.

2.5 CONCEPT OF GLOBAL ORGANISATIONAL CULTURE

Globalisation is a major factor for change in the organisation. There is an urgent need of the global outlook in the organisational culture represents the national character and is a reflection of the institutional circles that people have built together. These institutions represent the family, religion, literature, education, and so on.

A person and his culture are so interwoven with each other that it is difficult to distinguish the individual from his cultural context. Cultural upbringing will make for the difference in the attitudes of people concerning issues such as work habits, risk taking, introducing or accepting change, value of time, concept of authority, material gains, employment of physically or mentally challenged workers, firing of less productive workers, attitudes towards women in general and women workers in particular, and so on.

Owing to these cultural differences, it is important that the management be aware that respect for differences in attitudes towards issues is necessary to achieve harmony among workers. These attitudes are so emotionally energised that lack of understanding and acceptance of these attitudes could cause an undesirable conflict. Respect for diversity in the work environment has gained further ground because of multinational and transnational business organisations which operate in many countries with differing cultural characteristics.

The values that reflect organisational culture should support the global view because expanding business and industrial horizons would necessarily incorporate the diversity in the global cultural backgrounds and expressions. S.H. Rhinesmith has suggested six specific guidelines that assist in creating a global culture within an organisation.

a. Create a clear and simple mission statement. A shared mission could unite individuals from diverse cultural backgrounds.

b. Create systems that ensure an effective flow of information. Co-ordination councils and global task forces can be used to ensure that information flow throughout a geographically dispersed organisation is consistent.
c. Create "matrix minds" among mangers, that is, broaden their minds to allow them to think globally. IBM does this through temporary overseas assignments. Managers with international experience share that experience when they return to home organisations.
d. Develop global career paths. This means ensuring not only that home country executives go overseas but also that executives from other countries rotate into service in the home office.
e. Use cultural differences as a major asset. Digital Equipment Corporation, for example, has transferred its research and development functions to Italy to take advantage of the free-flowing Italian management style that encourages creativity. Its manufacturing operations go to Germany which offers a more systematic management style.
f. Implement worldwide education and team development programmes. Unified training efforts that emphasise corporate values can help establish a shared identity among employees.

These guidelines assist organisations to create a global organisational culture through proper change in its constituting factors. The whole world is shrinking into a single global village; hence multinational business and social interactions require the integration of various diverse cultures into organisational philosophy and operations.

2.6 ORGANISATIONAL CLIMATE

Even though organisational culture and organisational climate are sometimes use interchangeably, their respective importance in change management is very significant. They have some important differences between them that have been recognised. According to Bowditch and Buono, "organisational culture is concerned with the nature of beliefs and expectations about organisational life, while climate is an indicator of whether those beliefs and expectations are being fulfilled."

Basically, organisational climate reflects a person's perception of the organisation to which he belongs. It is a set of characteristics and factors that are perceived by the employees about their organisation which serve as a major force in influencing their behaviour. These factors may include job description, organisational structural format, performance and evaluation standards, leadership style, challenges and innovations, organisational values and culture, and so on.

Richard M. Hodgetts has classified organisational climate into two major categories. He compares organisational climate with an iceberg where a part of it can be seen above the surface of water and the rest of it is under water and, therefore, not visible. The visible part of the iceberg that can be observed or measured is akin to the structure of hierarchy, goals, and objectives of the organisations, performance standards and evaluations, technological state of the operations, and so on. This is the first category. The second category contains factors that are not visible and quantifiable and includes such subjective areas as supportiveness, employee's feelings and attitudes, values, morale, personal and social interaction with peers, subordinates and superiors and a sense of satisfaction with the job. Both these categories are shown below in the form of an iceberg (Fig. 2.3).

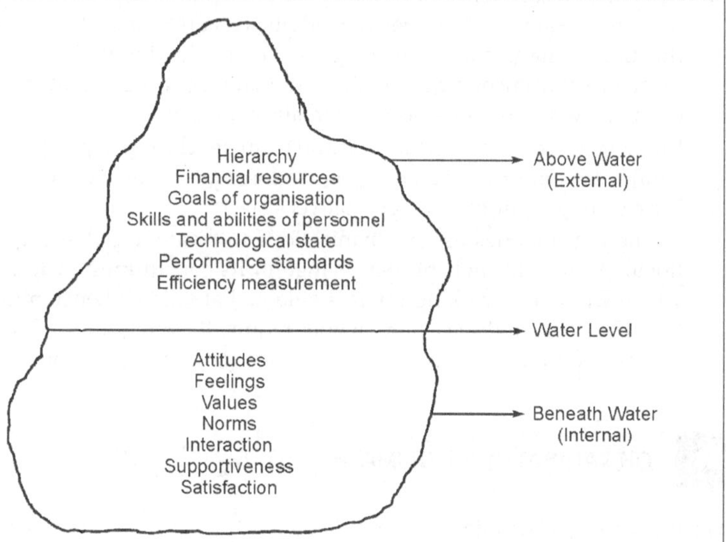

Fig. 2.3 Iceberg model of organisational culture

While some of the factors can be easily measured by quantitative methods, others have to be assessed subjectively by asking employees relevant questions about how they feel about certain factors relating to organisational climate. A questionnaire is given to the workers to respond. Their responses are measured on a scale of 1 to 5 where 1 means a strong disagreement with the essence of the question and 5 means a strong agreement. For example, a statement such as "In this organisation, promotions are given entirely on the basis of merit and contribution to the organisation," could elicit a response on the following scale:

1. Strongly disagree
2. Moderately disagree
3. Neutral (No opinion)
4. Moderately agree
5. Strongly agree

These responses can then be tabulated and conclusions drawn about how the employees feel about the process of promotion.

Likert, who developed a profile of organisational climate by isolating six variables, with each variable having four dimensions and each dimension containing five degree or levels, has done considerable work in this area. For example, one of the variables is decision-making—"At what levels are decisions made?" The four dimensions to this variable are:

a. Mostly at the top
b. Policy is set at the top; some delegation occurs
c. Broad policy is set at the top; considerable delegation occurs
d. Decisions are made throughout the entire organisation

Each of these dimensions can be answered on a scale of 1 to 5 as discussed above. Other organisational variables in a particular profile developed by Likert are: leadership style, motivation, communication, goal setting, and control.

Based upon the inputs received from its employees, an organisation can determine the type and state of the existing climate and the changes that can be undertaken to achieve the desired climate. For example, an organisation with a climate of autocratic leadership might find that the workers are unhappy with the situation and would prefer a more democratic style of management. It may thus decide to make the decision making more participative which is expected to be more conducive to higher productivity.

2.7 FUNCTIONALITIES AND DYSFUNCTIONALITIES OF CULTURES

For effective management of change in an organisation, a comprehensive understanding of the functionality and the dysfunctionality in the organisational culture is required (Fig. 2.4).

We shall briefly mention the functionality and dysfunctionality of nine aspects of the culture of most developing countries. A similar analysis can also be done for industrialised countries. In most cases, the same aspect can be functional if used in one way (or within limits), and can become dysfunctional if used in another way (or beyond some limits). In mentioning functionality and dysfunctionality of cultures, some examples from Indonesian culture are cited in the next section.

2.7.1 Fatalism

Functionality

Fatalism as a mode of surrendering to circumstances is dysfunctional for managing change. In this mode, a person or a group has high external locus of

Fig. 2.4 Functionalities and dysfunctionalities in culture

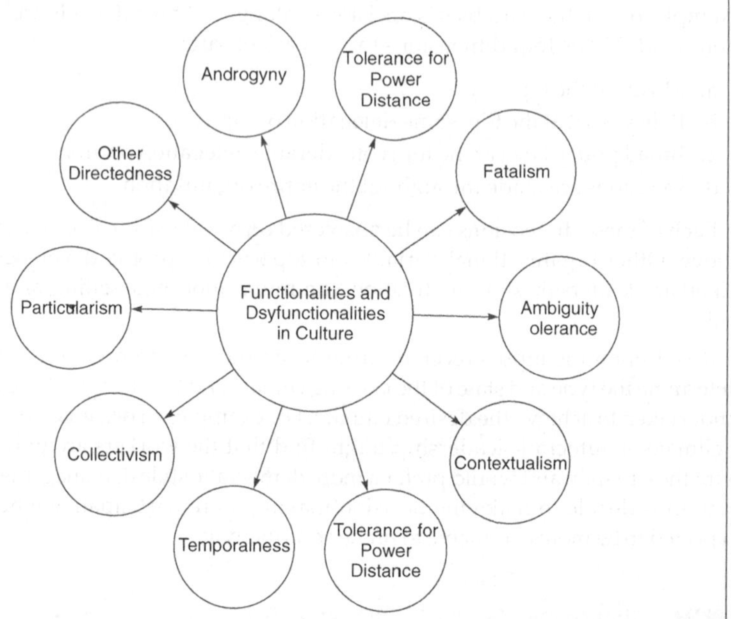

control (believing that control of the outcome of action lies outside in nature or significant persons). However, this orientation makes a group more realistic and helps it to hibernate and survive. In some societies an absence of this mode of externality may lead to frustration and dysfunctional conflicts. It helps persons to perceive constraints about which nothing can be done.

Dysfunctionality

Fatalism is obviously dysfunctional, making individuals and groups passive, reactive, and unrealistically tolerant of conditions that need to be changed. It lowers self-confidence and reduces exploratory tendencies to search for solutions to problems.

2.7.2 Ambiguity Tolerance

Functionality

Ambiguity tolerance helps a culture to develop several rich traditions, which are not seen as necessarily conflicting. It develops tolerance for differences. There is also a much higher role flexibility in such cultures.

Dysfunctionally

In a culture with a high tolerance of ambiguity, there is less respect for structure and time. Many areas in which structuring is necessary are left unattended, causing confusion, delays, and anxiety.

2.7.3 Contextualism

Functionality

High-context cultures develop much more insight into social complexities, and have higher empathy for others who may differ in their behaviour from the known norms. Persons in such a culture are more sensitive to other persons and groups. They are able to understand the contextual factors faster.

Dysfunctionality

In high-context societies and organisations, common norms and procedures take time to develop. There may be confusion in interpreting the events or behaviour because different persons may use different contexts to understand these.

2.7.4 Temporalness

Functionality

Emphasis on the present and a tendency to live in the present results in high involvement of individuals in the current activities. The emphasis on "here and now" may help in dealing more effectively with current problems. Present-oriented cultures are likely to develop competencies of working with and using temporary systems.

Dysfunctionality

Present-oriented cultures are likely to develop competencies of working with and using temporary systems.

2.7.5 Collectivism

Functionality

The following are the strengths of this orientation contributing to individual and organisational strengths.

i. Good relations are maintained and affiliation needs are satisfied.
ii. There is high trust amongst the members of the collectivity with high potential for collaboration.
iii. Consensus is attempted more frequently. For example, in Indonesia, the tradition of *musyawarah* (team building) is a very useful one.

iv. There is sharing of work and reward. In Indonesia, the practice of *gotongroyong* (shared work) is a good example of this.
v. Members have a high sense of belonging to the collectivity.

Dysfunctionality

Collectivism produces several handicaps for the individuals and society.

i. People find it difficult to tackle their seniors in matters requiring confrontation and exploration.
ii. There is lack of initiative by individuals and groups.
iii. There is lack of self-confidence and lack of effort for individual development. Individuals do not develop autonomy and personal identity.

2.7.6 Particularism

Functionality

Particularist cultures have strong in-groups, and the persons belonging to them have a very high sense of identity with their groups.

Dysfunctionality

The in-group/out-group feeling reduces objectivity of the members who are generally prejudiced in favour of their in-groups and against the out-groups. Favouritism and clique formations are encouraged, taking attention away from the achievement of results.

2.7.7 Other Directedness

Functionality

Giving importance to norms laid down by society may help to reduce "improper behaviour" of individual members. The concern to save face may also contribute to behaviour useful for the maintenance of the collectivity.

Dysfunctionality

The greater dysfunctionality is in terms of lack of inter-nalisation of the values and developing criteria which are internally consistent of oneself. People in such cultures are afraid of taking risks if this involves some possibility of loss of face.

2.7.8 Androgyny

Functionality

Androgyny contributes to the values of the future human society. It helps groups to value (and develop) interpersonal trust, caring, harmony, concern for the weak, and collaboration.

Dysfunctionality

Overemphasis on such values may reduce the effectiveness of competition which is also needed in societies and organisations.

2.7.9 Tolerance for Power Distance

Functionality

There are some strengths in societies with high tolerance of power distance. Respect for seniority and age may help persons to learn from experienced people. Conformity may be high and is needed for effective functioning of groups.

Dysfunctionality

High tolerance for power distance may result in stress on form against substance. There may be higher centralisation with little autonomy for lower level units and individuals. A scribed status is valued more, leading to lack of value for achievement. There may be much higher dependence on authority.

2.8 STRENGTHS AND WEAKNESSES OF INDIAN CULTURE

As already discussed, for organisational change societal culture is an important context. Organisations exist in society; they are a part of the society and they derive strength from it. In order to be effective, it is necessary that organisations are aware of the major cultural characteristics of the society in which they exist. We shall now discuss how organisations can use this knowledge and whether they should adapt to the culture or try to change it.

In order to understand the cultural context of Indian organisations, it may be useful to pay attention to some important cultural characteristics of India. seven cultural characteristics have been selected for this focus (Fig. 2.5). The first two characteristics are examples of the strengths of India's culture. The negative characteristics help to focus attention on the dimensions that require change.

2.8.1 Extension Motivation

One important characteristic of Indian culture has been its high extension motivation which is reflected in several traditions in the country. In Indian culture, there has always been concern for others. This concern has, however, not acquired the same character as in western society, namely, concern for the community. Concern for others in India has been much more general, even though this has been a strong trend. The concern has also been for society in general; when it comes to specific aspects, the concern has not been as prominent.

Fig. 2.5 Strength and weaknesses of Indian culture

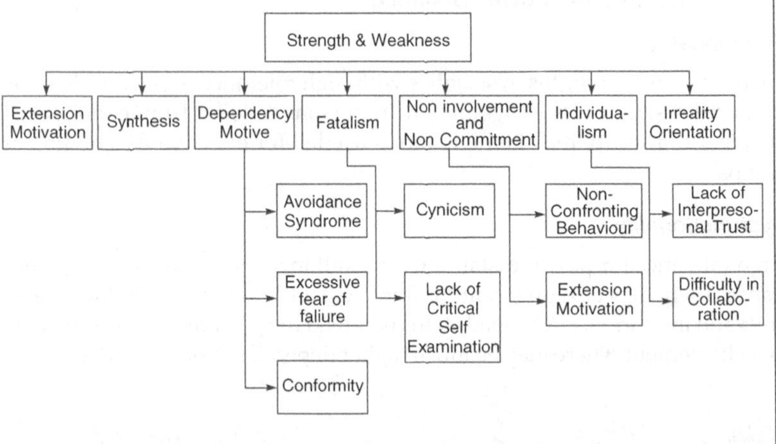

2.8.2 Synthesis

Indian culture is characterised by a tendency towards synthesis, absorbing various influences, which impinge on the culture, and internalising them. Similarly, conflicting points of view are also synthesised. In many cases, the synthesis may go to the extent of several contradictions existing at the same time. This may be a result of a combination of several characteristics. The characteristic of synthesis has helped the culture to survive over thousands of years, and has helped to develop a tradition which is quite unique in the world.

2.8.3 Dependency Motive

Being a feudal culture, the dependency motive has been fairly strong in India. Dependency motive is characterised by a tendency to depend on and please the authority figure, and to expect others who are lower in authority to do the same thing in turn. This is reflected in various forms. When dependency is high, it results in some of the following behaviours.

Avoidance Syndrome

Lack of initiative is one symptom of the avoidance syndrome. In a dependency situation, the individual does not take the initiative to make a decision. He merely carries out a decision. Similarly, a person does not take responsibility for an action because he himself is not responsible for the action. Another characteristic of the avoidance syndrome is an exaggerated view of obstacles.

When a person faces problems, he exaggerates them, and is overwhelmed by them; such an exaggerated view would justify the person not taking the necessary action. Such syndromes can be seen in organisations also. In many cases the obstacles loom large before a person take action. Difficulties come up first and there is an unrealistic obsession with such difficulties. The tendency is to avoid trying out something new because that would require taking responsibility and risks which people find difficult to face.

Excessive Fear of Failure

In a dependency culture, the main concern is to be acceptable to the authorities. As a result, a person does not want to be seen as failing at all. This results in excessive fear of failure. (Everyone fears failure to some extent, but the way out is to tackle it head on, not avoid failure.) Risk taking is completely avoided in the face of such a fear and easy targets are kept so that there may be no chance of failing at all.

Conformity

In a dependency culture, the tendency is to conform to a given framework, rather than try out a new framework. Creativity is low in dependency, because creativity involves taking risks, initiative, and responsibility for both success and failure. Such conformity is quite evident in most organisations where the tendency is to do what is given, rather than take the initiative and try out something new.

2.8.4 Fatalism

The tendency to depend on or refer to unknown factors is very high in India. This is known as fatalism. The general tendency is to see outside forces as highly important. There have been historical reasons for this, and because of long experience of dependency on various factors, this tendency has persisted. It is seen in two ways in organisations.

Cynicism

In many organisations, fatalism (which, by implication, means lack of faith that one can do something about certain things and that their control lies somewhere outside) leads to a general cynical tendency that things are bad and cannot be improved. Such cynicism is stronger amongst intellectuals. If the internal locus of control in people is low and their ability is high, they tend to be more cynical. We find bright young people feeling frustrated in organisations and talking about their organisations in cynical terms. For example, they may feel that they are only passing time in the organisation, that not much can be done in the organisation.

Lack of Critical Self-examination

Because of the exaggerated importance given to outside factors in determining things, there is a tendency to avoid taking responsibility for certain actions. In such a case the person need not examine what he or she lacks and no appropriate action needs to be taken to improve. This is reflected in the analysis of stories written by managers from various organisations. In their stories, the element of what is called a personal block (perceived difficulties of personal nature for which the person himself may be responsible) was found to be very low.

2.8.5 Non-involvement and Non-commitment

This characteristic may have some spiritual-religious roots. For example, it is reflected in the tendency of most Indians not to take clear and strong positions on issues, if such positions are in conflict with other points of view. When it comes to discussions or expressing opinions, there is a tendency to take the "golden mean," as it is the safest position to avoid confrontation. It results in the following two characteristics of the Indian organisations.

Non-confronting Behaviour

Non-involvement and non-commitment would make a person take a more compromising position and avoid any position which would lead to a confrontation. This tendency is seen in people when discussions are held and when some uncomfortable opinions need to be shared.

Excessive Tolerance

Another result of non-commitment and non-involvement is tolerance. Tolerance is a positive quality because it reflects the respect people have for others' views, and a tendency to see the good aspects of another point of view. However, tolerance creates problems when it becomes excessive. Our tendency of excessive tolerance is reflected in general social behaviour. In organisations, this tendency may result in not being bothered with some disturbing things. For example, people may tolerate lack of standards or a behaviour like lateness, and so on.

2.8.9 Individualism

Indian culture by nature is individualistic, even though there has been a tendency to show concern for others. Usually, Indian culture emphasises individual spiritual pursuits. This results in two main characteristics.

Lack of Interpersonal Trust

When the basic concern of the individual is for the self, the tendency to trust others is low. This results in a more or less unstated and underlying suspicion of other people. It is often reflected in organisations where collaboration may be low because the tendency to trust the other person is low.

Difficulty in Collaboration

As a result of an individual's orientation, the tendency to work together is rather low. One foreign behavioural scientist made a profound remark about Indian organisations and people. He said that while Indians as individuals could be compared with the best and most competent persons anywhere in the world, they formed poor organisations and found it difficult to work in groups. Collaboration, which requires the skill to work together on problems, is lacking in most cases.

2.8.10 Irreality Orientation

This is an interesting characteristic of the Indian culture. There is a tendency to avoid reality, resulting in what may be called "irreality orientation." This is primarily reflected in the difficulty we in India have in anticipating problems and failures. During planning, people find it difficult to anticipate the kind of problems that are likely to come up and therefore, they find it difficult to prepare a plan to cope with such organisational planning and planning at the national level. We tend to prepare plans which cannot be realised. Targets are kept too high, without keeping the possible difficulties and obstacles in view. Of course some organisations prepare realistic plans and achieve them. But the general tendency in India is to see the brighter side of things and neither expect nor be prepared for problems and difficulties.

2.9 TOP MANAGEMENT AND ORGANISATIONAL CULTURE

For any organisation to grow and prosper, it is important that its mission and its philosophy be respected and adhered to by all members of the organisation. Even when an organisation has a strong and established culture, the dynamics of environment may require changes, subcultures may have to be encouraged to support and enhance the organisational culture, or counter-cultures may have to be controlled to minimise their harmful effects.

Since culture is an important aspect of organisational success, it is important that managers play a significant role in keeping values and behaviour of the organisational members under control. This means that the leaders pay continuous attention to maintaining the established standards and send clear signals to all the members about what is expected of them so that corrective action can be taken before any damage is done. Cultural consistency and strong adherence to cultural values becomes easy when leaders themselves act as strong role models. Employees often emulate leader behaviour and look up to them for guidance. By being strong role models and by guiding, teaching, and coaching, leaders reinforce the values that support organisational culture. A leader's cultural strength is measured especially by the way he handles crisis situations. Emotions are heightened during a crisis. Proper handling of a crisis sends a powerful message about culture. A classic example is Lee Iacocca's handling of the financial crisis faced by Chrysler Motor Company during the 1970s. He articulated Chrysler's mission as protecting American jobs and asked the government for a bail-out of the crisis situation. The American government does not believe in protecting private business with government funds but Iacocca was successful in obtaining these funds by emphasising the strong culture of commitment to its employees.

How managers handle their less productive workers or reward their more productive employees also speaks about their ability to maintain a certain strength in their culture. Some managers may simply reassign a less productive worker to another job which may be more suitable to the person's skills or retrain the employee instead of firing him. High turnover in any company is an indication of poor cultural standards.

Good managers are able to support and reinforce an existing strong culture by being strong role models and by handling situations that may result into cultural deviations with great diplomacy.

2.9.1 Managing Organisational Culture

Managers are increasingly recognising the power and effects of culture on the behaviour of people in organisations. They are becoming interested in trying to manage it as a way of contributing to the effectiveness of the firm. However, while there is agreement that cultures exist in every organisation and that they

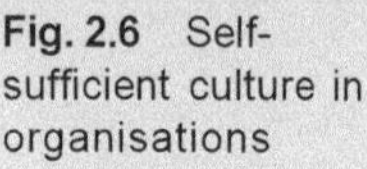

Fig. 2.6 Self-sufficient culture in organisations

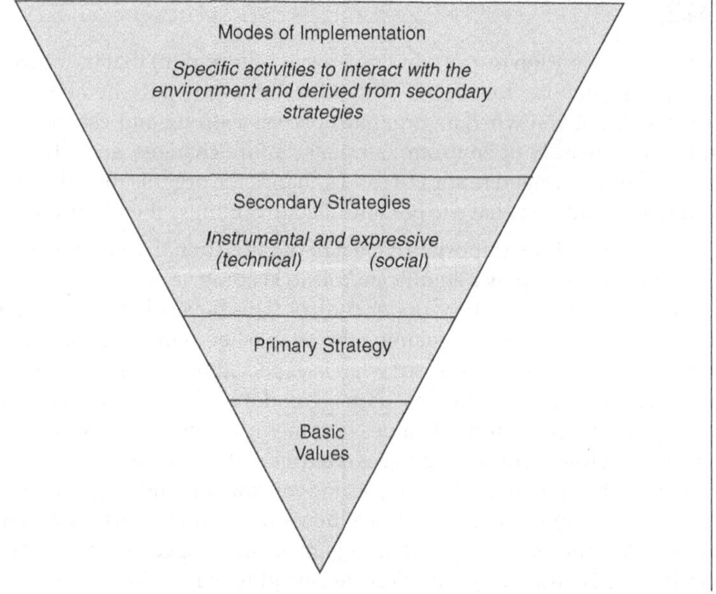

do change, there is disagreement over the degree to which they can be managed. In new organisations, it is possible to shape the culture through carefully designed selection programmes, socialisation strategies, and consistent use of symbols and language. Very quickly though, the members of the organisation modify the values intended by the management, and a culture emerges. It is more difficult to affect the culture of an existing organisation, especially when an entrenched management attempts to change it by using consultants and through formal change programmes. The reason for this difficulty is illustrated in Fig. 2.6 and Fig. 2.7 usually, attempts to modify culture centre around revision of activities and practices, that is, modes of implementation and secondary instrumental strategies. Suppose, for example, a firm was headed by a compulsive chief executive who thought that productivity might be increased through some of the currently popular high worker involvement approaches. He might decide to move from a bureaucratic culture to a creative one. Trainers and consultants, who use a set of team-building development approaches that give managers experience in working together, might be retained. There might be some organisational redesign to facilitate activities among groups by creating new interdependencies. However, because the basic values of the dominant managerial group are not consistent with these practices, the change effort would fail. The modes of implementation and the secondary strategies required for a creative culture are not consistent with the primary strategy of maintaining values consistent with a compulsive personality. Cultural shifts occur when the top management

Fig. 2.7 Why cultural change fails?

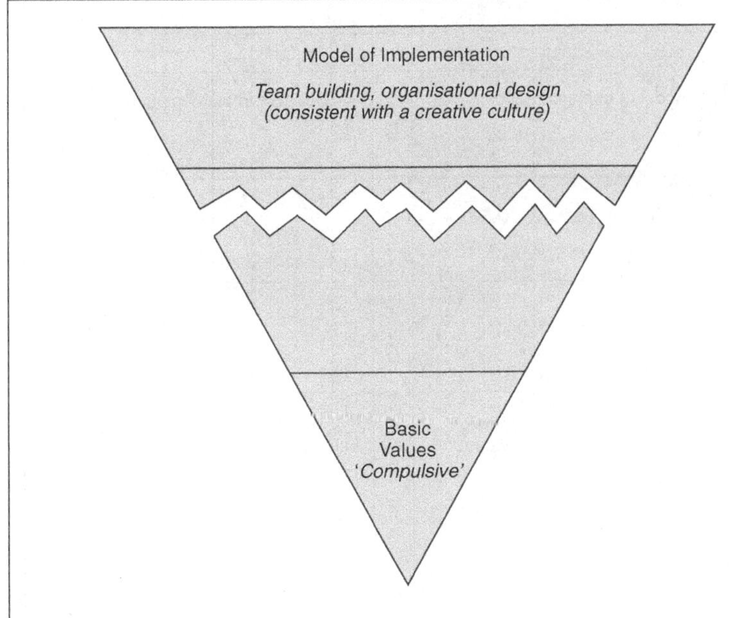

changes or when there is a significant change in the firm's environment to which it must adapt in order to survive. Fig 2.8 illustrates the case in which an environment shift could require a modification of the organisation's culture.

Suppose that at one time (T_1) a company is operating effectively in the environment as shown bracketed by A. This means that the modes of implementation and the values (basic values A) from which they are derived are congruent. Suppose, however, that over time the external environment changes and at another time (T_2) the environment now is shown bracketed by B. This would require different modes of implementation, along with value set B, to operate effectively. In many ways, the modes of implementation for a new environment may be similar to those required by the old one, shown by the area of overlap in Fig. 2.8. However, the problem of adjustment occurs in those areas where there is no overlap with the previous secondary strategies and modes of implementation.

An example of this situation is the business of publishing college textbooks. In many respects, neither the target market for textbooks (students) nor the means of finding authors has changed much over the years. What has changed is the channel of distribution for used books, which is now so well-organised that it has significant effects on the way publishers must now do their marketing. Now there are "used book" companies that buy large quantities of textbooks and sell them to bookstores. The original publisher does not control these sales. While traditional publishers believe that the actions of the

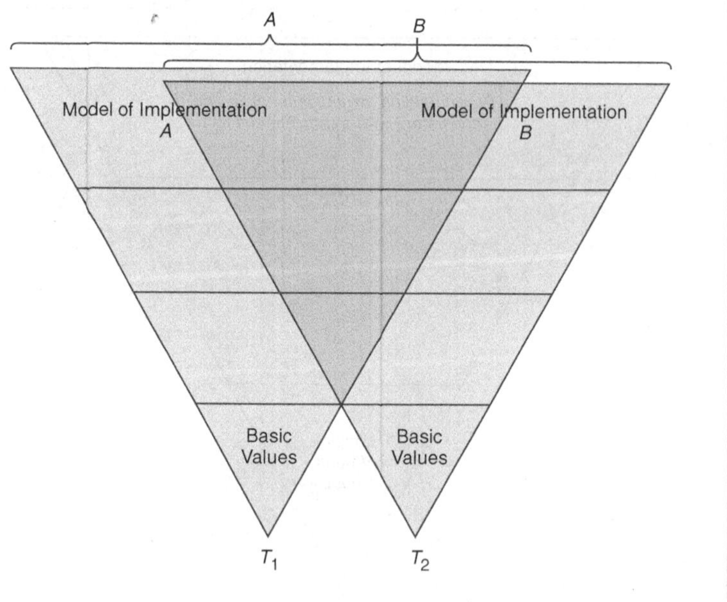

Fig. 2.8 Change in organisation culture due to change in the environment

used book company are unethical and professional, they are entirely legal. Publishers must change the way they do business, perhaps by entering the used book market themselves. However, such a business approach (a new mode of implementation) is inconsistent with traditional publishing values which the managers of these firms wish to maintain.

Three companies that have been affected by the changing environment are Ford, AT & T, and Gillette. In all these firms not only were product, market, and customer value-related changes made, but also the organisational attitude was transformed by the management to align the organisational culture with the environment.

2.10 A PROACTIVE APPROACH TO CULTURE AND CHANGE

To bring the sustainable change in the organisation, there is often a conflict between the traditional culture and the demands of a modern management. Two extreme views are taken on the subject, some advocating that management practices should be designed to suit the culture, and others advocating that modern management practices should be uniformly adopted to suit the goals of the organisation (Fig 2.9). A proactive action strategy would involve the following steps.

a. Determine the direction It is necessary in the beginning to be quite clear about where the organisation wants to go. The direction should be defined not only in terms of specific systems like performance feedback, counselling, potential appraisal, career planning, and so on, but also in terms of process movement, for example, towards more openness, more collaborative action, and consulting each other. An open discussion psychological preparation for accepting the system. Thoughts for the new directions should be widely shared.

b. Share possible consequences of the journey Introduction of the human appraisal system is like starting a new journey. The fact that the journey is not likely to be very pleasant should be known from the beginning and understood very clearly. Usually, consultants who work on the introduction of such a system not only communicate it verbally to the client but also make the possible consequences clear in their written reports. For example, it should be made known and should be communicated that the appraisal system may increase dissatisfaction to some extent, because individuals will begin to voice some problems when the system becomes open. It should be understood that these processes are part of the "teething problems" experienced in introducing the system. If these are not communicated and understood, the organisation may by unduly disturbed when it faces such problems. Instead of taking these problems as a necessary part of the introduction of the system, they may be taken as signs of failure, and the system may be abandoned. Those who are introducing a new system should clearly anticipate such problems and be prepared to deal with them.

Fig. 2.9 Proactive aproaches in building sound organisational culture

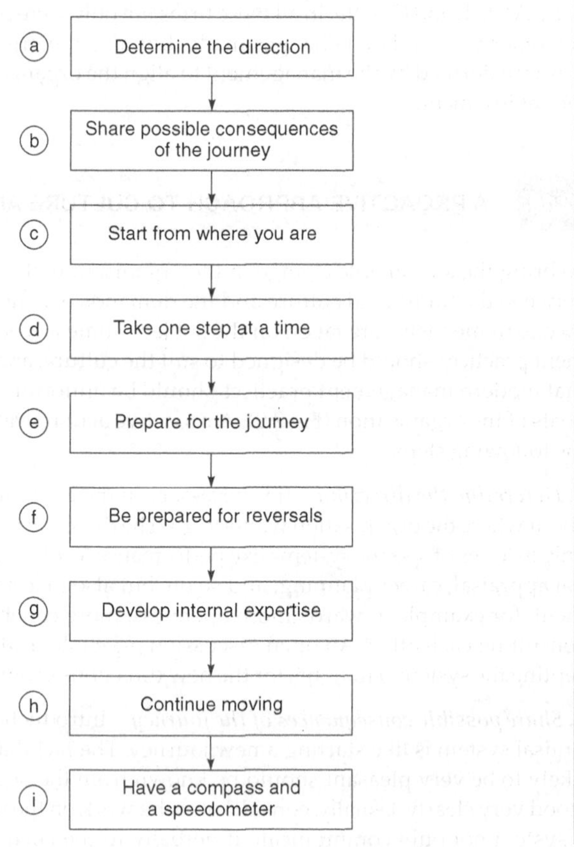

c. Start from where you are Each organisation has a tradition and some rudimentary form of a particular system. The design of a new system will be different for each organisation. While the direction may be determined so that the organisation knows in which direction it has to move, the nature of the system will naturally differ. It may be useful for the organisation to understand this and start from the level where it stands in terms of the sophistication of the system.

d. Take one step at a time Organisations should prepare a careful plan for introducing various steps. Various elements of a system cannot be introduced simultaneously. For example, while introducing an appraisal system, a simple appraisal form may be introduced at first. After the form has been properly understood and used, a counselling and feedback system may be introduced, followed by analysis of the critical attributes of various jobs and a system of assessing these attributes. A full appraisal system may be introduced later. This kind of phasing may be done for various subsystems.

e. Prepare for the journey The introduction of a system requires preparation. The system needs changes in the orientation and attitudes of the people in the organisation as well as skills to implement and use the system. In the absence of these the system is likely to fail. Various complications may arise if the skills and competence to run a system are lacking. Problems may arise if necessary training does not precede the introduction of a system. If the organisation argues that it will introduce a system only after necessary conditions have been fulfilled, then it may have to wait for ever. Sometimes this may be used as a pretext for not introducing the system. Action to provide such preparation is necessary. The preparation may also be phased. This may be done at various stages of introduction, not at the beginning alone.

f. Be prepared for reversals The introduction of a system would produce certain changes. The introduction of a new system may create confusion, give rise to suspicion, create doubts, and result in more problems of communication. This may be a necessary part of the change, which is rarely smooth, easy, and pleasant. Any change, especially when it intervenes in the culture of an organisation, creates disturbance. Secondly, at several stages it may seem as if preliminary work has been wanting and the organisation is back to "square one." Such reverses may appear especially when progress is not according to schedule but should not arouse anxiety. It should be understood that reverses are likely to occur and the organisation should be prepared to deal with them and move forward.

g. Develop internal expertise It is necessary that while a system is being designed and implemented there is enough internal expertise which increases with the development of the system. A system cannot be implemented with the help of external expertise alone. Outside help may be useful, either in the beginning or at a later stage, when some dimensions need attention. However, continuous work will have to be done through internal resources alone. If enough attention is not paid to developing such expertise in the enthusiasm of accepting a system, the system is likely to fail.

h. Continue moving Persistence in the implementation of the system is important for various sequences, with certain reverses, and for phasing the system. Such perseverance is possible if the organisation is able to prepare a long-term plan and identify one person or a small group of persons to attend to the introduction of the system and its implementation. The main responsibility of these people may be to take necessary steps to deal with the problem and not let these come in the way of the final implementation of the system.

*i. **Have a compass and a speedometer*** Monitoring mechanisms in the implementation of the system are necessary. At each step, enough information should be collected about the progress of the system and the direction in which the system is going. An individual or a small group of persons may be given the responsibility to monitor progress. For example, special interview schedules/questionnaires can be designed to gather information about the quality of employee feedback and counselling after performance appraisal forms have been completed. Such information will help in taking corrective action.

To sum up, proactive strategy requires planned and persistent work. Past experiences of failure and problems in implementing some system confirm these needs. Advocates of reactive strategy adopt these as defences to argue that such systems are not suited to the culture and that they should be evolved to "suit" the culture. Such a strategy may not help an organisation to take necessary steps for change.

SUMMARY

- In this chapter we have discussed the concept of organisational culture. The sources of organisational culture are—environmental influences, social and natural values, and organisation-specific values.
- We have studied various types of organisational cultures – (a) Charismatic and self-sufficient cultures (b) paranoid and trusting cultures; (c) avoidant and achievement cultures; (d) politicised and focused cultures; and (e) bureaucratic and creative cultures.
- Culture plays an important role during the change process. In the first place, a reasonable degree of stability is required as a setting for planned change. In the context of a global organisational culture, the requirement of a global outlook in culture is discussed.
- A significant difference between organisational climate and culture has been discussed for a better understanding of the concept.
- For effective management of change in organisations, the functionality and dysfunctionality of the culture on the basis of fatalism, ambiguity tolerance, contextualism, temporalness, collectivism, particularism, other directedness, androgyny, and tolerance for power distance are discussed.
- The strength and weakness of organisational culture have been discussed on the basis of motivation, synthesis, dependency motive, fatalism, non-involvement, non-commitment, individualism, and irreality orientation.
- The top management plays an important role in building and maintenance of the organisational culture. Their commitment towards culture determines the success of change in the organisation.
- In a proactive approach for the effective management of change direction, time and journey (process of change)-oriented guidelines are given.

 Case Study: A Fortune 500 Financial Services Company Supported by Offshore Services in India

History

A Fortune 500 financial services company developed an offshore outsourcing relationship with Indian vendors for the development and support of its software and online services. This involved ongoing interactions between the US-based project and technical support staff and counterparts at vendor sites in India. To facilitate interactions and head off communication problems, the client company desired to have all of the relevant US-based staff receive basic India-US cross-cultural training.

Task

Working closely with the client, customise an appropriate "Indian Cultural Awareness" training programme, and deliver it to groups of US-based staff over a period of several months.

Intervention

Management consultants India Practice customised for this company a half-day face-to-face Indian Cultural Awareness training. The training was delivered to different groups of managers and employees by a bi-cultural India Practice team. Feedback and recommendations to the client were made after each training.

Result

Gradual improvement in the communications and effectiveness of the working relationships between the US-based personnel and the project and support team members in India.

Key-Disciplines

Cross-cultural Training, Training Programme Development.

 Case Study: "Globax" A High-tech Start-up Company

History

A high-tech start-up company was developing web-based applications and services for the financial services industry, that is, banks, insurance, mutual funds, stock broking, and so on. This venture required bringing together a highly diverse team of talent from two very different industries (financial services and information technology) and a wide range of company backgrounds, including a key contingent of software engineers from India.

Task

Help the company develop and implement a positive organisational culture, improve interdepartmental integration, and facilitate cross-cultural communication.

Intervention

Globax HR Department worked one-on-one with the CEO to define his values and draft an organisational culture vision statement. Through questionnaires and interviews, the ideas of management team members and other key employees were elicited. A company-wide feedback process was deployed to create broad buy-in and ownership of the vision.

Globax HRD also carried out a number of diagnostics to bring to the surface incipient organisational issues and provided the CEO with a set of action recommendations. Finally, Globax HRD provided consultation, troubleshooting, facilitation, and training sessions around the multi-cultural team-building challenges of the company.

Result

This process helped the company move into its rapid growth phase with a more focused corporate culture, an integrated team, and positive approaches to the cultural diversity among its workforce.

Key Disciplines

Organisation Development, Cross-cultural Consulting, Cross-cultural Training, Team Building.

REVIEW QUESTIONS

1. What are the sources and types of organisational culture?
2. What do you understand by significance of culture during change?
3. What is the difference between organisational climate and organisational culture?
4. Write brief notes on:
   a. Concept of organisational culture
   b. Strengths and weaknesses of Indian culture
   c. Top management and organisational culture
5. What do you understand by functionality and dysfunctionality of a culture?
6. Illustrate a proactive approach to culture for successful change.

EXERCISE

This practical play is for better understanding the individuality and the culture factor of the organisation. It is a very simple game for groups of all sizes, and people of all ages and levels of seniority. People can work as individuals, pairs, or teams of three or more, depending on the situation and outcomes and development required. Playing the game with individuals will limit team discussion and co-operation but will produce individual expression; working in teams will prompt team discussion and generate collective expression.

The object of the exercise is for the team members to embellish or decorate a big word on a sheet of flip-chart paper. The word can be the same or different for each person/team, and can be chosen by the delegates or the facilitator, depending on the outcomes and particular focus required. Short words work better than long words.

The word can be prepared before the exercise, that is, it can be enlarged and printed in a plain font such as arial, 3-6 inches high, preferably in outline to optimise the scope for decoration. Then the printed sheet can be pasted to the flip-chart sheet breadthwise. Alternatively, agree on the word with the individuals/team and instruct them to draw it as a simple black outline on the flip-chart sheet. The word should be plain and simple, it is the decoration that matters for it to be very revealing.

Participants must use materials provided, for example, pens, paints, crayons, glitter, glue, or cloth, to decorate and embellish the word to emphasise what the word means to them, in whatever context the facilitator suggests. The context can be anything that pertains to the session, for example, the organisation's values and positioning, the delegate's personal philosophy (if working as individuals), management culture, or customer service effectiveness. This exercise is also ideal for very young people as well as people at work.

The exercise gives participants the opportunity to express their feelings about the given context, in the way that they choose to decorate the word.

Examples of themes/contexts Organisation, customers, customer service, inter-departmental communications, career opportunities, school, training and development.

Examples of words for decoration Team, boss, staff, teacher, student, school, service, talk, hear, ideas, change, me, us, work.

Chapter

Concept of Change

CHAPTER OUTLINE

- Introduction
- Meaning of Organisational Change
- Nature of Organisational Change
- Pressure for Change
- Planned Change
- Types of Planned Change
- Levels of Change
- Change Cycle
- Organisational Barriers to Change
- Performance-driven Organisational Change
- Rate of Change
- Different States of Change
- Creating Change
- Implementation of Change
- General Guidelines for Effective Change
- Summary
- Case Study
- Review Questions
- Exercises

> "Progress is impossible without change; and those who cannot change their minds, cannot change anything."
>
> "We must always change, renew, rejuvenate ourselves, otherwise we harden."
>
> —Goethe

3.1 INTRODUCTION

We live in an age of transition. What is constant is change. It has become an inescapable fact of life, a fundamental aspect of historical evolution. Everything changes continually. What is history indeed but a record of change? If there had been no changes in the past, there would have been little of history to write.

Change is inevitable in a progressive culture. There is constant evolution in political, scientific, and technological areas. Sophisticated communication techniques, robots performing jobs done by humans; man reaching the moon are some examples that bear testimony to the fast pace of change.

Organisations cannot completely buffer themselves from this change. They must respond to the change in order to survive. In fact, the present day philosophy is "change or perish."

Change can be defined as an alteration in the existing field of focus which tends to affect the equilibrium. The history of organisation is littered with the corpses of enterprises which failed to respond appropriately to the innumerable demands of the environment for change. Organisations are, of course, learning to cope with the rate of internal and external change with the help of some fundamental shifts in management philosophy and organisational technology. Modern organisations are highly dynamic, versatile, and adaptive to the multiplicity of changes.

There are plenty of definitions of organisational change. However, this definition provided by the Organisation Development and Research Organisation, a consulting firm with more than 23 years of experience in helping organisations successfully implement change, is a good starting point. "Organisational change is the implementation of new procedures or technologies intended to realign an organisation with the changing demands of its business environment, or to capitalise on business opportunities."

3.2 MEANING OF ORGANISATIONAL CHANGE

Change is a kind of learning process. New ideas, new values, new skills, and ways of behaviour have to be learned if significant change is to take place. One of the basic findings about learning is that its rate is not uniform throughout. Although the rate pattern differs for different kinds of learning, it generally goes through several stages: slow start, acceleration, rapid rate, and levelling off. On a graph, the line of learning speed appears as an S-shaped curve. This is called the learning curve as shown in Fig. 3.1.

Fig. 3.1 Learning curve

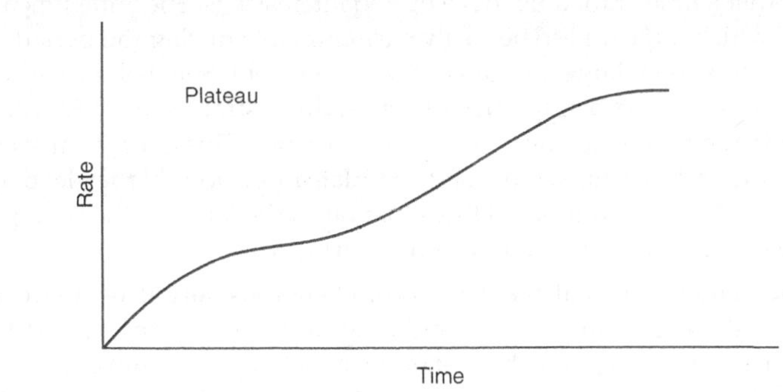

Learning takes place slowly during the early, experimental period. The learner is getting adjusted to the task of learning. This is not a passive period; it is a period of preparation. If the individual is properly motivated and adequately guided to understand the learning task and what is required of him, the next stage is one of acceleration and rapid learning. There is a sudden growth in the rate of learning. This period is followed by a decrease. This may be due to many factors. When the greater part of the task is accomplished, interest may taper off. The learner's attention may be distracted by other new challenges. A feeling of satisfaction may set in because much of the task is finished. Or the learner may feel that he needs a period to consolidate his learning.

The learner may be experiencing some difficulty. Or the needs of the learner may have changed during the process, or the goal may have been judged to be no longer appropriate or worthwhile. Whatever the reason, learning tends to level off and enter a plateau during which little new is learned.

The plateau requires careful watching. If it occurs near the achievement of full learning or change, then there is little reason for concern—the learning task will probably be rounded off at a slower, normal rate. If, however, the plateau period arrives prematurely, special steps may be required to revive the rate of learning. The causes of the early plateau should be studied and appropriate action planned by the teacher. New motivation may be required. Assistance may be needed in digesting what has already been learned. The goal and the learning task may require adjustment in keeping with the new insights and purposes developed by the learner. The learner may need help in overcoming certain learning blocks that have developed. Improved communication may be required among learners working on the same task or between teachers and learners. When the situation has been accurately diagnosed and proper action taken, learning should move at an increased rate once more, towards fulfillment of the learning objectives.

Change often follows a path similar to the learning curve. After a slow start, change programmes often excite a great deal of enthusiasm, resulting in rapid progress. After a time, difficulties develop and interest lags. The impediments to change, which appeared to be easily surmountable during the period of enthusiasm now loom large and cause discouragement. Some of the earlier, rapid change is found to be superficial. Or, the administrators may lose interest and their attention taken up by other programmes. This is a critical stage where the programme moves beyond the plateau on to a higher level of achievement. Many illustrations of this situation can be found in the attempts to introduce varieties of crops among Indian farmers.

It can be generalised that the process of change usually takes place in stages, each stage growing out and building on the experience of earlier stages. Sometimes the steps are those of problem-solving. Sometimes they are those of an individual who becomes aware of a new practice and eventually adopts it. Sometimes they can be described as learning stages, including the plateau stage. However, we view the steps or stages of change, it is important to keep in mind that most people who are expected to make a change must experience all the stages themselves. In this way, it is possible for them to grow with the process, to change qualitatively rather than in form or appearance only. While there may be some people who require less evolutionary development than others, even those who are most change-prone need help in adjusting to significant changes in attitudes and practices.

However, it is not always possible for everyone to go through all the stages involved in a change programme. This is particularly true where a programme is initiated at the national or state levels. In such programmes, the early stages must be planned by seniors at the top and passed down to lower levels for implementation. In such cases, it is critically important that every effort be made to help persons at the level of implementation to experience a new one will thinking that has gone into the earlier stages. This can be done in a number of ways. One way is for clients to be allowed and encouraged to replan the programme, in terms of the local situation. Through rethinking and adapting the innovation, the clients will develop some understanding of the earlier stages through which the change programme has evolved. As indicated earlier, such participation at the local level assumes that the plan developed at higher levels is in no sense a "master-plan", but procedures for replanting at lower levels in the national or state plan. Another way to provide for growth of clients, parallel with the earlier stages of a centrally initiated scheme, is for them to carry on a study and discussion of the problem area to which the programme will contribute. For instance, before introducing a new syllabus planned at the state level, it is desirable to help teachers, through study and discussion, to understand why the syllabus should be changed. Or before the introduction of a new scheme for the inspection of local schools, which was evolved in a national research project, will be helpful for local inspectors to study some of their own problems in relation to the fundamental purposes of inspection.

Typically, the concept of organisational change bears relation to organisation-wide change, as opposed to smaller changes such as adding a new person, modifying a programme and so on. Examples of organisation-wide changes might include a change in mission, restructuring operations (restructuring to self-managed teams and layoffs), new technologies, mergers, major collaborations, "rightsizing", new programmes such as total quality management, re-engineering, and so on. Some experts refer to organisational transformation. Often this term designates a fundamental and radical reorientation in the way an organisation operates.

Change is an important aspect in the study of organisational viability. The right kind of change enables an organisation to maintain its viability in its changing environment. On the other hand, the wrong kind of change can destroy an organisation. For example, death, destruction, and deterioration are all changes, yet it can hardly be maintained that they are generally constructive. True, the demise of one system might work to the benefit of other systems. For instance, a competitive firm might benefit from the failure of another. Revolutionaries also may view the destruction of an old political system as necessary if their ideal is to be implemented. Despite such exceptions, it is clear that change per se may be dysfunctional as well as functional. The challenge is to create change that increases or renews the viability of an organisation's position in its environment. "Renewal is not just innovation and change. It is also the process of bringing the results of change in line with [the organisation's] purposes."

3.3 NATURE OF ORGANISATIONAL CHANGE

Any alteration that occurs in the overall work environment is called change. Keith Davis beautifully explains the nature of work change by drawing a parallel with an air-filled balloon. He explains when a finger (which represents change) is pressed against the exterior of the balloon (which represents the organisation), the contour visibly changes at the point of impact. The molecules of air in the balloon represents the firm's employees. Repeated pressure at a point may unnecessarily weaken the balloon at that point and motion creates friction and heat. Eventually, a rupture occurs and the organisation collapses. But an organisation is much more complex than a balloon, and real people are quite different from the molecules in the balloon. This comparison is merely intended to emphasise the point that just as molecular equilibrium is essential, an organisation also seeks equilibrium in its social structure. By equilibrium we mean that people come to expect various relationships within their working surroundings. The essence is that change requires new adjustments and new equilibrium.

Fig. 3.2 Nature of change

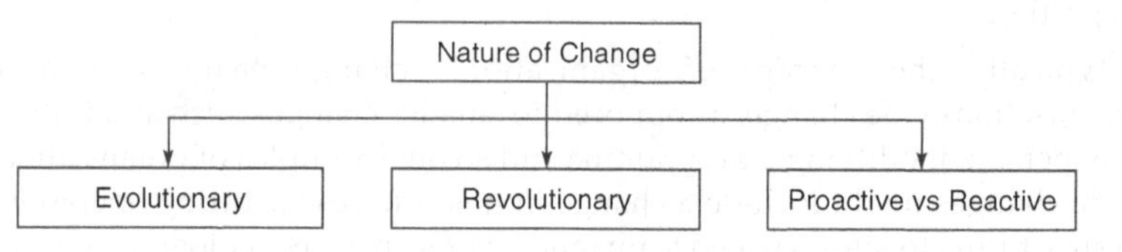

There are a variety of changes (Fig. 3.2).

3.3.1 Evolutionary Change

Some changes are evolutionary in nature and do not greatly violate the tradition and status quo expectations. They usually take place one by one. They seldom promote great inclusion, evoke deep resistance, or give dramatic results. One limitation of this change is that it is very slow and the organisation may fall behind the expectations.

3.3.2 Revolutionary Change

Sometimes, change may be cataclysmic. A revolutionary change results in overturning the status quo arrangement and causes violation, rejection, or suppression of old expectations. The revolutionary churning generally faced strong resistance and sometimes only an exercise of power can implement such changes. Revolutionary changes are rarely introduced except where the situation becomes highly intolerable and there are no other acceptable options.

3.3.3 Proactive vs Reactive Change

Proactive change is change that is initiated by an organisation because it is desirable to do so. Reactive change is change initiated in an organisation because it is made necessary by outside forces. For instance, introduction of a new employee benefit scheme is proactive as the management strongly believes that it enhances the satisfaction and motivation of employees. The change would be reactive if the benefit plan was introduced because of demands made by the employees.

3.4 PRESSURE FOR CHANGE

As we have already discussed in Chapter 1, an organisation works in an ever-changing business environment. To survive, it needs to adapt to the factors of external, operational, and internal environment.

Change should not be made for the sake of change—it is a strategy to accomplish an overall goal. Usually organisational change is brought about by some major outside driving force, for example, substantial cuts in funding, addressing new markets/clients, need for dramatic increases in productivity/services, and so on. Typically, organisations must undertake organisation-wide change to evolve to a different level in their life cycle; for example, going from a highly reactive, entrepreneurial organisation to a more stable and planned organisation. A new chief executive, for example, can provoke organisation-wide change when his new and unique personality pervades the entire organisation.

3.4.1 Nine Winds of Change

Nine new discontinuities have identified, all or some of which may be in play at any one time.

a. *Global* In the next century companies will need to look and deal beyond national borders as the makeup of the global economy changes. Experts predict that as China and India emerge as economic powerhouses, multinational companies will need business units there.
b. *Deregulation and privatisation* One only needs to look at the financial and telecommunications industries to see how deregulation has snowballed, particularly as the focus of these sectors has become international. Mergers and takeovers will continue to be commonplace, as companies seek to position themselves and their assets to the best advantage.
c. *Resizing* Public sector firms continue to move into the private domain, resulting in unemployment and rationalisation of assets. Resizing has become a synonym for downsizing.
d. *Volatility* The demand for greater efficiency, reduction in product development times, and flexibility on the part of producers will see a significant shift in the new economy. Shifting markets mean companies can no longer justify concentrating production on a single product (so-called "focussed factories"). Instead, they must adapt to dealing with more than one product to become "flexible factories." Suppliers will play a key role in business success.
e. *Convergence* As business sectors converge, firms must learn to move beyond their traditional areas of expertise to survive. The impact of digital technology will have a profound effect. No organisation can afford not to respond to the changes it sets in motion.

f. ***Indeterminate business boundaries*** The lines between sectors will continue to blur in the next century. Competition may come from unexpected quarters, so identifying potential threats may be difficult. For example, supermarkets will bring their own skills to bear in the financial market. The boundaries between suppliers, competitors, and customers will be less defined. Traditional market measures may no longer suffice. Size will not necessarily imply influence and power.

g. ***Standards*** There will be a change in the way industry standards are created, as market drivers, not policy-makers, take charge. Companies will set their own standards, and the most successful will become industry-wide. Competing coalitions of companies will decide the fate of any given set of standards.

h. ***Disintermediation*** The distance between producer and customer is shrinking. E-commerce and other new channels emerge as traditional links in the supply chain disappear. In this deregulated business zone, "the expert" will wield considerable influence—checking on the authenticity of claims and acting as a new kind of intermediary.

i. ***Eco-sensitivity*** A new system will emerge which uses world resources to the best advantage in both an economic and environmental sense. In other words, moving from a "compliance-orientated" perspective to one that is "business-opportunity-driven".

"We live in the audit of constant change" has become a well-worn and relevant fact. Pressure for change in an organisation is created internally and externally.

3.5 PLANNED CHANGE

A group of employees that worked in a small retail women's clothing store confronted the owner. "The air pollution in this store from cigarette smoking has a rotten effect," said their spokeswoman. "We won't continue to work here if you allow smoking in the store. We want you to post no smoking signs on the entrance of the floor. If people have to smoke, they can go outside the mall." The owner listened carefully to the group's ultimatum and agreed to the request. The next day the owner posted the no smoking signs and advised all the employees to follow the new rule. This issue never came up again and seemed to have been solved forever.

A major automobile manufacturer spent several million dollars to install state-of-the-art robotics. One area that would receive the new equipment was quality control. Sophisticated computer-controlled equipment would be put in place to significantly improve the company's ability to find and correct defects. Since the new equipment would dramatically change the job of the people working in the quality control area, and since management anticipated considerable employee resistance to the new equipment, executives were developing a programme to help people become familiar with the equipment and to deal with any anxiety they might be feeling.

Both of the above scenarios are examples of change. That is, both are concerned with making things different. However, only the second scenario describes planned change. In this section, we want to clarify what is meant by planned change, describe its goals, contrast first order and second order change, and consider who is responsible for bringing about planned change in the organisation.

What are the goals of planned change? Essentially there are two. First, it seeks to improve the ability of the organisation to adapt to changes in its environment. Second, it seeks to change employee behaviour.

If an organisation is to survive, it must respond to changes in its environment. When competitors introduce new products or services, government agencies enact new laws, important sources of supply go out of business, or similar environmental changes take place, the organisation needs to adapt. Efforts to stimulate innovation, empower employees, and introduce work teams are examples of planned change activities directed at responding to changes in the environment.

Since an organisation's success or failure is essentially due to what its employees do or fail to do, planned change is also concerned with changing the behaviours of individual and groups within the organisation.

Planned change will be effective if the following points are considered.

a. ***Qualitative change*** It occurs when the employees working in an organisation have the desire to change themselves.

b. ***Direction-oriented change*** The main objective of any organisation is to accomplish its goal; for this it is necessary to have a positive approach towards change. It has been rightly said, "It's not so much where you stand in life but in what direction you are moving."

c. ***Variation in the adoption rates*** Studies have shown that people who accept a particular change fall into five categories (Fig. 3.3).

   i. Innovators They contribute towards 2.5 percent of the total consumer base and they are the first ones to adopt any change readily.

Fig. 3.3 Variation in the adoption rate

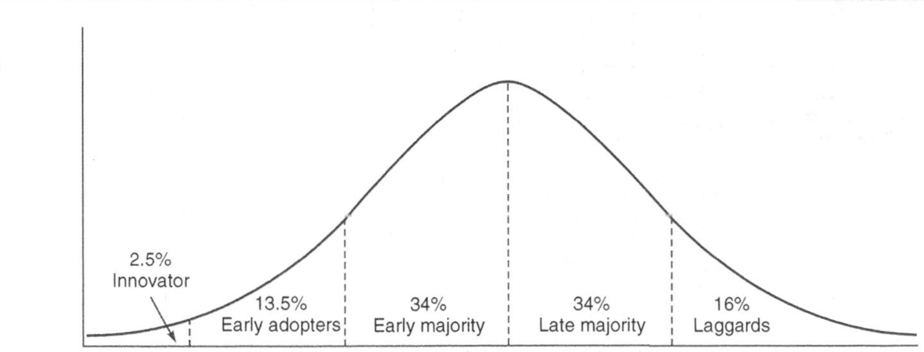

ii. *Early adopter* They constitute 13.5 percent of the total and they are highly motivated persons. They need little persuasion and can easily become a part of change.

iii. *Early majority* They constitute 34 percent of the total group. They require some time to prepare themselves for a change.

iv. *Late majority* They also constitute 34 percent of the total group but are very slow in accepting a change.

v. *Laggards* They constitute 16 percent of the group and they accept change very late and there are some who never accept change.

3.6 TYPES OF PLANNED CHANGE

There are three types of planned change—individual, group, and organisational (Fig. 3.4). A planned change at the individual level could stem from:

- Change in job assignment
- Transfer of an employee to a different location
- Change in the maturity level of a person in the organisation

A planned change at the group level could take place due to:

- Trade unions
- Inefficient work design
- Lack of communication in the organisation work environment

Planned organisational change could happen due to or be:

- Strategic change
- Structural change

Fig. 3.4 Different types of planned change

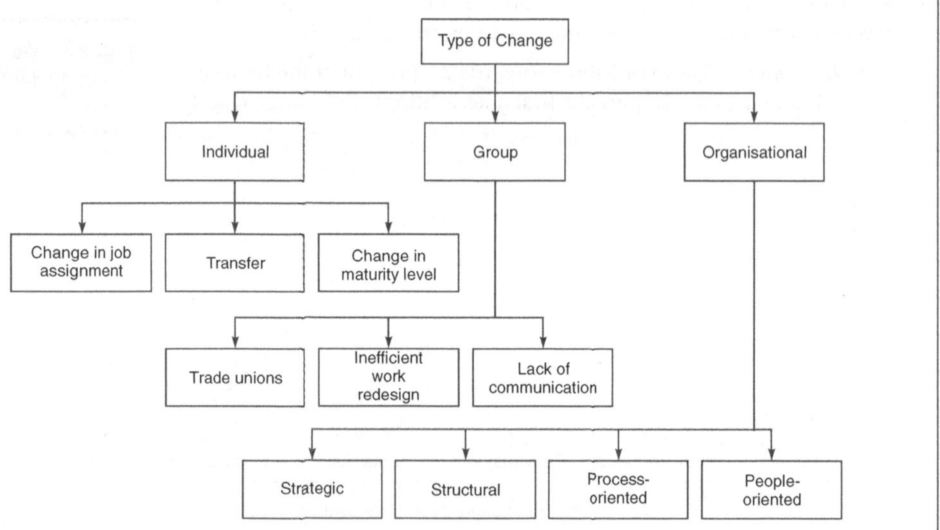

- Process-oriented change
- People-oriented change

Now let us examine some major organisational changes in detail.

a. ***Strategic change*** It refers to change in the basic objectives or missions of the organisation.

b. ***Structural change*** It involves change in the internal structure of the organisation. This change means change in the whole set of relationships, work assignment, and authority structure.

c. ***Process-oriented change*** It relates to the recent technological developments, information processing, and automation.

d. ***People-oriented change*** It is directed towards performance improvement, group cohesion, dedication and loyalty to the organisation as well as developing a sense of self-actualisation among members. This could be done by closer interaction with employees and by behavioural training.

Fig. 3.5 Different types of change on the basis of magnitude

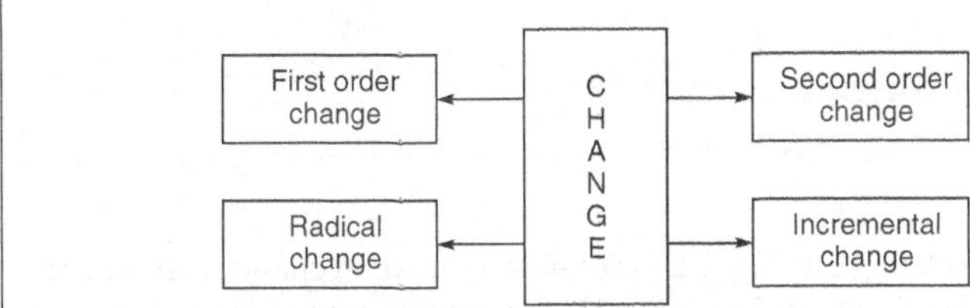

It also helps to think of planned change in terms of magnitude (Fig. 3.5).

a. ***First order change*** is linear and continuous. It implies no fundamental shifts in the assumption that organisational members hold about the world or how the organisation can improve its functioning.

b. ***Second order change*** is a multi-dimensional multi-level, discontinuous, radical change involving re-grading of assumptions about the organisation and the world in which it operates.

c. ***Radical change*** means that a firm stops doing things in old ways and begins to do things in fundamentally new ways. Radical change is about pursuing new and different strategies, structures, capabilities, and resources supported by new and different core values.

d. ***Incremental change*** helps to improve operations by improving the alignment among organisational structure, systems, and environment. It does not challenge the firm's core values; it builds on them. Incremental change does not imply any change in the basic assumptions and values about how the organisation should be run.

3.7 LEVELS OF CHANGE

Change is a broader phenomenon; it has four interdependent levels of change in the people.

Knowledge changes
Attitudinal changes
Behavioural changes
Group or organisational performance changes (Fig. 3.6).

Fig. 3.6 Levels of change

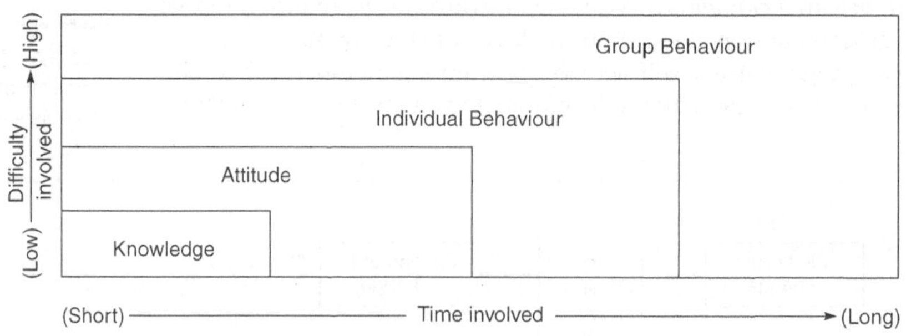

a. ***Knowledge changes*** tend to be the easiest to make. A change can occur as a result of reading a book or an article or hearing something new from a knowledgeable person.
b. ***Attitudinal changes*** differ from knowledge changes in that they are emotionally charged in a positive or negative way. The addition of emotion often makes attitudes more difficult to change than knowledge.
c. ***Behavioural changes*** seem to be significantly more difficult and time consuming than either of the two previous levels. For example, managers may have knowledge about the advantages of increased follower involvement and participation in decision-making and may even feel that such participation would improve their performance. Yet, they may be unable to delegate or share decision-making responsibilities significantly with subordinates. This discrepancy between knowledge, attitude, and behaviour may be a result of their own authoritarian management-subordinate upbringing. Past experience may have led to a habit pattern that feels comfortable.

   While individual behaviour is difficult enough to change, it becomes even more complicated when you try to implement change within groups or organisations.
d. ***Group or organisational performance changes*** The leadership styles of one or two managers might be effectively altered, but drastically chang-

ing the level of follower participation throughout an organisation might be a very time-consuming process. At this level you are trying to alter customs and traditions that have developed over many years.

3.8 CHANGE CYCLE

The level of change becomes very significant when you examine two different change cycles—the *participative change cycle* and the *directive change cycle.*

3.8.1 Participative Change Cycle

This change cycle is implemented when new knowledge is made available to the individual or group. It is hoped that the group will accept the data and will develop a positive attitude and commitment in the direction of the desired change. At this level, an effective strategy may be to involve the individual or group directly in helping to select or formalise the new methods for obtaining the desired goals. This is group participation in problem-solving (see Fig. 3.7).

The next step will be to attempt to translate this commitment into actual behaviour. This step is significantly more difficult to achieve. For example, it is one thing to be concerned about follower participation in decision-making (attitude) but another thing to actually get involved in doing something (behaviour) about the issue. An effective strategy may be to identify the informal and formal leaders among the work group(s) and concentrate on gaining their behavioural support for the desired change. Once this is accomplished, organisational change may be effected by getting other people to begin to pattern their behaviour after those persons whom they respect and perceive in leadership roles.

Fig. 3.7 Participative change cycle

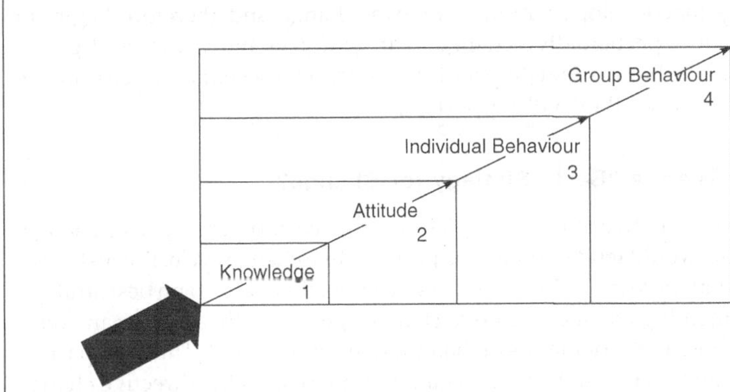

3.8.2 Directive Change Cycle

Many of us probably been faced with a situation at work when there is an announcement on Monday morning that "as of today all members of this organisation will begin to operate in accordance with Form 10125." This is an example of a directive change cycle. It is through this change cycle that many managers in the past have attempted to implement such innovative ideas as management by objectives, job enrichment, and the like (Fig. 3.8).

Fig. 3.8 Directive change cycle

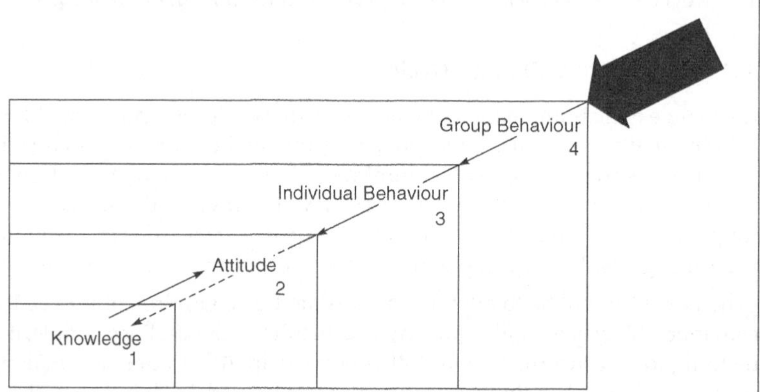

This change cycle is imposed on the entire organisation by some external force, such as higher management, community, or new laws. It tends to affect the interaction network system at the individual level. The new contacts and modes of behaviour create new knowledge, which tend to develop a predisposition towards or against the change.

In some cases where change is forced, the new behaviour creates the kind of knowledge that develops commitment to the change, and, therefore, begins to approximate a participative change as it reinforces individual and group behaviour. The hope is that "if people will only have a chance to see how the new system works, they will support it".

3.8.3 Is There a "Best" Strategy for Change?

Given a choice between the polarities of directive and participative change, most people would tend to prefer the participative change cycle. But just as we all know that there is no "best" leadership style, there is also no best strategy for implementing change. Effective change agents are those who can adapt their strategies to the demands of their unique environment. Thus, the participative change cycle is not a better change strategy than the directive change cycle and vice versa. The appropriate strategy depends on the situation, and each has its advantages and disadvantages.

3.8.4 Advantages/Disadvantages of Change Cycles

The participative change cycle tends to be more appropriate for working with individuals and groups who are achievement motivated, seek responsibility, and have a degree of knowledge and experience that may be useful in developing new ways of operating. In other words, people with task-relevant readiness. Once the change starts, these people are capable of assuming the responsibilities of implementing of the desired change. Although these people may welcome change and the need to improve, they may become very rigid and opposed to change if it is implemented in a directive (high task/low relationship) manner. A directive change style is inconsistent with their perceptions of themselves as responsible, self-motivated people who should be consulted throughout the change process. When they are not consulted and change is implemented in an authoritarian manner, conflict often results. Examples of this occur frequently in organisations in which a manager recruits or inherits competent, creative staff that is willing to work hard to implement new programmes and then proceeds to bypass the staff completely in the change process. This style results in resistance.

A coercive, directive change style might be very appropriate and more productive with individuals and groups who are less ambitious, are often dependent, and who are not willing to take on new responsibilities unless forced to do so. In fact, these people might prefer direction and structure from their leader to being faced with decisions they are not willing or experienced enough to make. Once again, diagnosis is important. It is just as inappropriate for a manager to attempt to implement change in a participative manner with a staff that has never been given the opportunity to take responsibility and has become dependent on its manager for direction as it is to implement change in a coercive manner with a staff that is ready to change and willing to take responsibility for implementing it.

There are other significant differences between these two change cycles. The participative change cycle tends to be effective when introduced by leaders who have personal power; that is, they have referent information and expert power. On the other hand, the directive cycle necessitates that a leader have significant position with power, that is, coercion, connection, reward, and legitimate power.

If managers decide to implement change in an authoritarian, coercive manner, they would be wise to have the support of their superiors and other sources of power or their staff may effectively block them.

A significant advantage of the participative change cycle is that once the change is accepted, it tends to be long lasting. Since everyone has been involved in the development of the change, each person tends to be highly committed to its implementation. The disadvantage of participative change is that it tends to be slow and evolutionary—it may take years to implement a significant change.

An advantage of directive change, on the other hand, is speed. Using position power, leaders can often impose change immediately. A disadvantage of this change strategy is that it tends to be volatile. It can be maintained only as long as the leader has position power to make it stick. It often results in animosity, hostility, and, in some cases, overt and covert behaviour to undermine and overthrow the leader.

The directive change cycle could be utilised if the power of the driving forces pushing for change far outweighed the restraining forces resisting change. On the other hand, a directive change cycle would fail if the power of the restraining forces working against the change were more frequent and powerful than the power of the driving forces pushing for change.

A participative change cycle that depends on personal power could be appropriate in either of the cases just described. With frequent and powerful driving forces pushing for change in a situation, a leader might not have to use a high task, directive change cycle since the driving forces are ready to run with the change already and do not have to be forced to engage in the new desired behaviour. At the same time, when the restraining forces can easily overpower the driving forces, managers would be advised to begin with participative change techniques designed gradually to turn some of the restraining forces into driving forces or at least immobilise their influence on the situation. In other words, when things are stacked against organisation, it would be more effective to try to re-educate the forces against the change than to try to force change in a situation when little power is on the side of the change effort.

These two change cycles have been described, as if they are were either/or positions. The use of only one of these change cycles exclusively, however, could lead to problems. For example, if managers introduce change only in a directive, high task/low relationship manner without any movement toward participative change, members of their staff—if they decide to remain—may react in one of two ways. Some may fight the managers tooth and nail and organise efforts to undermine them. Others may buckle under their authority and become passive, dependent staff members, always needing the manager to tell them what to do and when to do it before doing anything. These kinds of people say yes to anything the manager wants and then moan and groan and drag their feet later. Neither of these responses makes for a very healthy organisation. At the other extreme, managers who will not make a move without checking with their staff and getting full approval also can immobilise themselves. They may establish such a complicated network of "participative" committees that significant change becomes almost impossible.

Thus, in reality, it is more a question of a proper blend of the directive and participative change cycles, depending on the situation, than a forced choice between one or the other.

3.9 ORGANISATIONAL BARRIERS TO CHANGE

Typically there is strong resistance to change. People are afraid of the unknown. Many people think things are already fine and do not understand the need for change. Many are inherently cynical about change, particularly from reading about the notion of "change" as if it is a mantra. Many doubt there are effective means to accomplish major organisational change. Often there are conflicting goals in the organisation, for example, to increase resources to accomplish change yet concurrently cut costs to remain viable. Organisation-wide change often goes against the very values held dear by members in the organisation, that is, the change may go against how members believe things should be done. That is why much of organisational change literature discusses needed changes in the culture of the organisation, including changing members' values and beliefs and in the way they enact these values and beliefs.

During the process of change, individual, group, and organisation show resistance to the process of change due to physical, psychological, social, and economic reasons. These are explained in brief in the following units.

3.10 PERFORMANCE-DRIVEN ORGANISATIONAL CHANGE

Organisational change is driven by organisational performance. The different effects of high and low organisational performance can be distinguished with low performance causing organisational adaptation and high performance leading to organisational growth. Thus, there are basically two aspects of organisational change.

a. Organisational adaptation
b. Organisational growth

Organisational adaptation occurs whenever an organisation alters some attribute of itself to bring about a better fit with its situation to improve organisational performance. For example, organisational adaptation occurs when a diversified firm with a functional structure that is inappropriate adopts instead a divisional structure that is appropriate, thereby raising performance.

Organisational growth, on the other hand, refers to an increase in organisational size or scale such as number of employees, sales, or number of branches.

Many factors such as strategy, human resources, product marketing, production, logistics, and procurement shape organisational performance.

As explained above, organisational adaptation means to bring about changes in the organisation to improve its performance. This means that low performance triggers organisational adaptation. If the performance of organisation is not satisfactory, then it will have to make changes in the organisation, that is, organisational adaptation will take place.

Similarly, higher levels of performance encourage growth of an organisation that is in fit, by making additional resources available. An organisation in fit will have a structure and other attributes that are well suited to its situation, for example, in size, strategy, and environment so that it operates effectively and can make correct decisions. Therefore, the organisation can grow and will do so as long as it is the strategic intent of its managers. When the organisation also simultaneously enjoys high performance, it will have surplus resources. These resources are therefore available to find growth in the organisation such as hiring new employees, opening new branches, launching new products or services, purchasing more advanced technology, and acquiring other firms. Therefore, the higher the performance of an organisation in fit, the greater is the resulting growth rate.

3.11 RATE OF CHANGE

Although the environment of an organisation is constantly changing, the required rate of change of a viable organisation may vary depending on the type of organisation. A company manufacturing a toy that is a fad can expect a short viable relationship with its environment, whereas a firm producing a staple item as salt might prosper for many decades with comparatively little change.

To gain efficiencies of expertise and standard operating procedures, it is necessary that an organisation adopt, for a time, a particular way of doing things step by step (step function). Thus, its method of operations may be relatively static in relation to its environment. Instead of constantly making the incremental changes necessary to maintain perfect adaptation, the organisation may instead, from time to time, make a number of structural or technological changes at once. This idea is illustrated in Fig. 3.9, which depicts the adaptation of a long-term viable organisation to its environment. The steep portions of the curve represent periods soon after the organisation made major successful changes. The flatter portions represent the periods of relatively stable operations that were becoming obsolete.

Organisational changes that improve its adaptation can be of several types:

a. Technological changes including new products and new processes
b. Structural changes including new policies or procedures
c. Human changes including new promotional techniques or new personnel. None of these is necessarily the most important; what counts is their total mix.

Fig. 3.9 Rate of change

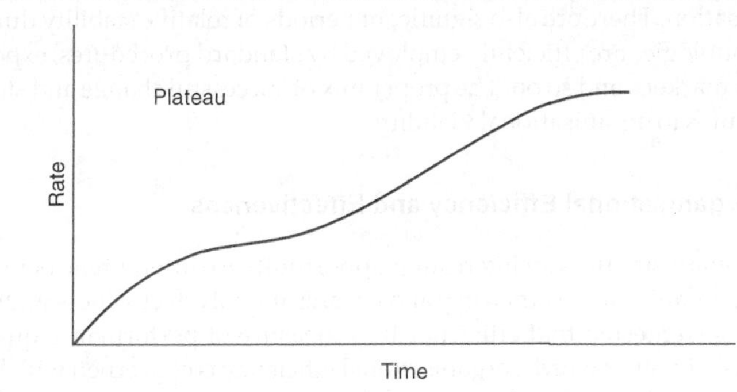

The step-function idea of adaptation just described frequency can be seen in organisations that make major changes in their operations after experiencing unsatisfactory results. In extreme cases, the old management may be discharged in favour of new ideas.

In some cases an organisation may virtually dominate its environment. It may then control the environment in such a way as to maintain itself indefinitely, even though it may be contributing little to its environment. Such conditions may be found in despotic governments and in the perpetuation of vested interests by control of the decision-making process. In the long-term view, such situations are unstable; they are the stuff of which violent revolutions and wars are made. Unfortunately, there is no assurance that a replacement system will be any better. Thus, an apparently endless chain of despotic governments can be observed in some countries. Stable, viable organisations of any kind or size can exist only if there is continuing satisfaction of the interests of all parties concerned.

Long-term viability may require periodic replacement of declining technologies with those that are viable in an evolving environment. Fig. 3.9 illustrates the life phases that successful technologies such as products, processes, principles, programmes, policies, procedures, and persons go through. The question might be raised: Why does something that is successful eventually decline? The answer is fairly simple: because the demands of the environment change.

As long as an organisation replaces declining technologies with new, viable ones, it can remain profitable. On the other hand, failure to introduce new technologies will eventually cause the organisation to decline. Organisations do not have a fixed life span, but the technologies upon which they are based do. Thus, an organisation that fails to change is headed towards certain extinction, although its death may be far away if its present technologies have relatively long-term viability. Progress is a process of changing from one favoured technology to another.

Too frequent changes, even if they are "good" ones, may not bode well for the organisation. There are also significant periods of relative stability during which technologies are efficiently employed by standard procedures, experts, developed markets, and so on. The proper mix of successful change and stability contributes to organisational viability.

3.11.1 Organisational Efficiency and Effectiveness

The above analysis offers an interesting opportunity to differentiate between two terms: organisational efficiency and organisational effectiveness with the change. It is suggested that efficiency be a measure of performance quality within a task. In other words, organisational efficiency is concerned with how well an organisation performs a given task.

Organisational effectiveness can be taken to mean a measure of the quality of relationship of an organisation with its environment. Paradoxically, an organisation may be effective (a viable relationship with its environment) but inefficient (internally wasteful). An organisation can also be highly efficient (fine, standardised internal procedures, for example) but ineffective (outmoded product, for instance).

As previously noted, some degree of internal efficiency is clearly necessary for viability. However, trade offs exist between efficiency (perhaps doing old things better) and effectiveness (doing other better things). Often, there is a clear preference for increased effectiveness at the cost of efficiency because many technological advances (increases in effectiveness) are order-of-magnitude improvements. For instance, computers can perform some numerical manipulations a million times faster than a person. Merely focusing on trying to improve the efficiency of manual computations could never offer the promise of such increases in speed as can a computer. Even to increase efficiency by doubling the speed of the manual computations (which might be quite difficult) would not begin to compare with the million-fold speed of the computer for certain operations.

The futility of some efficiency improvements has been noted succinctly by Peter Drucker: "There is surely nothing quite so useless as doing with great efficiency what should not be done at all." Perhaps this line of thinking explains why some efficiency techniques seem to be becoming less important. More organisations are recognising that "breakthrough" effectiveness gains may be far more significant than mere improvements in procedures (efficiency). Total concern with how to improve current technologies can be fatal to an organisation, just as too much change can be.

3.12 DIFFERENT STATES OF CHANGE

Everyone knows that re-engineering is about processes. To the great relief of many workers, the focus is taken off of them and put on the work.

"Let's not blame people, let's look at where the process failed."

"If there is a problem, it's because the process has broken down. The people are doing their best to make it work."

The workers knew these things all along; they are pleased that you have finally figured that out!

So, if we are going to change the processes, improve them, fix them, the workforce should be happy. Right? Well, there is a problem. The workforce is people and re-engineering the processes means change and people have a lot of problems with change. Any re-engineering project that does not figure in the difficulties people have with change and address the change issues in a systematic, structured way, is bound to fail.

Why, if we are fixing what they wanted fixed, would the workforce resist these changes? Several possibilities exist (Fig. 3.10).

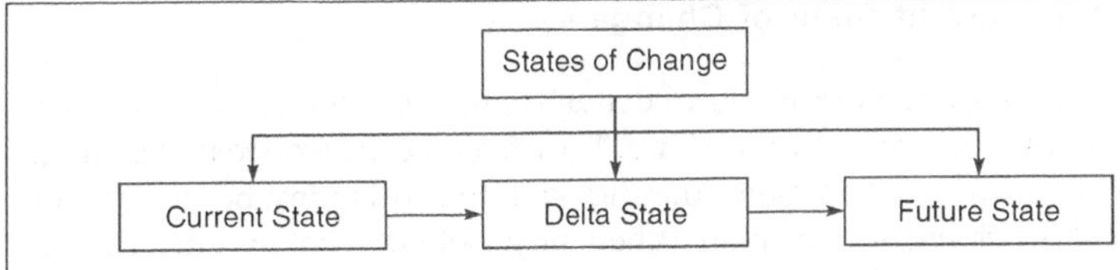

Fig. 3.10 Different states of change

Business process re-engeering uses a rigorous and disciplined methodology to identify the current state, determine the optimum future state, and design an implementation plan. Too often, however, this methodology ignores human resistance issues and the need to address them in the implementation plan. When that happens, people who are targets of the change end up expending the majority of their time and energy figuring out how to stop the change, or change it until it looks like something they can live with, not what the engineers developed. This is how re-engineering fails. What can we do about this problem? If we are thoughtful and listen well, the targets of the change will tell us what to do.

3.12.1 The Future State of Change

They may want change, but not necessarily the changes in the plan. They may have their own ideas about what should change, and frequently it revolves around someone else changing, not them. If the problem is that the desired state is not very desirable, we need to find out why. Are the targets making this judgement based on incomplete information? Then communication is the key. Is the problem that as the targets look closely at the change, they see some things that, from their perspective, are not very desirable? For example, maybe now they will have to work in partnership with the purchasing department.

After years of blaming that group for all the problems, they may have some pretty strong opinions about the skills, knowledge, and personal characteristics of purchasing. Now you want them to work with those people? It will never work. They see purchasing as a group that makes life worse, not better. They see themselves having to expend tremendous amounts of energy and resources to compensate for the deficiencies in purchasing. They would be much better off staying the way they are. The new way will never work.

While communication may help a little here, what is called for is changing the perspective people have about purchasing through education and providing both departments with the skills to integrate with people they have until now seen so negatively. As they move towards that co-operative working environment, they need to see that there are rewards for changing. In other words, "what's in it for them."

3.12.2 The Current State of Change

While the new way of working may be much better, workers do not see much wrong with the current way of working. They may see the way to make things better as just adjusting and manipulating what they do today, not the drastic and wrenching changes in the plan. When the problem is that the current state just does not seem that bad and the question is why go through all this effort, the change agents, those engineers planning the change, need to communicate the why—in the language and from the perspective of the worker. Many companies have gone to the well too often with bad or incomplete information. If every year the workers have heard the same message, "We need to change or we will go out of business", but every year they continue to be employed, they distrust the message.

Go back and check those messages from previous years. Were they an honest and accurate appraisal of the company's situation? Were they designed for understanding by the workforce and to engage people as partners in change or were they really targeted at Wall Street or to scare the workforce into accepting change with incomplete or even inaccurate data?

Sometime, the first step in getting people to accept the need to change is to educate them about the state of the business and how to understand what the current state is. In addition, they need to clearly see how their current rewards in the form of pay cheques, job stability, and reinforcement for the current way they do their job is going away in the marketplace. The worker needs to know the real situation. What are the rewards in terms of performance reviews, merit increases, and promotions that would keep people operating in the current state? These rewards need to be systematically removed when they are rewarding behaviours, actions, processes, and results that will not support the new environment.

3.12.3 The Delta State of Change

The new way may appear highly desirable, and the current way very unsatisfactory, but the process of going from here to there, the process of changing, looks too hard, will take too much energy, and is confusing and frightening. Moreover, it may appear that there are not enough resources of time, people and money. The above mentioned two steps, defining the future state and showing the dangers in the current state are not enough, however. Even the most committed workers will find it difficult to go through the delta of change required in a re-engineering effort. Therefore, it is critical to build into the implementation plan attention to the three change elements that have surfaced in this discussion: communication, education/training and rewards/reinforcements.

Companies and people have no choice: they must change to survive. They do have a choice, however, in how they change. Deciding to manage change by applying an organised, structured methodology is the clear choice of successful companies. When they do this, changes are implemented faster, cheaper (economically), and with a minimum of pain and disruption to people. Since every company is struggling to make changes, those that can do it successfully have a strong edge over their competitors who struggle and often fail. Change management is a key factor in making the changes from business process re-engineering successful.

3.13 CREATING CHANGE

One focus of the interest in creating organisational change has been on the elements of individual creativity. Work here has focused on the process of creative thought, including stages such as conception of the problem, accumulation of information, intensive thinking, frustration, relaxation, and illumination.

The term organisation development (OD) has been applied to many behavioural techniques and techniques used to approach conflict and change in organisations. Specifically, Bennis says that OD is intended to change the beliefs, attitudes, values and structure or organisations so they can better adapt to new technologies, markets and challenges, and the dizzying rate of change itself." Techniques such as job enrichment, management by objectives (MBO), behaviour modification, leadership evaluation, and modification may be considered part of OD. Further, sensitivity and grid training are two techniques very closely associated with OD. Sensitivity, or T-group training, has the simultaneous goals of increasing self-awareness, sensitivity to others, self-expression, self-direction, personal and conceptual insights, and behavioural effectiveness in the organisational environment. The managerial grid developed by Blake and Mouton, and discussed later, can be effectively utilised in OD. The dual concern for both human and production by managers can be developed in an organisational setting by integrating individual manager development with inter-group development, organisational goal-setting, goal attainment, and system stabilisation. Clearly, such a technique should promote organisation development and adaptability to change.

A number of other techniques using groups to produce creativity have been developed. A key feature of many such techniques is to get individuals to break out of habitual ways of thinking which may impede progress. For this reason non-experts frequently can offer creative solutions to problems. A non-expert often sees something in a new light; experts often are so close to the problem that they miss such insights. Experts may tend to offer improvements in efficiency, but effectiveness gains made by non-experts may be much more significant.

3.14 IMPLEMENTATION OF CHANGE

Successful change must involve top management, including the board and chief executive. Usually there is a champion who initially introduces the change by being visionary, persuasive, and consistent. The role of a change agent is to translate the vision in to a realistic plan and carry out the plan. Change is usually best carried out as a team effort. Communication about the change should be frequent and with all organisation members. To sustain change, the structure of the organisation itself should be modified, including strategic plans, policies, and procedures. This change in the structures of the organisation typically involves an unfreezing, change, and refreezing process.

The best approaches to address resistance is through increased and sustained communication and education. For example, the leader should meet with all managers and staff to explain reasons for the change, how it will generally be carried out, and where they can go for additional information. A plan should be developed and communicated. However, plans do change. Communicate that the plan has changed and why. Forums should be held for organisation members to express their ideas for the plan. They should be able to express their concerns and frustrations as well.

3.14.1 Practical Tools to Understand Change

Steps can be taken to increase knowledge and understanding. These include the following.

- SWOT (Strengths, Weaknesses, Opportunities, and Threats) analysis

- TQM (Total Quality Management) exercises
- Group planning exercises
- Programmes by visiting speakers
- Training needs analysis
- Environmental scanning
- User surveys
- Internal staff surveys
- Away days
- External seminars, conferences, and workshops
- Shared experience sessions

3.15 GENERAL GUIDELINES FOR EFFECTIVE CHANGE

The following basic guidelines work as the foundation for carrying out any of the methods associated with organisational change.

a. Consider using a consultant. Ensure that the consultant is highly experienced in organisation-wide change. Ask to see references and check the references.
b. Widely communicate the potential need for change. Communicate what you are doing about it. Communicate what was done and how it worked out.
c. Get as much feedback as practical from employees, including what they think are the problems and what should be done to resolve them. If possible, work with a team of employees to manage the change.
d. Do not get wrapped up in making a change for the sake of change. Know why you are making the change. What goal(s) do you hope to accomplish?
e. Plan the change. How do you plan to reach the goals? What will you need to reach the goals? How long might it take? How will you know when you have reached your goals?
f. Focus on the co-ordination of the departments/programmes in your organisation, not on each part by itself. Have someone in charge of the plan.
g. End up having every employee ultimately reporting to one person, if possible, and they should know who that person is. Job descriptions are often complained about, but they are useful in specifying who reports to whom.
h. Delegate decisions to employees as much as possible. This includes granting them the authority and responsibility to get the job done. As much as possible, let them decide how to do the project.
i. The process will not be an "aha!" It will take longer than you think.

j. Keep perspective. Keep focused on meeting the needs of your customers or clients.
k. Take care of yourself first. Organisation-wide change can be highly stressful.
l. Do not seek to control change, but rather to expect it, understand it, and manage it.
m. Include closure in the plan. Acknowledge and celebrate your accomplishments.
n. Read some resources about organisational change, including new forms and structures.

Any technique for creating creativity must produce ideas to enable organisations to meet their current objectives more efficiently or to develop new objectives that offer a more viable relationship with the environment.

SUMMARY

- Change is inevitable if an organisation wants sustainable development. Compatibility between the organisation and the environment is at the core of this concept of change. Change is a kind of a learning process.
- Organisational change has been defined as evolutionary, revolutionary, proactive, and reactive in nature. The environmental factors are responsible for the introduction of change in the organisation.
- In planned change, a systematic approach of change implementation is given. Then the change can be classified into individual, group, and organisational level change.
- The interdependent levels of change in people are defined as knowledge, attitude, behaviour, and group performance change.
- In change cycle, the dynamics of different levels of change have been explained in terms of participative and directive change cycles.
- In organisational barriers to change, the forces which hamper the pace of change have been introduced.
- In performance-driven organisational change, organisational adaptation, and organisational growth have been defined as a key areas to work upon.
- In different rates of change, the concept of long-term organisational viability, efficiency, and effectiveness are discussed.
- In different states of change, the change processes are catagorised into future, current, and delta state of change.
- In creating change, the concept of organisational development and MBO are important.
- In implementation of change, practical tools to understand change are introduced.
- Finally, there are certain valuable guidelines for understanding the concept of change.

Case Study: A Semiconductor Solutions Company with an Offshore Development Centre in India

History

A US-based global company supplying process control and yield management solutions for the semiconductor and related microelectronic industries had a large number of expatriate software engineers from India working on its projects, through an India-based vendor of IT staffing services and an Offshore Development Center (ODC) in India. A number of US managers were experiencing communication and cross-cultural difficulties in working effectively with the Indian IT staff, both on-site and at the ODC in India.

Task

Conduct a "Working with Indians" consultation with the US managers to identify issues and develop solutions. Evaluate the Indian vendor's pre-departure orientation processes in order to make recommendations for improvement.

Intervention

Consultant India Practice conducted a "Working with Indians" consultation with the US managers and representatives of the Indian vendor firm to identify issues for communication and other problems, the reasons these problems exist, and strategies for addressing them through management training, cross-cultural orientation and structural arrangements. Subsequently, they visited the Offshore Development Centre in India and conducted interviews, examined training materials and processes, and held consultations with those responsible for the pre-departure orientation of the Indian engineers going to the USA. A comprehensive report with action recommendations was prepared for the guidance of both the client company and the Indian vendor company.

Result

Increased awareness on the part of both the client company and the Indian vendor company about why and how cross-cultural differences in work-related behaviours and expectations affect work interactions and effectiveness. Adoption of policies, practices, and training programmes to address these issues in a systematic manner.

Key Disciplines

Concept of Change, Cross-cultural Consulting, Training Needs Assessment, Organisational Needs Assessment, Human Resources Strategy, Employee Orientation, Cross-cultural Training.

REVIEW QUESTIONS

1. What do you understand by organisational change?
2. Comment on planned change and types of planned change.
3. What are the different organisational barriers to change?
4. What are the different states of change and how can change be implemented?

5. Write short notes on:
   (i) Levels of change
   (ii) Change cycle
6. What do you understand by performance-driven organisational change?
7. What are the general guidelines to the management for effective incorporation of change?

EXERCISE 1

Team members are given a couple of minutes to consider and decide three types of food that they would choose to live on for a year, if stranded on a deserted island, with nothing else to eat or drink other than water. After considering their selection and reasons, each participant takes turns to tell the group what three foods he would choose and why.

The facilitator can determine the finer points of the rules, such as if there is anything to cook with, if there are any condiments, and "Does 'chicken tikka masala' count as one food type?" or "Can we choose processed readymade meals as one food type?", and so on.

The point of the exercise is to get delegates thinking about something completely different, in a way that allows them to express their own personality, likes, dislikes, weaknesses, and so on to the group. For large groups, people can be made to form teams of three and come up with a selection of three foods that satisfy each member of the team. Other than obviously unsuitable selections like "whisky, lager, and magic mushrooms" or "burgers, chips, and eggs", there are no right or wrong answers. It is simply an exercise in personal preference.

EXERCISE 2

We can use this game to support the training of any new task, particularly if participants feel unsure about their ability to learn the new task and apply it along with existing activities and change in the situation. The game works extremely well, and trainees love it because it is different and fun. This exercise will also help participants understand and deal with the uncomfortable feeling when they join a new team, experience change within their own team, or are forced to adjust to a change in procedure or policies. It emphasises the understanding of "what is now new and will soon become the normal" and helps demonstrate how the transition from new to normal can flow naturally. Amongst other things, this great team building game can be used to develop multi-tasking ability, for example, for people who are unsure of their ability to talk to customers and work on the computer at the same time.

How it works A group of 6 to 20 stand in a circle facing each other. The facilitator must participate as well. The facilitator explains to the group that he will call out a person's name and toss a ball (such as a stress ball or juggling ball; any soft object, even a fruit or a cuddly toy will suffice) to the named person.

The person must then call out another person's name in the circle (who has not yet had the object tossed to him) and throw the object to that person. This continues until everyone in the circle has thrown and caught the object. Each person must remember his catcher. When the object has been thrown to everyone in the group, the ball returns to the facilitator, and is then thrown around the circle again, in the same order as before. This cycle continues until the facilitator is happy that the whole group is comfortable with the exercise. (You will know this because people are actually listening for their name to be called out and catching the object.)

When the group is competent with the first ball, the facilitator introduces a second ball (or suitable object), which must follow the same order as the first, so that two objects are being passed around the group. When competence is reached with the two objects, a third is introduced.

At some stage between three objects and saturation point (that is, as many objects as people in the group), without warning, the facilitator instructs the group to begin tossing the objects in the reverse order (that is, catchers call out the names of, and throw the object to the people who previously threw to them). This results in chaos at first, but gradually people learn, which after all, is the point of the game.

Points to review How did you feel when the exercise began? After you reached a comfort level with the task, how did you feel when more objects were added? How soon did you achieve comfort level when new objects were introduced, and did this timescale change for each new object? Did anyone in the team begin encouraging or helping others by telling them to just focus on the person tossing the object to them? When the order of tossing the object was reversed, did you expect it? How did you handle it? Did the group eventually perform well at it and get a constant flow of objects in the air? You will think of more questions to ask and points to review, especially when seeing the game played.

Chapter 4

Organisational Resistance to Change

Chapter Outline

- Introduction
- Core Facts of Resistance to Change
- Individual and Group Resistance to Change
- Overcoming Resistance to Change
- Strategies for Introducing Planned Change
- Techniques to Manage Resistance during Change
- Other Strategies for Introducing Change
- Summary
- Case Study
- Review Questions
- Exercises

> "It is the nature of man as he grows older to protest against change, particularly change for the better."
>
> — John Steinbeck

4.1 INTRODUCTION

Change originates from vitality and is a positive and necessary sign of growth and progress. People resist change because it is easier to continue with what you are doing rather than learn something new. People resist change because it is difficult for us to understand one another. People resist change for highly personal and unique reasons. Today, change seems to be faster than in the past. This is so because of higher levels of education, communication, and greater human aspiration about what we should have as an expected part of our life. In industry, change is related to automation, obsolescence, competition, new technologies, computerisation, information technology, and liberalisation of economy.

Resistance to change does not necessarily surface in standardised ways. Resistance can be hidden, implicit, immediate, or deferred. It is easiest for management to deal with resistance when it is practical and immediate in nature. For instance, a change is proposed and employees quickly respond by voicing complaints, engaging in a work slowdown, threatening to go on strike, or the like.

The greater challenge is managing resistance that is implicit or deferred. Implicit resistance efforts are more subtle—loss of loyalty to the organisation, loss of motivation to work, increased errors or mistakes, increased absenteeism due to "sickness"—and hence more difficult to manage. Similarly, deferred actions cloud the link between the source of resistance and the reaction to it. A change may produce what appears to be only a minimal reaction at the time it is initiated, but the resistance may surface weeks, months, or even years later. Reaction to change can build up and then explode in some response that seems totally out of proportion to the change action it follows.

4.1.1 Reactions to Change

When employees realise that changes will benefit them, they welcome the changes. For instance, the vast majority of employees will welcome a reduction in work hours without a reduction in salary. However, most of us are generally uncomfortable with changes that are not perceived as directly beneficial to us or if we are uncertain about how they will affect us personally. The ambiguity of the unknown compared to the comfort of living with the known procedures and systems of the present is difficult for many of us to look forward to. Also, if it is a small change which results in slight discomfort, we may not mind it very much. For example, an office order is issued stating that from January 1 of the following year, all employees have to come to work 15 minutes earlier and leave 15 minutes earlier because the city is trying to stagger the work hours of all the organisations to put less strain on the city's public transport system. Employees will tend not to resist this too much despite the fact that coming to work 15 minutes earlier might pose some problems for them at home. They understand that this is a city ordinance, and neither they nor the organisation can do much about it. Thus, certain types of changes that elicit resistance can be overcome through knowledge of the unavoidable necessity for change.

There have been instances where employees have accepted cuts in pay without much resistance because they have known that this is the only way the company can survive and they can hold on to their jobs. In this case, even though the change would affect their standard of living, the resistance is small because the alternative is worse. In other words, there is a logic, or rationale, for understanding why the change is necessary which makes it easier to accept the change.

However, there is another kind of change, which would elicit emotional resistance because of fear, suspicion, insecurity and extreme levels of anxiety. If these fears cannot easily be allayed by facts or logic, either because the facts are not readily available for dissemination, or if available and disseminated but facts are not accepted by the employees as "true", the change will be resisted. The effort to bring in IBM computers to computerise the routine transactions of India's banking industry in the three decades starting from the 1950s is a case in point. Though to the management, the computer was only to be used for simple and routine payroll type of work to reduce the monotonous labour and clerical errors, to the bank employees the computer meant loss of jobs and less job opportunities for the future in a country which already has a high unemployment rate. Employees conjured up visions of being jobless and starving. The result was that the perceived magnitude of the adverse consequences of the change that was to be introduced was matched by the magnitude of the resistance by employees which took the form of strikes and picketing. Thus, changes which touch the emotional or psychological chords of fear and insecurity will be resisted much more than concerns that can be addressed and understood by pure logic.

4.2 CORE FACTS OF RESISTANCE TO CHANGE

Resistance to change is perhaps one of the baffling problems a manager encounters because it can assume many forms. The effects of resistance may be overt, implicit, subtle, or cumulative. Implicit resistance may be manifested in resignation, tardiness, loss of motivation to work, increased absenteeism, request for transfer, and so on. Overt resistance, on the other hand, assumes the form of wild-cat strikes, shoddy work, reduction in productivity, and so on.

Resistance to change may, further, be individual or organisational. Individual resistance may be due to personal, economic, or social reasons. Organisational resistance, on the other hand, generally centres around the structure, organisational constraints, threats to power and influence, and sunk costs.

Changes may be resisted for several different reasons—economic, social, security, fear of losing authority and status, having to make additional efforts to overcome technological obsolescence, comfort with the status quo, and not having had a say in deciding what changes will be introduced (Fig. 4.1). Let us examine these in more detail before looking at other reasons for resistance to change.

a. Resistance due to economic threat Sometimes, as just discussed, changes may be perceived to threaten the economic well-being of individuals. The technological sophistication of the modern era is perceived as a threat to the job and the economic security of an individual. In an over populated country such as India, better ways of doing things carry with them the fear that fewer people will be needed to do the same jobs. Thus employees might fear losing their jobs. The economic threat then becomes very real in the minds of employees, who, as a result, tend to resist changes, despite the fact that a number equivalent to

Fig. 4.1 Sources of resistance to change

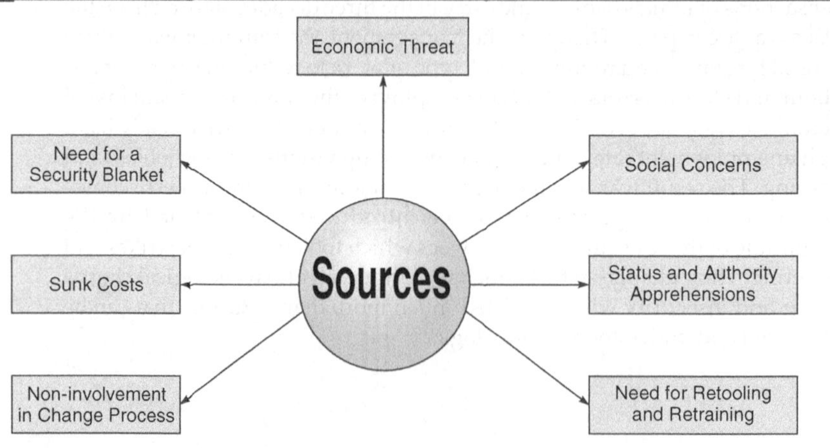

the displaced employees will be hired to manufacturing the new technology which would replace the old.

b. Resistance due to social concerns Sometimes even simple changes in the layout of the work place could be resisted by employees because it upsets their social set-up. Social relationships established among members of a group are motivators of behaviour since group norms get established. Members of a close-knit group look forward to coming to the work place because of the special relationships they have established with each other, and employees experience satisfaction at the work place because of their interactions with close colleagues. We find transfers from one department to another or from one city to another traumatic for the same reasons.

c. Resistance because of the need for a security blanket Apart from economic and job security, we all like to have some predictability and structure in our lives. The need for this security blanket (Gray and Starke, 1984) also makes us apprehensive about changes. For instance, most of us know how to do our present jobs very well. When changes are introduced, it causes us some apprehension that a new way of doing things will have to be learnt. We are not sure that we will become as adept at the new method (even after practice) as we now are with the current method. The unpredictability of our effectiveness in the new system gives rise to a sense of insecurity, which most of us try to resist as much as we possibly can.

d. Resistance due to status and authority apprehension An added fear is that when changes in technology or improvements in work methods eliminate a layer of supervision, supervisors might feel that their authority and status has been undermined. Recently a bank decided that supervisors did not have to exercise a 10 percent random check on the work done by coders which was already checked for accuracy by a senior clerk. This caused widespread concern among the supervisory staff as to whether they were being stripped of their authority and power. The fear that arises in the minds of those in authority is, "I have no control over the subordinates and they will not respect or obey me."

e. Resistance stemming from need for retooling and retraining Closely allied to the need for a security blanket is the concern for retooling and restraining oneself. In other words, knowing that one has perforce to learn new things might also be a factor in resisting change. For instance, technological changes mean the retooling and retraining of people in various jobs. Many professionals, even with doctoral degrees who had their education prior to the advent of the computer era and personal computers, are scared to interact with the "black box." Constant updating of knowledge and retooling, especially in certain kinds of professions which have a fast rate of obsolescence is, therefore, imperative. However, most of us become comfortable with the way things have been all along and prefer the status quo. This adds to our resistance to change.

f. Resistance because of non-involvement in the change process Frequently, resistance stems from the fact that employees are not consulted regarding the changes initiated by managers. When changes are incorporated with very little input from those who are affected by the changes, people have very little stake in ensuring that the new system will work. On the other hand, if contemplated changes have been the result of employees' ideas and inputs, they will be personally interested in making the change work. Thus, not only will they not resist change, but also they will work hard to ensure its success!

The danger of not involving employees in change processes can be illustrated by the following anecdote. Recently, a university made certain changes (and for very good reasons!) in the reward systems for faculty members in terms of their performance in the areas of teaching, research, and service. However, most of the faculty was not consulted about the change and their votes were not obtained in advance. This led to some key faculty members, who were nationally reputed, leaving the university within the next year!

g. Resistance due to "sunk costs" In many cases, if older employees seem to resist changes more than younger employees, it may not be due to the "rigidity and inflexibility of old age." Employees who have been with the organisation for a long time have obviously invested a lot of time and effort in learning, getting used to, and perfecting the older ways of doing things than have the younger people who have recently joined the system. Thus, the older employees have more of a psychological investment in older traditions. Kerr and Kerr (1972) refer to this as "sunk costs" of energy and experience. Thus, there is a greater resistance in changing to new methods, abandoning the "tried and tested ways of doing things." Some people might also resist change more than others, due to their personal predisposition. Individuals who have a low tolerance for ambiguity and low propensity to take risks and challenges are more likely to resist change than those who have higher levels of tolerance for ambiguity and are greater risk takers (Nedd, 1971).

A combination of factors discussed so far operates in any given situation for most organisations, which makes change a rather difficult phenomenon to readily accept.

4.3 INDIVIDUAL AND GROUP RESISTANCE TO CHANGE

Now in trying to be more specific in this regard, let us understand the resistance at the individual level as individual resistance and at the group level as organisational resistance.

4.3.1 Individual Resistance

One aspect of humankind that has remained more or less constant over time is its innate resistance to change. It is a fact of life and leadership; people resist change. By its very nature "change" is disconcerting. It is true that when the prevailing posture is "don't rock the boat", change may be resisted. Unfortunately, many a time a manager's efforts towards change in an organisation run in terms of human resistance. It is because almost all people who are affected by change experience some sort of emotional turmoil. Further, an individual prefers to maintain the status quo. Additionally, positive threats from habit or custom, fear of unknown, security and attractiveness of the familiar, displacement of human skills by the technological advancements are all the conditions that favour the status quo. In fact, there may be near-infinite reasons why people resist change in organisations (Fig. 4.2).

Fig. 4.2 Factors of individual resistance to change

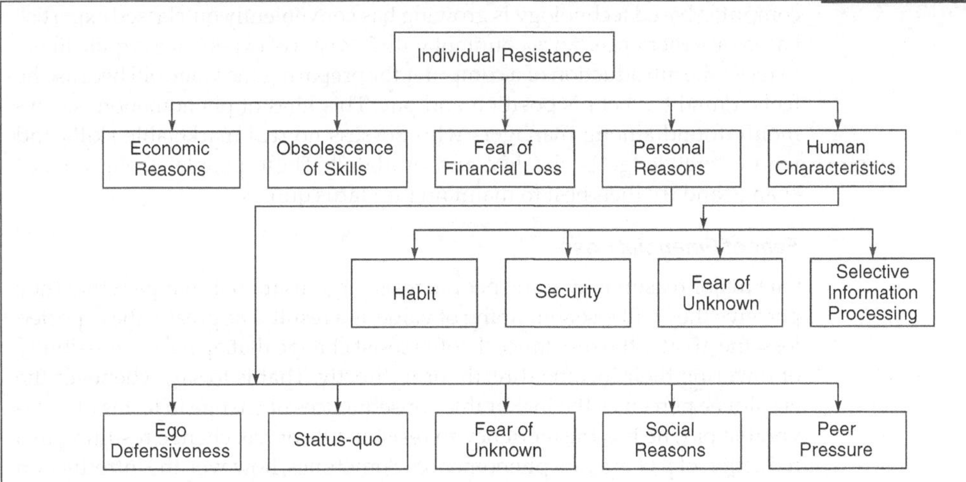

Economic Reasons

i. Fear of technological unemployment
ii. Fear of reduced work hours and consequently less pay
iii. Fear of demotion and thus reduced wages
iv. Fear of speed-up and reduced incentive wages

Many workers are justifiably afraid of being phased out of their jobs by automation. Their resistance to change can be quite effective. For instance, as Dowling and Sayles observe, "The machine looms destroyed the jobs of thousands of handloom weavers. They were introduced without consultation, without regard to human values, and they had dire consequences for the men directly concerned." In the past century, perhaps as many time-honoured occupations have disappeared from the economic sector as new ones have been born. Technological advancement (change) has always meant the destruction of old and outdated industry and the creation of new ones. Two factors are worth noting as far as economic reasons for resistance are concerned—namely, obsolescence of skills and fear of economic loss.

Individual resistance stems from concern that changes will lower one's income. Changes in job tasks or established work routines can also arouse economic fears if people are concerned that they will not be able to perform the new tasks or routines to their previous efficiency levels, especially when the pay is closely tied to productivity.

Obsolescence of Skills

The rate at which the knowledge is exploding is incredible. As a result, knowledge in any particular field quickly becomes obsolete. Whenever people sense that new machinery (change) poses a threat of replacing or degrading them, they simply resist such a change. For instance, the subsonic rate at which computer-based technology is growing has conveniently outclassed expertise based on experience. An accountant with 20 years of experience is quite likely to resist the introduction of a computer for preparing the wage bill because he feels it might affect his position and pay. This kind of phenomenon is commonly found among managers who possess no real marketable skills and whose knowledge is obsolete and outdated. These people strongly resist change and try their best to maintain the status quo.

Fear of Financial Loss

One major reason why some people resist organisational change is that they perceive they will lose something of value as a result. The greater the expected loss, the greater the resistance. People resist change that opens the possibility of lowering their income directly or indirectly. That is to say, whenever the employee perceives the inexorable consequences of change in terms of unfavorable pay, he has the tendency to resist it. Of course, change resulting in a reduction of pay is a rare phenomenon. Sometimes, however, the introduction of new technology takes people away from doing important jobs (or demanding work) to less-important or dead-end ones, where no skills are required as such. More realistically, when people perceive psychological degradation of the job they are performing, they resist such a change. In this connection, Keith Davis rightly remarks, "People fear technological unemployment, reduced work hours, demotion, reduced wages and reduced incentives and resist change."

Personal Reasons

Ego-defensiveness Sometimes, change may be ego-deflating. An ego-defensive subordinate or manager always tries to resist change. For instance, a profitable suggestion by a sales person to the marketing manager regarding the expansion of sales may be turned down because the manager perceives that his ego may be deflated by accepting the suggestion.

Status Quo Perhaps the biggest and most sound reason for resistance to change is the status quo. People have a vested interest in the status quo. A change may disturb the comforts of status quo. It is because people typically develop patterns for coping with or managing their current structure and situation. Change means they will have to find new ways of managing them and their environment—ways that might not be successful as those currently used. Venturing to change may involve uncertainty and risk and may be at the cost of the convenience and happiness of the employees.

Fear of the Unknown Change presents the unknown, which causes anxiety. Whenever people do not know exactly what will happen, they are likely to resist it. People fear any untoward and uncomfortable change and its consequences. For instance, a sales manager may wonder what might happen if he is relocated to the company headquarters in another state. He might wonder if his family would like it and if he would find friends. Uncertainty in the situation arises not from the change itself, but from the consequences surrounding the change. To avoid making a decision and fearing the unknown consequences of the move, the sales manager, may refuse the promotion that accompanies relocation. Further, any gap in the information about the move and its consequences will give rise to uncertainty about the future and the sales manager might decide that it is better to say "no" to moving to the company headquarters.

Social Reasons The introduction of change often results in disturbance of the existing social relationships. It may also result in breaking up of work groups. Normally people in the working environment develop informal relationships. When friendship with fellow-members is interrupted, then there is a possibility for the employees to experience a psychological let down. Research reveals that in combat situations, soldiers often fight the tendency to make friends with the other members of their platoon, because if one is killed or injured, the effect on the group can be disastrous. Thus, when social relationships develop, as normally is the case, people try to maintain them and fight social displacement by resisting change.

Social displacement and peer pressure are among the important social reasons that a manager must consider when dealing with resistance to change.

Peer Pressure It is not rare to find situations where individuals are prepared to accept change at an individual level, but refuse to accept it for the sake of the group. Whenever peers are unwilling to accept change, they force the subordinate individual employees who are willing to accept the change to resist it. Cohesive groups tend to resist some changes collectively.

Human Characteristics

Individual sources of resistance to change reside in basic human characteristics such as perceptions, personality and needs. The five reasons below summarise why individuals may resist change.

Habit Every time you go out to eat, do you try a different restaurant? Probably not. If you are like most people, you will find a couple of places you like and return to them on a somewhat regular basis.

As human beings, we are creatures of habit. To cope with the complexities of life, we rely on habits or programmed responses. But when confronted with change, this tendency to respond in our accustomed way becomes a source of resistance. So, for instance, when your department is moved to a new office building across town, it may mean that you have to change many habits: wake up ten minutes earlier, take a new route to work, find a new parking place, adjust to the new office layout, develop a new lunchtime routine and so on.

Security People with a high need for security are likely to resist change because it threatens their feeling of safety. When Sears announces that it is laying off 50,000 people or Ford introduces new robotic equipment, many employees in these firms may fear for their jobs. The sense of safety in the present job, makes people fear and resist change.

Changes substitute ambiguity and uncertainty for the known Regardless of how much you may dislike attending college, at least you know what is expected of you. But when you leave college and venture out into the world of full-time employment, regardless of how much you want to get out of college, you have to trade the known for the unknown.

Employees in organisations hold the same dislike for uncertainty. If, for example, the introduction of TQM means production workers will have to learn statistical process control techniques, some may fear they will be unable to do so. They may, therefore, develop a negative attitude towards TQM or behave dysfunctionally if required to use statistical techniques.

Selective information processing Individuals shape their world through their perceptions. Once they have created this world, it resists change. So individuals are guilty of selectively processing information in order to keep their perceptions intact. They hear what they want to hear. They ignore information that challenges the world they have created. To return to the example of the production workers who are faced with the introduction of TQM, they may ignore the arguments their bosses make in explaining why a knowledge of statistics is necessary or the potential benefits the change will provide them.

4.3.2 Organisational Resistance

Organisations, by their very nature, are conservative. They actively resist change. You do not have to look far to see evidence of this phenomenon. Government agencies want to continue doing what they have been doing for years, whether the need for their service changes or remains the same. Organised religions are deeply entrenched in their history and attempts to change doctrines may require great persistence and patience. Educational institutions, which exist to open minds and challenge established doctrines, are themselves extremely resistant to change. Most school systems are using essentially the same teaching technologies today as they were 50 years ago. The majority of business firms, too, appear highly resistant to change.

Seven major sources of organisational resistance have been identified. They are shown in (Figure. 4.3).

*a. **Structural inertia*** Organisations have built-in mechanisms to produce stability. For example, the selection process systematically selects certain people in and certain people out. Training and other socialisation techniques reinforce specific role requirements and skills. Formalisation provides job descriptions, rules and procedures for employees to follow.

The people who are hired into an organisation are chosen to fit; they are shaped and directed to behave in certain ways. When an organisation is confronted with change, this structural inertia acts as a counterbalance to sustain stability.

Some organisational structures have an inbuilt mechanism for resistance to change. For instance, consider a typically bureaucratic structure where jobs are narrowly defined, lines of authority are clearly spelled out, the flow of information is from top to bottom. In such an organisation, the channels of communication make it difficult for a new idea to travel. Eventually the new idea/innovation will probably be screened out because it is not suitable for the structure of the organisation.

b. Limited focus of change Organisations are made up of a number of interdependent subsystems. You cannot change one without affecting the others. For

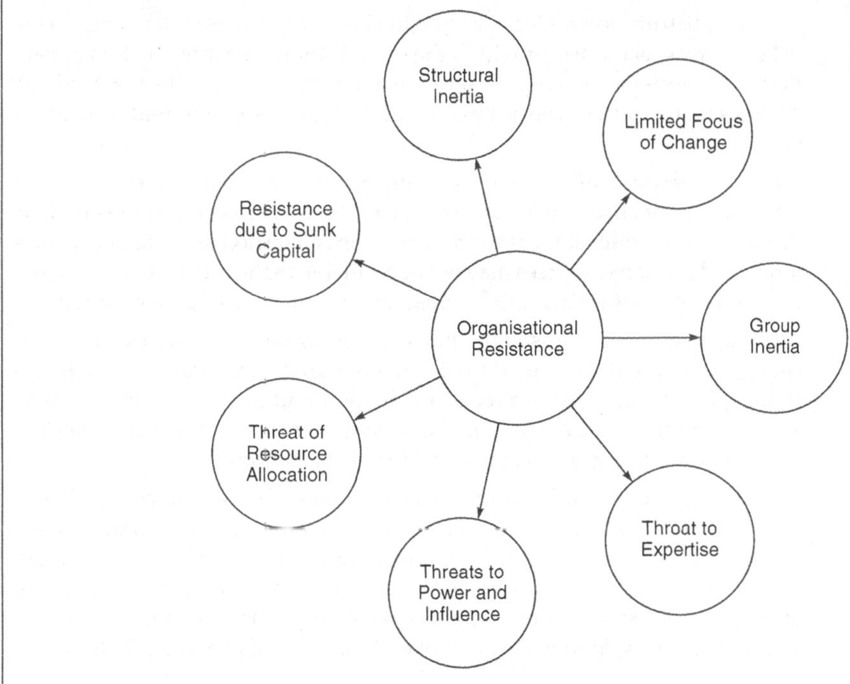

Fig. 4.3 Sources of organisation resistance

example, if management changes the technological processes without simultaneously modifying the organisation's structure, the change in technology is not likely to be accepted. So limited changes in subsystems tend to get nullified by the larger system.

c. Group inertia Even if individuals want to change their behaviour, group norms may act as a constraint. An individual union member, for instance, may be willing to accept changes in his job suggested by management. But if union norms dictate resisting any unilateral change made by management, he is likely to resist.

d. Threat to expertise Changes in organisational patterns may threaten the expertise of specialised groups. The introduction of decentralised personal computers, which allow managers to gain access to information directly from a company's mainframe, is an example of a change that was strongly resisted by many information systems departments in the early 1980s. Why? Because decentralised end-user computing was a threat to the specialised skills held by those in the centralised information systems department.

e. Threats to power and influence Some people consider change as a potential threat to their position and influence in the organisation. Novel ideas and the new use of resources can disrupt power relationships and, therefore, are often resisted at the organisational level. This is especially so in the case of people who occupy the top ranks in the organisation.

Any redistribution of decision-making authority can threaten long-established power relationships within the organisation. The introduction of participative decision making or self-managed work teams are the kinds of changes that are often seen as threatening by supervisors and middle managers.

f. Threat of resource allocation If an organisation has plenty of resources, the introduction of change is rarely a problem. However, organisations may, at times, operate under some resource constraints. The necessary financial, material, and human resources may not be available to the organisation to make the needed changes. Therefore, inadequate resources also hinder change.

Groups in the organisation that control sizeable resources often see changes as a threat. They tend to be content with the way things are. Will the change, for instance, mean a reduction in their budgets or a cut in their staff size? Those that most benefit from the current allocation of resources often feel threatened by changes that may affect future allocations.

g. Resistance due to sunk capital The plight of some companies is such that their heavy capital is blocked in fixed or permanent assets. If an organisation wishes to introduce a change, these sunk costs present a difficulty. Sunk costs are not restricted to physical assets alone; they can also be expressed in terms of people. For instance, some members in the organisation retain their jobs by virtue of seniority, though they do not make any significant contribution. Unless they are motivated to higher performance, the payments for their services (for example, fringe benefits, salaries, and so on) represent sunk costs of the organisation.

4.3.3 Consequences of Resistance to Change

If organisations do not overcome employees' resistance to change, they may have to pay a price. The consequences to the organisation may be drastic, depending on the extent of resistance exhibited by the employees. Employee reactions to change can be overt, subtle, implicit, immediate, or deferred. Sometimes, where changes of great magnitude are introduced without employee acceptance, the consequences may be overt, such as a strike. Needless to say this would cost both the organisation and the employees a lot of pain. Employees need not always be as overt in their resistance to change as to strike, but they could react in very subtle and dysfunctional ways. They could, for instance, introduce errors in their work deliberately and mess up the end product. On the other hand, the reaction of employees could be very implicit and not easily visible on the surface. An example of this is alienation or psychological withdrawal of employees from the job. When employees are there only in body and not in spirit, it will ultimately show in their organisational loyalty and quality of performance. Immediate resistance to change would be reflected in absenteeism and tardiness. Deferred reaction will be reflected in high rates of turnover.

4.4 OVERCOMING RESISTANCE TO CHANGE

A manager need not always be saddled with the task of change in organisations where resistance is strongly prevalent. He is wedded to some techniques to overcome resistance. One thing he should keep in mind is not to underestimate the variety of ways people react to change, and the ways they can positively influence specific individuals and groups during the change process.

Change creates tension and emotional turmoil in the minds of employees. According to Harris, some people attempt to avoid tension by creating barriers whereas some others tend to minimise tensions by a quick adjustment to change. Negative reactions bode ill for the success of the change programme especially when a manager is unable to handle it properly. A manager should also note that individuals and groups react very differently to change from passively resisting it to aggressively trying to undermine it to sincerely embracing it.

To overcome resistance is no mean task. Probably that is why Niccolo Machievalli rightly contended, "...it must be considered that there is nothing more difficult to carry out, nor more doubtful of success, nor more dangerous to handle, than to intimate a new order of things." Managers have to grapple with continuous uncertainty and change especially because of resistance.

Therefore, the very first thing to consider is the source of resistance. According to experts, understanding the root of the problem is half the solution. Understanding the sources of resistance to change is the first step in designing a programme to help an organisation accept change. These are the most common causes for resistance (Fig. 4.4).

Fig. 4.4 Common causes of resistance to change

a. Ignorance When people have insufficient knowledge, they are uncertain about the causes and effects of change. This uncertainty, in turn, causes stress and resistance. As with walking in the dark, most people would rather stay put than venture into the unknown. Also, when people are uncertain about reality, they try to make guesses about it, sometimes adding imaginary problems to real ones. For example, if employees learn via the office grapevine that management is considering merging some departments to streamline operations and cut costs, they are likely to resist the change because they fear losing their jobs or having new reporting relationships.

b. Desire for security People often want to retain the status quo even when they know it is inferior to the change that will happen. The security of the "known" makes them resist change. The faster or more major the change, the more powerful the lure of the comforting status quo. This phenomenon was first discussed extensively by Alvin Toffler in his bestselling book, *Future Shock*.

c. Fear and lack of ambition Another source of resistance to change is people's unwillingness to learn the new skills or behaviour that change may require. There are two reasons for this. First, workers fear in inability to learn new skills or behaviour. Therefore, change signifies failure. This fear is especially prevalent in older workers who have developed their skills over a long period. Second, some workers simply may not want to exert the energy, time and mental effort required to imbibe new learning and skills.

d. Informal group pressure Most organisational changes have some impact on the informal networks in the formal set up of organisations. Breaking up a closely knit work group or changing social relationships can provoke a great deal of resistance. Managers often overlook this source of resistance because the informal network is not the focal point of organisational change. This often unplanned, secondary spillover effect can cause resistance to change.

e. Eroding powder bases When people expect their status or power to decline as a result of change, resistance is inevitable. Besides the direct loss of status or power, there are power and status considerations in the change process itself. That is, change often invites criticism from other employees and causes workers to question their own abilities and self-worth.

f. Potential loss of job security Advances in technology have made concern for job security an especially strong source of resistance. A change that can eliminate jobs is a threat for employees. Two examples are the worker whose job will be taken over by a machine or a middle-level manager who is afraid that computers will eliminate his duties.

g. Personality conflicts These conflicts often are the result of misunderstandings, lack of trust, or past resentments. For instance, if employees whose personalities conflict must have daily personal contact because of a structural change, they are likely to resist the reorganisation. This resistance can be strong enough to override the best of changes. Conflicts among workers, between positions, or with management in general can all inhibit acceptance of change.

4.5 STRATEGIES FOR INTRODUCING PLANNED CHANGE

Illuminating researches and theoretical constructs have been developed to understand and explain of resistance to change. There are at least six conditions, which have been found to be conducive to resistance:

a. Resistance can be expected if the nature of change is not made clear to the individual who is going to be influenced by the change.
b. Different people see different meanings in the proposed change.
c. Resistance can be expected when those influenced are caught between strong forces pushing them to make a change and equally strong forces deterring them from making the change.
d. Resistance may be expected to be in proportion to the pressure put on the people for change.

e. Resistance may be expected if the change is made on personal grounds rather than impersonal requirements or sanctions.
f. Resistance may be expected if the change ignores the already established institutions in the group.

On the basis of the above conditions Chin and Benne (1976) describe three strategies that managers commonly use to introduce change. They are: empirical-rational, normative-reductive and power-coercive (see Fig. 4.5).

Fig. 4.5 Core strategies for planned change

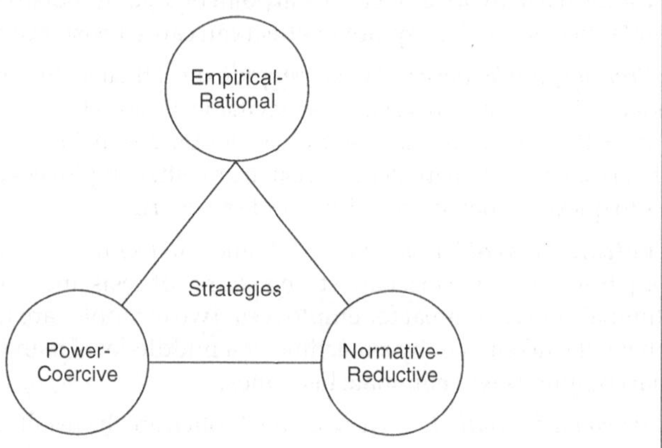

4.5.1 Empirical-rational Strategy

Managers who act as change agents might subscribe to the belief that people are rational and if they understand that the change to be introduced will benefit them, their self-interest will guide them to accept the change. In other words, the rational human being who is motivated by self-interest will react positively to change if the benefits of the change to the individual or the group are properly understood. So, if the manager explains the benefits of change to the employees and then introduces it, it is likely to be a success.

4.5.2 Normative-reductive Strategy

In this strategy the belief is that people are guided by the socio-cultural norms that they subscribe to. Changes do not always take place merely because they make sense to people at the rational or cognitive level but changes become acceptable because they are in keeping with the personal values and belief system of the people. Thus, when changes appeal to the socio-cultural norms of individuals affected by the change, they are successfully implemented. Hence, when the necessary changes to be made are identified, the change agent and those who will be influenced by the change should participatively and collaboratively plan and implement the necessary changes. This will ensure that successful changes occur in the system because people have internalised the need for changes as they worked together in developing and implementing them.

4.5.3 Power-coercive Strategy

These strategies are used by change agents who operate under the assumption that people with less power will comply with the changes brought about by those with more power in the system. This strategy will utilise legitimate authority, rewards, and punishments as the means to enforce change. Though people may respond out of fear, they may resist the changes psychologically and react in subtle ways, as discussed earlier. The compliance to any order imposing changes will be temporary in nature and once the change agent is out of sight, people will revert to their old ways of doing things.

4.6 TECHNIQUES TO MANAGE RESISTANCE DURING CHANGE

4.6.1 Education and Communication

Resistance can be reduced by communicating with employees to help them see the logic of change. This tactic basically assumes that the source of resistance lies in misinformation or poor communication. If employees receive the full facts and clear any misunderstandings that may arise, resistance will subside. Communication can be achieved through one-on-one discussions, memos, group presentations, or reports. Does it work? It does, provided the source of resistance is inadequate communication and that management-employee relations are characterised by mutual trust and credibility. If these conditions do not exist, the change is unlikely to succeed.

One of the most easy and prescribed techniques to overcome resistance is to educate the people who resist it. People are the essential ingredients of the organisation and in most of the cases it is individual resistance that is the quite common and a threatening phenomenon. Many people do not properly understand change and hence underscore the consequences and resist change. Misunderstandings can be resolved by explaining exactly what is to happen.

A manager or change agent, who is interested in introducing change successfully, must carefully evaluate the change consequences and educate the employees about these. It is essential that individuals who will be affected be convinced of the necessity of change lest they resist. The manager in this connection should exhibit appropriate leadership style. Most importantly, a manager should explain

i. What the change is
ii. When is it to be introduced

iii. How will it be implemented
iv. Why is the change needed
v. The basic objectives of change

While educating the employees on the change and its consequences, communication plays an important role. Communication of ideas help people visualise the need and logic of change.

Education as a method of overcoming resistance to change is commonly used in situations where there is a lack of information and analysis. It is an ideal solution where resistance is based on inadequate or inaccurate information and analysis, and the initiator needs the resistor's help in implementing change effectively.

The chief merit of this method is that once persuaded, people will often help in the implementation of change. However, one potential drawback of this method is that it can be very time-consuming if many people are involved. It requires a significant amount of time, effort, and money.

Fig. 4.6 Techniques to manage resistance to change

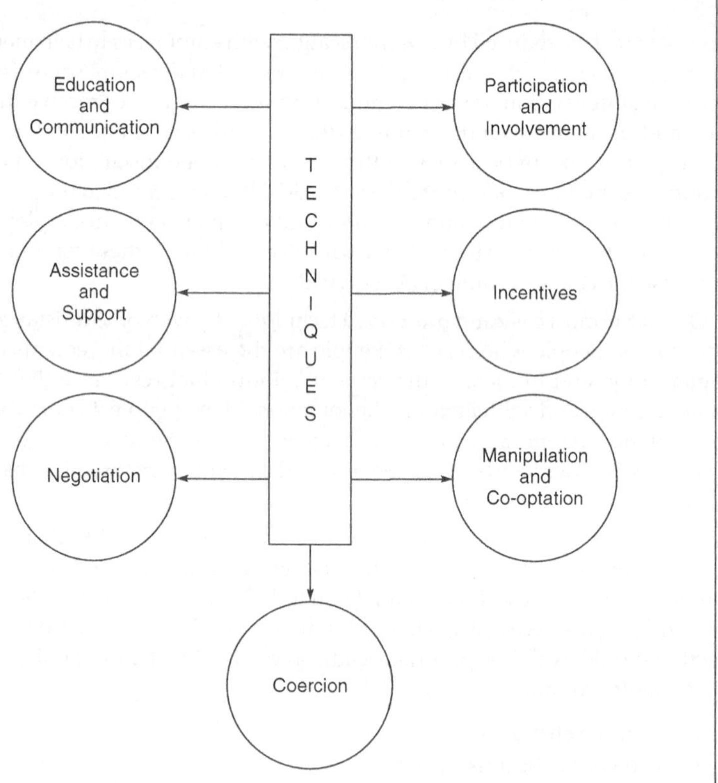

4.6.2 Sense of Participation and Involvement

It's difficult for individuals to resist a change decision to which they are party. Prior to making a change, those opposed to it can be brought into the decision process. Assuming that participants have the expertise to make a meaningful contribution, their involvement can reduce resistance, obtain commitment and increase the quality of the change decision. Get people involved in the change process by including them in the design and implementation of the change processes. Once people have had an opportunity to contribute ideas and become a part of the change process, they will be less inclined to see it fail. Working in committees or task forces is a time-consuming activity. Hence it will take a longer time to bring about changes. However, against these advantages are the negatives: potential for a poor solution and time consumption.

In order to overcome resistance, a manager may resort to the technique of participation and involvement. Here the basic strategy of the manager is to involve the resistors in some aspect of design and implementation of the change so that he can forestall resistance. The manager, in this connection, will have a dialogue with his subordinates, and encourage and allow them to air their views, on the change and its implementation. When the subordinate is allowed to participate and involve himself in the change process (decision-making regarding the implementation of the change), he generally feels satisfied and does not oppose change. Participation will also be instrumental in clearing any misunderstanding in the mind of a subordinate about the change and its consequences. With participative change efforts, the initiators listen to people's views about what change involves and use their advice.

Considerable research has demonstrated that participation leads to commitment, not merely compliance. It should be noted that commitment is vital for change to be a success.

This method works best when the initiator does not have all the information he needs to design or implement change. It is also used where others have considerable power to resist and where a high level of commitment is needed to introduce change successfully in the organisation.

The main advantage of this method is that people who participate will be committed to implementing change, and the relevant information they possess will be integrated into the change plan. The negative point of this method is that it is a very time-consuming exercise. Sometimes participation results in designing inappropriate change.

4.6.3 Assistance and Support

Change agents can offer a range of supportive efforts to reduce resistance. When employees' fear and anxiety are high, employee counselling and therapy, new skills training, or a short paid leave of absence may facilitate adjustment. The drawback of this tactic is that, as with the others, it is time consuming. Additionally, it is expensive, and its implementation offers no assurance of success.

Managers sometimes deal with potential resistance by being supportive. This includes listening, providing emotional support, providing training in new skills or giving employees time off after a certain demanding period, and so on. The support may be facilitative and emotional.

Assistance and support attempt to remove organisational barriers that might hamper change or implementation of organisational policies to facilitate change. It includes assistance offered by the organisation (for example, appropriate tools, materials, advice, and training) to help make the change work effectively.

Emotional support addresses an individual's concerns as opposed to technical concerns about change. A manager can assist employees experiencing anxiety induced by change through compassionate listening and helping them work out their concerns.

This technique, facilitation, is commonly used where people put up resistance because of adjustment problems. Facilitation and support are most helpful when fear and anxiety lie at the heart of resistance. Though reasonable managers often overlook or ignore this kind of resistance, as well as the efficacy of facilitative ways of dealing with it. The potential limitation of this method is that it can be expensive, time consuming, without any guarantee of success.

4.6.4 Incentives

Offering incentives to those who resist change is another fruitful way of overcoming resistance to change. For instance, if the resistance is centred in a few powerful individuals, a specific reward package can be negotiated that will meet their individual needs and ensure that the change is not blocked.

4.6.5 Negotiation

Where some persons in a group clearly lose out following a change, and where a group has considerable power to resist, negotiation and agreement are helpful. Negotiation as a tactic may be necessary when resistance comes from a powerful source. Its costs are high. Additionally, there is the risk that once a change agent negotiates with one party to avoid resistance, he is open to the possibility of being blackmailed by other individuals in positions of power.

Though in some instances negotiation may be the relatively easy way to gain acceptance, it is possible that this could be an expensive way of effecting changes. Also, if the use of this strategy becomes public knowledge, others might also want to try to negotiate before they accept the change.

4.6.6 Manipulation and Co-optation

Manipulation refers to covert influence attempts. Twisting and distorting facts to make them appear more attractive, withholding undesirable information, and creating rumours to get employees to accept a change are all examples of manipulation. If corporate management threatens to close down a particular manufacturing plant if its employees fail to accept an across-the-board pay cut, and if the threat is actually untrue, management is being manipulative.

Co-optation, however, is a form of both manipulation and participation. It seeks to buy off the leaders of a resistance group by giving them a key role in the change decision. The leaders' advice is sought, not to seek a better decision, but to get their endorsement.

To obtain maximum support for the contemplated changes, covert attempts to influence others may sometimes have to be resorted to. This could include such tactics as selectively sharing information and consciously structuring certain types of events that would win support. Managers generally indulge in manipulation when all other tactics are infeasible or have failed.

Both manipulation and co-optation are relatively inexpensive and easy ways to gain the support of adversaries, but the tactics can backfire if the targets become aware they are being tricked or used. Once discovered, the change agent's credibility may drop to zero.

4.6.7 Coercion

The application of direct threats or force on resistors is called coercion. Sometimes people may have to be forced to accept change by threatening those who resist with undesirable consequences. This strategy can be resorted to when changes have to be speedily enforced, when changes are of a temporary nature, or when the initiator of change weilds considerable power. Though speedy and effective in the short run, it may make people angry and resort to mean behaviour in the long run.

If corporate management is determined to close a manufacturing plant, if its employees do not acquiesce to a pay cut, then coercion would be the label attached to its change tactic. Other examples of coercion are threats of transfer, loss of promotion, negative performance evaluations and a poor letter of recommendation. The advantages and drawbacks of coercion are about the same as those mentioned for manipulation and co-optation.

When managers do not have other ways to end resistance to change, they, sometimes resort to coercion. They essentially force people to accept a change by explicitly or implicitly threatening them (with the loss of their jobs, promotion possibilities and so forth) or by actually firing and transferring them.

One definite advantage of this method is that it is fast, and can overcome any kind of resistance. At the same time, it can be risky if it leaves people angry at the initiators.

The most common mistake managers commit is to use only one approach or a limited set, regardless of the situation. For example, the hard-boiled boss who often coerces people, the people-oriented manager who consistently tries to involve and support his people, the cynical boss who always manipulates and co-opts others, the intellectual manager who relies heavily on education and communication, and lawyer like manager who usually tries to negotiate. What is important to note is that the manager concerned with the implementing the change must be appropriate technique for overcoming resistance.

4.6.8 Other Strategies for Introducing Change

Gray and Strake (1984) explain that in addition to communicating the advantages of proposed changes less traumatic for employees.

Frequent Changes

When frequent changes becomes the norm in the organisation and when changes are managed well, people get more used to adapting to changes and their fear of new situations successively reduces with each change.

Introducing Multiple Changes

This strategy is also good, since the incremental resistance to several changes is only slightly greater than adjusting to a single change. Also when multiple changes are introduced, the potential benefits from several different changes are substantially greater than the potential negative effects spread across them.

Use of Informal Leaders

Since informal leaders have a lot of power in the group, by co-opting them in the change processes, changes can be introduced with least resistance from employees.

If a system-wide change is contemplated, the best place to start the process is where the restraining forces are the least and there is an inclination for change.

SUMMARY

- We studied the reaction to the change process by the organisation. This reaction can be positive as well as negative. A positive reaction helps the management in facilitating the process of change within the organisation. A negative reaction creates a resistance to the introduction of change in the organisation.
- The core factors of resistance to change are economic and social—the need for security due to status and authority apprehensions, need for retooling and retraining, non-involvement in the change process, and sunk costs.
- The resistance to change can be divided into individual and organisational.
- Individual resistance is due to economic reasons, obsolescence of skills, fear of financial loss, personal reasons (ego, status, fear of unknown, social reasons, and peer pressure) and due to human characterstics (habit, insecurity, fear of unknown, selective information processing).
- Organisational resistance is due to structural inertia, limited focus of change, group inertia, threat to expertise, threat to power and influence, threat of resource allocation, and sunk capital.
- To overcome resistance, a manager must know the common causes of resistance. These are ignorance, desire for security, fear and lack of ambition, informal group pressure, eroding power bases, potential loss of job security, and personality conflicts.
- To introduce a resistance-free change, a manager can use empirical-rational, normative-reductive, or power-coercive strategies. At the same time some techniques of these strategies are also available to confront the problem of change. These are education and communication, participation and involvement, assistance and support, incentives, negotiation, manupulation and co-optation, and coercion.
- For the effective management of change in the organisation, effective management of resistance to change is an essential prerequisite. How management channelises individual and organisational resistance determines the success of change management.

Case Study: A Student Services Division of "National University"

History

A Student Services Division of a large public university had undergone an internal self-assessment process. This assessment resulted in identifying four priority issues that hampered the effectiveness of the division: leadership, organisation, decision-making, and communication.

Task

Guide and assist with the implementation of a comprehensive change management initiative to address the issues of leadership, organisation, decision-making, and communication

Intervention

A change agency conducted interviews with all senior and middle managers to assess the structural, cultural, management, resource, and communication dimensions of these issues. A detailed set of action recommendations was prepared for a restructuring based on client service needs, a shift to team leadership, clarification of roles and authority, and effective decision-making processes.

They also assisted in the creation of a comprehensive restructuring and change management plan. Finally, for the transition to the new structure, they operated as change management coach to senior management, guiding and advising on both strategy and tactics, and "shadow-managing" to help the organisation move from concept to action plan to implementation.

Result

The result was a major change in the leadership structures of the division, and significant progress towards a more streamlined, integrated, and client-oriented operation.

Key Disciplines

Organisational Needs Assessment, Change Management, Organisational Culture, Organisational Structure and Design, Executive Coaching.

Review Questions

1. What is meant by resistance to change? Explain its functionalities and dysfunctionalities.
2. What are the basic reasons of organisational resistance?
3. Differentiate between individual and group resistance to change from the organisation's point of view.
4. Suggest some strategies for the introduction of change in an organisation.
5. What techniques are available to manage resistance during change?

EXERCISE 1

This is simple but sophisticated game for a team of six to ten people to understand the concept of resistance. The scenario is that the team is stranded on a life-raft which is too small to hold everyone without sinking. Someone (or two or three people, it's flexible) must to be thrown overboard.

The group must decide who is/are to be the victim(s). First participants have the opportunity to present their reasons why they should stay on board (the facilitator can decide what media are to be used, but watch out for the time; this part needs to be reasonably brief). Participants can be directed either to base their presentations on their own real selves, or if a less emotive approach is required, to adopt the personality of a character from history, a TV soap, and the like. The facilitator must decide how best to instruct the team on this aspect.

After presenting individual cases, the group then debates people's relative values and strengths. Within this debate individuals can continue to argue their own cases if they wish, after which the group makes its decision. Set a time limit for each presentation, the debate, and the decision, for example, 2 minutes per presentation; 20-30 minutes for the debate; 5 minutes for the decision or vote.

The facilitator can guide the group on the decision method, for example secret ballot, show of hands, or preferably leave it to the group to decide on the decision process, as this highlights other interesting behaviours and capabilities within the team.

Points to Review

- Quality and effect of individual presentations
- How individuals behave and respond to threat and possible rejection
- How different personality types within the group react in different ways to the debating and decision process
- How the group organises itself to manage the difficult discussion process
- The different perceptions in the team of relative strengths, weaknesses, values, and so on
- The way the group decides on how to make the decision (unless told how to by the facilitator).
- The reaction of the team members and colleagues of the victim(s) after the vote—balance between relief and sympathy

Other points to observe, especially if using this as an interactive group selection recruitment game

- Individual behaviour and style
- Participation levels
- Constructive, supportive input ("How can we best approach this...?") versus negative contributions ("This is a stupid game...")
- Natural leaders
- Natural process checkers
- Result driven players
- Compassion and empathy
- Presentation skills
- Negotiation skills
- Awareness of process and consensus principles
- Logical and objective assessment of relative values and capabilities
- Integrity
- Awareness of need to preserve mix of team abilities
- Bullying, ganging-up, and defence and reaction to these
- Sexism, racism, prejudice, and defence and reaction to these

EXERCISE 2

This exercise is meant to help understand the concept of resistance.

First facilitate a brainstorming session with the group to create the scenario, with as many variables (tradables) as possible for each side. This is a very helpful exercise in itself since staff and managers who to learn and practise negotiating rarely appreciate all the issues and opportunities for negotiation that exist in any particular situation. Having the group construct the scenario also gives the trainer or facilitator the chance to guide the development of the scenario, so that it is workable, and to identify the development needs of the team that warrant most attention later as the session unfolds. Use a template as a guide for the group for the scenario design brainstorming session.

Here is an example of a template for a negotiation scenario.

- Situation description
- People involved on each side, their level of influence, their personal and corporate aims, and comment about personality and negotiating styles
- Variables (tradables) for each side with values or notional priority ranking for each side (because each side will place a different value on each variable)
- Alternative options for each side (competitor offers with pros and cons, and comment on opportunity for either side to simply walk away)
- External pressures and time-sensitive factors (for example, seasonal or contractual aspects)
- Anything else of bearing to either side

Having constructed the scenario, you can then run the negotiation role-play in any way you choose. The negotiation activity can be organised for individuals or teams, with stages and responsibilities built in to increase the complexity and challenge. Or simply run the activity with two teams facing each other across a table, with a suitable time limit to achieve a creative win-win (collaborative) outcome.

A flip chart is an essential tool for this exercise, because it allows ideas and criteria for the negotiation to be clearly agreed upon and shown at all times. As the negotiation role-play unfolds it is likely that questions will arise which require the facilitator's arbitration. So expect to have to manage and control the activities closely and pragmatically. In this respect there is some similarity with real negotiations, which rarely proceed as anticipated.

The aim of the exercise and the role-play negotiation is not to create a confrontation or a winner-takes-all result. The aim—which should be reinforced frequently with the team members—is for the delegates to seek and develop new ways of arriving at better collaborative outcomes, by thinking creatively and together with the other side, ideally based on a realistic (perhaps historical) work negotiation situation. As such, you can facilitate an enormous amount of learning and ideas with this format, in the way the scenarios are developed and discussed, and especially in the way the negotiating teams can be encouraged to take a creative and co-operative approach to finding better solutions than might first appear possible or have historically been achieved.

Every negotiation, when viewed creatively, entrepreneurially, and collaboratively, provides an excellent opportunity to develop and improve synergies between and benefiting both sides, within the negotiated outcome.

Chapter 5

Organisational Change and Change Agents

CHAPTER OUTLINE

- Introduction
- Change Agent: Definition and Meaning
- Types of Change Agents
- Key Roles in Organisational Change
- Difference between External and Internal Change Agents
- Characteristics of a Good Change Agent
- Timing the Entry of the Agent/Consultant into the Organisation
- What Can a Change Agent Change?
- Summary
- Case Study
- Review Questions
- Exercises

> "When dealing with people, let us remember we are not dealing with creatures of logic. We are dealing with creatures of emotions, creatures bristling with prejudices and motivated by pride and vanity."
>
> —Goethe

5.1 INTRODUCTION

History is full of examples in each country of rulers and kings seeking the advice of experts and wise men of various kinds in the process of handling/ solving problems. The very desire to consult someone knowledgeable and respected when faced with a tricky problem is an eternal human need.

Change agents have become an influential force in changing the way businessmen operate. Change and resistance to change is the nature of human beings. Organisations do fall into deep problems sometimes, trying to manage change. This change may be of any type and magnitude; what is more important here is the very perception of the problem. If the problem is looked at as an opportunity, the problem acquires an altogether different dimension as compared to it being handled casually.

Organisational change is a complex phenomenon involving several people. Organisational change goes through several phases. Several internal and external roles contribute to the different phases of change.

In summons consulting/hiring external mangement experts on a formal and professional basis is however, a relatively recent phenomenon. As the body of management knowledge and complexities grow, so does the professional. This professional is commonly known as a management consultant and the profession has become popular as management consultancy.

5.2 CHANGE AGENT: DEFINITION AND MEANING

Change agent is a person who acts as catalyst and assumes the responsibility for managing change activities in the organisation.

The initiator of changed behaviour is known as a change agent. Change agents can be managers or non-managers, employees of the organisation or outside consultants.

By change agent we mean a change plus agent, that is, a representative who brings change or introduces change. He is the one who works for the accomplishment of the goals or objectives of the organisation, conflict resolution, increased understanding, and more leadership.

This means the change agent can work with the internal executives of any organisation as a consultant for the establishment of a collaborative relationship that includes mutual trust, and influence and jointly determine the organisation's goals.

The change agent also determines the techniques to be used initially in starting the analysis and interaction organisational development.

The change agent is mainly an expert who may be an outsider or an internal person of any organisation who aims to work to identify the grey areas where change is required in an organisation (diagnosis) and then suggests different alternative changes for betterment.

A change agent is a consultant who

- identifies need of change
- identifies area where change is required
- identifies what change should be made
- helps the management in the implementation process if required.

The role of change agent is very important because he not only needs to be a technical expert but also an expert in human behaviour and that means lots of skills to manage.

5.3 TYPES OF CHANGE AGENTS

Change agents can be classified into two types.

a. Internal change agent
b. External change agent

5.3.1 Internal Change Agent

As the name suggests, the internal change agent is an insider. These change agents are very effective compared to an outside consultant because the latter may not have as good an understanding of the organisation.

As an insider the internal change agents understand the organisation, the nature of management as well as the employees, and are aware of where the change is required and what change is required. The internal change agent not only works for identification of the change but in the process of implementing change he works for the betterment of his own organisation, that is, for his own betterment.

Thus his future benefit is attached with the organisation's upliftment which makes the internal change agent more involved.

5.3.2 Role of Internal Change Agent

a. The primary role of an internal change agent is to act or work as a link between the consultant and the organisation. He is the person who produces the familiarisation and learning time of the consultant.
b. He plays a significant role in communication within the organisation. He communicates the objectives of the change programme to interested persons in formal and informal discussions. This helps in reducing resistance of individuals to change significantly.
c. He also works as a researcher and analyst whose in-depth awareness and knowledge of the organisation helps make the diagnosis richer and close to reality.
d. He plays a key part as a role model for changing behaviour and style.
e. As a role model, he can facilitate change in others through motivation.
f. He can play the role of a trainer to train people for effective change.

The internal change agent's expertise, knowledge, and experience could be an asset to any organisation (a learning organisation especially) which is looking ahead for change.

5.3.3 External Change Agent

The external change agent is the expert who comes from outside the organisation to diagnose its change areas and provide change alternatives.

He is the consultant who with his knowledge, previous experience, and efficiency in bringing and identifying change, helps the organisation to bring in change.

It can be defined as a service provided by an independent and qualified person/s in identifying and investigating problems concerned with policy, organisation, procedures and methods, recommending appropriate action and assistance in implementation.

5.3.4 Need for an External Change Agent

There are some good reasons for hiring an outsider to usher change in an organisation.

a. He has the expertise and specialised knowledge to diagnose the problem.
b. He has a wider experience to draw from. If the outside consultant has worked for other organisations, he would be aware of their problems and how they were overcome or could not be overcome due to specific reasons.
c. Persons within the company may not be able to devote themselves wholly to the new problem while an outsider would be able to do so.
d. The external change agent may have a fresh point of view. This does not necessarily mean that he is more imaginative, but being an outsider he would not have the same biases as those in the company.
e. An outside consultant would have better access to infrastructure, for example, reference libraries as well as colleagues from who he can get assistance.

5.4 KEY ROLES IN ORGANISATIONAL CHANGE

Organisational change is a collaborative effort and to implement it smoothly, several roles come into play. These include both external and internal roles. Six main roles, relevant for organisational change are discussed here (Fig. 5.1). They are:

Corporate management
Consultant(s)
Internal resource persons
Implementation team
Chief Implementor
Task forces

Fig. 5.1 Key roles in organisational change

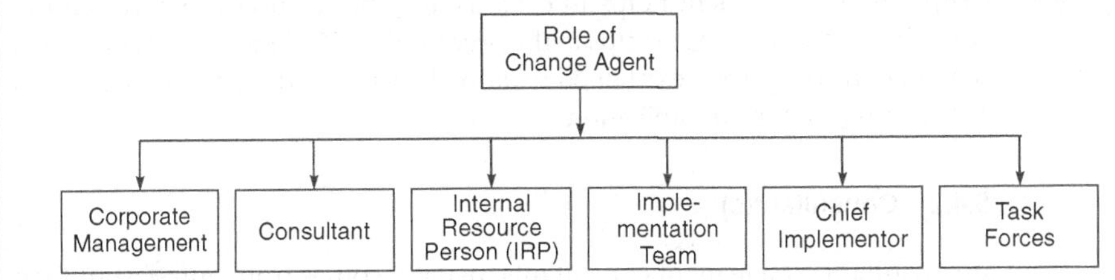

5.4.1 Corporate Management

The chief executive and several top executives who are involved in policy decision are included in those who comprise corporate management. The following are the main functions of corporate management in relation to organisational change (Fig. 5.2).

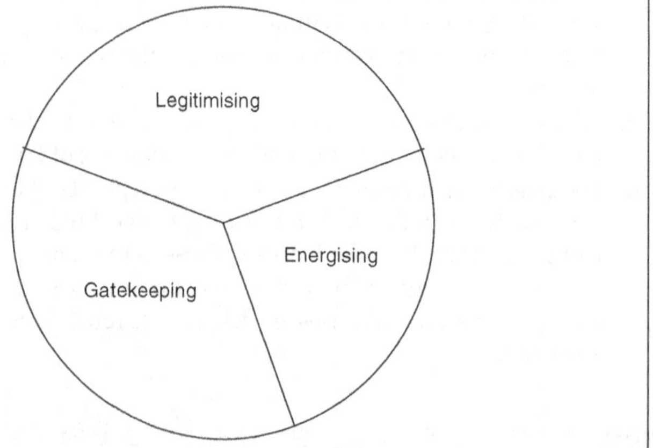

Fig. 5.2 Functions of the corporate management

Legitimising

Corporate management legitimises the change being planned, recommended, and implemented. The more actively the corporate management promotes the change, the more legitimate it becomes and the quicker it is likely to be accepted.

Energising

Organisational change is a difficult process. It may slow down at several stages. In many cases the enthusiasm may go down. In other cases, difficulties arising in the natural course of things may discourage people who may find it difficult to deal with such problems and may like to take the line of least resistance by reverting to the older methods or ways of management.

Gatekeeping

Corporate management helps in establishing the relationship between the consultants and various groups in the organisation. Calling various meetings in which the purpose is explained usually does this and then the consultants get an entry into the organisation.

5.4.2 Consultant(s)

A consultant, or a team of consultants, usually comes from outside but they can also be insiders. The consultant's role is that of an expert, who has both knowledge and experience in the field in which change is proposed. There are some advantages in having outside consultants for some time. Insiders, even though they may have the necessary expertise, are likely to be inhibited by their own perception of the problem. Also, they may be restrained by the internal dynamics. This may make the insiders less effective. Therefore, even organisations with a very high quality of expertise in a particular field invite outside consultants at times. Consultants perform the following functions (see Fig. 5.3).

Fig. 5.3 Functions of a consultant

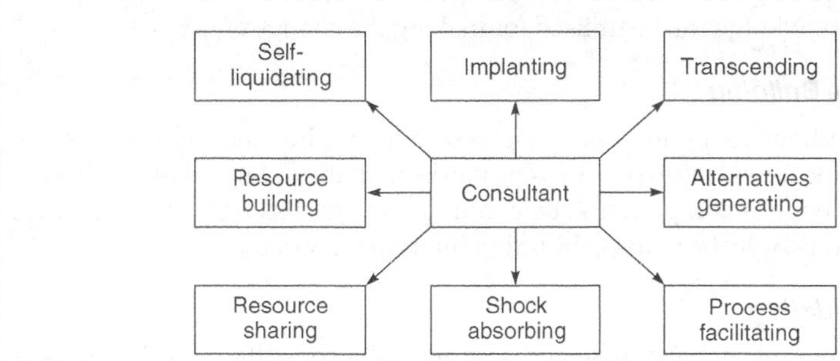

Implanting

The consultant does not supplant the internal expertise available but supplements such expertise. It is necessary that the consultant carries along with him the various people during the different states of the process of organisational change. Then the consultant is successful in making change a part of the organisation.

Transcending

One great advantage of the consultant is that he is not bound by the constraints of the organisation. He takes an overall view. He transcends both the ecology of the organisation, that is the various units and departments, to be able to take an overall view of the organisation, and also transcends the time and people into the future of the organisation.

Alternatives Generating

The consultant is hired not as much for working out a specific solution as for helping the organisation develop the capability of evolving solutions. The consultant does this by generating several alternatives.

Process Faciliting

The consultant is primarily a process facilitator. He has to be perceptive of the reality in the organisation. There is nothing like an ideal or a best one. The consultant may see the repercussions of a solution, and may like to make the necessary modifications to suit the situation.

Shock Absorbing

During the planning of change and making necessary recommendations, much unpleasant feedback may be required to be given to the organisation. This is easier for an outside consultant to do than for an insider.

Resource Sharing

The consultant brings with his background, the latest knowledge and a wide variety of experience, which he uses in making organisational change effective. He collects such resources and shares them with the internal people so that the knowledge can be utilised for making the change effective.

Resource Building

The consultant helps in generating resources within the organisation by building the necessary expertise as he works with the organisation by sharing his knowledge and experience. By continuously discussing matters with the concerned people, he helps in building internal resources.

Self-liquidating

By building internal expertise and resources the consultant works towards withdrawing from the organisation and liquidating his role and indispensability. In many cases the consultant enjoys the influencing function so much that he may continue to play this role in the organisation. This is not good either for the organisation or the consultant. The consultant must deliberately refrain from using undue influence on internal executive decisions. And as the work of organisational change is over he must take definite and deliberate steps to withdraw and wean the organisation from depending on him.

5.4.3 Internal Resource Persons

Even if the expert is from outside the organisation, some people from the organisation work with him. These people either have the same expertise as the consultant has or, at least, they propose to develop that expertise. In many organisations, these persons are called Internal Resource Persons (IRP), or facilitators. This role may already exist in an organisation, or it may have to created (Fig. 5.4).

Several important aspects of the development of the IRP deserve attention. These are mentioned below.

Support of the Community

The role of the IRP has to be legitimised in the organisation. It is necessary for various important persons in the organisation to sit together and define the role of the IRP. The person selected for such a role should have some qualities for functioning as a change agent. There must be some preparation of the person for this role.

Fig. 5.4 Functions of an internal resource person

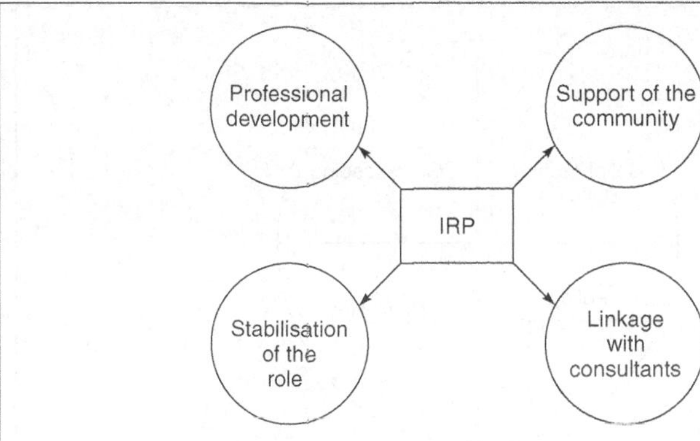

Linkage with Consultants

IRPs should have linkages with several outside consultants. The initial linkage should be with the external consultant associated with the change from the beginning.

Stabilisation of the Role

It is necessary that the role is stabilised in the system through sharing of successes and failures. The work of the IRP can be reviewed from time to time by the organisation.

Professional Development

It is necessary to attend to the continuous professional development of the internal OD facilitators. This can be achieved by helping the IRP attend some advanced programmes, become a member of professional organisations, and work with other organisations in a helping role.

5.4.4 Implementation Team

This team consists of a group of people from various departments or areas of the organisation who are given the responsibility for monitoring, deliberating, and making necessary recommendations from time to time. Such a team ensures proper motivation of people throughout the organisation and takes necessary steps for effective implementation. The functions of an implementation team are given below (Fig. 5.5).

Fig. 5.5 Functions of an implementation team

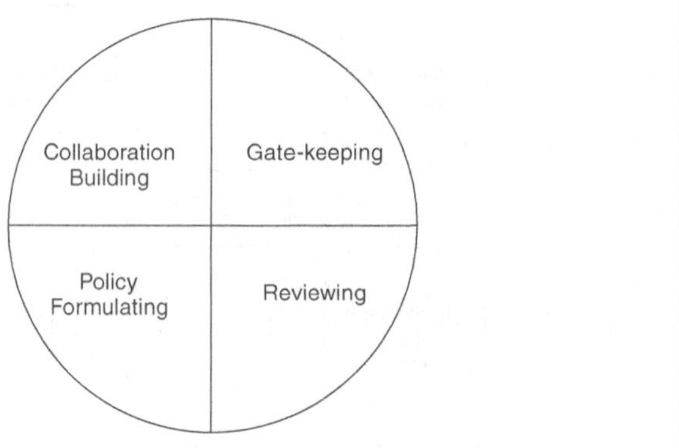

Collaboration Building

The implementation team helps various sections and departments of the organisation collaborate for the change programme. Every member of the team should have respect for the others, and collectively think and evolve a consensus in spite of differences in view points. An effective team is one which has a representation of various kinds of expertise and diverse experiences relevant for the change. And yet people are prepared to listen to each other and take collective decisions which are not necessarily unanimous or majority decisions, but decisions by consensus.

Gate-keeping

The implementation team helps to keep the communication between those who are planning and implementing change and the rest of the organisation open. This is done by developing a liaison among the various departments and sections of the organisation. Since the team has representatives from every department and section, it is able to carry various matters to the departments and raise various questions there. Similarly, the team can get some feedback from the departments for discussion.

Reviewing

From time to time the implementation team reviews the progress of the change programme, and makes necessary adjustments in the programme so that the implementation is effective. The reviewing function helps to take stock as well as to make necessary modification so that implementation is not hampered.

Policy Formulating

The implementation team, in the light of the review, makes necessary recommendations and formulates policies to ensure that the programme of change is both effective and smooth.

5.4.5 Chief Implementor

Any organisational change has to be implemented and those who are working in a particular area need not do this. In fact, it is better to make implementation independent of the functional responsibility in an organisation. The chief implementor is usually the chairman of the implementation team. But his responsibility is not confined to discussing problems and making recommendations. He takes the responsibility of monitoring the change and ensuring proper implementation. The main difference between the role of the chief implementor and the implementation team is that a group can never take on executive responsibility.

The chief implementor performs the following functions (Fig. 5.6).

Fig. 5.6 Functions of a chief implementator

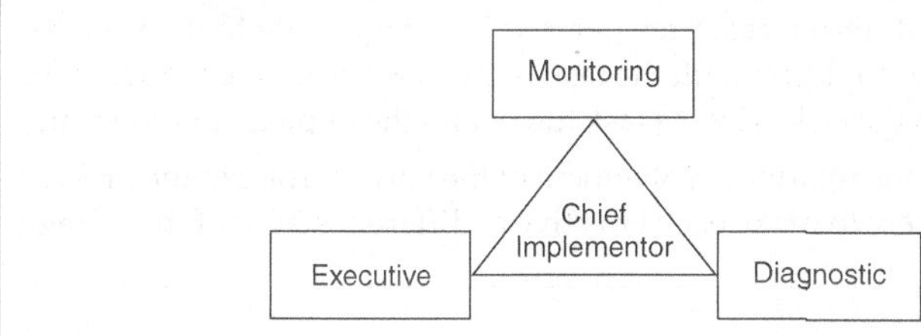

Monitoring

The chief implementor monitors the programme of change. He ensures that the programme design and the time schedule that has been laid down are followed.

Diagnostic

From time to time the chief implementor examines the programme to find out what, if anything, is preventing the smooth functioning and progress as planned. He collects the necessary information through specially designed questionnaires or through interviews, and uses these to discuss the necessary action that needs to be taken with the implementation team.

Executive

The chief implementor has the responsibility of implementing the programme. This is an executive function. It involves not only making recommendations but ensuring that action is taken on whatever has been decided.

Qualities of a Successful Implementor

The chief implementor should be systematic in his approach. He should have a head for systematic planning and going into the details of the various steps planned. At the same time he should be flexible.

The chief implementor needs to be creative, resourceful, and imaginative. He may come across several problems and has to find solutions for them. He should try various ways of dealing with the problem sometimes even unconventional ways can be successful.

5.4.6 Task Forces

These bodies are set up for specific purposes in order to prepare material, collect information, generate ideas, and take specific responsibility which is time bound and which is completed very fast.

The six roles suggested above are involved both in the process and the task. However, their emphases differ. For example, corporate management and the consultant primarily contribute to the process. Their major function is to facilitate the process so that the necessary movement towards organisational change is possible. Internal resource persons also contribute to the process, although their preoccupation with the task is greater. The greater concern for and involvement in the task is by the task forces and the implementation team.

Fig. 5.7 indicates the relative involvement of the various roles in the process or task, which is likely to make each effective at different stages of the change

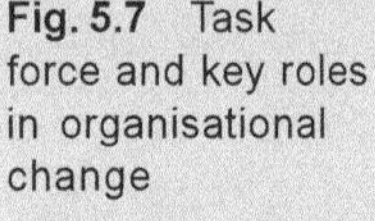
Fig. 5.7 Task force and key roles in organisational change

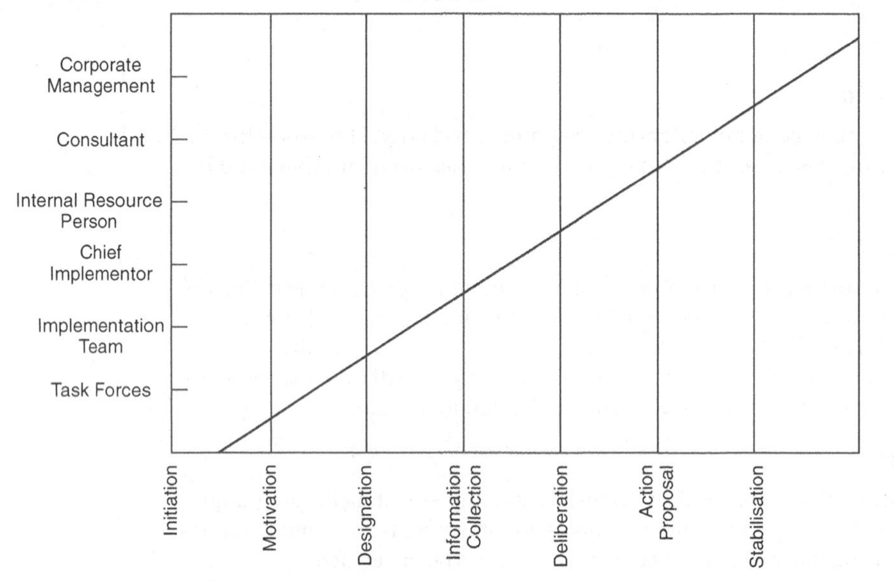

process. In the initial phases, the involvement required in the process is greater than in the subsequent phases when gradually more involvement in the task will be possible. When the change process is being started, all roles concerned with it should pay more attention to the process. If it is properly executed task performance becomes easier. Towards the end, all roles can pay attention to the task. The figure also indicates that even towards the end, top management has to be concerned with the process though the intensity and the time spent by them on this will be less. As a matter of fact, the involvement of top management will be predominantly with the process whereas the task force would need to pay attention mainly to the emergent tasks. The relative focus of the different roles in orienting themselves in this proportion of the process-task continuum will be useful.

5.5 DIFFERENCES BETWEEN INTERNAL AND EXTERNAL CHANGE AGENTS

External Change Agent	*Internal Change Agent*
1. He is the outside consultant hired by any organisation.	1. He is the inside consultant who is an employee of the organisation.
2. He is always a professional.	2. He is not always a professional.
3. He works for a limited period of time for any organisation.	3. His working period is not limited.
4. Hiring external change agent is expensive.	4. Working with an internal change agent is economical for an organisation.
5. External change agent only outlines the change process.	5. An internal change agent works for the implementation of the change process as well.
6. He primarily gives recommendations. He does not work as a linkage person.	6. He primarily works as a linkage between the consultant and the organisation.
7. He only gives the objectives of the change process.	7. He works as a medium between the consultant and the organisation. He communicates the objectives of the change process.
8. At times he does not have in-depth knowledge of practices in an organisation.	8. He always has a in-depth knowledge about his organisation
9. He has the necessary expertise and knowledge to diagnose the problem.	9. He has less expertise and knowledge than the outside consultant to diagnose the problem.
10. He is experienced.	10. He is less experienced.

11. He works full time as a consultant.	11. Being an employee of the organisation, he is not always able to work full time as a consultant.
12. Being an outsider, he has new and fresh ideas. He is less biased.	12. Being an insider, he might have a bias.
13. Being a professional, he has better access to infrastructure such as libraries.	13. Being an insider and a non-professional, he does not have infrastructure of that level.
14. He has a wider outlook about any problem and change.	14. He has a limited outlook about any problem and change.

5.6 CHARACTERISTICS OF A GOOD CHANGE AGENT

According to various authors and researchers an effective change agent is an extrovert with considerable interpersonal skills, who has an ability to conceptualise, be creative, take risks, present ideas clearly, is good at organising activities, and so on.

However, it is impossible to have all these qualities in one person.

Havelock and Sashkin (1983) identified a set of characteristics of an effective change agent. These characteristics are more related with the change process than with personality (Fig. 5.8).

Fig. 5.8 Characterstics of a good change agent

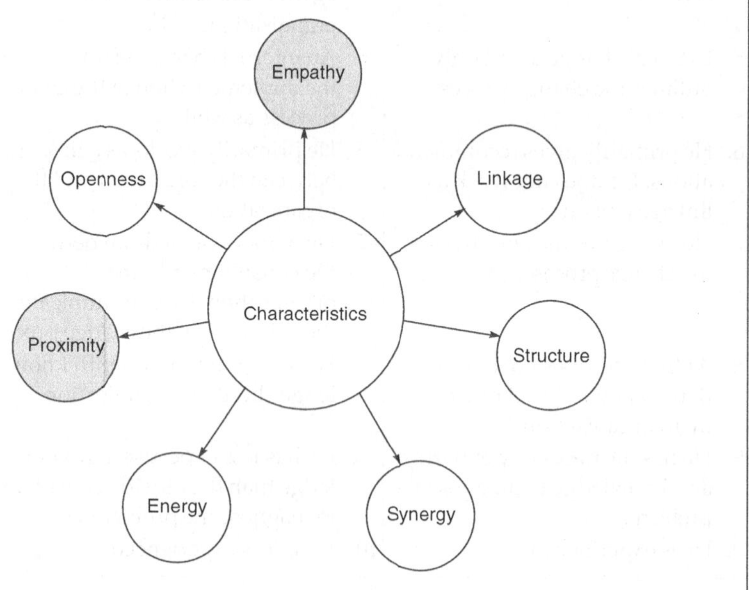

Empathy This is the skill of understanding the feelings and thoughts of another person. It is actually related to improved communication and understanding between the change agent and the employees of the organisation. This characteristic can be easily adopted or learned.

Linkage This refers to the degree of collaboration or the extent to which the change agent and others are linked to each other as equal participants in the change process. The greater the linkage, the more likely it is that the change agent will be successful.

Proximity This refers to the accessibility of a change agent. The greater his accesibility, the greater the chance of success. The increased proximity leads to easy development of collaborative linkage.

Structure This refers to a very important ability of any change agent. The ability to clearly plan and organise the change activity or activities. When the change effort is outlined and presented clearly, it becomes easy to understand the effort. When the change agent is clearly organised, it facilitates the implementation process. Thus work progresses in a structured step-by-step manner.

Openness This refers to the degree to which the change agent is receptive to ideas, needs, and feelings. The former qualities would work only if openness is present in the change agent. If it is absent, it will block the development process between the change agent and client.

Energy This refers to the amount of effort needed for any change activity by a change agent. More energy is needed for greater efforts and vice versa. If the change agent uses his energy in an appropriate manner then he will be successful.

Synergy This factor refers to the reinforcing effects that each of the preceding six characteristics have upon each other. It means when all these factors work individually and with each other, then the efforts of a change agent will bear fruit and the change would be introduced and lead to the success of the OD effort.

5.7 TIMING THE ENTRY OF THE AGENT/CONSULTANT INTO THE ORGANISATION

5.7.1 How to get the Best from the Consultant

For an organisation, it is not "how excellent" a consultant's recommendations are but "how well" the consultant can put them to use.

To get the best out of the consultant, it would be useful if the organisation decides on the timing of his entry. This could be determined on the basis of the following points.

a. If the organisation has just undergone a major crisis, it may be advisable to wait till all the dust settles and work resumes as usual. Frequent changes leave a bad impression on employees and executives and they become suspicious and insecure. These circumstances would act as hurdles for the consultant in his collection of information, and analysis.

b. What is the work load on the execution employees? That is, when the consultant's recommendations are introduced, would the employees be able to handle any extra load or stress. And would the organisation itself be able to overcome any resistance to the change?
c. When a company or organisation is doing well financially is the best time to introduce a change because the change would be easier and the employee would be co-operative.

However, this does not happen most often and change is introduced when either the organisation has reached a plateau or is on the decline. During such times, desire for introducing change is the most but implementation is difficult. Sometimes even worse conditions occur and companies go on for adopting change anyhow.

5.7.2 How Do Consultants Work

All outside consultants are hired for a fixed period of time. They study the organisation, give their recommendations, and help in the implementation if required. Thereafter it is the insider who would either use or misuse the recommendations.

Therefore, from the beginning, the outside consultant should be associated with a few insiders. This helps the insider to broaden his view and improve his skills and also leads to a better implementation of the recommendations provided by the consultant.

The joint effort by the outside consultant and the insider has some other advantages as well.

a. It provides insight to the consultant about the company's procedure, realities, and character.
b. It shortens the time span from collecting information to diagnosis to solution.
c. It is rewarding as consultants can more easily gauge how much the organisation can cope with.
d. The consultant and the organisation both analyse each other as references to check out the viability of their tentative solutions.

5.7.3 Importance of the Consultant

With change being as inevitable as the resistance that accompanies it coping and managing change is an important area of operation these days. Mergers and acquisitions, that are frequent occurrences these days, let loose huge all-round changes. These might be met with serious resistance. Management needs help in handling the change and resistance at such times. An insider may not be useful under the circumstances for they may lack vision or an objective point of view. He may not be able to put across his opinions freely either. It is at such a time that an external consultant is of use. With no stake in the organisation, he can bluntly put the facts before management and recommend drastic solutions too. The consultant can help the insiders cope with change, help the management choose among conflicting issues, and help people learn the truth—all of which will help the organisation accelerate its growth.

5.8 WHAT CAN A CHANGE AGENT CHANGE?

Just as a French proverb tells us to "try and make that place beautiful wherever you live", change agents also make the working environment employee-friendly, so that change can be successful and sustainable.

To do so, what can a change agent change? The options essentially fall into five categories: structure, technology, physical setting, work place, and people (Fig. 5.9). Changing structure involves making an alteration in authority relations, co-ordination mechanisms, job redesign, or similar structural variables. Changing technology encompasses modifications in the way work is processed and in the methods and equipment used. Changing the physical setting involves altering the space and layout of the work place. Changing people refers to changes in employee attitudes, skills, expectations, perceptions and/or behaviour.

5.8.1 Structure

In Chapter 1, we discussed structural issues such as work specialisation, span of control, and various organisational designs. But organisational structures are not set in concrete. Changing conditions demand structural changes. As a result, the change agent might need to modify the organisation's structure.

An organisation's structure is defined by how tasks are formally divided, grouped, and co-ordinated. Change agents can alter one or more of the key

Fig. 5.9 Areas in which a change agent can work

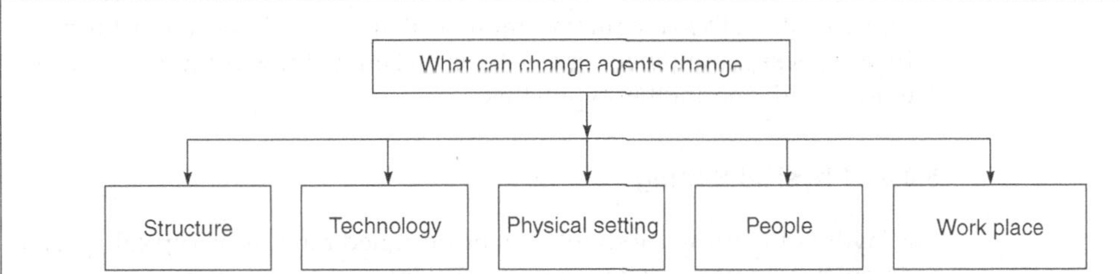

elements in an organisation's design. For instance, departmental responsibilities can be combined, vertical layers removed, and spans of control widened to make the organisation flatter and less bureaucratic. More rules and procedures can be implemented to increase standardisation. Greater decentralisation can be introduced to speed up the decision-making process.

Change agents can also introduce major modifications in the actual structural design. This might include a shift from a simple structure to a team-based structure or the creation of a matrix design. Change agents might consider redesigning jobs or work schedules. Job descriptions can be redefined, jobs enriched, or flexible work hours introduced. Still another option is to modify the organisation's compensation system. Motivation could be increased by, for example, introducing performance bonuses or profit sharing.

5.8.2 Technology

Most of the early studies of management and organisational behaviour dealt with efforts aimed at technological change. At the turn of the century, for example, scientific management sought to implement changes based on time and motion studies that would increase production efficiency. Today, major technological changes usually involve the introduction of new equipment, tools, or methods; automation, or computerisation.

Competitive factors or innovations within an industry often require change agents to introduce new equipment, tools, or operating methods. For example, many aluminium companies have significantly modernised their plants in recent years to compete more effectively. More efficient handling equipment, furnaces, and presses have been installed to reduce the cost of manufacturing a ton of aluminium.

Automation is a technological change that replaces people with machines. It began with the Industrial Revolution and continues as a change option today. Examples of automation are the introduction of automatic mail sorters by the U.S. Postal Service and robots on automobile assembly lines.

As we noted in previous chapters, the most visible technological change in recent years has been expanding computerisation. Many organisations now have sophisticated management information systems. Large supermarkets have converted their cash registers into input terminals and linked them to computers to provide instant inventory data. The office of 2005 is dramatically different from its counterpart of 1975, predominantly because of computerisation. Desktop microcomputers that can run hundreds of business software packages and network systems that allow these computers to communicate with one another typify this.

5.8.3 Physical Setting

The layout of work space should not be designed randomly. Typically, management considers work demands, formal interaction requirements, and social needs when making decisions about space configurations, interior design, equipment placement, and the like.

For example, by eliminating walls and partitions and designing an open office, it becomes easier for employees to communicate with each other. Similarly, management can change the quantity and types of lights, the level of heat or cold, the levels and types of noise, the cleanliness of the work area, as well as interior design dimensions like furniture, decorations, and colour schemes.

Evidence indicates that change in the physical setting, in itself, does not have a substantial impact on organisational or individual performance. But it can make certain employee behaviours easier or harder. In this way, employee and organisational performance may be enhanced or reduced.

5.8.4 People

Change agents help individuals and groups within the organisation to work more effectively together. This typically involves changing the attitudes and behaviours of organisational members through communication, decision-making, and problem-solving. The concept of organisational development has come to encompass an array of interventions that are designed to change people and the nature and quality of their work relationships. We review these people-changing interventions in our discussion of organisational development.

5.8.5 Work Place

The working world is changing fast. New technologies and realigned work environments are altering the way companies do business and the relationships between workers and their employers. Longer work hours, increased levels of work/stress, downsizing, mergers and buyouts have made building and maintaining employee morale a challenge. At the same time, more and more employees are now looking at non-traditional work arrangements to achieve a better balance in their professional and personal lives. Traditional work structures are no longer enough, and companies that fail to be flexible are finding that keeping employees and recruiting new talent is increasingly difficult. Surveys show that the fastest-growing concern of employees in all types of organisations is lifestyle balance. Several factors are causing the issue to loom larger today than in the past.

i. Getting ahead and money alone do not drive people in their 20s as much as previous generations.
ii. Many people in their 30s are now starting families and establishing different types of goals.
iii. Baby boomers either have attained their work goals or know they will not.

iv. The average professional work week has increased to 48 hours, meaning that for every person working 40 hours a week, there is someone working 56 hours a week.

5.8.6 Flexible Work Options

Telecommuting, flex-time, job sharing, and compressed work weeks are some of the work schedule arrangements companies are making available to employees to provide them with a better work/life balance. Forward-thinking companies have come to realise that flexible work arrangements are a strong recruitment tool, a great boost for employee morale, and an effective means for decreasing employee turnover.

Over the last several years, many federal and state governmental agencies in the US have also begun offering their employees flexible work arrangements. In New Jersey, the Department of Labor offers both flex-time and telecommuting options to employees. The telecommuting programme is a pilot programme that has been in effect for three months. The arrangement already has resulted in significant rent savings in office space, according to the department. Officials also report that employee morale has increased significantly since the two programmes began. The NJ Department of Transportation has offered a compressed work week programme for employees since 1997 that allows them to work five days one week and four days the next week. The Department of Transportation credits the programme with reducing sick leave and with increasing employee satisfaction. The Department of Health and Senior Services also offers an alternative work week programme that lets employees complete their regular hourly schedule in nine days so they can get the tenth day off. As with the Department of Labor and Department of Transportation, Health and Senior Services officials report they have seen a definite increase in employee morale.

5.8.7 Telecommuting

Propelling the change in work arrangements are new technologies that have helped to redefine office boundaries. In the beginning of the 1980s, the introduction of new technologies was limited to a few specific business sectors. But by the end of the decade, there was a significant increase in the penetration of computers and computer-based technologies on a vast array of business functions. The advent of fax machines, email, voice mail, and the growth and popularity of the Internet has created a global work environment that is fast-paced and aggressive, and which is changing where, when, and how people work. Statistics gathered by the International Telework Association and Council show that there was a 60 per cent increase in telecommuting between 1996 and 1998, with almost 16 million workers spending at least one day per week outside the traditional work environment. Telecommuting is the concept of performing work on a regular basis in a location other than the office, usually at home. There are many advantages to telecommuting for both companies and employees.

Employees both feel they have more control of their lives and enjoy the benefits of less time spent commuting to work. Employers benefit as their employees increase their use of new technologies and as their organisations gain an advantage for recruiting and retaining top professionals.

Some important points to keep in mind when offering a telecommuting option are training, equipment, and communication. Without proper training and equipment, implementing a telecommuting programme can be more trouble than it is worth. The time and effort invested in providing proper equipment and training will pay off many times over once employees are out on their own. Also, establishing clear communications and expectations with telecommuting employees is essential. Employees also need to be able to access company information as easily as if they were in the office.

5.8.8 Flex-time

This is a popular work option that is easy for management to institute and monitor. Flex-time allows for flexibility in starting and quitting time within limits established by management. In most flex-time situations, there is a set amount of hours everyone must work. For example, if the normal hours are 9:00 am–5:00 pm, a flex schedule could be 7:30 am–3:30 pm or 10:00 am–6:00 pm. The total number of hours worked remains the same for other similar positions. Another way that flex-time can be used, which is popular in many accounting firms, is to reduce daily time during slower periods to compensate for the increased hours during busy seasons.

5.8.9 Compressed Work Weeks

A variation of flex-time is the compressed work week. This generally squeezes the hours of a "normal" work week into a shorter period to allow for a regular day off. Examples include four 10-hour days with the fifth day off, or nine-hour days with the tenth day off. Many other different hourly combinations can be created to meet the needs of the employee and the business. For example, the New Jersey Environmental Protection Agency offers an alternative work week programme that provides employees with the option of working four 10-hour days so they can have the fifth day off, or working 70 hours in nine days so they can have the tenth day off. Employers benefit from such arrangements by being able to provide employees with a zero-cost benefit. Such arrangements can also be used to save one day a week of operating costs or to provide more overall hours of coverage without running additional shifts or accruing overtime.

5.8.10 Job sharing

Yet another arrangement that has been growing in popularity is job sharing. Job sharing involves allowing two people to share one job, each working part-time so that their combined schedule equates to one full-time job. Unlike flex-time and compressed work weeks, job sharing is an employee-initiated arrangement. Typically, one employee is the official "holder" of the job and has first rights to the job on a full-time basis. In allowing such arrangements, management needs to be careful in evaluating the employees looking for such an arrangement and the job itself. Questions that need to be considered are whether the job can be carried out successfully in such a manner and whether the employees have the communication and organisational skills required of such arrangements. Generally, job-sharing agreements are for limited periods, which may be renewed.

Though job sharing tends to be applicable only in a limited range of situations, there are a number of benefits for employers. Since both employees are part-time, the need to pay overtime is eliminated, benefit costs are contained, and customer service hours can be expanded. Job sharing also can help to decrease employee absenteeism and tardiness.

5.8.11 New Rules for Managers

To reap the full value of flexible arrangements, employers need to involve employees in the work process and let them know they are valued. Managers taking the time, outside of performance reviews, for career discussions can accomplish this. Such discussions can help employees clarify the fit between themselves and their work schedules and, in turn, uncover and address lifestyle issues that impact their jobs, while demonstrating that the company is willing to step "outside-the-box" to assist them in getting ahead.

While it may be difficult at first to gauge the bottom-line benefits of new work arrangements, many employers report they quickly noticed an elevation in morale and commitment to the organisation. Just as significantly, flex-time arrangements have been shown to provide a competitive advantage for attracting and retaining top professionals.

SUMMARY

- The role of a change agent is very crucial in the introduction and implementation of the change process in the organisation.
- The change agent works as a consultant in bringing due change for the success of the organisation. The change agent is basically classified into two categories—internal change agent and external change agent.
- The key roles during organisational change can be played by corporate management, consultants, internal resource persons, implementation team, chief implementor, and task forces.
- Corporate management performs legitimising, energising, and gatekeeping functions.
- The consultant performs the functions of implementing, transcending, alternative generating, process facilities, shock absorbing, resource sharing, resource building, and self-liquidating.
- The internal resource person works for the support of community, linkage with consultants, stabilisation of the role, and professional development.
- The implementation team performs collaboration building, gatekeeping, reviewing, and policy formulating functions.
- Task forces are set up for a specific purpose and can perform any of the above mentioned functions.
- There is a difference between an external and an internal change agent based on the purpose and the requirement of the changing needs of the organisation.
- Characteristics of a good change agents are: empathy, linkage, proximity, structure, openness, energy, and synergy.
- The timing of the entry and the mode of operation within the organisation also determines the performance of a change agent.
- During the management of change a change, agent can introduce changes in the organisational structure, technological operations, physical setting, attitude and behaviour of people, and working environment or work place.

Case Study: "Taj Mahal Group of Hotels" A Hospitality Company

History

A new Director of Human Resources in a Taj Mahal hotel decided that the approach to training had been too haphazard, thereby wasting money and failing to align training with the company's priorities of performance improvement and business expansion.

Task

Perform a TQM-based training needs assessment for the hotels to determine priority training targets and develop a selective directory of external training resources suitable for meeting these targets.

Intervention

A change agency developed a customised training needs questionnaire, conducted a survey, and prepared an analytical report summarising identified needs and ranking priorities for action. This was followed by targeted research to identify a range of the best possible training resources for each category of needs (ranging from computer skills/IT training to TQM training, communication training, performance evaluation, and ISO 9002 Management Representative training).

Result

Within a short time, the company gained the vital information necessary to develop and budget for a comprehensive training plan in support of its business goals and commitment to performance improvement.

Key Disciplines

Training Needs Assessment, Training Resource Identification, Training Resource Evaluation.

REVIEW QUESTIONS

1. Who are change agents? Define different types of change agents.
2. Differentiate between external and internal change agents from the organisational point of view.
3. The success of a change is determined by the quality of a change agent. Discuss.
4. How does a consultant work in an organisation?
5. In what areas of an organisation can a change agent bring some changes?
6. Who plays the major roles in facilitating change in an organisation?

EXERCISE 1

This simple short exercise is adaptable for a wide variety of situations, and illustrates how we tend to go through our lives in a routine manner, not noticing things around us, when we should all be more alive to our surroundings (and our own selves). Awareness is a prerequisite for response and action in the case of a change agent, especially effective communication. Self-awareness is essential for personal effectiveness and change. This activity demonstrates that we can all improve in these areas.

The facilitator should prepare a list of 5–20 questions (depending on the duration of activity required) about details of the particular work or meeting environment (and optionally about the participants' own selves). For example,

- What colour are the floor tiles in the reception?

- What was the name of the lady who served you coffee on arrival (it was on her name-badge)?
- According to the plaque by the entrance, who inaugurated the building and in what year?
- What is featured in the big landscape picture that hangs in the reception?
- Where is the fire extinguisher in the hallway outside this room?
- What products are featured in the pictures in the elevator?
- What was the colour of the receptionist's jacket/hair/blouse?
- What is printed on your room key fob aside from the number?
- How many plastic cards are there in your purse/wallet?
- And so on.

The exercise is an enjoyable and different way to illustrate the opportunities that we all have for improving our awareness, and therefore responsiveness.

To give the activity an extra edge, you can make it competitive, in which case ask team members to exchange their answer sheets for scoring while the facilitator calls out the answers. You can also award a prize for the most amusing wrong answer. The observation/awareness emphasis of the exercise is slightly different if the situation is a one-off conference venue, compared with the group's normal working environment. Try to make the questions fair for all, especially if participants have quite different levels of familiarity with the location. Select questions and adjust the positioning of the purpose and review accordingly.

EXERCISE 2

This innovative group activity can be used for exploring the dynamics of a team and developing mutual awareness in the process of change and development of the organisation through the agency. The exercise can be used with teams of four, up to a maximum of twenty, although such a large group size increases the time required. Larger groups can be split into teams (ideally work teams) of 4–10 members.

Each person must be asked before the activity session to bring along three objects or items that have some personal meaning and which also relate to the team. (This is an interesting exercise in itself if the items are shown and their personal and team significance discussed by the team.)

Next, use a suitably sized table or a piece of cloth on the floor to act as the base for the sculpture. Team members must then, in their own time, place their objects either all at once or one at a time onto the base. Team members should be instructed to place and adjust the position of their objects in meaningful relation to other team members' objects, and at any time any person can move any object on the base provided none is removed altogether. Participants should be encouraged to move around the sculpture as it is evolving. This is all done in silence for a period stated beforehand or decided during the activity according to the situation by the facilitator, typically 20–40 minutes.

The sculpture is complete at the end of the fixed time period when team members have finished moving the objects and are satisfied with the sculpture. (Alternatively, participants can be permitted to discuss the positioning of the objects, which on one hand encourages active team-working during the exercise, but on the other hand will reduce the effect of interference and "violation", obviously a potentially interesting discussion area for later. So choose what you think will be most helpful for the team concerned, or ask the team whether it would prefer the sculpture build to be silent or openly discussed.

The facilitator then encourages the team to view the sculpture from different angles and discuss the meaning of the finished work, and how it symbolises the team (dynamics, personality, strengths, weaknesses, style, relationships, mix, opportunities, threats, and so on). Then the facilitator encourages the participants to talk about the process—the significance of their personal objects and how they felt about them being moved around.

A significant aspect of this fascinating exercise is to reveal hidden personal values and needs, plus the risks of unintentional violation, and the opportunities for nurturing through each person's own needs and desires. This exercise can be used for fun and creative activity, and certainly to promote increased mutual awareness and support. Teams which are able to use their imagination, and are able to extract meaning from what is quite an abstract process, should be able to gain substantial insight into the team's dynamics from this activity.

Chapter

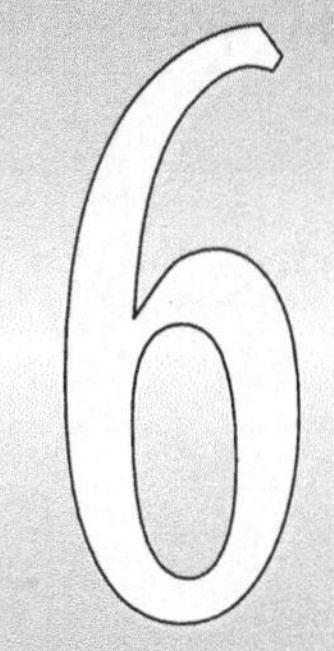

Strategic Management of Change

CHAPTER OUTLINE

- Introduction
- Three Basic Definitions
- Strategic Management of Change
- Sequential Process of Change
- Change Process as a Problem-solving and Problem-finding Approach
- Change Management: Skill Requirements
- Change Management: Four Basic Strategies
- Factors in Selecting Change Strategy
- Change Strategy Formulation and Implementation
- Evaluation in the Strategic Change Process
- Process of Transformational Change
- Guidelines to Management of Effective Change
- Summary
- Case Studies
- Review Questions
- Exercises

> "A sound change strategy looks for change, knows how to find the right changes and knows how to make them effective both outside the organisation and inside it."
>
> — Anonymous

6.1 INTRODUCTION

Organisations are highly specialised systems and there are different schemes for grouping and classifying them. Some are said to be in the retail business, others are in manufacturing, and still others confine their activities to distribution. Some are profit-oriented and some are not for profit. Some are in the public sector and some are in the private sector. Some are members of the financial services industry, which encompasses banking, insurance, and brokerage houses. Others belong to the automobile industry, where they can be classified as original equipment manufacturers (OEM) or after-market providers. Some belong to the healthcare industry, as providers, as insured, or as insurers. Many are regulated, some are not. Some face stiff competition, some do not. Some are foreign-owned and some are foreign-based. Some are corporations, some are partnerships, and some are sole proprietorships. Some are publicly held and some are privately held. Some have been around a long time and some are newcomers. Some have been built up over the years while others have been pieced together through mergers and acquisitions. No two organisations are exactly alike.

The preceding paragraph points out that the problems found in organisations, especially the change problems, have both a content and a process dimension. It is one thing, for instance, to introduce a new claims processing system in a functionally organised health insurer and quite another to introduce a similar system in a health insurer that is organised along product lines and market segments. It is different thing altogether to introduce a system of equal size and significance in an educational establishment that relies on a matrix structure. The languages spoken differ. The values differ. The cultures differ. The problems differ. However, the overall processes of change and change management remain pretty much the same, and it is this fundamental similarity of the change processes across organisations, industries, and structures that makes change management a task, a process, and a practice.

A classic example of success through effective change management involves the global communications giant Motorola. The Space and System Technology Group at Motorola gradually introduced self-managing teams as a work change initiative. This came about from listening to employees and from a pressing need to improve the quality of output and cycle times. As a result of a well-communicated and carefully implemented change, Motorola was able to boast a figure of 22 defects per million, as compared to 750 defects per million before the change—a considerable improvement by any standards!

At the end of the day, change boils down to people. People make things happen, and people will carry out the changes. However, this is only likely to occur if management properly communicates a change initiative. The organisations that succeed at change are the ones that are able to consider the people who will be affected by the change and that will be crucial to their long-term chances of success.

Change usually involves the introduction of new procedures, people or ways of working which have a direct impact on the various stakeholders within an organisation. The key to successful change management lies in understanding the potential effects of a change initiative on these stakeholders. Will employees be scared, resistant, pessimistic, or enthusiastic about your proposed changes? How can each possible reaction be anticipated and managed?

With such widespread change occurring, handling all the various issues that arise becomes a priority for a manager and naturally some are better at it than others. But keeping pace with the rate of change is fast becoming a necessity of modern management. If a change programme is not handled appropriately despite the best of intentions, an organisation is unlikely to achieve any of its desired goals or objectives.

6.2 THREE BASIC DEFINITIONS

Change management is defined as "the systematic approach of planning, organising, coordinating and controlling of organisational resources to make them compatible to the ever changing environment for the sustainable development of the organisation".

In thinking about what is meant by "change management", at least three basic definitions come to mind. On the basis of these three core issues, strategic change management is:

a. The task of managing change
b. An area of professional practice
c. A body of knowledge

6.2.1 The Task of Managing Change

The first and most obvious definition of change management is that the term refers to the task of managing change. The obvious is not necessarily unambiguous. Managing change is a term that has at least two meanings.

One meaning of managing change refers to the making of changes in a planned and managed or systematic fashion. The aim is to more effectively implement new methods and systems in an ongoing organisation. The changes to be managed lie within and are controlled by the organisation. However, these internal changes might have been triggered by events originating outside the organisation, in what is usually termed "the environment".

Hence, the second meaning of managing change, namely, the response to changes over which the organisation exercises little or no control (for example, legislation, social and political upheaval, actions of competitors, shifting economic tides and currents, and so on). Researchers and practitioners alike typically distinguish between a knee-jerk or reactive response and an anticipative or proactive response.

6.2.2 An Area of Professional Practice

There are dozens, if not hundreds, of independent consultants who will quickly and proudly acknowledge that they are engaged in planned change, that they are change agents, that they manage change for their clients, and that their practices are change management practices. There are numerous small consulting firms whose principals would acknowledge these same statements about their firms. And most of the major management consulting firms claim to have a change management practice area.

Some of these change management experts claim to help clients manage the changes they face, the changes happening to them. Others claim to help clients make changes. Still others offer to help by taking on the task of managing changes that must be made. In almost all cases, the process of change is treated separately from the specifics of the situation. It is the task of managing this general process of change that is laid claim to by professional change agents.

6.2.3 A Body of Knowledge

Stemming from the view of change management as an area of professional practice, there arises yet a third definition of change management: the content or subject matter of change management. This consists chiefly of the models, methods and techniques, tools, skills, and other forms of knowledge that go into making up any practice.

The content or subject matter of change management is drawn from psychology, sociology, business administration, economics, industrial engineering, systems engineering, and the study of human and organisational behaviour. For many practitioners, these component bodies of knowledge are linked and integrated by a set of concepts and principles known as General Systems Theory (GST). It is not clear whether this area of professional practice should be termed a profession, a discipline, an art, a set of techniques, or a technology. For now, suffice it to say that there is a large, reasonably cohesive albeit somewhat eclectic body of knowledge underlying the practice and on which most practitioners would agree—even if their application of it does exhibit a high degree of variance.

6.3 STRATEGIC MANAGEMENT OF CHANGE

Strategic management of change is defined as a continuous, iterative process, aimed at keeping an organisation as a whole appropriately matched to its environment.

The definition of strategic management of change we have proposed emphasises that managers engage in a series of steps. These steps, which we will discuss individually, are (Fig. 6.1):

Performing an environmental analysis
Establishing organisational direction
Formulating organisational strategy
Implementing organisation strategy
Exercising strategic control for the effective application of change in the organisation.

The definition also suggests that the strategic management process for change is continuous—it never really stops within the organisation. Although different strategic management activities may receive more or less em-

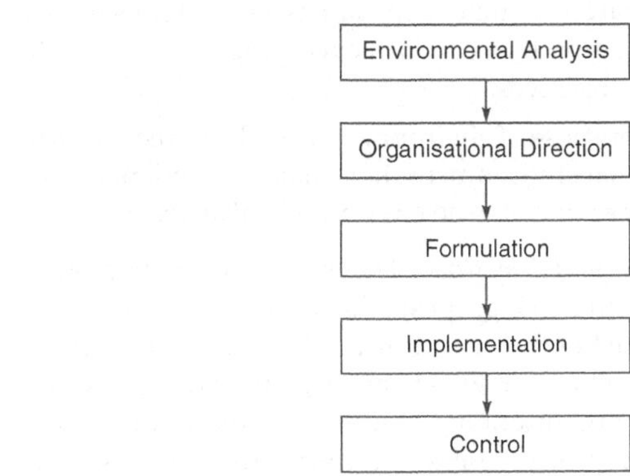

Fig. 6.1 Strategic management of change

phasis and may be pursued with different intensities at different times, management should virtually always be focusing or reflecting on some aspect of strategic change.

The term "iterative" in the definition of strategic management for change indicates that the process of strategic management starts with the first step, ends with the last step—and then begins again with the first step. Strategic management, then, consists of a series of steps that are repeated in cyclical fashion.

The last part of the definition of strategic management states that the purpose of strategic management is to ensure that an organisation as a whole is appropriately matched to its environment—that is, to its operational surroundings. Organisational environments are constantly changing, and organisations must be modified accordingly to ensure that organisational goals can be attained. Legislation affecting the organisation, changes in the labour supply available to it, and actions taken by its competitors are examples of changes within the organisation's environment that are normally addressed by the management.

Although the definition of strategic management seems clear and simple, actually implementing the process in an organisation is usually very complicated. Strategic management is a series of efforts adopted by the organisation for the achievement of its objectives.

6.3.1 Strategic Management Process

We have defined strategic management as a process or series of steps. Let us now take a look at each of these steps and its relationship to the strategic management system.

Step 1 Environmental analysis The strategic management process begins with environmental analysis, the process of monitoring the organisation's environment to identify both present and future threats and opportunities. In this context, the organisational environment encompasses all factors both inside and outside the organisation that can influence progress towards the attainment of organisational objectives.

Managers must grasp the purpose of environmental analysis, recognise the various levels of organisational environment that exist, and understand the recommended guidelines for performing an environmental analysis.

Step 2 Establishing organisational direction The second step of the strategic management process for effective change is establishing organisational direction, or determining the thrust of the organisation (Fig. 6.2). There are two main indicators of the direction in which an organisation is moving: organisational mission and organisational objectives. Organisational mission is the purpose for which, or the reason why an organisation exists. Objectives are the targets the organisation has chosen.

Fig. 6.2 Organisational direction (Top-D)

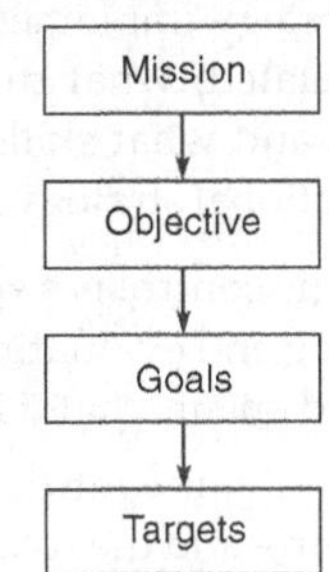

After the management has performed an environmental analysis to pinpoint the organisation's strengths, weaknesses, opportunities, and threats, it is often better able to establish, reaffirm, or modify its organisational direction. In order to establish organisational direction appropriately, however, management must know what comprises an organisational mission statement, understand the nature of organisational objectives, and adopt an effective and efficient process for establishing organisational direction. A proper understanding of the mission and the objective helps the organisation in its adaptability to change.

Step 3 Strategy formulation Strategy is defined as a course of action aimed at ensuring that the organisation will achieve its objectives. Strategy formulation, then, is the process of designing and selecting strategies that lead to the attainment of organisational objectives of successful change. The central focus of organisational strategy is how to deal better with competition. Once the environment has been analysed and organisational direction stipulated, management is able to chart alternative courses of action in an informed effort to ensure organisational success.

In order to formulate organisational strategy properly, managers must thoroughly understand various approaches to strategy formulation such as Critical Question Analysis, Strength/Weakness/Opportunity/Threat (SWOT) Analysis, and so on.

Step 4 Implementing organisational strategy This step involves putting into action the logically developed strategies that emerged from the previous steps of the strategic management process. Without an effective implementation of strategy, organisations are unable to reap the benefits of performing an organisational analysis, establishing organisational direction, and formulating organisational strategy.

In order to implement organisational strategy successfully, managers must have a clear idea of several diverse issues: how much change is necessary within an organisation when it implements a new strategy, how best to deal with organisational "culture" in order to ensure that a strategy will indeed be implemented smoothly, how strategy implementation and various types of organisational structures are related, what different implementation approaches a manager can follow, and what skills are necessary in managers who hope to implement organisational strategy successfully.

Step 5 Strategic control Strategic control is a special type of organisational control that focuses on monitoring and evaluating the strategic management process in order to improve it and ensure that it is functioning properly.

To successfully perform this strategic control task, managers must understand the process of strategic control and the role that strategic audits (assessments of the organisational environment) normally play in it. In addition, managers must understand the intricacies of management information systems and how such systems can complement the strategic control process. The strategic management process within any organisation is only as good as the information on which it is based.

For the purposes of analysis, we have presented the strategic management process for change as a series of discrete steps. The process is presented in this fashion to facilitate learning about what the process entails and to describe how the steps commonly relate to one another. In practice, however, managers sometimes find that applying strategic management effectively within an organisation entails performing several steps simultaneously or performing them in a different order from that suggested here. Managers must be creative in designing and operating strategic management systems for change and flexible enough to tailor their use of such systems to the organisational circumstances that confront them.

6.4 SEQUENTIAL PROCESS OF CHANGE

As we have seen, change takes place in steps or phases. By this we mean that the process through which a given innovation becomes an accepted part of the personality and way of working of individuals, is usually evolutionary. Seldom does a new idea or practice become accepted in one step, small or large. Perhaps a better way of putting it is that people who accomplish successful change go through a number of sequential stages in reaching their goal. This latter way of putting the matter is important because it implies that people, not the innovation, go through the steps. This point is often lost sight of in large-scale development projects. Sometimes the planning is done by one group, usually a group, of high-level administrators. Try-out, or experimentation, if included at all, is turned over to the lower-level administrators, and those who are expected to use the innovation may have experienced none of the development thinking involved. This is very likely to lead to uninformed, insensitive, and indifferent implementation, if implementation takes place at all. The dangers of this way of handling the stages of development can be minimised by indirect involvement in planning and evaluation, and by good communication among all the people who will eventually be touched by the new practice. But the problem needs to be kept in mind in the planning and steering of any development effort.

Several models of sequential steps or stages in change have been suggested. All these models envisage change as a continuous process involving several stages. The following eight stages are proposed as a framework of organisational change (Fig. 6.3).

a. Initiation This is the stage of vocalisation of the need for change. Organisational change starts when someone takes the initiative of proving that something has to be done at the level of the corporate management where the concern for some dimension of organisational functioning is shared and discussed. The idea may be mooted at the level of corporate management, at times based on observations or recommendations by some other level of organisation, and sometimes as a result of discussion at the level of corporate management. This usually leads to the hiring of a consultant from outside, or discussion with the appropriate set of people within the organisation.

b. Motivation This is the stage of the involvement of people in detailed thinking about the proposed change. At this stage, both the corporate management

Fig. 6.3 Sequential process of change

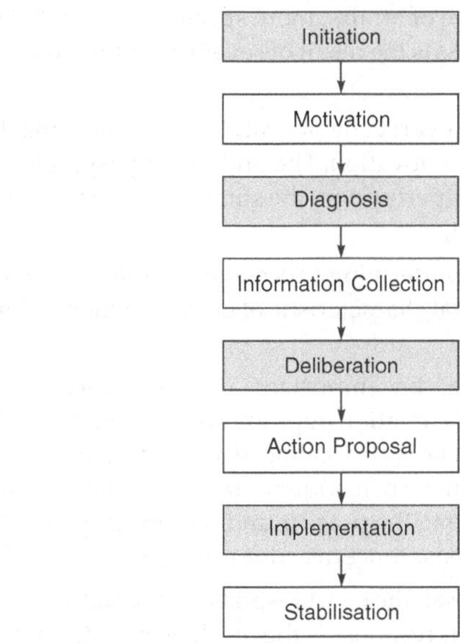

and the expert in organisational change take necessary steps to involve a larger section of the organisation in thinking about the various dimensions of the change process.

c. Diagnosis This is an attempt to search for the main cause of the symptoms encountered.

d. Information collection At this stage, detailed information is collected on the dimension indicated by the diagnosis.

e. Deliberation This stage is concerned with evaluation of various alternatives generated for change.

f. Action proposal This is the stage of framing an action proposal.

g. Implementation This is concerned with translating the proposal into action.

h. Stabilisation This is the stage of internalising change and making it a part of the organisation's normal life.

The various stages in the process of organisational change may be useful to pay much more attention to the process in the beginning and this will help to pay less attention to the process as organisational change proceeds further. Later, much more attention can be given to the task.

It is necessary to understand the psychological processes behind each stage of change, and the behavioural outcomes or indicators. These are suggested in Figure 6.3a.

As can be seen from the figure, the underlying psychological process at the initiation stage is arousal, resulting in readiness and characterised by dissatisfaction with the present state of affairs, more specifically with the practice being used currently. Readiness is the result of several maturational and environmental factors.

At the motivation stage, the overt behavioural characteristic is that the individual sees or hears about the innovation. The underlining psychological process is selectivity and stimulus perception, the stimulus being the practice the individual sees or hears about.

The diagnosis state has an underlying process of orientation and exploration reflected in the behavioural characteristic of gathering more information about the practice.

At the deliberation stage, an important process called perceptual reorganisation takes place. The relationships are shifting and the individual sees a number of patterns, as if he were looking at a kaleidoscope. These shifts in relationships are reflected in the behaviour of the individual who is weighing the pros and cons of adopting the practice and who meets people to check with them about his perceptions, concerns, ideas, and so on.

At the stage of action proposal, the overt response is a tentative action plan in details, with its pay offs. This response is the result of expectancy of results.

Fig. 6.3a Dynamics of the sequential process of change

Stage of adoption	Psychological (cover) process	Behavioural outcomes
1. Intiation	Arousal	Readiness: dissatisfaction with the present
2. Motivation	Selectivity and stimulus perception	Seeing or hearing about innovation
3. Diagnosis	Orientation and eoploration	Gathering information and data
4. Information collection	Exploration	Collecting more relevant data
5. Deliberation	Cognitive reorganisation and reinforcement	Discussion and planning
6. Action Proposal	Expectancy	Presenting a proposal with pay off and detailed planning acceptance by the group
7. Implementation	Acquiring new-learned drives	Extended use of the innovation
8. Stabilisation	Generalisation of the learned behaviour and inhibition of older modes of behaviour: consummatory response	Change of attitude and acceptance as a part of the total behavioural complex with secondary changes in other forms of behaviour communication reinforcing adoption

At the stabilisation stage, characterised by change of attitude as a part of total behaviour, there is generalisation of the learned behaviour and inhibition of older modes of behaviour.

6.5 CHANGE PROCESS AS A PROBLEM-SOLVING AND PROBLEM-FINDING APPROACH

A very useful framework for thinking about the change process is problem-solving. Managing change is seen as a matter of moving from one state to another, specifically, from a problem state to the solved state. Diagnosis, or problem analysis, is generally acknowledged as essential. Goals are set and achieved at various levels and in various areas or functions. Ends and means are discussed and related to one another. Careful planning is accompanied by efforts to obtain buy-in, support, and commitment. The net effect is a transition from one state to another, in a planned, orderly fashion. This is the planned change model.

The word "problem" carries with it connotations that some people prefer to avoid. They choose instead to use the word "opportunity." For such people, a problem is seen as a bad situation, one that should not have been allowed to happen in the first place, and for which someone is likely to be punished—if the guilty party (or a suitable scapegoat) can be identified.

From a rational, analytical perspective, a problem is nothing more than a situation requiring action but in which the required action is not known. Hence, there is a requirement to search for a solution, a course of action that will lead to the solved state. This search activity is known as "problem solving".

"Problem-finding" is thus the search for situations requiring action. Whether we choose to call these situations "problems" (because they are troublesome or spell bad news), or whether we choose to call them "opportunities" (either for reasons of political sensitivity or because the time is ripe to exploit a situation) is immaterial. In both cases, the practical matter is one of identifying and settling on a course of action that will bring about some desired and predetermined change in the situation.

6.5.1 The Change Problem

At the heart of change management lies the change problem, that is, some future state to be realised, some current state to be left behind, and some structured, organised process for getting from the one to the other. The change problem might be large or small in scope and scale, and it might focus on individuals or groups, on one or more divisions or departments, the entire organisation, or on one or more aspects of the organisation's environment.

At a conceptual level, the change problem is a matter of moving from one state (A) to another state (A'). Moving from A to A' is typically accomplished as a result of setting up and achieving three types of goals: transform, reduce, and apply. Transform goals are concerned with identifying differences between the two states. Reduce goals are concerned with determining ways of eliminating these differences. Apply goals are concerned with putting into play operators that actually affect the elimination of these differences.

As the preceding goal types suggest, the analysis of a change problem will at various times focus on defining the outcomes of the change effort, on identifying the changes necessary to produce these outcomes, and on finding and implementing ways and means of making the required changes. In simpler terms, the change problem can be treated as smaller problems, having to do with the how, what, and why of change.

6.5.2 Change as a "How" Problem

In the change management process, the change problem is often expressed, at least initially, in the form of a "how" question. How do we get people to be more open, to assume more responsibility, to be more creative? How do we introduce self-managed teams in Department W? How do we change over from System X to System Y in Division Z? How do we move from a mainframe-centred computing environment to one that accommodates and integrates PCs? How do we get this organisation to be more innovative, competitive, or productive? How do we raise more effective barriers to market entry by our competitors? How might we more tightly bind our suppliers to us? How do we reduce cycle times?

In short, the initial formulation of a change problem is means-centred, with the goal state more or less implied. There is a reason why the initial statement of a problem is so often means-centred and we will touch on it later.

6.5.3 Change as a "What" Problem

As pointed out, to frame the change effort in the form of "how" question is to focus the effort on means. Diagnosis is assumed or not performed at all. Consequently, the ends sought are not discussed. This might or might not be problematic. To focus on ends requires the posing of "what" questions. What are we trying to accomplish? What changes are necessary? What indicators will signal success? What standards apply? What measures of performance are we trying to affect?

6.5.4 Change as a "Why" Problem

During the process of change, ends and means are relative notions, not absolutes; that is, something is an end or a means only in relation to something else. Thus, chains and networks of ends-means relationships often have to be traced out before one finds the "true" ends of a change effort. In this regard, "why" questions prove extremely useful.

Application Exercise

Consider the following hypothetical dialogue with yourself as an illustration of tracing out ends-means relationships.

1. Why do people need to be more creative?
   I'll tell you why! Because we have to change the way we do things and we need ideas about how to do that.
2. Why do we have to change the way we do things?
   Because they cost too much and take too long.
3. Why do they cost too much?
   Because we pay higher wages than any of our competitors.
4. Why do we pay higher wages than our competitors?
   Because our productivity used to be higher, too, but now it's not.
5. Eureka! The true aim is to improve productivity!
   No it isn't; keep going.
6. Why does productivity need to be improved?
   To increase profits.
7. Why do profits need to be increased?
   To improve earnings per share.

8. Why do earnings per share need to be improved?
   To attract additional capital.
9. Why is additional capital needed?
   We need to fund research aimed at developing the next generation of competencies.
10. Why do we need a new generation of products?
    Because our competitors are rolling them out faster than we are and gobbling up market share.
    Oh, so that's why we need to reduce cycle times.
11. Hmm. Why do things take so long?
    To ask "why" questions is to get at the ultimate purposes of functions and to open the door to finding new and better ways of performing them. Why do we do what we do? Why do we do it the way we do it? Asking "why" questions also gets at the ultimate purposes of people, but that's a different matter altogether, a "political" matter, and one we will not go into in this chapter.

6.5.5 Change Process as Unfreezing, Changing, and Refreezing

The process of change has been characterised as having three basic stages: unfreezing, changing, and refreezing. This view draws heavily on Kurt Lewin's adoption of the systems concept of homeostasis or dynamic stability, as shown in Fig. 6.4.

Fig. 6.4 Lewin's model for process of change

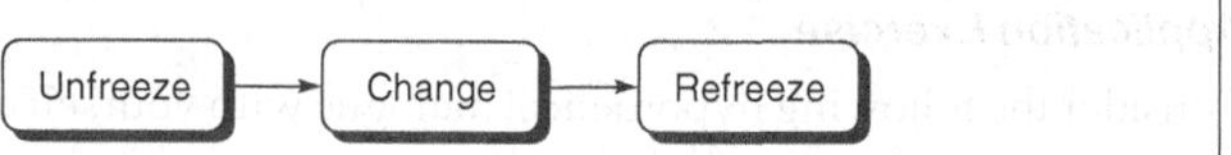

What is useful about this framework is that it gives rise to thinking about a staged approach to changing things. Looking before you leap is usually sound practice.

What is not useful about this framework is that it does not allow for change efforts that begin with the organisation in extremes (that is, already "unfrozen"), nor does it allow for organisations faced with the prospect of having to "hang loose" for extended periods of time (that is staying "unfrozen").

In other words, the beginning and ending point of the unfreeze-change-refreeze model is stability—which, for some people and some organisations, is a luxury. For others, internal stability spells disaster.

So we can say that the change process is a continuous process of problem identification and solving it to to get a sustainable development. Even the fastest of hares, if standing still, can be overtaken by a tortoise on the move.

6.6 CHANGE MANAGEMENT: SKILL REQUIREMENTS

Managing the kinds of changes encountered by and instituted within organisations requires an unusually broad and finely honed set of skills, chief among which are the following (Fig. 6.5).

6.6.1 Political Skills

Organisations are first and foremost social systems. Without people there can be no organisation. Lose sight of this fact and any would-be change agent will likely lose his head. Organisations are hotly and intensely political. And, as one wag pointed out, the lower the stakes, the more intense the politics. Change agents dare not join in this game but they had better understand it. This is one area where you must make your own judgements and keep your own counsel; no one can do it for you.

6.6.2 Analytical Skills

Make no mistake about it, those who would be change agents had better be very good at something, and that something better be analysis. Guessing will not do. Insight is nice, even useful, and sometimes shines with brilliance, but it is extremely difficult to sell and almost impossible to defend. A lucid, rational, well-argued analysis can be ignored and even suppressed, but not successfully contested and, in most cases, will carry the day. If not, then the political issues have not been adequately addressed.

Two particular sets of skills are very important here: workflow operations, or systems analysis, and financial analysis. Change agents must learn to take

Fig. 6.5 Skills required in change management

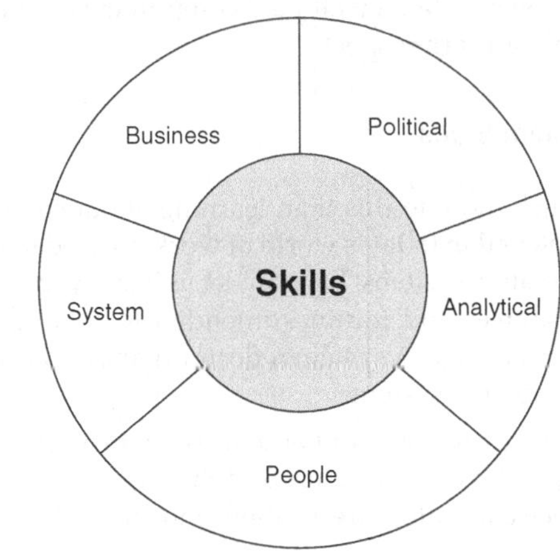

apart and reassemble operations and systems in novel ways, and then determine the financial and political impact of what they have done. Conversely, they must be able to start with some financial measure, indicator, or goal, and make their way quickly to those operations and systems that, if reconfigured a certain way, would have the desired financial impact. Those who master these two techniques have learned a trade that will be in demand for the foreseeable future. (This trade, by the way, has a name. It is called "Solution Engineering".)

6.6.3 People Skills

As stated earlier, people are the sine qua non of any organisation. Moreover, they come in all manner of sizes, shapes, colours, intelligence and ability levels, gender, sexual preferences, national origins, first and second languages, religious beliefs, attitudes towards life and work, personalities and priorities—and these are just a few of the dimensions along which people vary. We have to deal with them all.

The skills most needed in this area are those that typically fall under the heading of communication or interpersonal skills. To be effective, we must be able to listen and listen actively, to restate, to reflect, to clarify without interrogating, to draw out the speaker, to lead or channel a discussion, to plant ideas, and to develop them. All these and more are needed. Not all of us will have to learn Russian, French, or Spanish, but most of us will have to learn to speak Systems, Marketing, Manufacturing, Finance, Personnel, Legal, and a host of other organisational dialects. More important, we have to learn to see things through the eyes of these other inhabitants of the organisational world. A situation viewed from a marketing frame of reference is an entirely different situation when seen through the eyes of a systems person. Part of the job of a change agent is to reconcile and resolve the conflict between and among disparate (and sometimes desperate) points of view. Charm is great if you have it. Courtesy is even better. A well-paid compliment can buy gratitude. A sincere "thank you" can earn respect.

6.6.4 System Skills

There is much more to this than learning about computers, although most people employed in today's world of work do need to learn about computer-based information systems. For now, let us just say that a system is an arrangement of resources and routines intended to produce specified results. To organise is to arrange. A system reflects organisation and, by the same token, an organisation is a system.

A word processing operator and the word processing equipment operated form a system. So do computers and the larger, information processing systems in which computers are so often embedded. These are generally known as "hard" systems. There are "soft" systems as well: compensation systems, appraisal systems, promotion systems, and reward and incentive systems.

There are two sets of systems skills to be mastered. The first is the set most people associate with computers and it is exemplified by "systems analysis". This set of skills, by the way, actually predates the computer and is known elsewhere as "systems engineering." For the most part, the kind of system with which this skill set concerns itself is a "closed" system which, for now, we can say is simply a mechanistic or contrived system with no purpose of its own and incapable of altering its own structure. In other words, it cannot learn and it cannot change of its own volition.

The second set of system skills is the set associated with a body of knowledge generally referred to as General Systems Theory (GST). This set deals with people, organisations, industries, economies, and even nations as socio-technical systems—as "open," purposive systems, carrying out transactions with other systems, and bent on survival, continuance, prosperity, dominance, plus a host of other goals and objectives.

6.6.5 Business Skills

Simply put, you had better understand how a business works. In particular, you had better understand how the business in which and on which you are working works. This entails an understanding of money—where it comes from, where it goes, how to get it, and how to keep it. It also calls into play knowledge of markets and marketing, products and product development, customers, sales, selling, buying, hiring, firing, EEO, AAP, and just about anything else you might think of.

6.7 CHANGE MANAGEMENT: FOUR BASIC STRATEGIES

There are some basic strategies which are quite frequently used by business organisations for the effective introduction of change in the organisation, as propounded by Bennis, Benne, and Chin. They are as follows.

Fig. 6.6 Basic strategies for management of change

Rational-Empirical	Normative-Reductive
STRATEGIES	
Power-Coercive	Environmental-Adaptive

Strategy	Description
(1) **Rational-Empirical**	People are rational and will follow their self-interest—once it is revealed to them. Change is based on the communication of information and the offering of incentives.
(2) **Normative-Reductive**	People are social beings and will adhere to cultural norms and values. Change is based on redefining and reinterpreting existing norms and values, and developing commitments to new ones.
(3) **Power-Coercive**	People are basically compliant and will generally do what they are told or can be made to do. Change is based on the exercise of authority and the imposition of sanctions.
(4) **Environmental-Adaptive**	People oppose loss and disruption but they adapt readily to new circumstances. Change is based on building a new organisation and gradually transferring people from the old one to the new one.

Note: An excellent example of the fourth strategy in action, albeit on an accelerated basis, is provided by the way in which Rupert Murdoch handled the printers of Fleet Street. He quietly set about building an entirely new operation in Wapping, some distance away. When it was ready to be occupied and made operational, he informed the employees in the old operation that he had some bad news and some good news. The bad news was that the existing operation was being shut down. Everyone was being fired. The good news was that the new operation had jobs for all of them—but on very different terms. That there are also elements of the rational-empirical and power- coercive strategies at play here serves to make the point that successful change efforts inevitably involve some mix of these basic change strategies, a point that is elaborated below.

6.8 FACTORS IN SELECTING CHANGE STRATEGY

Generally speaking, there is no single change strategy. You can adopt a general or what is called a "grand strategy" but, for any given initiative, some mix of strategies serves you best.

Which of the preceding strategies to use in your mix of strategies is a decision affected by a number of factors. Some of the more important ones are mentioned here (Fig. 6.7).

a. ***Degree of resistance*** Strong resistance argues for a coupling of power-coercive and environmental-adaptive strategies. Weak resistance or concurrence argues for a combination of rational-empirical and normative-reductive strategies.

b. ***Target population*** Large populations argue for a mix of all four strategies, something for everyone so to speak.

c. ***Stakes*** High stakes argue for a mix of all four strategies. When the stakes are high, nothing can be left to chance.

d. ***Time frame*** Short time frames argue for a power-coercive strategy. Longer time frames argue for a mix of rational-empirical, normative-reductive, and environmental-adaptive strategies.

e. ***Expertise*** Having available adequate expertise at making change argues for some mix of the strategies outlined above. Not having adequate expertise argues for reliance on the power-coercive strategy.

f. ***Dependency*** This is a classic double-edged sword. If the organisation is dependent on its people, management's ability to command or demand is limited. Conversely, if people are dependent upon the organisation, their ability to oppose or resist is limited. (Mutual dependency almost always signals a requirement for some level of negotiation.)

Fig. 6.7 Factors in selecting change strategy

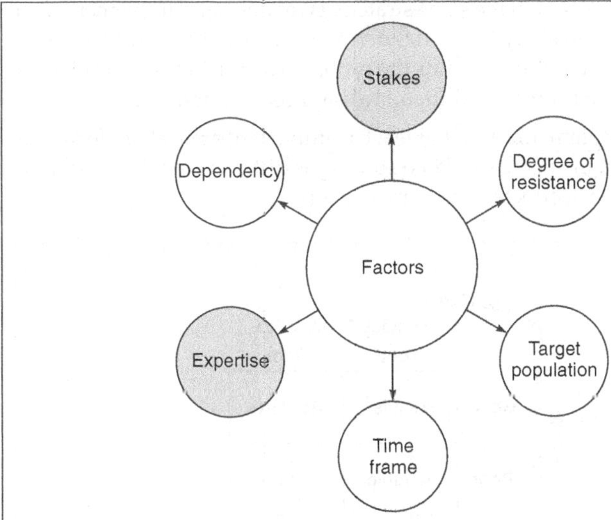

6.9 CHANGE STRATEGY FORMULATION AND IMPLEMENTATION

In order for an organisation to achieve its objectives, it must not only formulate but also implement its strategies effectively. If either of these tasks is poorly done, the result is likely to be failure of the overall strategy. The proper combination of strategy formulation and implementation can be understood in the following terms (Fig. 6.8).

a. Success This is the most likely outcome when an organisation has a good strategy and implements it well. In this case, all that can be done to ensure success has been done.

b. Roulette This involves situations wherein a poorly formulated strategy is implemented well. Two basic outcomes may ensue. The good execution may overcome the poor strategy or at least give management an early warning of impending failure. Thus, it is impossible to predict exactly what will happen to strategies in the roulette cell, and that is where it gets its name.

c. Trouble The trouble cell is characterised by situations wherein a well-formulated strategy is poorly implemented. Because managers are more accustomed to focusing on strategy formulation, the real problem with the strategy—faulty implementation—is often not diagnosed. When things go wrong, managers are likely to reformulate the strategy rather than question whether the implementation was effective. The new (and often less appropriate) strategy is then reimplemented and continues to fail.

d. Failure This is most likely to occur when a poorly formulated strategy is poorly implemented. In these situations, management has great difficulty getting back on the right track. If the same strategy is retained and implemented in a different way, it is still likely to fail. If the strategy is reformulated and implemented the same way, failure remains the probable result. Strategic problems in this cell of the matrix are very difficult to diagnose and remedy.

First, strategy implementation is at least as important as strategy formulation. Second, the quality of a formulated strategy is difficult if not impossible to assess in the absence of effective implementation.

Fig. 6.8 Performance matrix (relation between strategy formulation and implementation)

6.10 EVALUATION IN THE STRATEGIC CHANGE PROCESS

In today's world, organisations exist in a turbulent environment. Technical, economic, social, political, and cultural changes cloud the horizon with uncertainties. Only the fittest can survive. To remain the fittest, an organisation has to be a learning organisation. An organisation has to learn constantly about the ways it can adapt to demands from outside as well as from inside; about the ways it manages itself; about the programmes, procedures, processes systems, structures; about the difficulties it is trying to overcome; whether it is moving in the right direction; and what faults and blocks it needs to overcome.

It is better to use the term monitoring evaluation for the purpose. One of the main criteria of monitoring evaluation is the simultaneity of the change process and monitoring process.

6.10.1 Components of Evaluation

The basic components of evaluation are given below and depicted in Fig. 6.9.

a. ***Objectives*** deal with the 'why', that is, the ultimate purpose for which the evaluation is being undertaken. It is synonymous with mission, goals, or aims. It also keeps in view the needs of the stakeholders in general or of the specific need of a particular stakeholder.

   The objectives of an evaluation at the formative state, particularly when it is based on pilot studies, or at the initial stage of the main change programme, are to gain knowledge and insight about the efficacy of the main programme and about the designing of the main change programme. Objectives of intermediate evaluations at regular intervals would be to establish mile posts as benchmarks for time series analysis. So, the objectives of evaluation at the initial stage of a change programme, at the intermediate points, at the final stage, or at the completion of the change programme may be different.

b. ***Worth or value*** refers to the "what" of the focal variable(s). The focal variable(s) can be an individual, object, situation, a project, or a programme. Worth is the essence of existence of the variable. This is the here and now essence, that is, it does not refer to other time, place, and context, not what it was or it could be. Worth includes present quality, inherent potential and latent capability, and power of the variable for movement from the present state to the desired state.

c. ***Measurement*** refers to the "how much" of the worth. The technique of measurement of social variables has been very well developed in psychology and sociology, more particularly in psychometrics. It is a quantitative transformation of some dimensions of the variable, usually referred to as properties, using a scale that may be actual or notional.

Fig. 6.9 Evaluation in strategic management of change

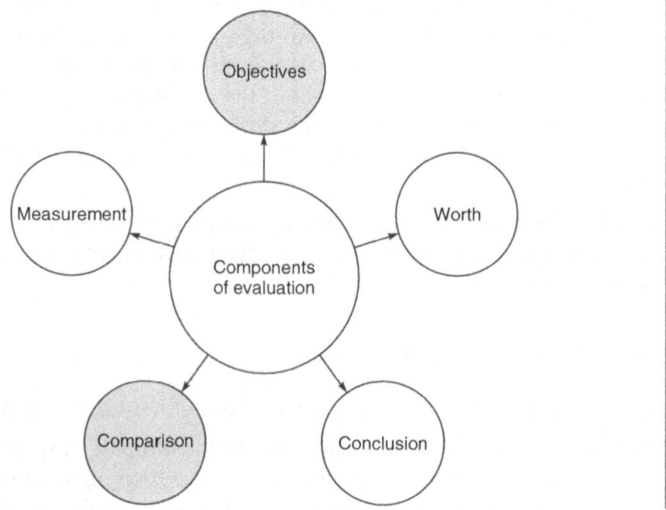

Estimate of work can also be made by other methods which are qualitative and non-metric. Observational methods, case methods, interviewing, simulation techniques, projective techniques, and so on can also provide valid data.

d. ***Comparison*** refers to positioning the data in relation to a chosen reference point. The data obtained from the measurement of the worth of the focal variable can be positioned with data evolved from the measurement of another significant variable chosen for reference. The post-treatment data can be related to the pre-treatment data. Qualitative description of what has happened can be matched with how it was when the programme was not introduced or at the initial stage.

e. ***Conclusion*** is arriving at a judgement after comparison is made. The conclusion can be made on the basis of objective logic or subjective preferences depending on what is warranted in a given situation depending on the time, place, and person. After taking a circumspective view of a large number of issues involved, it involves arriving at a final verdict as to the adequacy of the present attainment of worth for the final achievement of the desired objective of the change programme.

Example

The starting point in evaluation is to define what is to be evaluated. For example, as a part of planned organisational change, a training programme is to be launched with the participants drawn systematically from some or all levels of employees. In evaluation of the training programme, the focal variable can be one of the following.

- Individual participant
- Training sessions
- Trainers
- Design of the course
- Utilisation of the training centre
- Coverage of the participants
- Desired learning emerging out of the programme
- The Whole training programme including the effects it has generated in the organisation and the benefits the programme has brought to the organisation.

On the policy level the evaluation should be able to indicate whether the training programme is desirable or not. Even if it is assumed that the training programme should continue on the basis of the logical theoretical standpoints, or on consideration of many other factors like a belief that "training is always useful or it is a done thing in other organisations" and so on. Evaluation should be able to indicate what went right and what went wrong such that the same training programme or similar other training programmes can be improved.

6.11 PROCESS OF TRANSFORMATIONAL CHANGE

The process of change assumes qualitatively different dimensions in large and complex organisations. There are demands by external group and varying pressures from internal groups. In complex organisations, with rapid change in the environment, the process of change is one of transition from the present to the future. In such a case, vision becomes an important process of collectively creating models of the future, and helps most people to move towards these models. Changes are complex, involving the structure, systems, processes, and new norms and behaviour. Continuous monitoring is needed. Change has to continuously balance innovation with stability.

When an organisation undertakes to respond to a new challenge, to complex and changing environments, it needs to re-examine and redefine its mission, create a vision for the members of the organisation, and develop broad strategies for mobilising energies of most members of the organisation to move into the future. Such a change will be called transformational change. Beckhard (1989) suggests four types of changes: a transformational change that drives the organisation, a fundamental change in the relationship between and among organisational parts, a major change in the ways of doing work, and a basic change in means, values, or reward systems.

Beckhard suggests 10 prerequisites for success of (Table 6.1) and 8 steps in the process of transformational change (Table 6.2). The role of the top executives is critical in transformational change.

Table 6.1 Prerequisites for Success of Transformational Change

1. Communication of top leaders
2. Written description of the changed organisation
3. Conditions that preclude maintenance of the status quo
4. Likelihood of a critical mass of support
5. A medium- to long-term perspective
6. Awareness of resistance and the need to honour it
7. Awareness of the need for education
8. The conviction that the change must be true
9. Willingness to use resources
10. Commitment to maintaining the flow of information

Table 6.2 Steps in Transformational Change

1. Designing the future state
2. Diagnosing the present state
3. Extrapolating what is required to go from the present state to the transitional state
4. Analysing the work that occurred during the transitional state
5. Defining the system that is affecting the problem
6. Analysing each of the members of the critical mass with regard to readiness and capacity
7. Identifying the power relationships and resources necessary to ensure the perpetuation of change
8. Setting up an organisation (or structure or system) to manage the transformation

6.12 GUIDELINES TO MANAGEMENT OF EFFECTIVE CHANGE

How is management going to handle the task of change management? The honest answer is that you manage it pretty much the same way you would manage anything else of a turbulent, messy, chaotic nature, that is, you do not really manage it, you grapple with it. It is more a matter of leadership ability than management skill.

- The first thing to do is jump in. You can not do anything about it from the outside.
- A clear sense of mission or purpose is essential. The simpler the mission statement the better. "Kick ass in the marketplace" is a whole lot more

meaningful than "Respond to market needs with a range of products and services that have been carefully designed and developed to compare so favourably in our customers' eyes with the products and services offered by our competitors that the majority of buying decisions will be made in our favour."

- Build a team. "Lone wolves" have their uses, but managing change is not one of them. On the other hand, the right kind of lone wolf makes an excellent temporary team leader.
- Maintain a flat organisational team structure and rely on minimal and informal reporting requirements.
- Pick people with relevant skills and high energy levels. You will need both.
- Toss out the rule book. Change, by definition, calls for a configured response, not adherence to prefigured routines.
- Shift to an action-feedback model. Plan and act in short intervals. Do your analysis on the fly. No lengthy up-front studies, please. Remember the hare and the tortoise.
- Set flexible priorities. You must have the ability to drop what you are doing and attend to something more important.
- Treat everything as a temporary measure. Don't "lock in" until the last minute, and then insist on the right to change your mind.
- Ask for volunteers. You will be surprised at who shows up. You will be pleasantly surprised by what they can do.
- Find a good "straw boss" or team leader and stay out of his way.
- Give the team members whatever they ask for—except authority. They will generally ask only for what they really need by way of resources. If they start asking for authority, that is a signal they are headed towards some kind of power-based confrontation and that spells trouble. Nip it in the bud!
- Concentrate dispersed knowledge. Start and maintain an issues logbook. Let anyone go anywhere and talk to anyone about anything. Keep the communications barriers low, widely spaced, and easily hurdled. Initially, if things look chaotic, relax — they are.
- Remember, the task of change management is to bring order to a messy situation, not pretend that it is already well-organised and disciplined.

6.12.1 Twelve Principles for Managing Change

a. Thought processes and relationship dynamics are fundamental if change is to be successful.
b. Change only happens when each person makes a decision to implement the change.
c. People fear change, it "happens" to them.

d. Given the freedom to do so, people will build quality into their work as a matter of personal pride.
e. Traditional organisational systems treat people like children and expect them to act like adults.
f. "Truth" is more important during periods of change and uncertainty than "good news".
g. Those who demonstrate consistent behaviour and clearly defined values earn trust.
h. People who work are capable of doing much more than they are doing.
i. The intrinsic rewards of a project are often more important than the material rewards and recognition.
j. A clearly defined vision of the end result enables all the people to define the most efficient path for accomplishing the results.
k. The more input people have into defining the changes that will affect their work, the more they will take ownership for the results.
l. Commitment and participation of the people is the key to the success of change management.

SUMMARY

- This chapter elaborates on the importance of systematic approaches for sustainable change in the organisation.
- The three basic definitions of change management are the task of managing change, the area of professional practice, and the body of knowledge.
- In the strategic management of change, five basic functions are identified as
  a. Environmental analysis
  b. Establishing organisational direction
  c. Formulating organisational strategy
  d. Implementing organisational strategy
  e. Strategic control.
- In the sequential process of change, eight stages are identified: 1-Initiation, 2-Motivation, 3-Diagnosis, 4-Information collection, 5-Deliberation, 6-Action proposal, 7-Implementation, 8-Stabilisation.
- The change process is identified as problem-finding and problem-solving approaches.
- For effective change management, political, analytical, people, system and business skills are required.
- The four basic strategies for effective change management are a. Rational-Empirical, b. Normative-Reductive, c. Power-Coercive, d. Environmental-Adaptive.
- In the real relation between formulation and implementation of strategy, with the help of the performance matrix, success, roulette, trouble, and failure stages are identified.

- In the evaluation change management, the basic components of evaluation are objective, worth, measurement, comparison, and conclusion.
- Finally, the process of transformational change and guidelines to the management for effective change are mentioned.

Case Study: A Multi-department Academic Division of a University

History

A multi-department academic division of a large and prestigious research university, in an effort to streamline operations and create greater management accountability, had grouped a number of smaller departments into administrative units served by shared staff. Structural and authority issues, resistance to the change from some quarters, and weaknesses in management and supervision skills were preventing the transition from being successful.

Task

Consult with and advise the dean on change management approaches, identify implementation problems and recommend solutions, coach department chairs and administrative managers in management and supervisory methods, facilitate communications among the various stakeholders.

Intervention

Consultants met with the dean on long-term goals and strategies, worked with two units on developing better internal communication, management, and working protocols, helped facilitate communications between the units and the dean; and prepared a comprehensive report offering concrete suggestions for addressing overall issues around the new structure and departmental administration in the division.

Result

The dean's vision was clarified and more effectively communicated. The operations, morale, and functionality of the administrative units were substantially improved. The complex issues around resistance to the new structure were clarified and analysed in a way that could enable eventual resolution. Best practices for departmental administration were defined and promoted within all the units.

Key Disciplines

Change Management, Organisational Development, Organisational Structure and Design, Management Development, Executive Coaching, Management Development, Communications Strategy, Communications Facilitation.

Case Study: "MAX" A Health Care Improvement Organisation

History

A health care improvement organisation was poised to move into a new phase of rapid growth after large-scale downsizing, reorientation of mission, and reorganisation for team-based management.

Task

Design and facilitate a strategic planning process to support the change in direction.

Intervention

A change agent conducted a series of interviews to determine the readiness of the executive team for consensus and action. Then the agent worked one-on-one with the CEO to define key strategic and organisational process issues, designed and facilitated a planning retreat, and, after the retreat, drafted a report on the team's decisions, with action recommendations.

Result

This exercise resulted in the organisation's commitment to major goals, financial growth targets, implementation strategies, and individual department responsibilities to execute the plan. The organisation's business expansion and infrastructure development activities moved forward with clarity and timeliness.

Key Disciplines

Strategic Planning, Organisational Development, Executive Coaching, Retreat Facilitation.

Review Questions

1. Define management of change.
2. What do you understand by strategic management change and process?
3. Define sequential process of change and differentiate between the problem-solving and problem-finding approaches of change process.
4. Write short notes on:
    (a) The four basic strategies of change management
    (b) The factors responsible for selecting a change strategy
5. What do you understand by transformational change?
6. How can management of effective change be done?

EXERCISE 1

This exercise helps team members (and individuals) to identify their personal strengths, direction, aims, and goals, either in their personal life or for work-related development, or for both combined to effectively strategise upon a situation.

First ask participants to draw a line on a sheet of paper, (a large sheet is better than a small one, and a vertical line on a sheet along its length is probably easier if you are asked, although it is not critical).

Ask them then to map on it up to five major life events and/or the work achievements (either or both, depending on the purpose and focus of the activity).

Then ask them to list the qualities, skills, and attributes they used, and what experience, skills, and values they gained as a result, alongside each event or achievement.

When the participants have completed this task, ask the individuals to pair up or form teams of or three, and discuss in turn, using the other team members as a sounding board, possible future direction and aims (career, self-development, or both) that their strengths and experiences would enable and help them achieve.

EXERCISE 2

This is a SWOT-based role-playing exercise for one or more teams. Each team may have three or four members. Teams of five and more require a team leader. This is a motivational and empowering activity that can deliver immediate organisational and business benefits. The exercise lasts upwards of 30 minutes, depending on the complexity of the SWOT subjects issued to or agreed with the teams.

Ensure that all participants are issued with SWOT analysis instructions, and confirm their understanding of the process, which makes an ideal initial group exercise.

Identify suitable subjects for SWOT analysis before the session, or have the teams or team members do so at the start of the exercise. Let the teams choose a subject each, and then work as a team to produce the SWOT analysis, which should then be presented back to the group for discussion and review. It is important that the teams want the particular subjects.

Prior to the exercise the facilitator must clarify what will happen after the exercise to the teams' SWOT analysis findings, so that team members have an appropriate expectation for where their efforts and recommendations will lead.

This SWOT exercise is very flexible. Use it to suit the situation, the group, and what the organisation needs. Examples of SWOT subject areas (have some specific propositions, opportunities, or options handy in case you need them):

- Organisational or departmental change options
- Business development ideas
- Team restructuring

- Problem-solving options
- Customer service improvement ideas
- Production/distribution/technical support efficiencies or improvement ideas

EXERCISE 3

There is no better activity for diagnosis than a well-planned "treasure hunt." This one is an outdoor, daylong, planned exercise.

Treasure hunts can be based on solving clues, finding things, or a mixture. Teams have a set amount of time to collect a list of items from the hotel/office complex/local vicinity, for example, a restaurant menu with a fish dish, a box of matches with a phone number containing a seven, an acorn, a brochure with a yacht, a sports programme with a picture of green grass, and so on. This is fantastic fun and a supreme leveller. Ensure that the participants are warned not to do anything illegal or anti-social.

If you are planning a big event for more than twenty people, it is essential that the facilitator goes to the location in advance to sort out the clues and the route and to ensure it all works. It is easy when you are there. It is possible to think up some clues remotely, but the best clues will be specific local ones. Something of this scale must be planned and tested at the location.

Do some basic preparation remotely before you go there (start point, finish venue, rough area, and route) and then spend a day to find/create the specifics, design the whole thing, and be sure that it will all work in practice. Logistics (getting people from A to B) and timings (how long will it take the first and last to complete) are crucial.

Timings are always difficult to predict. Be aware that tourist venues are very busy during peak seasons, which will affect how quickly people can complete the task and the ease with which people can all meet up along the way and at the finish.

If it is an day long event, how you design the event will also depend on where everyone is staying and what you want to do before and after the treasure hunt. Ideally you should not have to worry about bussing people to and from the hunt. People should be staying where the hunt is and all together. If the activity is planned for the evening, avoid any necessity for driving. On foot is much more fun people can walk for miles without complaining provided the distance between stops for clues are not too far apart. The exercise helps too. You can may be have them catch a bus at most, but no driving at all.

The local tourist information office and library are always a useful reference points for ideas about a basic route, best areas, contact numbers, and so on.

It is necessary to plan an organised gathering for the end of the treasure hunt where you can give away prizes and relax as a group, particularly if the treasure hunt is in the evening. The finish venue needs to be reliable and under your control—you do not want everyone to be finally meeting up amongst hundreds of strangers.

For a large group of people it is best to have a few marshals along the route to help the lost and tardy.

Teams of four, five, or six at most, work best. The bigger the team, the quicker they solve the clues, although teams of seven would be too big and result in one or two being left out.

Think about your team-building priorities. If it is to improve inter-departmental team working, then create inter-departmental teams; if you want to build stronger relationships within departments, create departmental teams. If there are gender, race, or hierarchy barriers to break down, mix the teams accordingly.

Try to mix the clues so that they require different skills and knowledge, which will enable everyone in each team to shine. Some clues can be very cryptic; some can require observation; some can be historical, technical, or mathematical; some can require good persuasive or investigative skills, and always preferably with a local location reference/ingredient.

Whatever you do, remember, planning is vital.

Chapter 7

Organisational Diagnosis

Chapter Outline

- Introduction
- Concept of Organisational Diagnosis
- Methodological Planning
- Collection of Data
- Selection of Appropriate Method for Data Collection
- Summary
- Case Studies
- Review Questions
- Exercise

> "You never really understand a person until you consider things from his point of view—until you climb into his skin and walk around in it."
>
> —Anonymous

7.1 INTRODUCTION

As a human being passes through different stages in his life from infancy to old age there is no discontinuity in the passage from stage to stage yet each state has its own unique characteristics. In the same way, change is a continuous process characterised by certain stages. These stages are;

Initiation
Motivation
Diagnosis
Information collection
Deliberation
Proposal
Implementation
Stabilisation

They are direction-oriented rather than goal-driven, continuous, and specifically identified by stages.

In this chapter, we will examine the diagnosis stage with the information collection stage, as both stages supplement each other during the process of change. Diagnosis and intervention stage are the most crucial stages for the diagnostician. Diagnosis and intervention are two distinctly different phenomena. Diagnosis is concerned with knowing where the change is required and why, whereas intervention deals with the stages of implementation. Stabilisation means the practical application in the organisation. To maintain this distinction, a consultant is a diagnostician when he is occupied with diagnosis and intervention when he is occupied with interventions.

7.1.1 Meaning of Diagnosis

"To know" is the central concept in diagnosis. Most of the calculated management decisions are based on some sort of analysis of the situation or on diagnosis. In every organisation, the individual, irrespective of his level, is involved in an executive cycle. This executive cycle incorporates diagnosis, decision, action, and evaluation, as can be seen from Fig. 7.1.

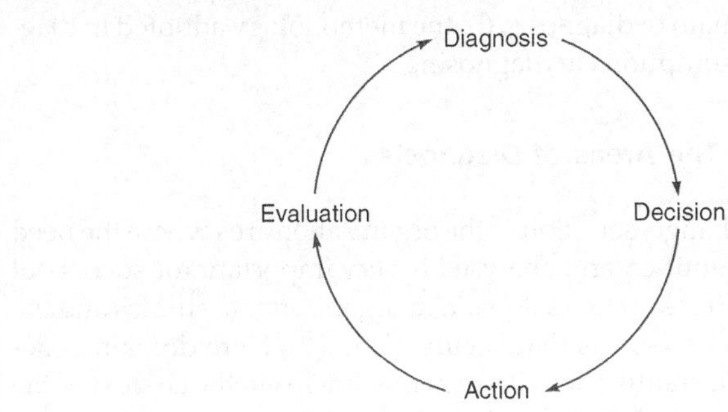

Fig. 7.1 Executive cycle

This cycle makes it very clear that as long as the executive's decisions and actions are not impulsive, his ability to diagnose directly affects his performance. Diagnosis means a cognitive analysis of the need to change, where the change is required, why it is required, and in which manner it is required.

7.2 CONCEPT OF ORGANISATIONAL DIAGNOSIS

A systematic process of diagnosis has been widely used in natural applied science, in applied sciences like medicine, engineering, agriculture, and in other fields. In these fields, diagnosis quite often ends when a name can be put to a distinguishable pattern of the mosaic of symptoms. For example, a criminologist's diagnosis is complete when he correlates all the facts of a case and concludes it to be a murder and not a suicide. In short, the diagnosis involves the following.

a. Defining the problem under study by picking up the relevant "symptoms"
b. Organising them into a pattern
c. Distinguishing them from other patterns

Organisational diagnosis essentially follows the same process but since organisational pathology has not been studied in any great detail, it is impossible at present to integrate symptoms into such precise and definite syndromes. Moreover, basic science has contributed a great deal to understand the cause-effect relationship in other fields of science and technology. Such contributions are limited in organisational science. That is why many heuristic approaches necessarily came into play. Because of these limitations, diagnosis should be based on the point of describing the present ailment and should be added with prognosis with an estimation of the likely consequences over a period of time. In addition to diagnosis and prognosis, recommendation for an active intervention is required. The approaches to organisational diagnosis vary not only with the nature of relationship between the diagnostician and the organisation, but in a very substantive way depend on: (a) the preference area or domain of diagnosis, (b) the methodology adopted in diagnosing, and (c) the assumptions in diagnosing.

7.2.1 Diagnocube: The Areas of Diagnosis

In the due process of change, selection of the organisation area where the need of change has to be identified and analysed is very important for successful change. This area is better known as domain in organisational studies and the systematic analysis is known, as diagnocube (Fig. 7.2). Here domain is defined as "the area of substantive activities or constituents in the context of the organisation." An organisation, defined as a synergistic aggregate of system and sub-system, offers different domains to work upon. The proper, regular, and supplemented execution of these domains ultimately leads to the organisation programme.

The domain of organisational diagnosis or diagnocube, can be conceived as surrounded by four dimensions as depicted by Fig. 7.2.

a. System

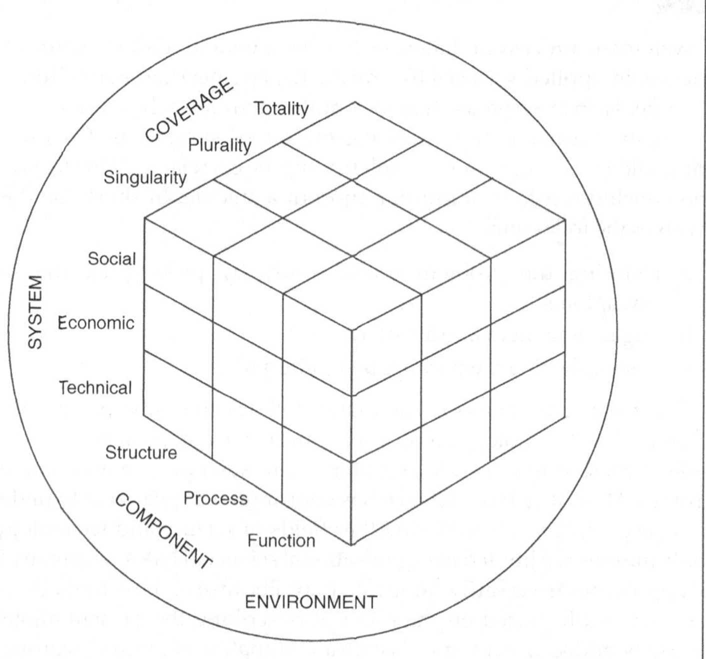

Fig. 7.2 Domains of organisational diagnosis (diagnocube)

b. Components of system
c. The area covered by the system, or systems coverage
d. The surrounding external environment

a. System Just as a job is a collection or grouping of similar tasks, so is the system. An organisation is a systematic integration of various internal systems. Every system has various interrelated, interdependent sub-systems within itself. In all, an organisation can be considered a combination of social-economic-technical (SET) systems (Fig. 7.2a).

Fig. 7.2a Types of systems in diagnocube

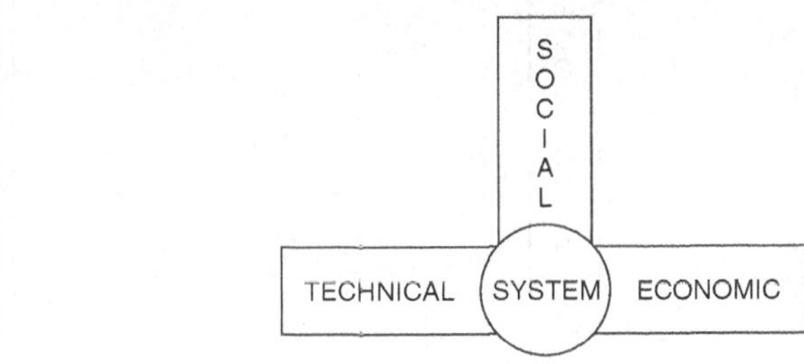

The *social system* is the people-oriented system. It consists of the employees-employers psychological framework and their social, cultural, and political values. These sub-systems arise out of people at work as individuals, groups, and multiple groups in the organisation framework.

The *economic system* including procurement, allocation, and utilisation of all resources, as a sub-system of economic system.

The financial aspect of all these activities are considered. For instance, how much financial viability and utility is involved in the due procurement of organisational resources, that is, man, money, material, machine in their proper allocation and utilisation. This system incorporates the resources and financial values of other systems as well.

The *technical system* includes the technology required to perform the work. Technology is the most feasible mode of execution and processing. It is the knowhow to get the task performed from man to machine. A technological system helps in the most feasible utilisation of the organisational resources.

b. Components of the system There are three components in each system where the diagnosis is undertaken (Fig. 7.2b). They are:

i. Structure
ii. Process
iii. Function.

Here structure means all the elements in the organisation and their comparatively enduring and lasting relationship and co-ordination within the formal network of organisation.

Fig. 7.2b Components in diagnocube

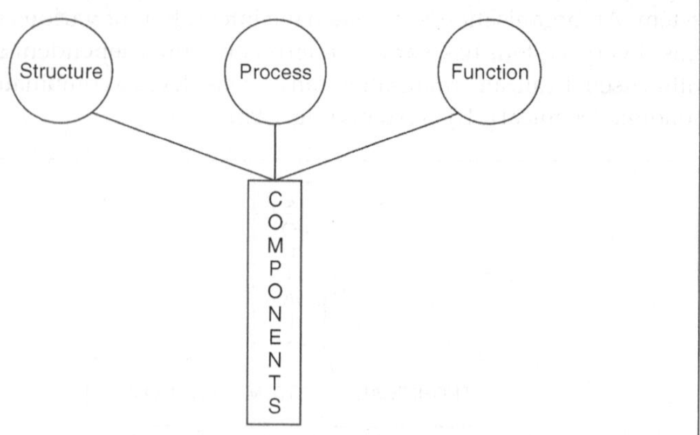

Process refers to the manner in which the tasks are performed and the events are conducted in a sequential and systematic manner.

Finally, function includes the different variables related to organisational performance or productivity. They are strategic variables, performance variables results, achievements, and end products of an organisation in a specific period and time span.

c. System coverage The coverage of domain refers to those areas of the organisation which are open for diagnostic investigation. This may be people, space, time, events, or phenomena occurring within the organisation. Coverage can be classified into three categories (see Fig. 7.2c).

i. Singularity
ii. Plurality
iii. Totality

For example, a doctor may be called upon to diagnose a single ailment (singularity), a number of episodes and ailments (plurality), and to examine the total health of the patient (totality).

Fig. 7.2c Areas of coverage in diagnocube

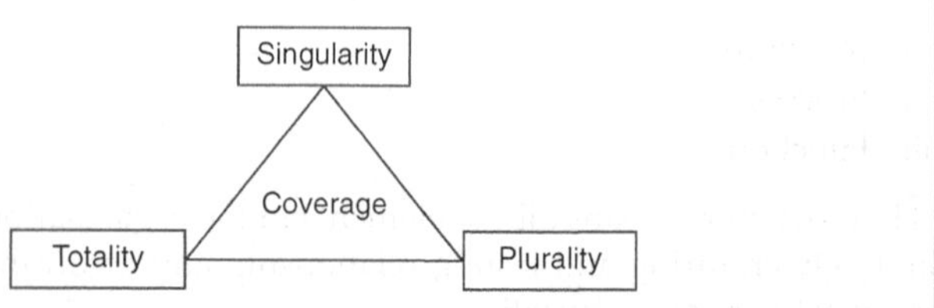

In the same way when a diagnostician is called upon to investigate a single issue, say, a strike, a relationship in a given department, marketing of a particular product, one decision of a particular investment, and so on, it is called singularity.

Plurality of coverage indicates the opening up of the organisation to more than one specific episode for investigation.

Totality of coverage denotes a diagnosis focussed on the entire organisation.

d. The surrounding external environment The environment encircles these domains. The environmental factors can be studied independently or in relation to any other factor of the organisational system, components, and coverage.

7.2.2 Theory in Action: Framework of Organisational Diagnosis

Beyond the diagnostic domain that the diagnostician selects to work upon, and the method that he chooses to use, are some of his basic assumptions regarding, man, organisation, man-in-the-organisation, quality of work life, and the interrelationships that are crucial in organisational life. These assumptions, in their turn, also influence the diagnostician to decide on the domain to work upon and to direct the process of diagnosis in a substantive manner.

In practice, diagnosticians have been observed to take different stances. The stance often taken in diagnosis is to examine the present state of affairs of the organisation in relation to its future goals; then the strategic variables take the topmost priority. However, the controversy arises in determining the goals of the organisation.

a. Any organisation pursues multiple objectives and these objectives need not necessarily be congruent.
b. The objectives at a given phase of development are not the same as those at another phase of development of the organisation.
c. The impact of different types of environment at different points of time will have different effects on organisational objectives. Taken together, one may see that the goal-oriented parameters of diagnosis are not really static but are in a state of continuous flux or change.

7.2.3 Normative Approach

Another approach pursued by the diagnostician is essentially normative. The organisation, at the point of time of diagnosis, is as if sick and, therefore, deviant from the normal. The role of the diagnostician is to find out where the deviation exists and also to estimate the nature and magnitude of these deviations such that ameliorative, corrective action can be taken to revert it back to the normal. This is the stance of the physicians in diagnosing patients' ailments. When they find that the deterioration is irreversible, they attempt to arrest or retard further progress of the disease. Some "business healers" tend to follow the same principle.

The assumptions about organisational diagnosis have been influenced by early views of organisations as a machine or organism. The fact of the matter is that an organisation is neither a machine nor an organism. The analogies are valid only up to a certain level. The mechanistic approach to find the optimal fit of factors leading to a normative existence, or the organismic approach to find adaptation to environment are, therefore, likely to be functional only up to a point.

Yet another approach, basically influenced by the practice of psychoanalysis, relies on the diagnostician analysing how he himself is made to feel at different stages of the relationship between the consultant and the client; and how those perceptions can be used to clarify the nature of the problems confronting the client (Bain, 1976). There are quite a few practitioners of this method. In this method also, the organisation-organism analogy is quite manifest; the client is ill; the ailment lies not in malfunctioning at the conscious level, but the cause is rooted somewhere deep down at the unconscious level of the organisation. Diagnosis of that mental block and the client's deeper realisation of it are what have to be aimed at.

One uses a concept like "health." But what is health? A sense of well-being. What is well-being? Diverse answers from various philosophies are possible. One talks about the guiding concepts, like dynamic homeostasis, coping ability, balance of integration and differentiation, negative entropy, equifinality, and so on. Concepts have been borrowed from sciences like philosophy, physics, chemistry, thermodynamics, ecology, and biology. There is nothing wrong in borrowing. The progress of science has been accelerated by such acculturation. But the fact that so many concepts from different disciplines are in active use suggests that a more comprehensive and satisfying explanation is yet to emerge. In its absence, one has to work with what is currently available and work towards finding a better concept. Accordingly, approaches to diagnosis will also be diverse. But some choice can still be exercised.

The process of diagnosis has a built-in enabling effect, which increases the ability of the managers to be better diagnosticians such that they can use the process continually in the cycle of diagnosis-decision-action-evaluation. This makes the organisation self-reliant, may be better in the long run. The process of diagnosis that does not reduce everything into inputs, outputs, and statistics, or into manipulative numbers, may provide a greater depth of vision and understanding about an organisation.

7.3 METHODOLOGICAL PLANNING

The process of diagnosis depends entirely on the theoretical constructs that the diagnostician works with. These constructs help one understand an organisation, its mode of functioning, its various sub-systems, its structure and design, and so on. They help in developing models focussing on individual, intrapersonal and interpersonal processes, on group and group processes, and on the total organisation and its macro processes.

The process of diagnosis includes two basic features, divergence and convergence. Divergence starts from the focal point of a theory. From the theory constructs are evolved; they lead to operational models; operational models indicate the network of variables to be studied; variables under study indicate the data to be collected. Up to this point, the operational area becomes wider and wider.

Once the data have been collected, the process of convergence starts. The data can be rational, quantitative, qualitative, unobtrusive, non-rational, or integrative (refer to unit 6). The volume of data has to be gradually reduced; analysers condense the data and ultimately they converge on the primary focal point—organisational need. In the process, some help is also rendered to theory building.

After data collection, analysis is undertaken. There may be measuring, or describing without measuring. Tabulation becomes a necessity if multi-method data collection has been resorted to. The next stage is interpretation. Through interpretation emerges the understanding of the reality of organisational functioning—the central aspect of the diagnostic process. Between the concepts and understanding the reality of organisational functioning one visualises two-way iterative relationships.

Lawler et al. (1980) consider that (a) concepts and theories for understanding organisations, (b) measurement tools to collect valid data about organisational effectiveness, and (c) technologies for changing organisations, are tools necessary for providing the capability to improve organisations. According to them, each set of tools aids in the development of other tools, but measurement tools are extremely central to the development and use of other areas.

Action intervention is also influenced, on the other hand, by empathising, caring, and experimenting flowing out of experiencing. Action intervention guided by proper technology of change brings about organisational change. Evaluation of change and the state of effectiveness achieved follow organisational change. This evaluation has a feedback loop to the action world of organising, on the one hand, and to further building of concepts and theories on the other.

It will be apparent that there are more than one major ways of diagnosing. From the emotional way of being one has to capture the experiences in a meaningful way. The psychoanalytical approach quite often takes this route between the clinician and the client. Psychoanalytical approach, and at times anthropological methods of understanding an organisation, are based on exploring the experiences emerging from the emotional world and identifying significant syndromes and patterns. The continuous involvement of the client managers in their action world gives them a direct understanding of what is happening. This understanding is valuable.

This kind of diagnosis is a regular instrument for a manager for his regular operation. He, therefore, may not be able to articulate this understanding in precise conceptual constructs. But the important fact is that he has made a diagnosis; and this diagnosis is valid enough. The problem arises when this diagnosis is not enough. For example, when various managers differ amongst themselves in terms of their personalised reality perceptions—where each one may have valid perceptions based on his particular assumptions and point of view. Normally, the inadequacy of the above approaches compels the organisation to take a third way—the path of inquiry. In the following discussion, emphasis will be accorded mainly to this mode.

In planning, some of the following points need to be considered.

- How to conduct the diagnosis
- The procedure to be followed
- The strategy to be adopted
- The resources (time, people, place, money, and so on) available
- The client's need(s)
- The extent to which the client system agrees with the plan
- The competence of the diagnostician
- The choice of the method(s) as the ideal fit

There are different trends in methodological planning. The trends range from hunches and educated guesses to applied organisational research. At this point, it may be worthwhile to ponder at what stage an external diagnostician is called in. The research by Bhattacharya, Chattopadhyay, and Sengupta obtained some interesting data from the study mentioned earlier. Out of the 85 chief executives, 26 percent said that before calling in the diagnostician, the organisation had already identified the problem; 54 percent said they had a reasonably clear idea of the problem; only 18% had some general notion and some uncertainty associated with it. Diagnosticians are not called in when the client organisation is uneasy or uncertain about the problem.

This implies that in many of the organisations, the management has already decided the domain of diagnosis and has a set of expectations regarding the possible diagnosis. Such a situation may help as well as hinder the actual process of diagnosis. It may help because it creates greater awareness and involvement on the part of the management to collaborate with the diagnostician. It is thus easier to accept his recommendations and reservations to associate him with implementation are less.

But the situation may hinder diagnosis in more than one way.

a. It may become a self-fulfilling prophecy.
b. If the diagnostician does not have a strong sense of professional adequacy, he may be sucked into compliance when a different viewpoint could have been pursued.
c. It may limit the possible search in diagnostic operation to a narrow field.
d. In case of a difference in points of view, the very fact of a difference may create a disturbance in the power dynamics within the organisation, even though the diagnostician may not like it or want to be a party to it. This may endanger the acceptance of a diagnosis.

7.4 COLLECTION OF DATA

An organisation is a dynamic system where things happen fast. A series of events move in a process. Collection of data at a given point of time is like taking a still shot of a moving object. It fails to capture the dynamic nature of the organisational reality.

Diagnostic data often provide still pictures of the company. For example, a part of a problem can be visualised even by looking at the organisational chart. The chart may represent the positional structure at a given point of time but the dynamics that it obtains may be different six months later, perhaps even after six days. A diagnostician faces an added dilemma in this situation. (a) In an ever-changing dynamic situation, what is relevant "here and now" is not relevant "there and then", in the past, or in the future. (b) A process is a continuity; the vision of the future together with the forces of the past mould the "here and now" of the organisation. The dilemma is in the choice between discontinuity and continuity. What kind of data collection then can be satisfying?

In an organisation, employees have clear differences in their demographic and orientational background. While developing an instrument to measure organisational environment (Somnath Chattopadhyay, 1975), it was found that what is relevant to the upper level of management is not relevant to employees at a lower level. Yet how would one arrive at a composite picture of the total organisation? It was also learnt that the questionnaire suitable for industries in the private sector loses some of its sensitivity when used in the industries in the public sector. There is hardly any instrument which is universally applicable.

7.4.1 Overview of Methods

The methods generally followed for data collection can be classified according to (a) the relationship between diagnostician and client organisation, (b) the nature of the methods, and (c) the basis of, and the data (Fig. 7.3).

a. The relationship between the diagnostician and the client organisation are normally of three types.

  i. The diagnostician plays the active, dominant role where conceptualisation, data generation, analysis and interpretation, and convergence of ideas to delineate the problem revolve around him. The client's involvement is only to the extent of providing data from his side, or from the organisation—from the records, files, and books in the archives, or by providing an opportunity to the diagnostician to collect the data directly.
  ii. The diagnostician and the client are interdependent in a mutually participative manner. In this situation, both may work together through the entire process of diagnosis or they may apportion the work between themselves and share it at selected phases.
  iii. The client plays an active role and the diagnostician plays a supportive role. The diagnostician often creates a situation where the client conceptualises, generates data, analyses and interprets, and formulates the problem.

b. The nature of the methods can be of two types.

  i. The methods may be more structured, instrumented, mechanistic, following the rules of scientific methodology with rigour.
  ii. The methods may be less structured, more open, more organic.

Fig. 7.3 Overview of data collection methods

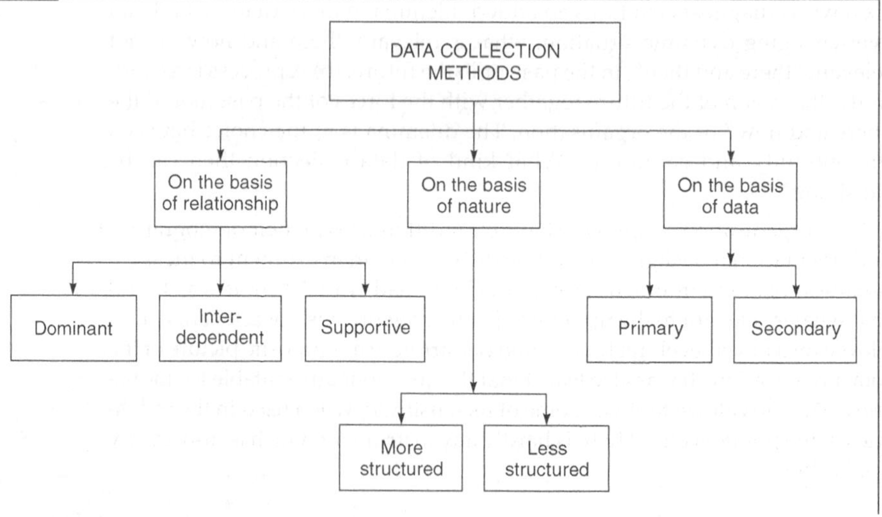

c. On the basis of the collection of data there can be two methods.

i. Primary data when data has been collected first hand by the dignostician.

ii. Secondary data when the diagnostician refers to the data reports (previously collected data) which are already existing in the organisation.

7.4.2 Instruments of Data Collection

Instruments required for data collection depend essentially on the variables identified for study. The nature and characteristics of the data indicate the type of instrument to be used. If the diagnosis starts from the final outcome variables, like performance or satisfaction, one would immediately recognise the need for different instruments. Many performance variables, like productivity, profit, and so on, can be measured by archival data. But for collection of data from archives and for unobtrusive measures, there cannot be a set pattern. The diagnostician's research background may be of some help to him in formulating his own instruments. Similarly, there is no ready-to-use tool for collecting data.

7.4.3 Methods of Data Collection

Primary data are data which are collected afresh and for the first time, and thus happen to be original and not already been collected by someone else and which have already been passed through the statistical process.

Collection of Primary Data

We collect primary data during the course of experiments for experimental research but in case of research of the descriptive type and surveys, whether sample surveys or census surveys, primary data can be obtained either through observation or through direct communication with respondents in one form or another or through personal interviews (Fig. 7.4).

Fig. 7.4 Methods for collecting primary data

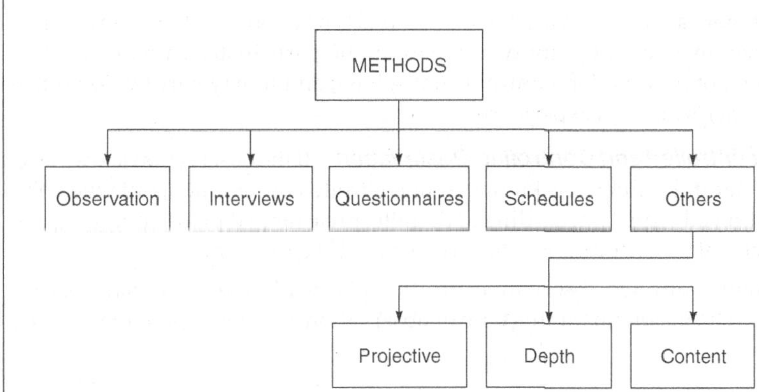

Important methods of collection of primary data are: (a) observation method, (b) interview method, (c) questionnaires, (d) schedules, and (e) other methods which include (i) projective techniques; (ii) depth interviews, and (iii) content analysis.

Observation Method

The main advantage of this method is that subjective bias is eliminated if the observation is done accurately. Secondly, the information obtained under this method relates to current happenings; it is not complicated by either past behaviour, future intentions, or attitudes. Thirdly, this method is independent of the respondents, willingness to respond and as such is relatively less demanding of active co-operation on the part of respondents which is the case in the interview or the questionnaire method.

The disadvantages of this method are, firstly, it is an expensive method. Secondly, the information provided by this method is very limited. Thirdly, sometimes unforeseen factors may interfere with the task of observation. At times, the fact that some people are rarely accessible to direct observation creates obstacles under this method to collect data effectively.

Participant and Non-participant Observation If the observer makes his observations by making himself, more or less, a member of the group he is observing so that he can experience what the members of the group experience, the observation is called participant observation. But when the observer makes his observations without any attempt to experience through participation what others feel, the observation is termed as non-participant observation. (In case of an observation where the observer's presence is unknown to the people he is observing, the observation is called a disguised observation.)

The participant type of observation has several merits. (a) The researcher is able to record the natural behaviour of the group. (b) The researcher can gather information which cannot easily be obtained if he observes in a disinterested fashion. (c) The researcher can even verify the truth of the statements made by informants in the context of a questionnaire or a schedule.

But there are also certain demerits of this type of observation, namely, the observer may lose objectivity to the extent he participates emotionally; the problem of observation-control is not solved; and it may narrow down the researcher's range of experience.

Non-controlled and Controlled Observation If the observation takes place in the natural setting, it is known as uncontrolled observation, but when observation takes place according to definite, prearranged plans, involving experimental procedure, it is called a controlled observation.

In non-controlled observation, no attempt is made to use precision instruments. The major aim of this type of observation is to get a spontaneous picture of life and persons. It has a tendency to supply naturalness and completeness of behaviour, allowing sufficient time for observing it.

In controlled observation, mechanical (or precision) instruments are used as aids to accuracy and standardisation. Such observation has a tendency to supply formalised data upon which generalisations can be built with some degree of assurance. The main pitfall of non-controlled observation is that of subjective interpretation. There is also the danger of feeling that we know more about the observed phenomena than we actually do. Generally, controlled observation takes place in various experiments carried out in a laboratory or under controlled conditions, whereas uncontrolled observation is resorted to in case of exploratory researches.

Some Basic Properties of Observational Methods Earlier it was stated that observation is planned, methodical, accurate watching. Some of the properties that make it so are indicated below.

a. What is being observed must be observable. For example, behaviours are observable; intentions are not, they are inferred. A process cannot be observed. Observation of discrete behaviour at a given point of time, repeated in sequence over a period of time, when conceptually linked up and integrated, helps to develop the idea of a process inferentially.
b. What can be observed are particular behaviours, settings, events, or things.
c. What is observed—a particular behaviour's settings, events, or things—must be relevant to the aims of the diagnosis directly, or indirectly through the variables interlinked in the conceptual construct that holds the aims of the particular diagnosis.
d. For enabling quantification, a set of behaviours is generally obtained. Composite measures can overcome the flaws of individual measures and can provide a more complete picture.
e. The origin of what is observed must be "in situ." If a person or persons are being observed, they must be in their natural setting as far as possible.
f. Observers may make subtle changes without destroying the dominant features of the natural setting. This is done to obtain greater clarity on the variable under study.
g. Observers make choices in selecting what they observe and edit the observed before, during, and after—knowingly or unknowingly. This property makes the observed particular and not general; the more explicit the choices, the greater the scope for improving the diagnosis.
h. All or extensive information about the observed phenomenon cannot be retained. Retention of information after meaningful reduction through careful selection and editing is called "recording". For example, continuous videotaped information by itself is not a "record." It contains much useless, extraneous, irrelevant information. When the relevant

portions in the film are selected, edited, extracted, and retained, they become "records."

i. Records by themselves are not data. When the records are encoded, that is, simplified through ratings, categories, or frequency counts, they yield data. So, the original bulk of material through recording and encoding generates data. Codes can be used in the course of observing the phenomenon when it occurs, or later, when a record is available.

j. An observational study may aim at only description. It can also come close to experiment when observational methods are employed for hypothesis testing or hypothesis formulation.

When to Use Observational Methods The properties indicated above may provide a good insight into why and when observational methods should be used. Some of these occasions are indicated below.

a. When a wide range of detail and immediacy are needed
b. When the observed phenomenon needs to be modular and whole
c. At the preliminary stages of an investigation to obtain information and an idea about the relevant parameters of the study
d. When any limitation of the subjects has to be offset, for example, when someone has to articulate his thoughts, say on values and norms, through subjective interpretation and reflection and which he is not capable of doing
e. When there is over-involvement of the subject in an activity rendering him unable to articulate his action
f. When the subject is not aware of the activities because they are habitual or culture determined
g. When the observed phenomenon is not an individual phenomenon (for example, many interpersonal and group activities may fall in this category)
h. When the phenomenon is fleeting and may not be noticed by the person
i. When the subject's report might be distorted for defensive purposes
j. When the subjects do not have the language to describe their actions
k. When other methods are not adequate to bring out data on variables like beliefs, values, attitudes, norms, and better data can be obtained from the "acting out" of these variables
l. When data needed are on the intimate relationship between the person and the setting, the contextual background of a behaviour, or on the environment in operation with the subject
m. Phenomena that are complex and multidimensional, whose naturalness is likely to be significantly altered by other methods
n. When individual behaviour and group setting need to be observed
o. When the variables are too dangerous to create in a laboratory, when excessive and distasteful demands need to be made of the subjects, and when laboratory inductions are unrepresentative of everyday life

p. When data from actual actions are more important than the throughts and feelings or self-reporting of intellectual responses which can be contaminated with errors from numerous sources

What is Observed What needs to be observed emerges from the aim of the diagnosis or from the construct formulating the aim. The observed phenomena can be extremely varied in keeping with the creativity, imagination, and skill of the diagnostician and the type of data that he requires; the need of the client organisation; and the resources available. Some broad indications of behaviours commonly observed are indicated in Table 7.1. These behaviours are generally classified into four groups:

a. Non-verbal behaviour
b. Spatial behaviour
c. Extra-linguistic behaviour
d. Linguistic behaviour

Table 7.1 Behaviours Analysed by Observational Method

	I. *Process dominant*
(a) Non-verbal behaviour	Focussed more Facial expressions Exchanged glances Body movements including gestures
(b) Spatial behaviour	Interpersonal distance Spatial relationship Spatial perception Architectural perception Ownership, acquisition, and defence of one's territory Conversational clustering
(c) Extra-linguistic behaviour	Vocal (pitch, loudness, timbre, and so on) Temporal (duration of speech, duration of utterances, rate of speaking rhythm, and so on) Interaction (tendencies to interrupt, dominate, facilitate, inhibit, and so on)
	II. *Content dominant*
(d) Linguistic behaviour	Interaction Process Analysis (IPA) Interaction process scores Member-leader analysis Behaviour scores system

It should be clear that what has been presented so far is the basic active ingredient of observational methods. It is like grains of wheat: whether one uses them as seeds, or for bread or cake is a matter of the mode of working with those grains.

Diagnostic Methods Employing Observational Methods Of the diagnostic methods mentioned in the previous unit, those that depend heavily on observational methods are presented here. This is not an exhaustive list but it provides an indication of applied modes. The methods are:

- Interaction process analysis
- Interpersonal behaviour analysis
- Small group interaction analysis
- Group process analysis
- Time study
- Motion study
- Work study
- Task analysis

Interaction process analysis is based on studies of peer assessment, content analysis of values statements, personality tests.

Interpersonal behaviour analysis takes into consideration various aspects of behaviour for analysis. For example, Mann (1967) developed a 16-category system of analysis divided into four areas: Impulse, Affection, Authority relation, and Ego states. Some others used categories like assertiveness, withdrawal, and support of the transactional analysis categories like parent, adult, child, and so on.

Small group interaction analysis focuses mainly on "members" communication with each other and its implications. Most often, this technique is employed in understanding the process involved in one or a series of meetings.

Group process analysis is very similar to group interaction analysis and often the distinction between the two are blurred. This method is useful when a group is evolving from a collection of strangers towards becoming a team or when an existing team is breaking up. It can be used to study some of the processes like inclusion-exclusion, exercising power, emergence of interpersonal affection, integration and disintegration, co-operation and conflict, leadership, cohesiveness, and emergence of norms, customs, and values in the group.

Time study, motion study, work study are basically borrowed from the Industrial Engineering discipline in which categorised reporting of actual engagement behaviour on job with machine, their sequencing, and flow are studied. These studies bring out the patterned behaviour of the observed as well as the efficacy of the system—their utilisation, blocks in the system and ways to simplify the system. This is most widely used on workers, or on the combination of worker and machine. It has been used to analyse utilisation of machines on a shop floor. The method has been used also with the management staff to analyse how managers spend their time and what they actually do. Often work norms, job description, job analysis, reward-punishment, and so on are determined using these methods.

Task analysis, a modification of the work study method, is used to analyse activities and tasks performed by employees in the perspective of the relevant mission, goals and objectives of the department, and the anticipated roles to be performed by them. The method brings out clearly the gaps between the professed, expected, and the actual in mission, goals, objectives, roles, activities, and tasks and enables locating the areas of change and ascertaining development needs.

Interview Method

Interviewing is a transaction between two persons in a face-to-face situation where one of them, the interviewer, asks the other person – the respondent, questions relevant to the aims of the diagnosis.

Diagnostic interview can be understood as a two-person conversation initiated by the interviewer, who is a diagnostician, with a respondent for the purpose of eliciting information about facts or responses indicating opinion and attitudes, interests, beliefs, values, or ideas related to the organisation and its functioning, commensurate with the objective of the diagnosis. The diagnostician is often an outsider but may be an insider. The respondent is most often an insider but may be an outsider too.

The interview method of collecting data involves presentation of oral-verbal stimuli and reply in terms of oral-verbal responses. This can be further illustrated with the following types of interviews (see Fig. 7.5).

Personal and Non-personal Interviews The personal interview method requires a person known as the interviewer asking questions generally in a face-to-face contact to the other person or persons. (At times the interviewee may also ask certain questions and the interviewer responds to these, but usually the interviewer initiates the interview and collects the information.) This sort of interview may be in the form of a direct personal investigation or an indirect oral investigation.

In the case of a direct personal investigation, the interviewer has to collect the information personally from the sources concerned. He has to be on the spot and has to meet people from whom data have to be collected. This method is particularly suitable for intensive investigations.

However, in certain cases it may not be possible or worthwhile to contact the persons concerned directly. Or, on account of the extensive scope of enquiry, the direct personal investigation technique may not be used. In such cases, an indirect oral examination can be conducted under which interviewer has to cross-examine other persons who are supposed to have knowledge about the problem under investigation. The information thus obtained is recorded. Most

Fig. 7.5 Types of interviews in diagnosis

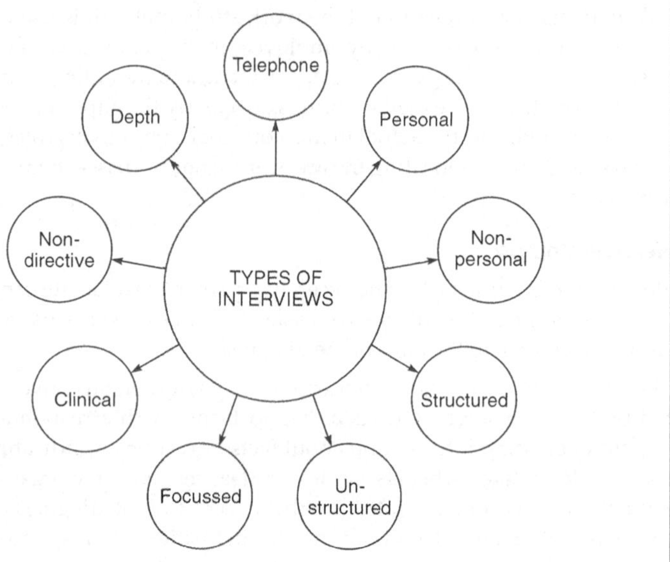

of the commissions and committees appointed by the government to carry on investigation make use of this method.

Structured and Unstructured Interviews The method of collecting information through personal interviews is usually carried out in a structured way. Hence the interviews are called structured interviews. Such interviews involve the use of a set of predetermined questions and highly standardised techniques of recording. Thus, the interviewer in a structured interview follows a rigid procedure that has been laid down, asking questions in the form and order prescribed.

Unstructured interviews, on the other hand, are characterised by a flexibility of approach to questioning. These interviews do not follow a system of predetermined questions and standardised techniques of recording information. In a non-structured interview, the interviewer is allowed much greater freedom to ask, in case of need, supplementary questions or, at times, he may omit certain questions if the situation so requires. He may even change the sequence of questions. He has relatively greater freedom while recording the responses to include some aspects and exclude others. But this sort of flexibility results in lack of comparability of one interview with another and the analysis of unstructured responses becomes much more difficult and time consuming than that of the structured responses obtained from structured interviews. Unstructured interviews also demand deep knowledge and greater skill on the part of the interviewer.

Unstructured interview happens to be the central technique of collecting information in case of exploratory or formulative research studies. But in case of descriptive studies, we quite often use the technique of structured interview because it is more economical, provides a safe basis for generalisation and requires relatively less skill on the part of the interviewer.

Focussed, Clinical, Non-directive and Depth Interviews A focussed interview is meant to focus attention on the given experience of the respondent and its effects. Here the interviewer has the freedom to decide the manner and sequence in which the questions would be asked and the freedom to explore reasons and motives. The main task of the interviewer in case of a focussed interview is to confine the respondent to a discussion of issues with which he seeks effective conversation. Such interviews are generally used in the development of hypotheses and constitute a major type of unstructured interviews.

The clinical interview is concerned with broad underlying feelings or motivations or with the course of individual's past experience. The method of eliciting information here is generally left to the interviewer's discretion.

In a non-directive interview, the interviewer's function is simply to encourage the respondent to talk about the given topic with a bare minimum of direct questioning. The interviewer often acts as a catalyst to a comprehensive expression of the respondents' feelings and beliefs and of the frame of reference within which such feelings and beliefs take on personal significance.

Depth interviews are not concerned with facts of what has happened in the past but focus on what is there in the mind of a person, even in its inner most recesses, beyond the observed and manifest. Depth interviews endeavour to bring out motivation, attitudes, beliefs, values, ideas of various kinds—even those that happen only during the period of interviewing concerning matters related to the past, present, and future. These may relate to what is there in the conscious mind of a respondent or what he has forgotten, what lies in the preconscious, or even in the unconscious.

Telephone Interview Here information is collected by contacting respondents on the telephone. It is not a very widely used method, but plays an important part in industrial surveys, particularly in developed regions.

The chief merits of such a system are:

a. It is more flexible in compared to the mailing method.
b. It is faster than other methods, that is, it is a quick way of obtaining information.
c. It is cheaper than the personal interviewing method; here the cost per response is relatively low.
d. Recall is easy; callbacks are simple and economical.

The main demerits are:

a. Little time is given to respondents for considered answers; interview period is not likely to exceed five minutes in most cases.
b. Surveys are restricted to respondents who have telephone facilities.
c. Cost considerations may restrict extensive geographical coverage.
d. It is not suitable for intensive surveys where comprehensive answers are required to various questions.
e. Possibility of the bias of the interviewer is relatively more.
f. Questions have to be short and to the point; probes are difficult to handle.

Advantages of Interview Method Despite the variations in interview techniques, the major advantages and weaknesses of personal interviews can be enumerated in a general way. The chief merits of the interview method are as follows:

a. More information and that too in greater depth can be obtained.
b. Interviewer can overcome resistance, if any, of the respondents; the interview method can be made to yield an almost perfect sample of the general population.
c. There is greater flexibility under this method as the opportunity to restructure questions is always present, specially in case of unstructured interviews.
d. Observation method can be applied to recording verbal answers to various questions.
e. Personal information can be obtained easily under this method.
f. Samples can be controlled more effectively as there arises no difficulty of the missing returns; non-response generally remains very low.
g. The interviewer can usually control which person(s) will answer the questions. This is not possible in the mailed questionnaire approach. If so desired, group discussions may also be held.
h. The interviewer may catch the informant offguard and thus may secure the most spontaneous reaction. This would not be possible if a mailed questionnaire is used.
i. The language of the interview can be adapted to the ability or educational level of the person interviewed and, as such, misinterpretations concerning questions can be avoided.
j. The interviewer can collect supplementary information about the respondent's personal characteristics and environment, which is often of great value in interpreting the results.

Disadvantages of Interview Method Among the important weaknesses of the interview method, mention may be made of the following.

a. It is a very expensive method, specially when a large and widely spread geographical sample is taken.

b. There remains the possibility of the bias of interviewer as well as that of the respondent; there also remains the headache of supervision and control of interviewers.
c. Certain types of respondents such as important officials, executives, or people in high income groups may not be easily approachable under this method and to that extent the data may prove to be inadequate.
d. This method is relatively more time consuming, specially when the sample is large and the respondents have to be called again.
e. The presence of the interviewer on the spot may over-enthuse the respondent, sometimes even to the extent of giving imaginary information just to make the interview interesting.
f. Under the interview method, the organisation required for selecting, training, and supervising the field staff is complex, with formidable problems.
g. Interviewing at times may also introduce systematic errors.
h. Effective interview presupposes proper rapport with respondents for free and frank responses. This is often a very difficult requirement.

Prerequisites and Basic Tenets of Interviewing For successful implementation of the interview method, interviewers should be carefully selected, trained, and briefed. They should be honest, sincere, hardworking, impartial, and must possess technical competence and necessary practical experience. Occasional field checks should be made to ensure that interviewers are neither cheating nor deviating from instructions given to them for performing their job efficiently. In addition, some provision should also be made in advance so that appropriate action may be taken if some of the selected respondents refuse to co-operate or are not available when an interviewer calls upon them.

In fact, interviewing is an art governed by certain scientific principles. Every effort should be made to create a friendly atmosphere of trust and confidence, so that the respondent may feel at ease while talking to the interviewer. The interviewer must ask questions properly and intelligently and must record the responses accurately and completely.

At the same time, the interviewer must answer legitimate question(s), if any, asked by the respondent and must clear any doubt the latter has. The interviewer's approach must be friendly, courteous, conversational, and unbiased. The interviewer should not show surprise or disapproval of a respondent's answer but he must keep the direction of interview in his own hands, discouraging irrelevant conversation, and must make all possible efforts to keep the respondent on track.

Interviews conducted for organisational diagnosis are a special category by themselves. Such an interview builds its technique from the techniques used in the above-mentioned classification, yet it has a distinct identity of its own.

Questionnaires

This method of data collection is quite popular, particularly in case of large-scale research. Private individuals, research workers, private and public organisations, and even by governments. In this method, a questionnaire is sent (usually by post) to the persons concerned with a request to answer the questions and return the questionnaire. A questionnaire consists of a number of questions printed or typed in a definite order on a form or set of forms. The respondents are expected to read and understand the questions and write down the reply in the space provided in the questionnaire itself. The respondents have to answer the questions on their own.

The method of collecting data by mailing questionnaires to respondents is most extensively employed in various economic and business surveys. The merits claimed on behalf of this method are as follows.

a. There is low cost even when the universe is large and is widely spread out geographically.
b. It is free from the bias of the interviewer; answers are in the respondents' own words.
c. Respondents have adequate time to give well-thought out answers.
d. Respondents who are not easily approachable, can also be reached conveniently.
e. Large samples can be made use of and thus the results can be made more dependable and reliable.

The main demerits of this system can also be listed here.

a. Low rate of return of the filled-in questionnaires; bias due to no response is often indeterminate.
b. It can be used only when respondents are educated and co-operative.
c. The control over the questionnaire may be lost once it is sent.
d. There is an inbuilt inflexibility because of the difficulty of amending the approach once questionnaires have been dispatched.
e. There is also the possibility of ambiguous replies or omission of replies to certain questions; interpretation of omissions is difficult.
f. It is difficult to know whether willing respondents are truly representative.
g. This method is likely to be the slowest of all.

Before using this method, it is always advisable to conduct a "pilot study" (pilot survey) for testing the questionnaires. In a big enquiry, a pilot survey is significant. Pilot survey is, in fact, a replica and rehearsal of the main survey. It brings to light the weaknesses (if any) of the questionnaires and also of the survey techniques. Improvement can be effected in the questionnaire before it is finally despatched to the respondents.

Main Aspects of a Questionnaire Quite often a questionnaire is considered to be the heart of a survey operation for change. Hence, it should be very carefully constructed. If it is not, the survey is bound to fail. This fact requires us to study the main aspects of a questionnaire, namely, the general form, question sequence, and question formulation and wording (Fig. 7.6).

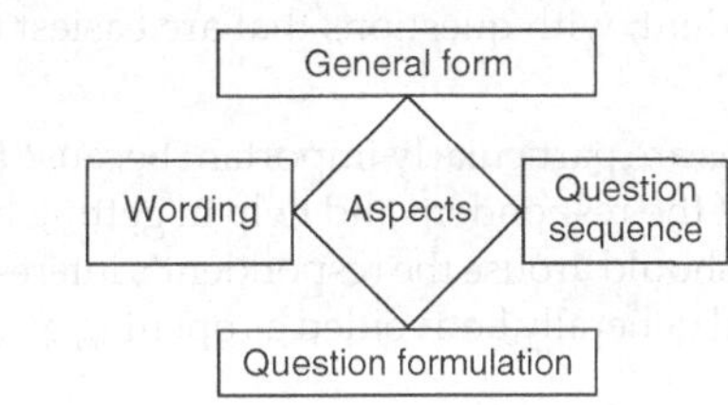

Fig. 7.6 Main aspects of a good questionnaire

a. General form As far as the general form of a questionnaire is concerned, it can either be structured or unstructured. Structured questionnaires have definite, concrete, and pre-determined questions. The questions to all respondents are worded and ordered the same way. This sort of standardisation ensures that all respondents reply to the same set of questions.

The form of the questions may be either closed (that is, of the type "yes" or "no") or open (that is, inviting free response) but should be stated in advance. Structured questionnaires may also have fixed alternative questions in which responses of the informants are limited to the stated alternatives.

Thus, a highly structured questionnaire is one in which all questions and answers are specified and comments in the respondent's own words are held to the minimum. When these characteristics are not present in a questionnaire, it is called an unstructured or non-structured questionnaire.

More specifically, we can say that in an unstructured questionnaire, the interviewer is provided with general guidelines on the type of information to be obtained, but the framing of questions is largely his own responsibility. The replies have to be taken down in the respondent's own words to the extent possible; in some situations, tape recorders may be used to achieve this goal.

Structured questionnaires are simple to administer and relatively inexpensive to analyse. The provision of alternative reply, at times, helps to understand the meaning of the question clearly. But such questionnaires have limitations, too. For instance, a wide range of data and that too in the respondent's own words cannot be obtained with structured questionnaires. They are usually considered inappropriate in investigations where the aim happens to be to a probe for attitudes and reasons for certain actions or feelings. They are equally not suitable when a problem is being first explored and working hypotheses sought. In such situations, unstructured questionnaires may be used effectively. Then on the basis of the results obtained in the pre-test (testing before final use) operations from the use of unstructured questionnaires, one can construct a structured questionnaire for use in the main study.

b. Question sequence In order to make the questionnaire effective and to ensure quality of the replies received, a researcher should pay attention to the question sequence while preparing the questionnaire. A proper sequence of questions considerably reduces the chances of individual questions being misunderstood. Each question must be clear and move smoothly to the next question, that is, the relation of one question to another should be readily apparent to the respondent, with questions that are easiest to answer being put at the beginning.

The first few questions are particularly important because they are likely to influence the attitude of the respondent and help in getting his co-operation. The opening questions should arouse the respondent's interest. The following type of questions should generally be avoided as opening questions in a questionnaire.

a. Questions that put too great a strain on the memory or intellect of the respondent
b. Questions of a personal nature
c. Questions related to personal wealth, and so on.

Following the opening questions must be those that are really vital to the research problem and a connecting thread should run through successive questions. Ideally, the question sequence should conform to the respondent's way of thinking. Knowing what information is desired, the researcher can rearrange the order of the questions (this is possible in case of an unstructured questionnaire) to fit the discussion in each particular case. But in a structured questionnaire the best that can be done is to determine the question sequence with the help of a pilot survey, which is likely to produce a good rapport with most respondents. Relatively difficult questions must be relegated to the end so that even if the respondent decides not to answer such questions, considerable information would have already been obtained.

Thus, question sequence should usually go from the general to the more specific and the researcher must always remember that the answer to a given question is a function not only of the question itself, but of all previous questions as well. For instance, if one question deals with the price usually paid for coffee and the next with the reason for preferring a particular brand, the answer to the latter question may be couched largely in terms of price differences.

c. Question formulation and wording The researcher should note that each question must be very clear, for any sort of misunderstanding can do irreparable harm to a survey. Questions should also be impartial to avoid a biased picture of the true state of affairs. Questions should be constructed so that they can form a logical part of a well-thought out tabulation plan.

In general, all questions should be (a) easily understood; (b) simple, conveying only one thought at a time; and (c) concrete and conform as much as possible to the respondent's way of thinking. (For instance, instead of asking,

"How many razor blades do you use annually?" A more realistic question would be to ask, "How many razor blades did you use last week?")

The form of questions, can be either multiple-choice or open-ended question. In the former, the respondent selects one of set of possible answers whereas in the latter he has to supply the answer in his own words. The questions with only two possible answers (usually "yes" or "no") can be taken as a special case of the multiple-choice question, or can be called a closed question.

There are some advantages and disadvantages of each form of question. Multiple-choice or closed questions are easy to handle, simple to answer, quick and relatively inexpensive to analyse. They are most amenable to statistical analysis. Sometimes, the provision of alternative replies helps to make clear the meaning of the question. But the main drawback of fixed alternative questions is that of "putting answers in people's mouths", that is, they may force a statement of opinion on an issue about which the respondent does not in fact have any opinion. They are not appropriate when the issue under consideration happens to be a complex one and also when the interest of the researcher is in the exploration of a process. In such situations, open-ended questions that are designed to permit a free response from the respondent rather than one limited to certain stated alternatives are considered appropriate. Such questions give the respondent considerable latitude in phrasing a reply. Getting the replies in the respondent's own words is, thus, the major advantage of open-ended questions. But one should not forget that, from an analytical point of view, open-ended questions are more difficult to handle, raising problems of interpretation, comparability, and interviewer bias.

In practice, one rarely comes across a case when one questionnaire relies on one form of questions alone. The various forms complement each other. As such, questions of different forms are included in one single questionnaire. For instance, multiple-choice questions constitute the basis of a structured questionnaire, particularly in a main survey. But even there, various open-ended questions are generally inserted to provide a more complete picture of the respondent's feelings and attitudes.

Researchers must pay proper attention to the wording of questions since reliable and meaningful returns depend on it to a large extent. Since words are likely to affect responses, they should be properly chosen. Simple words, which are familiar to all respondents, should be employed. Words with ambiguous meanings must be avoided. Similarly, danger words, catch-words, or words with emotional connotations should be avoided. Caution must also be exercised in the use of phrases which reflect upon the prestige of the respondent. Question wording must, in no case, bias the answer. In fact, question wording and formulation is an art and can only be learnt with practice.

Essentials of a Good Questionnaire To be successful, a questionnaire should be comparatively short and simple, that is, the size of the questionnaire should be kept to the minimum. Questions should proceed in a logical sequence, moving from easy to more difficult questions. Personal and intimate questions should be left till the end. Technical terms and vague expressions capable of different interpretations should be avoided in a questionnaire. Questions may be dichotomous (yes or no answers), multiple-choice (alternative answers listed), or open-ended. The latter type of questions are often difficult to analyse and hence should be avoided in a questionnaire to the extent possible. There should be some control questions in the questionnaire which indicate the reliability of the respondent. For instance, a question designed to determine the consumption of particular product may be asked first in terms of financial expenditure and later in terms of weight. The control questions, thus, introduce a cross-check to see whether the information collected is correct or not. Questions affecting the sentiments of respondents should be avoided. Adequate space should be provided in the questionnaire for answers to help editing and tabulation. There should always be provision for indications of uncertainty, for example, "do not know", "no preference", and so on. Brief directions for filling up the questionnaire should invariably be given in the questionnaire itself. Finally, since the physical appearance of the questionnaire affects the co-operation the researcher receives from the recipients, an attractive questionnaire, particularly in mail surveys, is a plus point for enlisting co-operation. The quality of the paper and the colours used must attract the attention of the recipients.

Schedules

This method of data collection is similar to collection of data through questionnaires. The difference lies in the fact that schedules (pro forma containing a set of questions) are filled in by the enumerators who are specially appointed for the purpose. These enumerators go to respondents, put to them the questions from the proforma in the order the questions are listed, and record the replies in the space meant for the answer in the pro forma. In certain situations, the schedules may be handed over to respondents and enumerators may help them in recording their answers. Enumerators explain the aims and objects of the investigation and also clear any doubts a respondent may have in the course of filling in the schedule.

This method requires selecting enumerators for filling up schedules or assisting respondents to fill up schedules. The enumerators should be very carefully selected. They should be trained to explain the implications of different questions put in the schedule. They should be intelligent and must be able to cross-examine the respondents to find out the trust.

This method of data collection is very useful in extensive enquiries and can lead to fairly reliable results. It is, however, very expensive and is usually adopted in case of investigations conducted by governmental agencies or big organisations. Population census all over the world is conducted through this method.

Difference between Questionnaires and Schedules

a. A questionnaire is generally sent through mail to informants. A schedule is generally filled out by the research worker or the enumerator, who can interpret questions when necessary.
b. To collect data through a questionnaire is relatively cheap and economical. To collect data through schedules is relatively more expensive since considerable amount of money has to be spent in appointing enumerators and in imparting training to them.
c. Non-response is usually high in case of questionnaires as many people do not respond and many return the questionnaire without answering all questions. Bias due to non-response often remains indeterminate. Non-response is generally very low in case of schedules. But there remains the danger of interviewer bias and cheating.
d. In case of a questionnaire, it is not always clear who replies, but in case of a schedule the identity of the respondent is known.
e. The questionnaire method is likely to be very slow, but in case of schedules the information is collected well in time as they are filled in by enumerators.
f. Personal contact is generally not possible in case of the questionnaire method as questionnaires are sent to respondents by post. But in case of schedules direct personal contact is established with respondents.
g. The questionnaire method can be used only when respondents are literate and co-operative. In case of schedules, the information can be gathered even if the respondents are illiterate.
h. Wider and more representative distribution of a sample is possible under the questionnaire method, but in the case of schedules there may be a problem in sending enumerators over a relatively wider area.
i. The risk of collecting incomplete and wrong information is relatively more under the questionnaire method, particularly when people are unable to understand questions properly. But in case of schedules, the information collected is generally complete and accurate as enumerators can remove any doubts a respondent may have.
j. The success of the questionnaire method lies more in the quality of the questionnaire itself, but in the case of schedules much depends upon the honesty and competence of the enumerators.
k. In order to attract the attention of respondents, the physical appearance of the questionnaire is important. This may not be so in case of schedules.
l. Along with schedules, the observation method can also be used but this is not possible while collecting data through questionnaires.

Projective Methods

A human being's inner world about which he may not even be aware, tends to find expression through projection which is a well-known psychological phenomenon. Motives, emotions, values, attitudes, and needs are quite often projected outside the individual on to some external object. This property of the human personality is utilised in the projective method. The more unstructured and ambiguous a stimulus, the greater the projection. When the stimulus is ambiguous and unclear, the subject "chooses" his own interpretation from within. Famous projective tests are Rorschach, TAT (Thematic Apperception Tests) P-F tests, role playing, sentence completion, draw picture, write-a-story, complete-a-story, writing essays using finger paints, and playing with dolls and toys.

Projective tests are categorised on the basis of types of response into (a) Association, (b) Construction, (c) Completion, (d) Choice ordering, and (e) Expression. Fig. 7.7 depicts the categorisation.

Fig. 7.7 Type of projective techniques used in diagnosis

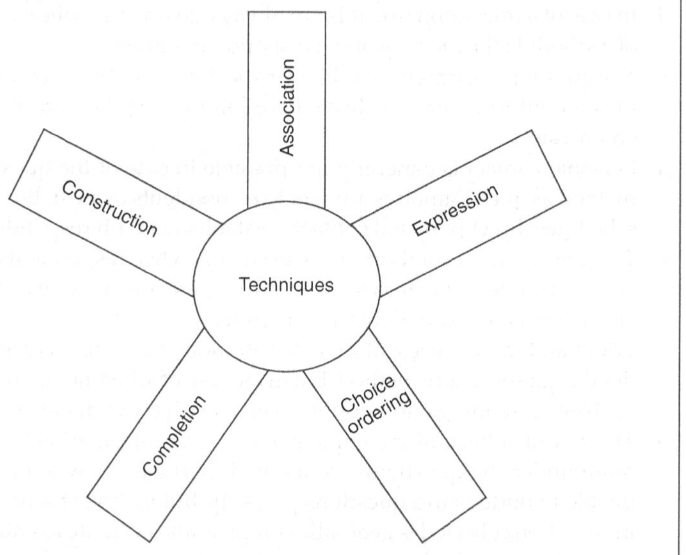

The *Association technique* requires the subject to write (or say) the first thing that comes to mind on being presented with a stimulus. For example, a series of inkblots of varying shapes and colours are used in Rorschach as the stimulus material.

Word association is another such method where the subject is asked to respond with the first word that comes to mind, or as many meanings as possible, on being presented words successively from a word list containing both emotionally tinged and neutral words.

The *construction technique* requires the subject to construct, to produce something, usually a story or a picture, on being presented with a stimulus, often a standardised one. An example is TAT, where subjects are shown an unclear picture for a few seconds and asked to develop a story on what they saw.

The *completion technique* requires the subject to complete a given task which can be a story, picture, event, and so on. How the subject correlates and concludes defines the result of the test.

The *choice ordering technique* requires the subject to choose an item that appears to him as most relevant, correct, attractive, preferred, and so on from among several items. It can be a choice from a pair of items. Or, the subject may be asked to rank the choices.

The *expressive technique* is like the construction technique but the emphasis here is on the process of construction: the manner in which it is done, not on what is done, not on the end product.

In Indian organisational studies, these techniques have been used widely to diagnose the motivational profile (achievement, power and affiliation in organisations). Cantril and Free (1962) devised a simple projective technique which they called a Self-anchoring Scale that consisted of utilising a picture of a 10-step ladder. The top and the bottom rungs are defined by the respondents from their own transactional view of their subjective worlds as life at its best and worst. The steps represent the life-positions between the two extremes. The respondent is asked where he stands on the ladder rung, with the top being the best life and the bottom rung being the worst life; where he stood in the past, and where he thinks he will stand in the future. The responses on the definitions of the best life and worst life are then subjected to content analysis. The specific positions on the ladder representing the present, past, and future, provide the quantitative measure. Cantril and Free used this technique to bring out the hopes and aspirations, fears and apprehensions, both at individual and national levels, in a multinational study and established the predictive validity of the test.

Chattopadhyay (1970, 1973) used this technique in several Indian organisations to measure aspirations and apprehensions of employees. Techniques like "draw a symbolic picture" of the organisation have been used quite often. For example, Nambudripad and Sigamoni (1980) mention using "Fantasy sharing" and "Drawing a picture of how each one saw himself in relation to the hospital" in the OD programme in a hospital.

Archival Methods and Unobtrusive Measures

Every organisation collects volumes of data from their day-to-day operations, for example, data about accounts and finance, material, productivity, rejects, repair costs, complaints, turnover, or employee behaviour like absenteeism, punctuality, turnover, accidents, grievances. These often vary systematically, and as a routine are collected and stored in the record books and in the computer. The data are not in one place; they are scattered but they are there. This store, with undefined location and boundary, can be conceived as a "data bank" or "archives"; hence, the name archival methods.

Similarly, Webb used the term unobtrusive measures. The measures are unobtrusive because in collecting them one does not thrust oneself upon a respondent to obtain ideas or information. A fingerprint on the dagger or the washerman's mark on a shirt can have a tale-telling effect in the courtroom. Sherlock Holmes, Hercule Poirot, James Bond and millions of their readers believe in it; doctors use it every day; the diagnosticians largely unutilised however, have this archive of unobtrusive data.

The major property of archival data is that they exist; there are records of behaviour, actions, events, and things, and their collection is relatively non-reactive. It does not disturb the person or the setting in which the information originated. The diagnostician's biases also do not influence it. Strictly speaking, these data do not have any subject or respondent.

Content Analysis

Content analysis as a technique has been mentioned earlier a number of times. A good example of content analysis is provided by Naisbitt (1982). Content analysis is a method of studying and analysing communication, information, or any symbolic behaviour in a systematic, objective, and quantitative manner to measure variables. Holsti (1968) defines it as follows. "Content analysis is any technique for making inferences by systematically and objectively identifying specified characteristics of messages." He provides an excellent coverage of the content analysis method.

In content analysis, the content of the information is subjected to coding. "Coding is the process whereby raw data are systematically transformed and aggregated into units which permit precise description of relevant content characteristics." The steps necessary for coding are: (a) defining the universe, (b) categories of analysis, (c) units of analysis, and (d) system of enumeration. These are briefly described below and shown in Fig. 7.8.

Fig. 7.8 Steps in content analysis

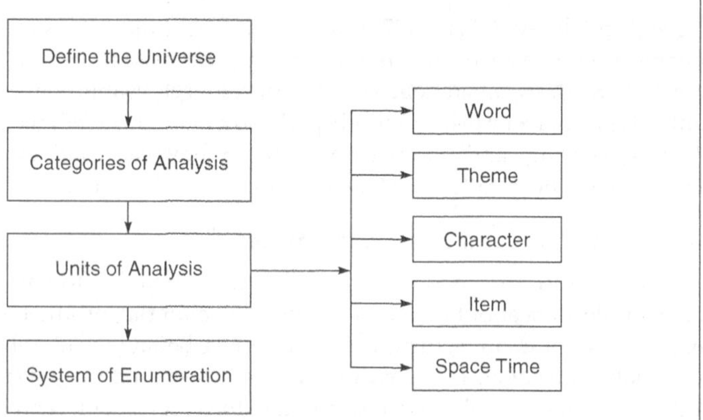

a. Defining the universe of the content Based on the theoretical construct and the hypotheses, the variables are decided and the relevant information is determined. Outlining the relevant source of the data in the universe is necessary. The categorisation of the universe, that is, the partitioning of the universe, depends on the variables and hypothesis. Partitioning itself also produces further refinement in spelling out the variables of the hypothesis.

b. Categories of analysis Selection and definition of categories, that is "pigeonholes" into which content units are classified from the critical part of content analysis. As many questions that the diagnostic purpose raises, in as many ways the categorisation may be made. Some of the types of categories generally used are listed below as an illustration:

A. *"What is said" categories*

(i) Subject matter, (ii) Direction, (iii) Standard, (iv) Values, (v) Methods, (vi) Traits, (vii) Actors, (viii) Authority, (ix) Origin, (x) Target, (xi) Location, (xii) Conflict, (xiii) Ending, (xiv) Time

B. *"How it is said" categories*

(i) Form or type of communication; what is the medium of communication (newspaper, radio, television, speech, and so on)

(ii) Form of statement. What is the grammatical and syntactical form of the communication?

(iii) Device. What is the rhetorical or propaganda method use?

c. Units of analysis Five major units of analysis are presented here: words, themes, characters, items, and space-and-time measures.

The word It is the smallest unit. Words can be simply counted and assigned to proper categories.

The Theme It is a more difficult unit. A theme is often a sentence—a proposition—about something. Themes are combined into sets of themes. It is a single assertion about some subject. It is the most useful unit of content analysis. Its self-reference is the larger theme; then the smaller themes making it up are sentences that use 'I', 'Me', or any other words referring to the writer's self.

The character In this case the coder tallies the number of persons in a written text, rather than the number of words or themes, into appropriate categories. It is mostly used in literary analysis.

The item In this case the entire article, film, book, or radio programme is characterised. It is useful for coding great amounts of material when gross categories will meet the need.

The space-time measures These are the actual physical measurements of content, for example, number of inches of pages, number of paragraphs, number of minutes of discussion, and so on.

d. System of enumeration This describes how numbers should be assigned to the units. The coder has to determine the unit in terms of which quantification is to be performed.

The first method is frequency which is similar to nominal measurement—count the number of objects in each category after assigning each object to its proper category. Stated otherwise, it is a method in which every occurrence of a given attribute is tallied.

The second method of quantification is ranking, that is, ordinal measurement; "judges" can be asked to rank the objects according to a specific criterion.

The third method of quantification is rating. This involves the issue of intensity of measurement which cannot necessarily be satisfied by pure frequency counts. Rating can be done by employing techniques of scaling like Thrustone's technique of paired comparison. Judgements are based on construct categories into which content units are placed. Both rank-order and rating methods assume that content units are sufficiently homogenous on a single continuum that they may be usefully compared.

Quantification becomes worthwhile when the materials to be analysed are representative and when the category items in the materials are insufficient numbers to justify counting. Careful counting of items is essential. These criteria determine the generalisability of the findings.

Collection of Secondary Data

Secondary data are data that are already available, that is, they refer to the data which have already been collected and analysed by someone else. When the researcher utilises secondary data, he has to look into various sources from where he can obtain them. In this case he is certainly not confronted with the problems that are usually associated with the collection of original data.

Secondary data may either be published data or unpublished data. Usually published data are available in (a) various publications of the central, state and local governments; (b) various publications of foreign governments or of international bodies and their subsidiary organisations; (c) technical and trade journals: (d) books, magazines, and newspapers; (e) reports and publications of various associations connected with business and industry, banks, stock exchanges, and so on, (f) reports prepared by research scholars, universities, and so on, in different fields, and (g) public records and statistics, historical documents, and other sources of published information.

The sources of unpublished data are many; they may be found in diaries, letters, unpublished biographies and autobiographies, and also may be available with scholars and research workers, trade associations, labour bureaus, and other public/private individuals and organisations.

A researcher must be very careful in using secondary data. He must make a minute scrutiny because it is just possible that the secondary data may be unsuitable or may be inadequate in the context of the problem which the researcher wants to study.

Before using secondary data, the researcher must see that they possess the following characteristics (Fig. 7.9).

a. Reliability of data Reliability can be tested by finding out such things about the said data as: (a) Who collected the data? (b) What were the sources of data? (c) Were they collected by using proper methods? (d) At what time were they collected? (e) Was there any bias of the compiler? (f) What level of accuracy was desired? Was it achieved?

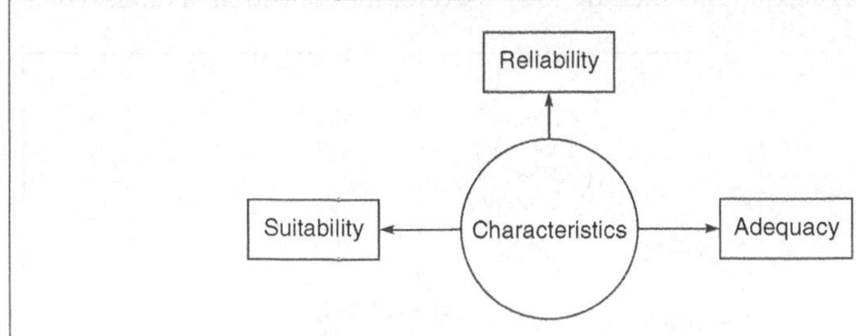

Fig. 7.9 Characteristics of secondary data

b. Suitability of data The data that are suitable for one enquiry may not necessarily be suitable in another enquiry. Hence, if the available data are found to be unsuitable, they should not be used by the researcher. In this context, the researcher must very carefully scrutinise the definition of various terms and units of collection used at the time of collecting the data from the primary source originally. Similarly, the object, scope, and nature of the original enquiry must also be studied. If the researcher finds differences in these, the data will remain unsuitable for the present enquiry and should not be used.

c. Adequacy of data If the level of accuracy achieved in data is found inadequate for the purpose of the present enquiry, the data must not be used by the researcher. The data will also be considered inadequate if they are related to an area which may be either narrower or wider than the area of the present enquiry.

7.5 SELECTION OF APPROPRIATE METHOD FOR DATA COLLECTION

A researcher must judiciously select the method/methods of data collection for his own study, keeping in view the following factors (Fig. 7.10).

a. Nature, scope and object of enquiry This constitutes the most important factor affecting the choice of a particular method. The method selected should be such that it suits the type of enquiry that is to be conducted by the researcher. This factor is also important in deciding whether the data already available (secondary data) are to be used or if data not yet available (primary data) are to be collected.

b. Availability of funds Availability of funds for the research project determines to a large extent the method to be used for the collection of data. When funds at the disposal of the researcher are very limited, he will have to select a comparatively cheaper method which may not be as efficient and effective as some other costly method. Finance, in fact, is a big constraint in practice and the researcher has to act within this limitation.

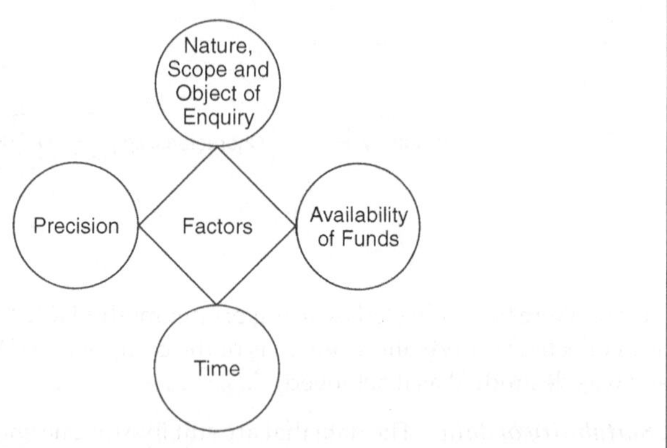

Fig. 7.10 Important factors in selection of appropriate method of data collection

c. Time factor The time at the disposal of the researcher has also to be taken into account in deciding a particular method of data collection. Some methods take relatively more time, whereas with others the data can be collected in a comparatively shorter duration.

d. Precision required The degree of precision of data required also needs to be considered at the time of selecting the method of collection of data.

But one must always remember that each method of data collection has its use and none is superior in all situations. For instance, a telephone interview method may be considered appropriate (assuming telephone population) if funds are restricted, time is limited, and the data is to be collected in respect of few items with or without a certain degree of precision.

In case funds permit and more information is desired, the personal interview method may be said to be relatively better. In case there is enough time but funds are limited and much information needs to be gathered with no precision, then the mail-questionnaire method can be regarded as more reasonable.

When funds and time are ample and much information with no precision is to be collected, then either the personal interview, or the mail-questionnaire, or the joint use of these two methods may be taken as an appropriate method of collecting data. Where a wide geographic area is to be covered, the use of mail-questionnaires supplemented by personal interviews will yield more reliable results per rupee spent than either method alone.

Secondary data may be used in case the researcher finds them reliable, adequate, and appropriate for his research. While studying motivating influences in market researches or studying people's attitudes in psychological/social surveys, we can resort to the use of one or more of the projective techniques stated earlier. Such techniques are of immense value in case the reason can be obtained from the respondent who does not want to admit it or the reason relates to some underlying psychological attitude and the respondent is not aware of it. But when the respondent knows the reason and can tell the same if asked, then a non-projective questionnaire, using direct questions, may yield satisfactory results even in case of attitude surveys.

Since projective techniques are as yet in an early stage of development and with the validity of many of them remaining an open question, it is usually considered better to rely on the straightforward statistical methods with only supplementary use of projective techniques. Nevertheless, in pre-testing and in searching for hypotheses, they can be highly valuable.

- Organisational diagnosis is a systematic process of identifying the need for change in the organisation with specific focus on where and why this need for change is required in the organisation.
- The concept of organisational diagnosis is based on (a) collecting information relating to the problem, (b) organising the information, and (c) distinguishing them from other patterns of problems. Diagnocube is a technique to perform this task with the four dimensions of business (a) system, (b) components of system, (c) area covered by the system, and (d) surrounding external environment.
- In the methodology for the diagnosis, the following points are considered the most important. (a) How to conduct it (b) Procedure (c) Strategy (d) Resources used (e) Clients need (f) Competence of the Diagnostician (g) Choice of method.
- For reliable diagnosis, the mode of collection of data is very important. The different methods which are available are (a) observation, (b) interview, (c) questionnaire, (d) schedule, (e) projective, (f) archival. Sources of secondary data are also explained. The relevance of the information relies on the nature, scope, and object of the inquiry, availability of funds, time, and precision required.
- Finally, the diagnosis is based on the quality of information which is collected. In this regard, the selection of appropriate matter is very essential.

Case Study: An Academic Department in a Public University

History

The administrative staff of a large academic department in a public university was a diverse group composed of both long-time career employees and new appointees from outside the institution. Changes of many sorts, including a new administrative manager, building renovations, and the use of new technology tools, contributed to a stressful atmosphere. The immediate symptoms of the stress were a breakdown in collegiality, and a culture of blame and complaint.

Task

Identify the root causes for the stress and best ideas within the organisation about how to address them. Develop a mini retreat to address the immediate teamwork, communication, and morale issues. Prepare a report for the chair and manager with longer-term recommendations for organisational improvement.

Intervention

OD agents interviewed the staff, manager, chair, and vice chairs with whom the staff had regular interactions. A retreat process was then developed and facilitated to help the staff examine its issues and determine areas for positive action. A comprehensive report outlined for the departmental leadership a number of actions to be taken in the areas of structures, processes, planning, management styles, behaviours and interactions, accountability, and skills development.

Result

The mini retreat had the immediate result of breaking the tension among the staff and between the staff and manager, setting the whole group on a positive direction to resolve problems. The report guided the chair and manager in a gradual and systematic improvement of the department's administrative structures, processes, and interactions.

Key Disciplines

Organisational Needs Assessment, Organisational Problem-solving, Change Management, Retreat Facilitation, Team Building, Process Improvement.

Case Study: "Ma Foi" An IT Staffing Company

History

An IT staffing company, founded and led by a CEO and management team from India, had been very successful in providing high technology personnel on a temporary basis to leading technology, consulting, services, and general manufacturing companies. The company's goals were to triple revenue, become a global enterprise with a culturally diversified management team, upgrade employee orientation processes, and change its business focus to e-business solutions.

Task

Evaluate management and organisational factors that might affect the executive team's capacity to carry the company to the desired higher level. Assist with the cultural orientation of new members of the executive team who were not Indians. Enhance the cross-cultural component and overall cohesiveness of employee orientation. Help the company assure a successful transition to its new business focus.

Intervention

A change agency on foreign origin practice and India Practice worked consecutively on these projects over the course of a year. Assessment was made of management and organisational issues, along with action recommendations for each identified issue. A customised cross-cultural orientation package was developed for the executive team. The orientation process for employees was reformulated and special cross-cultural modules developed. Finally, the change agency worked intensely with the CEO, executive team, and employees to enssure effective planning, communication, and buy-in for the transformation to the new business model.

Result

Change agency recommendations and interventions helped the company proceed rapidly and smoothly through a whole series of significant transformations needed to support its business goals.

Key Disciplines

Organisational Needs Assessment, Change Management, Employee Orientation, Cross-cultural Consulting.

REVIEW QUESTIONS

1. What do you understand by organisational diagnosis?
2. What is a diagnocube and how does it help in the process of diagnosis?
3. How can primary data or information related to organisational diagnosis be collected?
4. What is the observation method and when can this method be used in organisational diagnosis?
5. What are the essentials for effective interviews and the questionnaire method?
6. Differentiate between questionnaire and schedule methods used in diagnosis?
7. What are the projective and archival techniques of data collection?
8. What considerations should management keep in mind while selecting data collection methods for organisational diagnosis?

EXERCISE

The aim of the exercise is to share and develop best practices, ideas, and/or solutions to common problems. This provides a useful and collectively enjoyable experience, with some good outputs for the organisation when a best practice is identified or developed, and can then be implemented. Split large groups into teams of three or four. More than four members per team makes full involvement unlikely. For example, if the total group size is twelve, run four exercises concurrently in four teams of three. At the end of the exercise, each team leader presents the results of their discussions and ideas or solutions development to the whole group.

You could then look at implementing the most viable suggestions, create project groups, and then pilot groups. Establish an emphasis on working together to identify and implement constructive change through the sharing of ideas and experience. The activity can become a regular development forum; a place where challenges, opportunities, local problems, and so on, can be brought and collective ability used to find and apply solutions. Teams can be changed for each team-building session.

It is important to clarify the precise aims of each exercise before it begins. Teams can take a few minutes to do this prior to beginning the activity. Ensure that team members explain and understand each other's situations and processes (which in itself is another helpful output of the exercise). Ensure adequate support for all initiatives taken forward to the implementation stage, so that participants see that their work is resulting in some positive effect. Securing support from management prior to the process will help this, as will obtaining commitment where possible for initiatives considered worthy of implementation.

Chapter

Organisational Development

Chapter Outline

- Introduction
- Organisational Development Interventions and Their Classification
- Organisational Development Intervention Techniques
- Prerequisites for Effective Use of OD
- Summary
- Case Study
- Review Questions
- Exercises

"Not enjoyment, and not sorrow,
Is our destined end or way;
But to act, that each tomorrow
Bring us farther than today."

— H.W. Longfellow

8.1 INTRODUCTION

Organisations are complex systems comprising many sub-systems which must work together synchronously and in harmony. The fact that there are a number of variables that affect sub-systems and that the sub-systems themselves interact with each other makes the system even more complicated. Adding to the complication is the dynamic nature of the environment in which the organisation exists and the rapidly changing values of the variables affecting the system. Accordingly, management must be prepared to achieve a degree of organisational synthesis as well as change in the organisational environment to accommodate the change in the conditions. This organisational change must be pre-planned and not be a haphazard one. Harold Rush has defined organisational development as "a planned, managed and systematic process to change the culture, systems and behaviour of an organisation in order to improve the organisation's effectiveness in solving its problems and achieving its objectives."

The term Organisational Development (OD) was coined by Richard Beckhard in the mid-1950s, in response to the need for integrating organisational needs with individual needs. He described this dilemma as follows.

"If we are talking about the basic dilemma of managing work, the management problem has two horns. One horn is, how do you take all that human energy and channel it towards the organisation's mission? The other horn is, how do you organise the work, the communication patterns, the decision-making, the norms and values, the ground rules so that people's individual needs for self-worth, achievement, satisfaction and so on are significantly met at the work place?"

"A great deal of attention has been given to the second horn of the dilemma. But that alone does not solve the problem any more than the other way around. So the dilemma is, how do you manage the dilemma and not how you manage one horn of it. OD tries to work out and organise the interaction between the two."

The basic concept underlining Organisational Development then, is to improve organisational efficiency by modifying human behaviour rather than technological innovations, because without the committed involvement of human element, all technology has a limited meaning. OD theorists emphasise that the organic structure of an organisation, rather than the mechanistic and bureaucratic structure is more desirable in today's dynamic environment. It is accepted, however, that the mechanistic structure with its highly disciplined chain of command is more suitable under a stable environment. But the argument advanced by behaviourists is that there is no stable environment. The external environment is highly turbulent to be stable. Accordingly, the organic structure with its limited number of hierarchical levels, wide span of control, decentralised decision-making, open communication, interdependence among groups, high level of openness and trust and reliance on teams is the best organisation for today's situation.

Organisational development can then summarily be defined as, "An effort (a) planned, (b) organisation-wide, (c) managed from the top, in order to (d) increase organisational effectiveness and health, through (e) planned intervention in the organisation's 'processes' using behavioural science knowledge."

This definition was originally developed by Beckhard, who was an early proponent of behavioural science application to increase the health and effectiveness of the organisation. Again, according to Beckhard's view, "the healthy organisation manages according to established goals, the organisation is properly designed, decisions are made at the appropriate level, communications are relatively undistorted, win/lose activities are minimised, there is emphasis on helping each other grow and develop, the interpersonal difficulties are minimised and the organisation is open and adaptive."

In the above definition, effectiveness refers to establishment and attaining realistic organisational goals. Health refers to the motivation, integration, and utilisation of combined human resources within the organisation. The organisation development, as perceived, seems to be an answer to all organisational problems. Since the human element is the most important element in the success of any organisation, the reorganisation of any organisation along organic lines based upon openness and trust should ensure success. But does it ensure success? Even the behavioural theorists are beginning to doubt the rational applicability of this concept. This would explain why most organisations are still operating in a classical and mechanistic way and there does not seem to be any urgency to shift towards an organic structure. One of the major reasons for any lack of popularity of organic structures is that in such structures, the emphasis is primarily on human element which is most unstable and unpredictable and basically self-serving. Even Warren Bennis, who was a strong supporter of organisational development on the basis of human interaction, became sceptical after experiencing the realities and frustrations of serving as an administrator in two academic institutions. Based on his experience, he expressed his view that human nature is basically selfish, that people place self-interest above public interest, cannot tolerate ambiguity and frustration, and are more concerned with power and profit than with warmth and love. These traits run counter to what are desirable for organisation development. Still the trend towards organic structure indicates the optimistic belief that these self-oriented traits and attitudes can be changed through sustained efforts and motivation.

8.1.1 Objectives of OD Programmes

Some of these objectives are described as follows.

a. To build and enhance interpersonal trust, communication, co-operation and support among all individuals and groups throughout the organisation at all levels.
b. To encourage an analytical approach to problem-solving in a team spirit and open manner, where the problems and differences are confronted and resolved instead of a problem-avoiding or decision-postponing approach or "sweeping problems under the rug", as they say it.
c. To increase a sense of belonging to the organisation so that the organisational goals become the goals of the members of the organisation.
d. To assign decision-making and problem-solving responsibilities to skilled and knowledgeable persons who are closer to the scene of operations and the sources of information, rather than to a person with a particular role or at a particular hierarchical level.
e. To increase personal responsibility for planning, implementing the plans, and be aware of and responsible for the consequences. This will build enthusiasm individually and groupwise and will involve communication, feelings, open competition as well as compromise, conflict resolution, and so on. This will increase a sense of self-direction for all people within the organisation.
f. To help managers to manage according to the relevant objectives, rather than depending upon "past practices". The management should be goal-oriented rather than process-oriented. All efforts should be directed and channelled towards related objectives in the area of responsibility.

These objectives help the organisation in examining its current methods of operations, its norms and values, and in generating and evaluating alternative ways of operating and utilising the full potential of human resources.

8.1.2 Basic OD Assumptions

Organisational development has a number of underlying assumptions which can be examined to determine how OD programmes can be utilised to their fullest potential. These assumptions are laid down by French and Bell.

a. Most individuals have a drive towards personal growth and development. However, work habits are more a response to work environment rather than personality traits. Accordingly, efforts to change work habits should be directed towards changing the way the person is treated rather than towards attempting to change the person.
b. Highest productivity can be achieved when individual goals are integrated with organisational goals. This way, the workers will be highly devoted to quality output because they will take personal pride in optimum quality.
c. Co-operation is always more effective than conflict. Conflict tends to erode trust, prohibit collaboration, and eventually limit the effectiveness of the organisation. In healthy organisations, "efforts are made at all levels to treat conflict as a problem, subject to problem-solving methods."
d. The suppression of feelings adversely affect problem-solving, personal growth, and satisfaction with one's work. Accordingly, free expression of feelings is an important ingredient for commitment to work.
e. The growth of individual members is facilitated by relationships which are open, supportive, and trusting. Accordingly, the level of interpersonal trust, support, and co-operation should be as high as possible.
f. The difference between commitment and agreement must be fully understood. Agreeing to do something is totally different than being committed to do something. A sense of commitment makes it easy to accept change and the implementation of change is even easier when this commitment is based upon participation in the process.
g. OD programmes, if they are to succeed, must be reinforced by the organisation's total human resources system.

8.2 OD INTERVENTIONS AND THEIR CLASSIFICATION

OD interventions are the building blocks which are planned activities designed to improve the organisation's functioning through participation of the organisational members. The inventory of OD interventions is quite extensive. We will explore several classification schemes here to help you understand how various interventions "clump" together in terms of (a) the objectives of the interventions and (b) the targets of the interventions. Familiarity with how interventions relate to one another is useful for planning the overall OD strategy.

OD programmes are designed to achieve specific goals, and often several interventions are combined into a "package" to accomplish the goals. The following are the major "families" or types of OD interventions.

a. Diagnostic activities These are fact-finding activities designed to ascertain the state of the system, the status of a problem, the "way things are." Available methods range from projective devices such as "build a collage that represents you and your place in this organisation" to the more traditional data collection methods of interviews, questionnaires, surveys, and meetings.

b. Team-building activities These activities are designed to enhance the effective operation of system teams. They may relate to task issues, such as the way things are done, the needed skills to accomplish tasks, the resource allocations necessary for task accomplishments; or they may relate to the nature and quality of the relationships between the team members or between members and the leader. Again, a wide range of activities is possible. In addition, consideration is given to the different kinds of teams that may exist in the organisation, such as formal work teams, temporary task force teams, newly constituted teams, and cross-functional teams.

c. Intergroup activities Such activities are designed to improve the effectiveness of interdependent groups. They focus on joint activities and the output of the groups considered as a single system rather than as two sub-systems. When two groups are involved, the activities are generally designated intergroup or interface activities; when more than two groups are involved, the activities are often called organisational mirroring.

Fig. 8.1 Classification of OD interventions

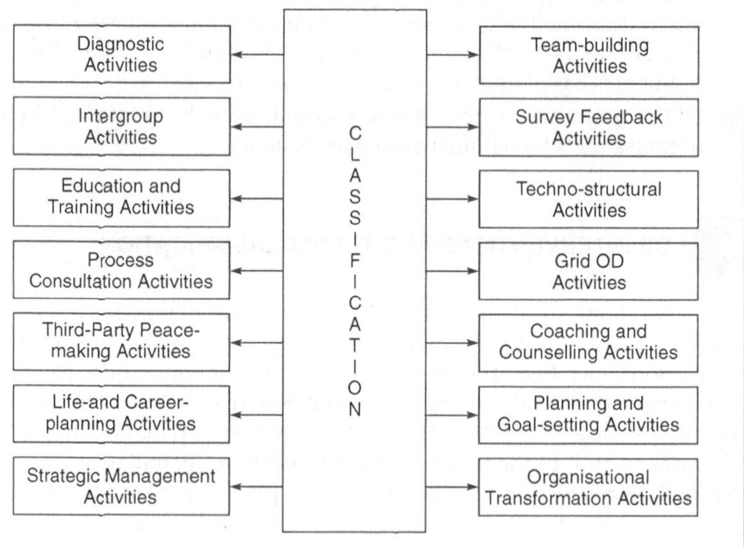

d. Survey feedback activities These activities are related and similar to diagnostic activities in that they are a large component of those activities. However, they are important enough in their own right to be considered separately. These activities centre on actively working the data produced by a survey and designing action plans based on the survey data.

e. Education and training activities Such activities are designed to improve skills, abilities, and knowledge of individuals. There are several activities available and several approaches possible. For example, the individual can be educated in isolation from his own work group (say, in a T-group, or Training-group, consisting of strangers), or one can be educated in relation to the work group (say, when a work team learns how better to manage interpersonal conflict). The activities may be directed towards technical skills required for effective task performance or towards improving interpersonal competence. The activities may be directed towards leadership issues, responsibilities, and functions of group members, decision-making, problem-solving, goal setting and planning, and so on.

f. Techno-structural or structural activities Such activities are designed to improve the effectiveness of the technical or structural inputs and constraints affecting individuals or groups. The activities may take the form of (a) experimenting with new organisation structures and evaluating their effectiveness in terms of specific goals or (b) devising new ways to bring technical resources to bear on problems. In Chapter 12 we discuss these activities and label them "structural interventions", defined as "the broad class of interventions or change efforts aimed at improving organisation effectiveness through changes in the task, structural, and technological subsystem." Included in these activities are certain forms of job enrichment, management by objectives, socio-technical systems, collateral organisations, and physical settings interventions.

g. Process consultation activities These activities on the part of the consultant "help the client to perceive, understand, and act upon process events which occur in the client's environment." These activities perhaps more accurately describe an approach, a consulting mode in which the client is given insight into the human processes in organisations and taught skills in diagnosing and managing them. The primary emphasis is on processes such as communications, leader and member roles in groups, problem-solving and decision-making, group norms and group growth, leadership and authority, and intergroup co-operation and competition.

h. Grid organisation development activities The activities were invented and franchised by Robert Blake and Jane Mouton and constitute a six-phase change model involving the total organisation. Internal resources are developed to conduct most of the programmes, which may take from three to five years to complete. The model starts with upgrading individual managers' skills and leadership abilities, moves to team improvement activities, then to intergroup relations activities. Later phases include corporate planning for improvement, developing implementation tactics, and concludes with an evaluation phase assessing change in the organisation culture and looking towards future directions.

i. Third-party peacemaking activities Such activities are conducted by a skilled consultant (the third party), and are designed to "help two members of an organisation manage their interpersonal conflict." They are based on confrontation tactics and an understanding of the processes involved in conflict and conflict resolution.

j. Coaching and counselling activities Such activities entail the consultant or other organisation members working with individuals to help them (a) define learning goals, (b) learn how others see their behaviour, and (c) learn new modes of behaviour to see if these help them to achieve their goals better. A central feature of this activity is the non-evaluative feedback given by others to an individual. A second feature is the joint exploration of alternative behaviours.

k. Life- and career-planning activities The activities enable individuals to focus on their life and career objectives and how they might go about achieving them. Structured activities lead to production of life and career inventories, discussions of goals and objectives, and assessment of capabilities, needed additional training, and areas of strength and deficiency.

l. Planning and goal-setting activities These activities include theory and experience in planning and goal setting, utilising problem-solving models, planning paradigms, ideal organisation versus real organisation "discrepancy" models, and the like. The goal of these activities is to improve skills at the levels of the individual, group, and organisation.

m. Strategic management activities The activities help key policymakers reflect systematically on their organisation's basic mission and goals and environmental demands, threats and opportunities, and engage in long-range action planning of both a reactive and proactive nature. These activities direct attention in two important directions: outside the organisation to a consideration of the environment, and away from the present to the future.

n. Organisational transformation activities Such activities involve large-scale system changes. They are activities designed to cause a fundamental change in the nature of the organisation. Almost everything about the organisation is changed—management philosophy, reward systems, design of work, structure of the organisation, organisation mission, values, and culture. Total quality programmes are transformational; so are programmes to create high-performance organisations or high-performance work systems. Socio-technical systems theory and open systems planning provide the basis for such activities.

In general, OD efforts are designed to bring changes in the conceptual environment of an organisation as well as in the outlook of the organisational members. Each member begins to see himself as a resource to others and is willing to lend his support to his colleagues when it is needed. The conceptual environment brings about open and free expression of feelings, emotions, and perceptions. It also helps members to develop interpersonal competence including communication skills and an insight into themselves and others.

8.3 OD INTERVENTIONS TECHNIQUES

The number of OD interventions is large. But they vary in the range and depth of their penetration into the organisational system and in the purpose they serve. No two interventions are alike and there is no single OD method capable of serving all the likely objectives of an organisation. Sometimes several methods of OD are used together.

Some of the most important and frequently used techniques of OD are listed below (Fig. 8.2).

Sensitivity training
Team building
Survey feedback
Grid training
Process consultation
Management by objectives (MBO)
Role analysis technique (RAT)
Role negotiation technique
Force-field analysis

Fig. 8.2 Intervention techniques

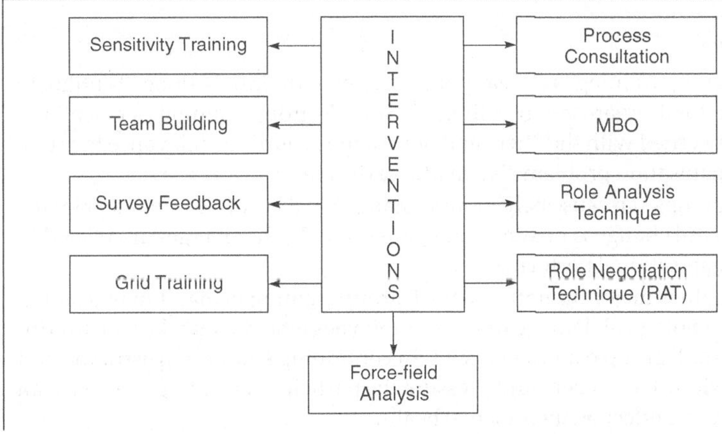

8.3.1 Sensitivity Training

One of the popular techniques in OD is sensitivity training. It is a method of changing behaviour through unstructured group interaction. Sensitivity training is sought to help individuals towards better relationships with others. The primary focus is on reducing interpersonal friction.

In sensitivity training, the actual technique employed is T-group. It is small group of 10 to 12 people, assisted by a professional behavioural scientist who acts as a catalyst and trainer for the group. There is no specified agenda. He merely creates the opportunity for group members to express their ideas and feelings freely. Since the trainer has no leadership role to play, the group must work out its own methods of proceeding. A leaderless and agenda-free group session is on. They can discuss anything they like. Individuals are allowed to focus on behaviour rather than on duties. As members engage in dialogue, they are encouraged to learn about themselves as they interact with others.

Features

a. The primary objective of sensitivity training is to break through the barriers of intellectualisation and verbalisation to facilitate the participants experiencing his own behaviour and its effects. It says, "Open your eyes. Look at yourself. See how you look to others. Then decide what changes, if any, you want to make and in which direction you want to go."
b. Sensitivity training emphasises the process rather than the content of the training and focuses upon emotional rather than conceptual training.
c. It is an experience-based methodology aimed at changing behaviour through unstructured group interaction.
d. It is not a set of hidden, manipulative processes, aimed at brainwashing individuals.
e. It is not intended to suppress conflict, it is not group therapy, and it does not guarantee change.

Criticism

a. T-group training lays heavy emphasis on individuals alone. Its utility to the total organisation is limited. Since T-group training is essentially concerned with the "here and now of the group", its relevance to actual organisation problems is a matter of debate.
b. T-groups can cause behavioural change but it is not clear whether (a) the overall change is positive or negative and (b) the changes are related to organisational performance.
c. Another major limitation with T group training is that it may result in psychological damage to some employees who do not take well to criticism. T-group experience can be a continuing source of frustration and anxiety. The anxiety and pressure the participants undergo can have an adverse effect on their mental health.

d. T-group training is impractical insofar as it is not consistent with the business and economic world we live in.

Where T-group Training is Suitable

a. In organic organisations where openness, trust, and willingness to work co-operatively are the essential features.
b. Where a climate of psychological safety prevails. For instance, where a person would feel safe to reveal himself in the group, to expose his feelings, drop his defences, and try to find new ways of interacting.
c. Where the group's feedback is articulate and meaningful for the organisation.

Necessary Conditions for the Success of T-group Training

Robert J. House recommends the following conditions so that T-group training can emerge as a successful and powerful tool for changing the behaviour of individuals.

a. Careful selection of participants so that the members do not have symptoms of emotional instability, low tolerance and anxiety, and psychiatric case histories.
b. Careful study of performance requirements.
c. Careful selection of the T-group leader.
d. Continued research to determine the participants' characteristics and conditions required for using T-group training.
e. Provision of reserve precautionary procedures to be instituted in the event of the programme failure.

Conclusion

Sensitivity training provides a mechanism for personal learning and development. If one can take the growth of intrinsic worth as the basis, then sensitivity training has passed the test of the market. The supporters of sensitivity training contend that the numerous potential pitfalls in sensitivity training are most likely to arise from using a poorly qualified trainer, failure to select the participants carefully, and improper fitting of the programme into the other developmental efforts. The critics point out the chief danger of "psychologically damaging the people" who are unable to endure the stress and tension induced by the training. Thus, both positive and sceptical assessments appear in the literature.

8.3.2 Team Building

It has received the most attention and OD practitioners have great faith in team building. Essentially, team building is an attempt to assist the work group in becoming adept by learning how to identify, diagnose, and solve its own problems. It directly focuses on the identification of problems relating to task performance and lays down concrete plans for their elimination. A team building programme deals with new problems on an ongoing basis. It is an effective technique by which members of an organisational group diagnose how they work together and plan changes that will improve their effectiveness.

The goal of team building is to perfect the operation of individuals as a team, not to teach each of them as an independent, isolated components of the organisation. Team building attempts to improve the effectiveness of a work group by allowing the group members to concentrate on

a. Setting goals or priorities for organisational groups
b. Analysing or allocating the way the work is performed
c. Examining the way the group is working
d. Examining the relationships among the people doing the work

Thus, the fundamental aim of team building is to help group members in examining their own behaviours and developing an action plan that fosters task accomplishment.

Team Building Cycle

Team building usually follows a logical cycle as shown in Fig. 8.3.

Fig. 8.3 Team building cycle

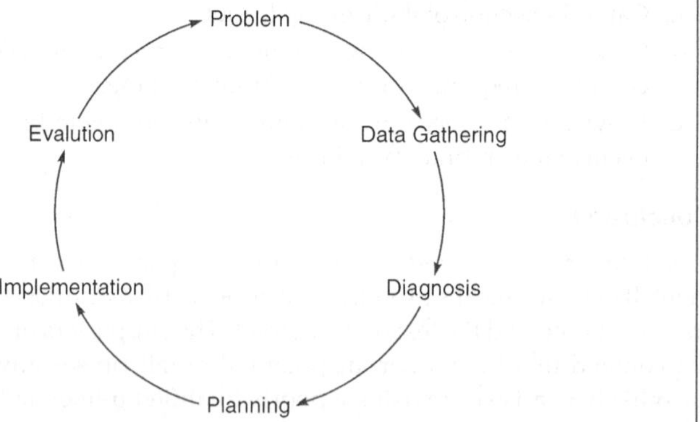

In team building, employees belonging to a work group gather and discuss problems relating to their task performance. In a typical team building exercise, the session starts with identifying current problems such as inefficient procedures, ineffective policies, use of faulty equipment, and role ambiguities. Members of the team contribute information concerning their individual perceptions of issues, problems, and task relationships. Having agreed on the key problems, discussion shifts to specific tactics for overcoming these problems/ difficulties. Assessments regarding the impact of these tactics are done in the final or concluding session.

Necessary Conditions for the Success of Team Building Programme

Before attempting to undertake a team building exercise, management has to ensure that

a. Basic interdependence among the members of the group exists (when task interdependencies do not exist, then team building is an inappropriate intervention)
b. The group members understand the stated goals clearly
c. The group members unanimously agree with the objectives
d. The group is capable of taking corrective action on the problems identified or at least will be able to tackle some reasonable percentage of them

Features

a. Team building improves the organisation's problem-solving ability and decision-making skills.
b. It results in effective interpersonal relationships.
c. It helps understand inter-group communication and remove barriers.
d. It provides a useful way for the group to examine interpersonal issues.
e. It provides a useful platform for the employees to get involved in their OD programme.
f. It increases the probability of occurrence of collaborative behaviour.

Team building, thus, contributes both to goal attainment and to building and solidifying positive interpersonal attitudes.

In spite of these benefits, team building as an OD intervention is severely criticised on the following grounds.

a. Team building focuses only on the work group.
b. Team building becomes a complicated exercise especially when new groups are formed.

Thus, when new groups are formed, they overemphasise the task problems ignoring the relationship issues completely. By the time relationship problems begin to crop up and come to the surface, the group may be unable to deal with them. This might adversely affect the performance of the group as well as the goals of the organisation.

Conclusion

As against sensitivity training where the primary focus is on individuals, the fundamental emphasis of team building is on work groups. The basic building blocks of organisations are groups of people and, therefore, the basic units of change are also groups, not individuals. Managers appreciate the logic that the focal point of improving the organisation's effectiveness is to improve the effectiveness of the building blocks—work teams.

8.3.3 Survey Feedback

The survey feedback intervention of OD is well-organised and systematic approach with a relatively long history of good performance. The technique is derived from a long and sound tradition of attitude measurement and survey research. It is an informational and efficient technique for fostering organisational effectiveness. As it does not involve a high degree of emotion and soul searching on the part of the participants, this technique is devoid of the main limitation of emotional instability or psychological damage of the participants.

This intervention, which enjoys widespread use nowadays, includes a package of four distinct steps as shown in Fig. 8.4.

Fig. 8.4 Steps in survey feedback

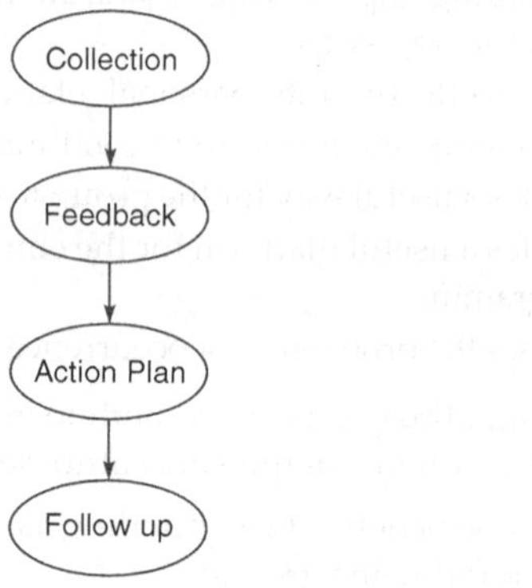

a. Collection of data First of all, information is gathered through a comprehensive questionnaire. The questionnaire consists of company-related multiple-choice items. The self-report questionnaire can be tailored to a specific organisation and designed to answer highly specific questions, or it can consist of standard questions that are useful in many organisational settings. The items contained in the questionnaire focus on such key organisational issues as employee satisfaction, quality and styles of leadership, and various facets of organisational climate like decision-making and co-ordination.

b. Feedback The survey feedback results are fed directly to the participants rather than to the top management. The information that is fed must be clear and accurate. Further, survey-generated results must be presented in a non-threatening and constructive manner to the employees. Usually, the data are fed back in group discussions and problem-solving sessions and the OD expert conducting the survey feedback programme summarises the findings in a clear-cut manner and elicits employee's reactions to them.

c. Develop an action plan A survey feedback programme will be rendered incomplete and meaningless if it does not contain the provision of developing an action plan to deal with the problems. In this stage, participants are asked about their recommendations, about how to resolve the problems that are uncovered in the survey.

d. Follow up Without continuous feedback and correction of the pro-gramme this intervention (or, for that matter, any intervention) will be short-lived. Normally, several months after the survey is conducted, a check should be made to determine whether the action plans are implemented or not.

The basic purpose of a survey feedback to organisation is in diagnosing problems and developing action plans for problem-solving. It also assists the group members to improve relationships through discussion of common problems.

The survey feedback starts by obtaining the commitment and endorsement of top management. The survey may be conducted with or without the help of an outside consultant. Participants in the first phase of the programme complete a standardised questionnaire.

One very important aspect of the survey feedback approach are the methods of feedback. Three basic methods of feedback are available. Every organisational members can obtain the data

a. Almost simultaneously.
b. In a "waterfall pattern" (that is, in which group meetings are held at the highest organisational levels first, followed by group meetings at each succeeding lower level).
c. In a "bottom up" fashion (that is, in which group meetings are held first at the lowest levels).

The typical approach is to feed the data back to higher levels and then to lower levels.

Necessary Conditions for the Success of the Survey Feedback Approach

Management must ensure that

a. The questionnaire it employs must be valid and reliable.
b. Employees must be willing to report their views and reactions honestly.
c. The OD consultant conducting the programme must be skilled at interpreting the survey data.
d. Top management must be willing to use the information it gathers.
e. The sessions are conducted in a factual, task-oriented environment.
f. Each group has enough discretion to consider and act upon its finding and analysis.
g. Organisational members trust each other (because distrust leads to response bias).
h. Participants do not feel deceived, manipulated, or misrepresented.

Empirical Assessment

Survey feedback has proved to be a fruitful OD technique. A study evaluating the effects of change techniques in organisations revealed that survey feedback was a more effective change strategy than many other types. Some other researchers have also noted that it is a cost-effective means of implementing a comprehensive programme, making it a highly desirable and better-rated technique.

The Institute for Social Research of the Michigan University has conducted a great amount of empirical investigation over the survey feedback method of OD intervention. After a detailed review of literature and research on survey feedback, Huse concludes "The available data seems to indicate that survey feedback can be an effective approach toward meeting organisational goals and individual needs."

Evaluation

Survey feedback as an OD technique is appreciated on many accounts.

a. It can yield a great amount of information and data efficiently and quickly.
b. Decision-making and problem-solving abilities of the organisation can be improved tremendously because this approach applies the competence and knowledge throughout the organisation.
c. It emphasises and promotes two-way communication in the organisation.
d. It can increase the influence of the lower-level managers.
e. It has a broad coverage and includes all the members of the organisation.
f. The information it provides often serves as the basis for concrete plans to enhance organisational effectiveness.
g. It is flexible and can be applied to many different organisations and to many different problems.

Conclusion

Finally, although it does not bring fundamental changes in the structure, task design, or technology of the organisation, a survey feedback may bring problems regarding these aspects to the surface and clarify them. Survey feedback is indeed an effective approach because it can meet both individual needs and organisational goals.

This approach may be counterproductive if the group can only discuss problems and perceptions without actually determining or strongly influencing corrective actions. If there is any information bias, then all the attempts to diagnose and solve the problems will be futile.

Above all, survey feedback method has the advantage of high motivation through involving the employees in studying matters that are at hand, and of practical interest and value, thus reducing the amount of resistance to change.

8.3.4 Grid Training

One of the most publicised techniques of OD is the grid organisation development. Grid identifies a range of management behaviours based on various ways in which task-oriented and people-oriented styles can interact with each other. Instead of decolonising the two dimensions of leadership—concern for production and concern for people—Blake and Mouton contend that managers should be concerned with both people and production in order to achieve effective performance results. They contend that in order to maximise organisational effectiveness, managers must be trained to develop this 9,9 style of leadership.

The specific objectives of a grid organisation development programme are to

a. Study the organisation as an interacting system and apply techniques of analysis in diagnosing its problems;
b. Understand the importance and rationale of systematic change in contrast to change by evolution and revolution;
c. Evaluate the styles of leadership and techniques of participation most likely to produce high-quality results.

Development of the manager's leadership skills through grid programme involves two parts and six overlapping phases, as shown in Fig. 8.5.

Fig. 8.5 Grid training

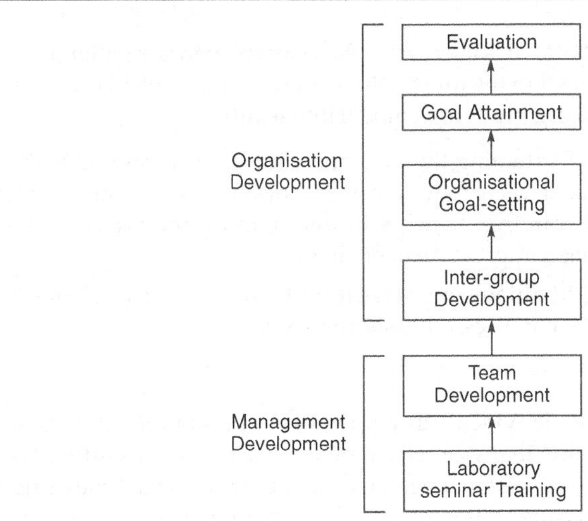

Part I Management Development

Phase 1 Laboratory-seminar Training First of all, grid concepts are introduced to the managers. At the outset of a grid seminar programme, each participant's leadership style is assessed, evaluated, and reviewed. The essence of this stage is that the managers are educated about the desirability of 9,9 style of the leadership.

Phase 2 Team Development Leaders learn here how to effectively function in group situations. They get familiar with such concepts as team work, team culture, team traditions, and the like. Managers learn how to foster team spirit.

An important objective of these two phases is to build more effective relationships among groups, co-workers, and between superiors and subordinates.

Part II Organisation Development

Phase 3 Inter-group Development The first two phases of grid training concentrates on individuals and single work groups. The next four phases throw light on the overall organisation. An important objective of the third phase is joint problem-solving. During this phase, the emphasis shifts to inter-group behavioural relations. Sources of inter-group conflict are carefully analysed, and ways of fostering co-operation are considered here.

Phase 4 Organisational Goal-setting During this phase, managers discuss and agree upon an ideal model for their organisation. Development of this blueprint involves developing convictions about ideal management practices, description of its major goals, structure and reward systems, and decision-making procedures.

Phase 5 Goal Attainment It is the crucial phase where managers attempt to accomplish the goals as set in the fourth phase. Participants seek to translate their thoughts about an organisational model into reality.

Phase 6 Evaluation Evaluating the pros and cons of grid training is the final fundamental phase. The current state of organisation is compared with its state prior to grid training. It helps in determining the areas of the organisation that still need improvement or alteration.

These six phases of grid training may take three to five years to implement, but in some cases, can be compressed to shorter spans.

Conclusion

Blake and Mouton cite some evidence in support of this programme and assert that the grid training aids many organisational participants in shifting towards the prescribed 9,9 style of management. However, in recent times, grid training is under fire because it is contrary to the contingency management theory. A frequent criticism of grid is that by espousing 9,9 orientation, this approach discounts the realities of contingency management. According to Hersey and Blanchard, even 1,1 style may be effective when employees are characterised by a high degree of maturity. In spite of these limitations, grid is a major contributor to OD and is probably a very effective and efficient tool for organisational change.

8.3.5 Process Consultation

Social psychologist Edgar Schein emphasised the role of a consultant in efficiently designing the methods to solve the problems faced by modern organisations. He defined the technique of process consultation as "the set of activities on the part of the consultant which help the client to perceive, understand, and act upon the process events which occur in the client's environment".

The assumptions underlying Schein's process consultation model are as follows.

a. Managers often need special diagnostic help in knowing what is wrong with the organisation.
b. Most managers have a constant desire to increase organisational effectiveness, but they need help in deciding "how" to achieve it.
c. Managers can be effective if they learn to diagnose their own strengths and weaknesses without an exhaustive and time-consuming study of the organisation.
d. The outside consultant cannot learn enough about the culture of the organisation to suggest reliable new courses of action. He should, therefore, work jointly with the members of the organisation.
e. The client must learn to see the problem for himself, understand the problem, and suggest a remedy. The consultant should provide new and challenging alternatives for the client to consider. However, the decision-making authority on these alternatives about organisational changes remains with the client.
f. It is essential that the process consultant is an expert in diagnosing and establishing effective helping relationship with the client. Effective process consultation involves passing those skills on to the client.

Steps in Process Consultation

According to Schein, process consultation normally proceeds along the following lines (Fig. 8.6).

a. *Initial contact* Here the client comes into contact with the consultant and specifies the problem that cannot be solved by normal organisational procedures or resources.
b. *Define the relationship* After identifying specific problem areas, the consultant and the client enter into a formal contract. The contract spells out the services, time, and fees of the consultant.
c. *Select the method of work* It involves a clear-cut understanding of where and how the consultant will perform the job. Each individual employee in the organisation is made aware.
d. *Collection of data and diagnosis* The consultant invests a great deal of time in collecting the relevant information.

Fig. 8.6 Step in process consultation

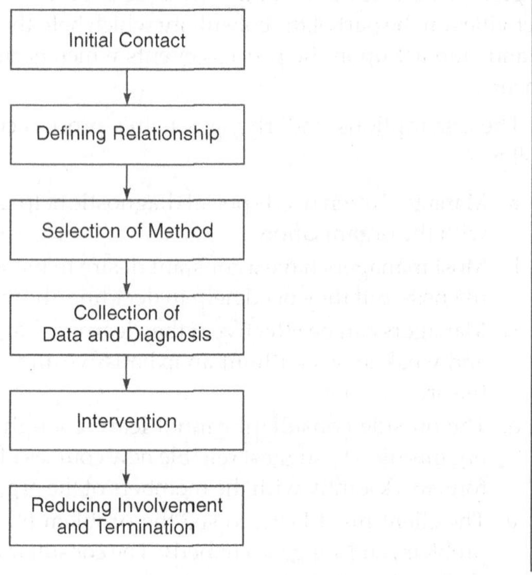

e. ***Intervention*** Various interventions by the consultant such as agenda setting, feedback, coaching, and structural suggestions are made in the process consultation approach.

f. ***Reducing involvement and termination*** When the goals of OD intervention have been successfully achieved, the consultant leaves the organisation by closing the formal contract with the client.

Features

Process consultation is designed to change attitudes, values, interpersonal skills, group norms and cohesiveness, and other process variables. Evidence shows that it is often effective in facilitating these changes. The professional consultant assists the organisational members in facing problems squarely and resolves the conflicts in a dispassionate way. However, the success of this technique depends, to a large extent, on the diagnostic skills of the consultant. If the consultant is lacking in the requisite experience and skills, the whole exercise may be self-defeating. Again, it is always not possible to ascertain how effectively the consultant works.

8.3.6 Management by Objectives (MBO)

Management by objectives emphasises participatively set goals that are tangible, verifiable, and measurable. It is not a new idea. In fact, Peter Drucker originally proposed it more than 40 years ago as a means of using goals to motivate people rather than to control them. Today, no introduction to basic management concepts would be complete without a discussion of MBO.

Goal specificity, participative decision-making, an explicit time period, and performance feedback make up the core of MBO.

As an OD technique it involves the following steps (Fig. 8.7).

a. People who are involved in the programme must be educated about the basic principles and procedures of MBO.
b. Employees and managers meet formally and agree upon clear-cut and quantifiable objectives.
c. Progress towards the chosen objectives is reviewed after some internal feedback is provided to employees.
d. An overall evaluation is made to assess the current progress for the next cycle of objective-setting and planning.

MBO is a comprchensive, overall managerial philosophy, the main emphasis being joint goals-setting. It tries to co-ordinate the efforts of individual employees with the organisational goals.

Strengths

Benefits for the Enterprise

a. Focuses the managers' efforts on the right objectives.
b. Improves the potential for achieving objectives such as profits, productivity, and satisfaction.
c. Provides the necessary data to reward managers "objectively."
d. Helps in pinpointing human development needs.

Fig. 8.7 Circular process of management by objectives

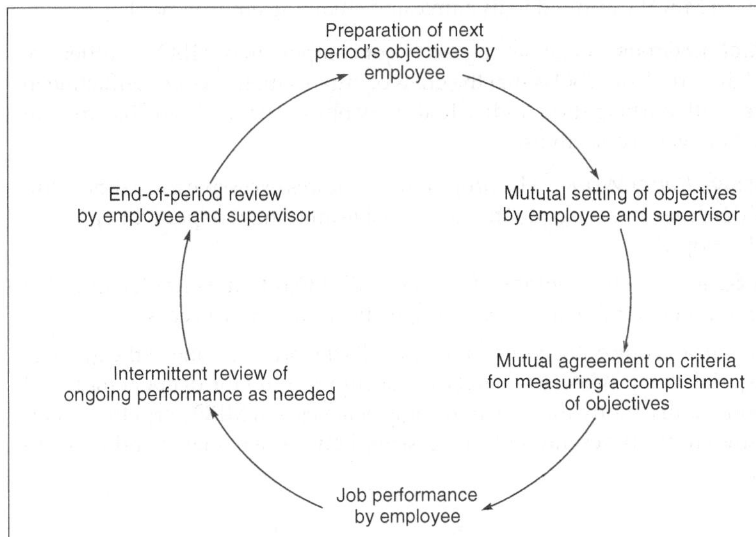

e. Assists in identifying managers who can be promoted.
f. Facilitates the enterprise's ability to change.
g. Helps in co-ordination of the efforts of the enterprise.

Benefits for Superiors

a. Helps in coaching subordinates.
b. Helps in eliminating vague and rigid performance appraisal tools.
c. Effectively motivates the subordinates to perform better.

Benefits for Employees and Lower-level Managers

a. It lets individuals know what is expected of them.
b. It makes individuals more aware of the organisation's goals.
c. It increases employee job satisfaction.
d. It also lets subordinates know how well they are doing in relation to the organisation's goals.
e. Provides measurable objectives that the employee is expected to achieve.

MBO thus has many advantages to offer to the individual employees, superiors, and also for top management. Since all levels of organisation are involved in goal-setting, the entire organisation will have the feeling of "unity."

Weaknesses

Some Questions

i. Is joint goal-setting among unequals really possible?
ii. Can MBO be applied at lower levels in an organisation?
iii. Does MBO aid in evaluating and rewarding the performance of the employees?
iv. Is setting objectives as explicitly as possible always functional?
v. Can MBO be applied to dynamic and changing environments?

Conflicting Goals Goal-setting is a major component of MBO. Another potential drawback of MBO is that the goals of organisation may be conflicting in nature. With participation, individuals may optimise their own objectives at the cost of overall objectives.

Excessive Paper Work The programme requires excessive formality in filling of documents. Consequently, an excessive amount of paper work and red tape develops.

Long Span Another notable drawback of MBO is that its implementation requires a considerably long span ranging from two to five years.

H. Levinson, one of the famous critics, calls the process "one of the greatest managerial illusions because it fails to take into account the deeper emotional components of a motivation". He strongly believes that MBO perpetuates and intensifies hostility, resentment, and distrust between a manager and subordinates.

Empirical Assessment

MBO is associated with improved planning and organisation of work. That MBO improved planning and utilisation of resources and interpersonal communication. He, however, contends that goal achievement is improved only when managers and superior are strongly pro-MBO.

Making MBO Effective

MBO programmes can be effective if properly implemented. Proper implementation of MBO can be done by removing the problems encountered in the use of it as a technique of OD. The following are the common problems the organisation encounters in implementing the MBO comprehensive programme (Fig. 8.8).

a. ***Inadequate top management support*** MBO is unlikely to work effectively without the participation and strong support of top management at the beginning and also during its implementation.

b. ***Inadequate explanation of MBO*** Organisations generally start off on the wrong foot and assume that employees have a thorough knowledge of MBO. Under this assumption they provide only short and cursory explanation. Probably this is the most important reason for the failure of MBO.

c. ***Poorly defined objectives*** MBO works only when the objectives are defined in clear-cut terms and these are jointly agreed upon.

d. ***Personality conflict*** Sometimes personality conflicts between superiors and subordinates create difficulties in setting up of an MBO programme.

e. ***Insincere commitment by managers*** In order to make an MBO programme successful, moderate leadership style is called for.

f. ***Inadequate reinforcement of MBO*** It is essential for the success of MBO that progress meetings are held and feedback is taken often after the programme is launched.

In spite of many problems associated with its implementation, MBO cannot be thrown out of the managerial tool kit. One simple but attractive reason to favour MBO is that it is self-correcting in nature. Since it states quantifiable

Fig. 8.8 Problems in implementation of MBO

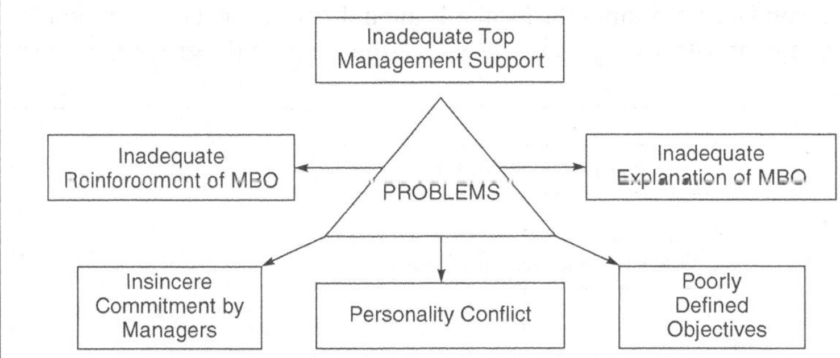

goals and insists on periodic assessment of progress towards them, it is a continuous process, making room for adjustment and feedback. Another important positive force in support of MBO is that it eventually leads to closer co-operation between employees and management.

8.3.7 Role Analysis Technique (RAT)

The role analysis technique intervention is designed to clarify role expectations and obligations of team members to improve team effectiveness. In an organisation, individuals fill different specialised roles in which they manifest certain behaviours. This division of labour and function facilitates organisational performance. Often, however, the role incumbent may not have a clear idea of the behaviour expected of him by others and, equally often, what others can do to help the incumbent fulfill the role is not understood. Iswar Dayal and John M. Thomas developed a technique for clarifying the roles of top management of a new organisation in India. This technique is particularly applicable for new teams, but it may also be helpful in established teams where role ambiguity or confusion exists. The intervention is predicated on the belief that consensual determination of role requirements for team members, consisting of a joint building of the requirements by all concerned, leads to a more mutually satisfactory and productive behaviour. Dayal and Thomas call the activity the role analysis technique.

In a structured series of steps, role incumbents, in conjunction with team members, define and delineate role requirements. The role being defined is called the focal role. In a new organisation, it may be desirable to conduct a role analysis for each of the major roles.

The first step, as shown in Fig. 8.9, consists of an analysis of the focal role initiated by the focal role individual. The role, its place in the organisation, the rationale for its existence, and its place in achieving overall organisation goals are examined along with the specific duties of the office. The specific duties and behaviours are listed on a chalkboard and are discussed by the entire team. Behaviours are added and deleted until the group and the role incumbent are satisfied that they have defined the role completely.

The second step examines the focal role incumbent's expectations of others. The incumbent lists his expectations of the other roles in the group that most

Fig. 8.9 Role analysis technique

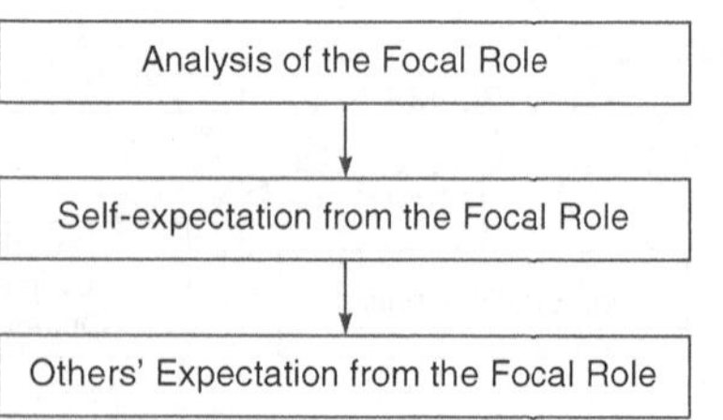

affect the incumbent's own role performance and these expectations are discussed, modified, added to, and agreed upon by the entire group.

The third step consists of explicating others' expectations and desired behaviours of the focal role, that is, the members of the group describe what they want from and expect from the incumbent in the focal role. These expectations of others are discussed, modified, and agreed upon by the group and the focal role person.

Upon conclusion of this step, the focal role person assumes responsibility for making a written summary of the role as it has been defined; this is called a role profile and is derived from the results of the discussions in steps 1 through 3. Dayal and Thomas describe the role profile thus. "This consists of (a) a set of activities classified as to the prescribed and discretionary elements of the role, (b) the obligation of the role to each role in its set, and (c) the expectations of this role from others in its set. Viewed in total, this provides a comprehensive understanding of each individual's 'role space.'"

The written role profile is briefly reviewed at the following meeting before another focal role is analysed. The accepted role profile constitutes the role activities for the focal role person.

This intervention can be a non-threatening activity with high payoff. Often the mutual demands, expectations, and obligations of interdependent team members have never been publicly examined. Each role incumbent wonders why "those other people" are "not doing what they are supposed to do." While in reality all the incumbents are performing as they think they are supposed to. Collaborative role analysis and definition by the entire work group not only clarifies who is to do what but ensures commitment to the role once it has been clarified.

From our experience, this procedure can be shortened if there is already high visibility and understanding of the current activities of various role incumbents. For example, if one of the problems facing an organisation is confusion over the duties of the board of directors, president, or executive director, the following sequence can be highly productive. This occurred in a workshop setting involving the board, the president, and the key subordinates in a team-building session.

a. With the board listening, the president and his staff members discuss the question: "If the board were operating in an optimally effective way, what would they be doing?"
b. During this discussion, responses are made visible on a chalkboard or on large newsprint, and disagreements are recorded.
c. After 45 minutes or so, the list is modified on the basis of general consensus of the total group.
d. The procedure is repeated, but this time the president listens while the staff and board members discuss the question, "If the president were operating in an optimally effective way, what would he be doing?" Again, responses are made visible during the discussion. The president responds, and then there is an attempt at consensus.

As with the longer technique, this procedure helps to clarify role expectations and obligations and frequently leads to some significant shifts in the whole network of activities of the management group, including the board. For example, we have seen this procedure result in boards shifting their activities almost exclusively to policy determination, pulling away from previously dysfunctional tinkering with day-to-day operating problems, and delegating operations to the president and the staff.

8.3.8 Role Negotiation Technique

When the causes of team ineffectiveness are based on people's behaviours that they are unwilling to change because it would mean a loss of power or influence to the individual, a technique developed by Roger Harrison called "role negotiation" can often be used to great advantage.

Role negotiation intervenes directly in the relationships of power, authority, and influence within the group. The change effort is directed at work relationships among members. It avoids probing into the likes and dislikes of members for one another and their personal feelings about one another.

The technique is basically an imposed structure for controlled negotiations between parties in which each party agrees in writing to change certain behaviour in return for changes in behaviour by the other. The behaviour relates to the job. Specifically, I ask you to change some of your behaviour so that I can do my job more effectively; and you ask me to change some of my behaviour so that you can do your job more effecitvely. Harrison states that the technique rests on one basic assumption: "Most people prefer a fail negotiated settlement to a state of unresolved conflict, and they are willing to invest some time and make some concessions in order to achieve a solution."

The role negotiation technique usually takes at least one day to conduct. A two-day session with a follow-up meeting a month later is best. The steps of the technique as given by Harrison are as follows (Fig. 8.10). The first step is contract setting. Here the consultant sets the climate and establishes the ground rules: we are looking at work behaviours, not feelings about people; be specific in stating what you want others to do more or do better, to do less of or

Fig. 8.10 Steps in role negotiation technique

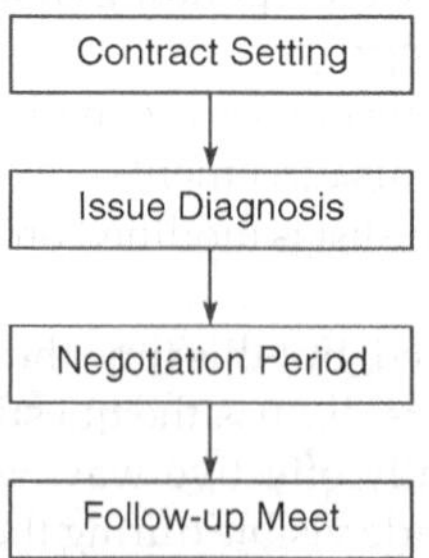

stop doing, or maintain unchanged; all expectations and demands must be written; no one is to agree to changing any behaviour unless there is a quid pro quo in which the other must agree to a change also; the session will consist of individuals negotiating with each other to arrive at a written contract of what behaviours each will change.

The next step is to issue diagnosis. Individuals think about how their own effectiveness can be improved if others change their work behaviours. Then each person fills out an issue diagnosis form for every other person in the group. On this form the individual states what he would like the other to do more of, do less of, or maintain unchanged. These messages are then exchanged among all members, and the messages received by each person are written on a chalkboard or newsprint for all to see.

The next step is the influence trade or negotiation period, in which two individuals discuss the most important behaviour changes they want from each other and the changes they are willing to make themselves. A quid pro quo is required in this step: each person must give something in order to get something. Often this step is demonstrated by two individuals with the rest of the group watching. Then the group breaks into negotiating pairs. "The negotiation process consists of parties making contingent offers to one another such as 'If you do X, I will do Y.' The negotiation ends when all parties are satisfied that they will receive a reasonable return for whatever they are agreeing to give." All agreements are written, with each party having a copy. The agreement may be published for the group to see or may not. The influence trade step is concluded when all the negotiated agreements have been made and written down. It is best to have a follow-up meeting to determine whether the contracts have been honoured and to assess the effects of the contracts on effectiveness.

Harrison's role negotiation technique is an effective way of bringing about positive improvement in a situation where power and influence issues are working to maintain an unsatisfactory status quo. We have used this technique successfully with several groups and have found that it is an intervention that leads to improved team functioning. It is based on the fact that frequently individuals must change their work behaviours for the team to become more effective.

8.3.9 Force-field Analysis

The oldest intervention in the OD practitioner's tool kit is the force-field analysis, a device for understanding a problematic situation and planning corrective actions. This technique rests on several assumptions: the present state of things (the current condition) is a quasi-stationary equilibrium representing a resultant in a field of opposing forces. A desired future state of affairs (the desired condition) can only be achieved by dislodging the current equilibrium, moving it to the desired state, and stabilising the equilibrium at that point. To move the equilibrium level from the current to the desired condition, the field of forces must be altered—by adding driving forces or by removing restraining forces.

This technique was first proposed by Kurt Lewin in 1947. It is essentially a vector analysis—an analytical tool learned in first-year engineering classes. But the genius of Lewin was to apply the device to social problems, social equilibria, and social change. Lewin proposed that social phenomena—productivity of a factory, morale of a sports team, level of prejudice in a community, and so forth—could best be understood as processes being influenced by social forces and events. Furthermore, social phenomena tend to stabilise at equilibrium points because opposing forces come into balance over time.

Force-field analysis involves the following steps (Fig. 8.11).

Step 1 Decide upon a problematic situation you are interested in improving, and carefully and completely describe the current condition. What is the status quo? What are the current conditions? Why do you want them changed?

Step 2 Carefully and completely describe the desired condition. Where do you want to be? What is the desired state of things?

Step 3 Identify the forces and factors operating in the current force field. Identify the driving forces pushing in the direction of the desired condition; identify the restraining forces pushing away from the desired condition. Identification and specification of the force-field should be thorough and exhaustive so that a picture of why things are as they are becomes clear.

Fig. 8.11 Steps in force field analysis

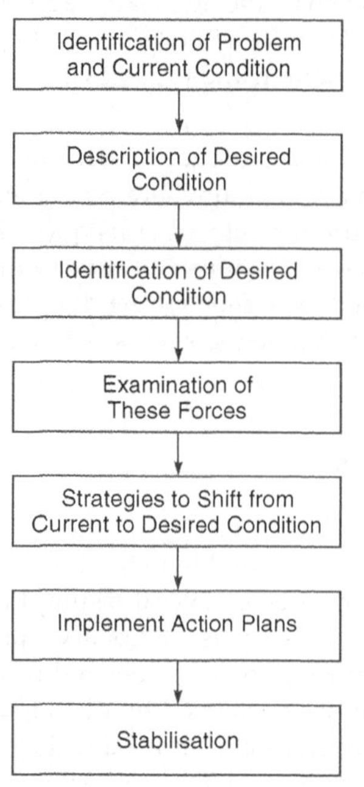

Step 4 Examine the forces. Which ones are strong, which are weak? Which forces are susceptible to influence, which are not? Which forces are under your control, which are not?

Step 5 Strategies for moving the equilibrium from the current condition to the desired condition are the following: add more driving forces; remove restraining forces; or do both. Lewin advises against simply adding new driving forces because that may increase resistance and tension in the situation. Therefore, at this step, select several important, adaptable restraining forces and develop action plans to remove them from the field of forces. As restraining forces are removed, the equilibrium shifts towards the desired condition. New driving forces may also be proposed and action plans developed to implement them.

Step 6 Implement the action plans. This should cause the desired condition to be realised.

Step 7 Describe what actions must be taken to stabilise the equilibrium at the desired condition and implement those actions.

This technique is excellent for diagnosing change situations. We label it as team intervention (although it is also a tool for individuals) because it can be powerful and exciting when used by groups. Group analysis typically yields a comprehensive understanding of what is happening to cause the problem and what must be done to correct it.

Force-field analysis is an old and valued friend of the OD practitioner.

8.4 PREREQUISITES FOR EFFECTIVE USE OF OD

Successful organisation development tends to be a total effort. It is not a programme with a temporary quality; it is rather aimed at developing the organisation's internal resources for effective change.

a. Support for OD programme should begin with top management OD is a system-wide concept requiring at least psychological involvement of all the parts of the system in the organisation. While all support for the programme is essential, this support should begin with top management. For the success of the programme, the support of individual members is also essential.

b. Organisation must communicate the objectives of programme clearly The objectives of the programme must be made crystal-clear to all the participants and organisational members before the programme is launched. If the organisation cannot communicate the objectives effectively then it is quite likely that the programme may be doomed to fail.

c. Enough time must be allowed so that the effects of an OD programme are realised Things in an organisation are not expected to change drastically over a brief period of time. Managers who introduce intervention to change

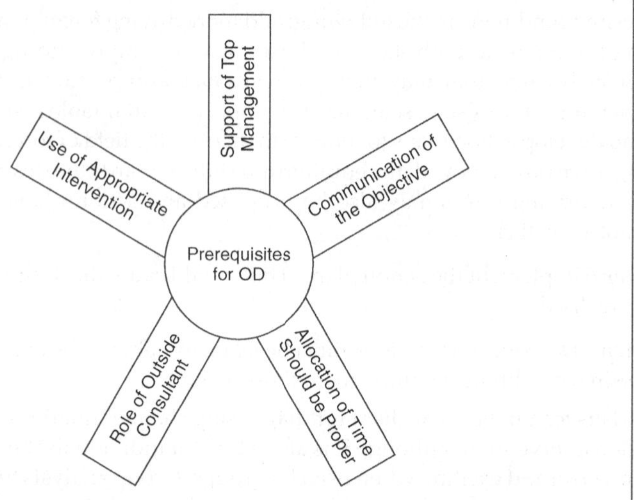

Fig. 8.12 Prerequistes for effective use of OD

will be invariably disappointed if they expect quick results of OD programmes. It is because OD aims at changing the conditioned behaviour of members, which is a rather difficult and time-consuming affair.

d. The role of outside consultant must be understood A consultant is an OD practitioner, often labelled as "interventionist", "change agent", or "process consultant." The OD consultant possesses the necessary behavioural knowledge, technical problem-solving abilities and clinical skills. He also possesses the personality and interpersonal skill competence to use himself as an instrument of change. But his role in the organisation must be properly understood to ensure the success of the OD programme. From the organisation's point of view, if the consultant's orientation is towards the problem-solving process and development of problem-skills of the employees, it is beneficial to the organisation.

e. Use the appropriate intervention For the success of an OD programme, use of appropriate intervention is essential. If the intervention is inappropriate, it will have undesirable consequences.

8.4.1 Criticism

OD, just like any new programme, suffers from lack of research and documentation, and far more heat than light. But it is a source of inspiration for whose who feel the need for a human-based approach to organisational change. But OD programmes have been subject to criticism by managers and researchers.

People are of the view that diagnostic interventions stir up discontent in organisations. Of all, the most frequently observed citicisms are the following (Fig. 8.13).

a. Discrepancy between the ideal and real As an ideal, OD programmes should begin at the top of the organisation. But in practice, OD efforts are often conducted many levels down in the organisation.

Further OD programmes often fail to recognise the organisational pressures and realities managers face in their jobs. Many managers struggle to achieve and maintain "bottom-line" performance and for them OD programmes may seem far removed from reality.

b. OD makes people unite for the real organisational world After attending OD workshops, many participants convert to such values as openness, trust, sharing of power, and so on, that are taught by OD practitioners. By exhibiting these features, however, the members are often punished rather than rewarded in the organisation.

c. OD makes the dichotomy between the "task" and "attitude" apparent Another major shortcoming of OD is the apparent dichotomy between "the task technique" and the "attitude" only adherents. The former is a sophisticated cost-cutting method of scientific management school whereas the latter is concerned primarily with developing positive and open interpersonal attitudes—which are difficult to measure.

d. OD is criticised because of the paucity of research about its effectiveness It is difficult to evaluate OD as it is still in its infancy. Further, it is difficult to measure the number, nature, and magnitude of confounding variables.

Fig. 8.13 Frequently observed negative points of OD

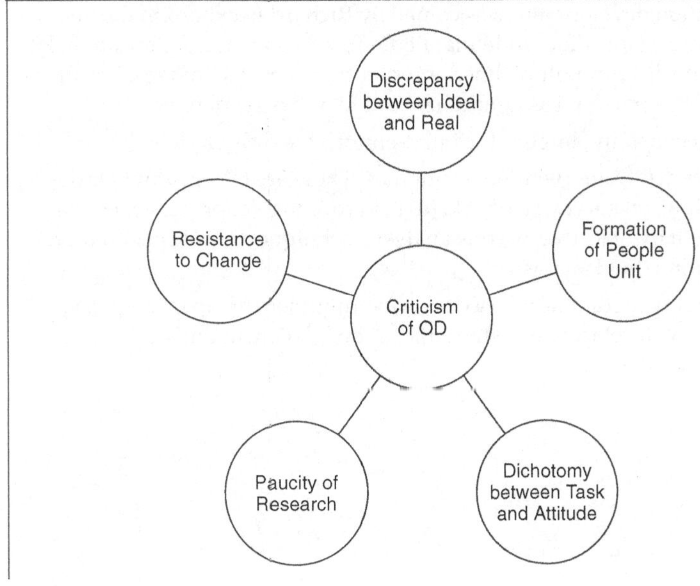

e. Resistance to change is a chronic problem to attain goals of OD The deep-seated resistance to change represents a serious obstacle to OD. According to Burrack and Smith "resistance at the top and firmly embedded at the middle of management." They observe that anti-planning attitudes, collective barganning to preserve outmoded jobs and technology in favour of technological changes more than social changes are the factors that the contribute to such resistance.

8.4.2 Conclusion

Organisation development offers some very attractive methodologies and philosophies to practising managers and academicians alike. OD has its devotees, its fanatical adherents, and also its detractors.

"If OD is to become a respectable applied profession, greater attention must be given to the integration of the theory and practice. Despite a few efforts, there has been no tradition of adding knowledge cumulatively or keeping a balanced perspective on change strategies, little interest has been shown in long-term profits to evaluate the development of organisation's overtime and searching questions have been raised about how to train competent practitioners."

SUMMARY

- OD is a systematic approach for the successful and sustainable management of change in the organisation.
- The term organisation development was coined by Richard Beckhard in the mid-1950s. An OD is an organisation-wide planned effort to increase organisational effectiveness and health through planned interventions and techniques. For the success of OD, its objectives and assumptions have to be clearly defined.
- On the basis of objectives and targets, the interventions are duly classified.
- There are a number of OD intervention techniques. These are (a) sensitivity training, (b) team building, (c) survey feedback, (d) grid training, (e) process consultation, (f) management by objective, (g) role analysis technique, (h) role negotiation technique, and (i) force-field analysis.
- The success of the OD programme is based on (a) commitment of top management, (b) communication of the objective, (c) time allocation, (d) consultant's ability, and (e) method of intervention.

 Case Study: An Electronic Imaging Technology Company

History

A company, a leader in the field of electronic imaging technology, had grown very rapidly. Then, with the downturn in high technology, the company had had to cut back on its workforce and reorganise some of its departments. Issues of "silo" mentalities and lack of co-ordination between departments were exacerbated by the need to do more with less people, and communication tensions at the employee as well as the manager level had reached a crisis point.

Task

Through an OD strategic partner, design and carry out a pilot intervention with two of the departments to address the co-ordination and communication issues and establish better protocols and attitudes towards working together as part of a team effort.

Intervention

To determine what the specific issues were, OD practice administered a questionnaire to all the employees of the two departments. The department heads were interviewed individually, and group interviews were held with the employees. OD then developed and facilitated a one-day off-site retreat process for the two departments, which involved developing a teamwork vision, practical teamwork exercises, focused work on defining and prioritising issues, brainstorming solutions, and commitment to a plan of action.

Result

An enthusiastic response from the participants in the retreat, leading to a reduction in communication tensions and a commitment to implementing the plan of action for improved co-ordination between the departments. The retreat's accomplishments were also brought to the company's executive team, which committed to implementing the action plan in the rest of the company as well.

Key Disciplines

Team Building, Organisational Development, Retreat Facilitation, Process Improvement.

Review Questions

1. Explain the concept of organisation development and how it is related to effective management of change.
2. What are OD interventions? Define and classify them.
3. Write a brief note on each of the following.
   (a) Sensitivity training
   (b) Grid training
   (c) Process consultation
   (d) Role analysis technique
4. Illustrate the management by objectives as a major OD intervention.

5. What are the reasons behind the success and failure of OD programmes?
6. On what basis does management decide which OD intervention technique is best suited for their organisation?

EXERCISE 1

Newspaper construction exercises are always reliable, flexible, and inexpensive activities for organisational development-oriented activities, ideas to cascade, or spread usage through organisations or departments.

Make teams and then split each team into two. The team task is for each half-team of three (or two) to build their half of a newspaper bridge so that it connects and can be joined to the other half of their team's construction, to meet in the middle between two tables.

Preferably (this is at the facilitator's discretion) sticky tape must not be used to fix each end of the bridge to the table, that is, bridges must be self-supporting. The winning team can be the quickest or one that builds the strongest supporting structure. The facilitator can add the requirement for the bridge to support an object, a lemon, or a chocolate bar, for example.

The secret is to build up and out so that each side of the bridge supports the other. Two horizontal halves generally collapse unless each is extremely strong. Tightly rolled struts make stronger constructions. Establish game rules that prevent both halves of the teams simply making a single bridge fixed to each table with sticky tape, which would defeat the challenge of the exercise. Control the level of difficulty of the game by the distance between the tables and the number of sheets issued.

EXERCISE 2

The task is to build a dome or roof structure/frame and cover it with newspaper and sticky tape, between as many tables as there are pairs/three somes. The whole group must be divided into pairs or threes. This is not a contest between the teams; it is a task for the whole group to co-operate and work together. For example, for a group size of 12, there could be six tables and six pairs, or for a group size of 15 five tables and five teams of three, each pair/threesome building one strut of a six- or five-strut dome frame. For a group of nine people, there could be three teams of three, and three tables, each team building a strut for a three-strut roof frame.

Each pair/threesome some should build their strut up and out from the table, connecting in the centre space with the struts from each of the other pairs/threesome. Struts can be fixed to the tables and joined in the centre space with sticky tape. For large frames (which will be required if the tables are placed far from each other), cross-struts can be used. The whole group can then cover the dome or roof frame with sheets of newspaper.

This activity requires a lot of thought, team-working, communication, sharing, best practice, assessment and feedback along the way, and leadership at key decision stages. The level of difficulty can be controlled by the distance between the tables and the number of newspaper sheets issued.

Chapter

Manager as Catalyst of Change

Chapter Outline

- Introduction: Role of a Manager
- Developmental Supervision
- Responsibilities of a Manager
- Motivation as the Soul of a Manager
- Manager as Motivator of Employees
- Using Power and Empowering Employees
- Managerial Control
- Coping Behaviour of a Manager
- Consultant Support during Change
- Manager and Group Dynamics
- Obstacles in the Middle of Change and How to Overcome Them
- Classic Skills for an Effective Change Manager
- Summary
- Case Study
- Review Questions
- Exercises

> "Six essential qualities that are the key to success: sincerity, personal integrity, humility, courtesy, wisdom, charity."
>
> — William Manninger

9.1 INTRODUCTION: ROLE OF A MANAGER

Managers have an important role to play in ensuring the realisation of organisation-wide change objectives. While top management should make available the resources required for investment on human resources and different departments must provide instruments and systems that can be used by the organisation to develop its human resources for change and its effectiveness, it is ultimately the managers who translate these into action.

To understand the role to be played by the managers in developing human resources during change, it is necessary to understand the concept of change and the conditions under which development takes place.

Development through change can be defined as the acquiring of new competencies. Such competencies may help in performing the existing tasks better or faster, or in performing new tasks. These competencies include cognitive abilities (acquisition of new information, new concepts, ideas, and so on), attitudes and orientations, values and skills. These may deal with managerial functions (co-ordination, planning, projecting, or technical areas, (designing a machine, servicing a product, and so on) or behavioural aspects (leading a group, building a team, motivating, and so on).

Development through a cognitive change of employees would require certain conditions.

a. The employee should perceive that acquiring new competencies help can him in fulfilling his psychological needs.
b. The employee should perceive opportunities for acquiring such capabilities.
c. The employee should be aware of the capabilities he needs to develop.
d. The employee should have mechanisms of assessing his own rate of growth in relation to such capabilities.
e. The employee should enjoy the process of growth itself.

A manager plays an important role in creating these conditions for his employees.

9.2 DEVELOPMENTAL SUPERVISION

Supervision is the basic managerial function during the change process. It is the process of facilitating and monitoring individual and team efforts to achieve organisational goals, and facilitating the growth of individuals and the team. This function has evolved over several periods of development of the service and practice of effective change management.

The traditional concept of supervision was to ensure that the tasks were done as planned by the supervisor, by the employees working under him. The concept of developmental supervision is radically different from the traditional one. The following four major factors define the concept of developmental supervision (Fig. 9.1).

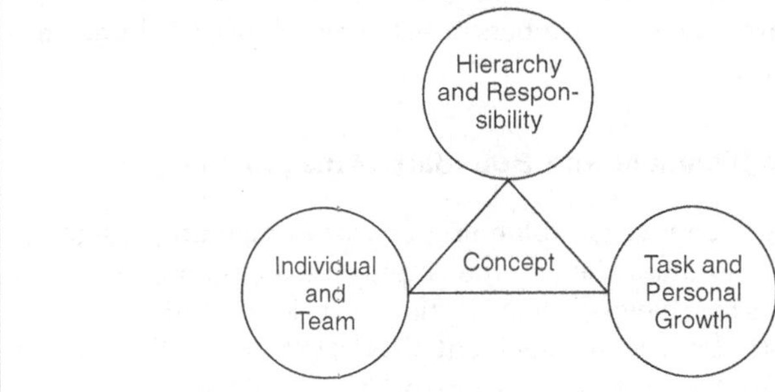

Fig. 9.1 Concept of developmental supervision

9.2.1 Hierarchy and Responsibility

The traditional concept and practice of supervision is based on the belief that the sense of responsibility increases with the increase in hierarchical level. The main role of the supervisor is to carefully plan, guide, and monitor the execution of the plan by his employees. The supervision has to be close and detailed, and very little freedom needs to be given to the operating employees.

Developmental supervision does not believe in this. It is based on the belief that although the level of responsibility may and does increase with the increase of managerial level (with the higher level competencies involved), the sense of responsibility is well spread out amongst all the levels of the organisational hierarchy.

In other words, workers are as much liable and responsible for change as are the managers. Consequently, the role of the supervisor is to develop this sense, and utilise it for the facilitation of change.

9.2.2 Task and Personal Growth

Traditional supervision makes a distinction between organisational tasks and development of employees and teams. The main focus of supervision is the achievement of the organisational tasks.

A developmental supervisor, in fact, integrates both. The accomplishment of organisational task is achieved by helping the concerned employees to develop needed task-related competencies and capability to face problems effectively.

9.2.3 Individual and Team

Traditional supervision is primarily concerned with individual employees. Since accountability is individual, the traditional supervisor's focus is the individual employee. Developmental supervision treats them as distinct units needing separate attention. Good individual performance may not ensure effective teamwork. A team has its own dynamics. A developmental supervisor pays attention to both, in fact, more attention to the team, because he believes that an effective team can help its members raise their levels of contribution for effectiveness of change.

9.2.4 Task Accomplishment and Boundary Management

A traditional manager emphasises planning of work (including assigning definite targets) to be accomplished by the employees, and giving them the necessary instructions to achieve the fixed goals. A developmental supervisor sees his main task as boundary management, that is, to facilitate the work of his employees, procure needed resources for working on the task, and remove difficulties which are likely to slow down the pace of the change process.

9.3 RESPONSIBILITIES OF A MANAGER

For the effective management of change within the organisation, a manager is required to perform certain activities, which are directly related to the process of change. They are as follows.

9.3.1 Managers and Appraisal System

The responsibilities of managers in relation to performance appraisal can be viewed under two roles: as appraisers and as appraisees.

As appraisers, managers have the following responsibilities.

a. Identify and clarify key performance areas of each employee.

b. Help the employees set challenging goals.
c. Identify support needed by employees and make the same available.
d. Help the employees experience success.
e. Help the employees recognise their strengths and weaknesses through periodic feedback.
f. Have regular appraisal and performance counselling discussions.
g. Understand the difficulties experienced by each employee in performing his functions and provide necessary support.
h. Generate a climate of mutuality, openness, and trust to encourage identification and use of competencies by the employees.
i. Conduct timely appraisals.
j. Invest time on performance appraisal and review discussion.

As appraisees, managers have the following responsibilities.

a. Set challenging goals for oneself.
b. Reflect periodically about one's strengths, weaknesses, and performance.
c. Identify problems hindering performance and communicate them to the supervisor.
d. Prepare for performance-review sessions.

This will help in identifying the key area for change.

9.3.2 Managers and Career Planning

Every employee would like to grow and build a career in his organisation or profession. Such growth is likely to be faster if it is purposeful and guided. More experienced and senior managers are in a better position to guide their juniors due to the larger perspectives and better understanding they have about the organisation as well as the outside world. Managers can lead their juniors by accomplishing the following.

a. Identify career opportunities in the organisation for each employee and assess competencies required for them.
b. Help the employees assess their own capabilities in relation to the possible career paths available for them.
c. Provide feedback to employees about their potential.
d. Encourage them to develop their potential.
e. Provide opportunities to employees to develop new competencies.
f. Help those who have reached a saturation level in the organisation and those who do not have any further career opportunities to become aware of their limitations and accept reality without any sense of inferiority and plan the future.
g. Motivate employees by helping them to recognise that their own contributions and performance facilitate change in the organisation and their growth.

The mentoring, responsibilities of managers are as follows.

a. Analyse to understand whether the manager can function as a mentor or not.
b. Get acquainted with the critical attributes of a mentor.
c. Spend enough time with respective employees for mentoring.
d. Give feedback and suggestions on the functioning of the mentoring system to the HRD department so that they can review, and if necessary, redesign the mentoring system.

These will help employees understand and accept the need for change.

9.3.3 Managers and Training System

Training is the most direct way of helping an employee acquire new competencies during change. Here the responsibilities of the manager include the following:

a. Analyse each role under him and list the detailed functions to be performed by the role occupants, outlining the managerial, technical, and behavioural competencies required to perform the role.
b. Identify training needs of each employee working with him against these functions and communicate these to the HRD department.
c. Encourage employees (and provide them with opportunities) to take responsibility and initiative, and try new things and learn on the job.
d. Provide continuous on-the-job coaching, and help each employee to develop problem-solving skills.
e. Sponsor employees for training with the help of the HRD department.
f. Get feedback from subordinates returning from training about the competencies developed during training, and have discussions with them about opportunities for trying out what they have learnt, and provide opportunities for their application.
g. Institute mechanisms like group discussions, meetings, and so on to help the employees learn to work as a team.

Training helps employees in acquiring skills which are necessary for the incorporation of change in the organisational working.

9.3.4 Managers and Work System

Regarding the quality of work life, the main responsibility of the managers includes the following.

a. Invite change/HRD experts to design and introduce participatory systems like autonomous work groups in one's unit.
b. Provide necessary support by critically reviewing the importance and progress of experiments being conducted.

c. Redesign supervisory roles to make them more supportive and facilitative.
d. Work on productivity and quality to be undertaken mainly by managers.

Organisations can only provide the process which helps managers to design quality circles, groups, and so on and make them more effective. The work system acts as a motivator for the readiness to change.

9.3.5 Managers and Cultural System

The managers have the following responsibilities with respect to culture and climate.

a. Analyse, with the help of an expert, implications of various practices in the department for culture and climate.
b. Request management and respond to their efforts if they initiate.
c. Pay attention to transitional periods in an employee's career, for example, induction in the organisation, change of job, promotion, retirement, or leaving the organisation. Develop appropriate rituals for such transitional occasions.
d. Use results of surveys of culture and climate for finding alternative ways of improving them.

Regarding communication, attention needs to be given to formal communication system, written communication, communication technology, and communication processes in various groups. The responsibilities of managers are to be sensitive and pay attention to the effectiveness of communication in various groups like committees, task forces, project groups, and so on.

9.3.6 Managers and Self-renewal System

Self-renewal systems are primarily concerned with organisational development and organisational learning. OD is a planned effort, initiated by process specialist(s) to help an organisation develop its diagnosis skills, coping capabilities, linkage strategies in the form of temporary and semi-permanent systems, and a culture of mutuality. Managers have the following responsibilities in this direction.

a. Identify sub-systems that need to be strengthened through OD efforts and bring them to the notice of the HRD department or top management.
b. Respond to organisational diagnosis and surveys freely and frankly.
c. Participate actively in discussions arranged by process specialists.
d. Prepare realistic action plans if required in some OD interventions and implement them.

9.3.7 Managers and Organisational Learning

Managers have following responsibilities for helping the organisation acquire new skills.

a. Use small groups appropriately to work on analysing problems and alternatives.
b. Have frank and critical discussions with employees on the progress and results of projects.
c. Conduct quick evaluation or appraisal of projects in progress.
d. Provide necessary support needed for proper implementation.
e. Record the experiences and share them in writing with top managers as well in forums of discussion.
f. Invite outside experts or persons from other companies or departments to discuss their experiences in similar tasks.

9.3.8 Managers and Stress Management

As a result of changes in the operational environment, many employees feel frustrated and stressed. Managers can help manage employee stress in the following ways.

a. Provide budget expenses for stress audit. Invite the HRD department to survey stress levels.
b. Discuss feedback of stress surveys with employees for dealing with the relevant issues.
c. Institute formal programmes wherever possible to deal with stress.
d. Request the HRD department's help in stress management programmes.

9.3.9 Managers and Research

With respect to change-related research, managers can help in the following ways.

a. Quickly respond to questionnaires or surveys undertaken by HRD department.
b. Send feedback to the HRD department on its procedures and systems.
c. Review the working and problems of HRD programmes in the department.
d. Invite the HRD staff to deal with the problems in HRD aspects.

9.4 MOTIVATION AS THE SOUL OF A MANAGER

Organisational success is based on the competence of the manager. If the manager has the ability, skill, and attitude, he can perform any task given to him but to become an achiever or a role model for the rest of the organisation, he requires a sense of motivation.

The eventual objective of motivation is to make an employee effective. The effectiveness of an employee depends on his potential effectiveness as a person, his technical competence and experience, and his role in organisational design. It is the integration of the person and the role that ensures an employee's effectiveness in the organisation. If the role does not allow him to use his competence, and if he constantly feels frustrated in the role, his effectiveness is likely to be low. The integration of the person and the role comes only when the role is able to fulfil the needs of the individual, and when the individual is able to contribute to the evolution of the role.

The more we move from role, the more we move from role taking (responding to the expectations of various other persons) to role making (taking initiative in designing the role more creatively such that the various expectations from others as well as the role occupant are integrated), the more the role is likely to be effective. The effectiveness of a person in an organisation, therefore, may depend on his own potential effectiveness, the potential effectiveness of the role, and the organisational climate.

Potential effectiveness is known as efficacy. Personal efficacy would mean the potential effectiveness of a person in personal and interpersonal situations. Role efficacy would mean the potential effectiveness of an individual occupying a particular role in an organisation. Role efficacy can be seen as the psychological factor underlying role effectiveness. In short, role efficacy is the potential effectiveness of a role. It is the key to motivating organisational roles.

9.4.1 Aspects of Role Efficacy

Role efficacy has several aspects. The more these aspects are present in a role, the higher the efficacy of that role is likely to be. One dimension of role efficacy is called role making as against role taking. The first is an active attitude towards the role (to define and make the role to one's liking), whereas the second is a passive attitude (mainly responding to others' expectations). The aspects in the second dimension are concerned with increasing the power of the role, making it more important. This can be called role centring as against role entering (accepting the role as given, and reconciling oneself to its present importance or lack of it). The third dimension is called role linking (extending the relationship of the role with other roles and groups) against role shrinking (making the role narrow, confined to work-related expectations). Fig. 9.2 depicts these three dimensions.

Dimension 1 Role Making

Self-role Integration Every person has his strengths—his experience, his technical training, special skills, some unique contribution he may be able to make. The more a role provides an opportunity for the use of such special strengths, the higher its efficacy is likely to be. This is called self-role integration. All of us want our special strengths used in roles so that it may be

Fig. 9.2 Three dimensions of role efficacy (for motivation)

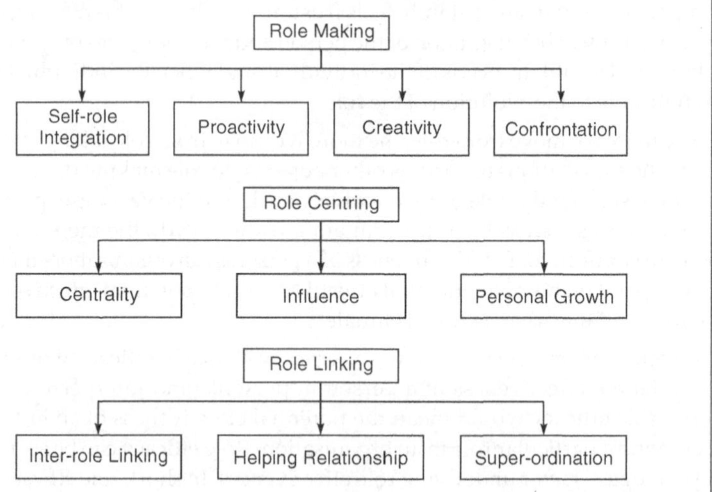

possible for us to demonstrate how effective we can be. As such, integration contributes to high role efficacy. On the other hand, if there is distance between the self and the role, efficacy is likely to be low.

Proactivity A person who occupies a role responds to the various expectations people in the organisation have from that role. This gives him satisfaction, and it also satisfies others in the organisation. However, if he also has to take the initiative in starting some activity, his efficacy will be higher. But if a person feels that he has no opportunity to take the initiative in the role he occupies in the organisation, his efficacy will be low.

Creativity It is not only initiative which is important for efficacy. An opportunity to try new and unconventional ways of solving problems or an opportunity to be creative is equally important. It increases their role efficacy and their performance improves. If a person perceives that he has to perform only routine tasks and there is no time or opportunity to be creative, his efficacy will be low.

Confrontation In general, if people in an organisation avoid problems, or pass them on to others to solve, their role efficacy will be low. A tendency to confront problems to find relevant solutions contributes to efficacy. When people facing interpersonal problems sit down, talk about these problems, and search for solutions, their efficacy is likely to be higher.

Dimension 2 Role Centring

Centrality Everyone in an organisation wants to feel that his role there is important. If a person feels that the role he plays is central to the organisation his role efficacy is likely to be high. If persons feel that their roles are peripheral, their potential effectiveness will be low.

Influence The more influence a person is able to exercise in the role, the higher his role efficacy is likely to be.

Personal Growth One factor which contributes effectively to role efficacy is the perception that the role provides an opportunity to grow and develop.

Dimension 3 Role Linking

Inter-role Linking Inter-role linkage of one's role with other roles in the organisation increases efficacy. If there is a joint effort in understanding problems, finding solutions, and so on, the efficacy of the various roles involved is likely to be high.

Helping Relationship The opportunity to receive and give help also increases role efficacy. If employees feel that they can get help from some source in the organisation in case of need, they are likely to have higher role efficacy.

Super-ordination A role may have linkages with systems, groups, and entities beyond the organisation. When a person performing a particular role is likely to be of value to a larger group, his efficacy is likely to be high. Roles which allow occupants to work for super-ordinate goals have the highest efficacy.

9.5 MANAGER AS MOTIVATOR OF EMPLOYEES

Managers can plan to increase their role efficacy as well as that of their employees. The following are a few practical suggestions, based on work in some organisations, for supervisors to increase the role efficacy of their employees (Fig. 9.3). These are the applied inferences of the different theories of motivation where motivation is expressed through efficacy.

9.5.1 Self-role Integration

a. Work with employees in redesigning their roles in which their strengths can be utilised.
b. Recommend replacement of a misfit in a job to where he can use his assets.

9.5.2 Productivity

a. Minimise supervision of employees and encourage them to ask for help when they need such help.

Fig. 9.3 Factors responsible for the motivation of employees

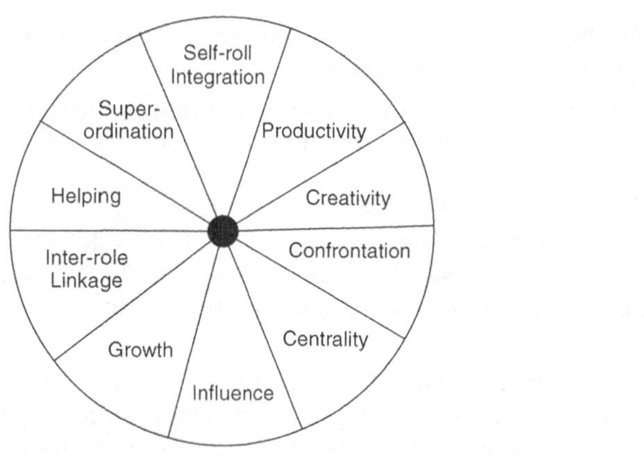

b. Reward initiative.
c. Listen to employees, respect their views, and use their ideas wherever possible.
d. Arrange for employee visits to other organisations.

9.5.3 Creativity

a. Encourage employees to give ideas to solve problems.
b. Create a climate which encourages people to generate ideas without fear of being criticised.
c. Appreciate and use new ideas given by employees.
d. Encourage and reward suggestions to solve problems.

9.5.4 Confrontation

a. Take employees into confidence while confronting a problem.
b. Support the action taken by an employee if it is within the rules and procedures.
c. Appoint a task group for a problem making a decision.
d. Use failure of an employee as an experience and help him to learn from it.
e. Encourage employees to bring up problems.
f. Anticipate problems together with employees.
g. Encourage subordinates to solve problems and report to you.
h. Follow the "buck stops here" dictum.

9.5.5 Centrality

a. Communicate the importance of the roles to their incumbents (the critical contributions of the roles).
b. Communicate the importance of the role as perceived by others.
c. Give enough freedom to each employee to set his objectives and decide on ways of achieving them.
d. Give increasingly difficult and challenging responsibilities.

9.5.6 Influence

a. Delegate enough authority.
b. Give relevant details of decisions made.
c. Send good ideas of employees to higher management.
d. Give feedback to employees on their suggestions.
e. Be willing to accept mistakes.

9.5.7 Growth

a. Appreciate employee's work
b. Do not ridicule employees for their shortcomings but help to improve them.
c. Delegate to them increasingly difficult and challenging tasks.

9.5.8 Inter-role Linkage

a. Encourage employees to seek/render co-operation with other departments.
b. Encourage employees to solve problems by working with their peers (and not refer the problems to you unless it needs your intervention).

9.5.9 Helping

a. Encourage employees to respond to requests by other departments.
b. Encourage them to seek help from peers in other departments.
c. Seek the help of employees in areas they can contribute.
d. Encourage your employees to come to you for help, and respond to them positively.

9.5.10 Super-ordination

a. Help employees to understand and appreciate the contribution of their role to society.
b. Help the employees link (and see the linkage) the objectives of their roles with organisational objectives.

c. Encourage them to include in their roles what may be useful for a larger section.
d. Encourage teamwork.
e. Communicate accessibility to employees.

9.6 USING POWER AND EMPOWERING EMPLOYEES

Managerial effectiveness depends on how well managers use power. With genuine practise of power, a manager directs organisational resources in the desired direction during the management of change. It may be useful to examine some concepts of power relevant for supervisory effectiveness as shown in Fig. 9.4.

Fig. 9.4 Managerial power wheel

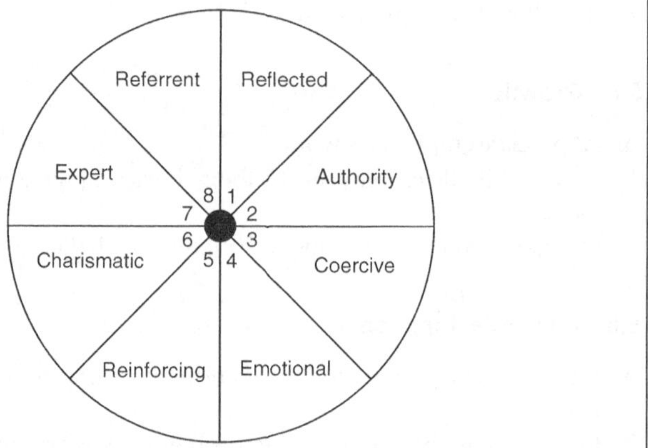

a. ***Reflected power*** is the power a person derives from closeness to a powerful person. Such power need not only be because of their status giving them special privileges, but also because of the opportunities they have of learning from the powerful persons as a result of the close association.
b. ***Authority*** is the power given to the status or role which a person occupies in a system. Every role has a relevant authority.
c. ***Coercive power*** is the power of the supervisor to punish his employees. The employees may obey or follow the instructions of a supervisor because he has the power to punish them.
d. ***Emotional power*** is used by people over those who are very close to them and would, therefore, carry out their wishes because of such close relationship.

e. *Reinforcing power* is exercised when a person (for example, supervisor) can reward others (employees) for their work.

f. *Charismatic power* is the influence a person has over others because of his ability to inspire them and move them emotionally. An inspiring supervisor may get things done by appealing to the emotions of people to contribute to the goals of the organisation.

g. *Expert power* grows out of the expertise of a person in his own field. For example, we accept and implement what the electrician tells us about electric fittings. He has the necessary expertise and people generally do not question him. Similarly, employees may do what the supervisor tells them to do because they may perceive him as an expert. Expert influence in an organisation reflects the ability of an organisation to develop such expertise and specialised skills. Expert power can generate more maturity since all people may look to the expertise of colleagues for guidance in specific fields.

h. *Referrent power* is the influence a person has because of high competence. His competence may not necessarily stem from his specific expertise; it may be a general sense of competence based on his effectiveness. Three considerations are relevant in this regard.

In the first place, supervisors need to be flexible in being able to use the various bases of power suggested above according to the needs of the situation.

Secondly, the eight bases may be regarded as a continuum, one end of the continuum being reflected power and the other end referrent power. This is also the continuum of maturity, use of referrent power showing higher maturity. Supervisors need to move towards the end represented by referrent power. The more they use the more mature bases of power, the more effective they are likely to be. For example, instead of using authority and coercive power, they may use expert and referrent power.

The eight bases of power can be classified into two main categories—coercive power (reflected power, authority, coercive power, and emotional power) and persuasive power (reinforcing power, charismatic power, expert power, and referrent power).

Thirdly, supervisors help their employees to be more flexible and mature in the use of these bases of power, moving towards referrent power.

Supervisors may examine their objectives in the use of power. If they want their employees to take initiative and responsibility, to be creative and innovative, their own style needs to be more of an indirect influence style. In other words, they need to use their power to empower employees, increase their initiative and autonomy, and help them take initiative and personal responsibility for results.

9.7 MANAGERIAL CONTROL

The purpose of supervisory control is to ensure that results are achieved according to the planned schedule (time, quantity, quality, use of input, and so on). The word control may be misleading if it is understood and interpreted in the sense of directing and commanding employees. In other words, supervisory control refers to the process and result of work (using co-ordinated mechanism to check the process and outcome of work against pre-determined norms/and taking corrective action) and not to people (directing and commanding them). Supervisory control is exercised with people concerned, not over them.

Supervisory control involves three processes: establishing norms or standards before any action is taken (including periodically planned performance indices), monitoring the level of periodic and taking corrective action progress (see Fig. 9.5).

Fig. 9.5 Process of managerial control

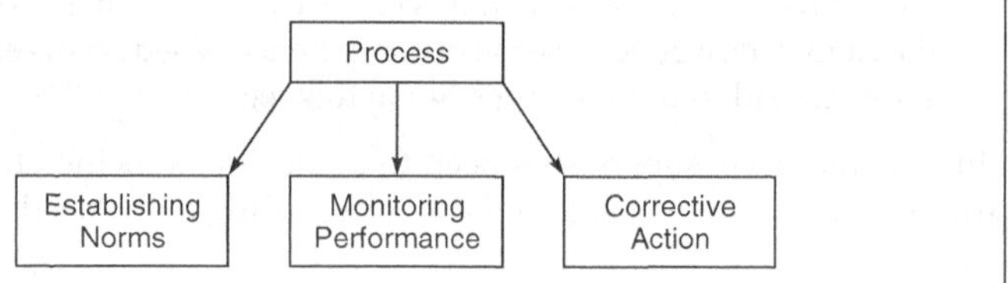

Establishing norms Norms or standards of performance are established in advance, so that monitoring may be possible. One system used in establishing norms is the performance appraisal system. The supervisor helps each employee to identify his key performance areas (KPAs) and then specific objectives or targets for the coming period (usually one year).

Monitoring performance This is a very important supervisory function. Monitoring is done through a system of periodic collection of critical information about quantitative and qualitative performance, and comparing that information with pre-determined standards.

Corrective action Such action is taken on the basis of monitoring of performance. Corrective action should establish accountability. It consists of identification of the extent of deviation from agreed standards, diagnosing causes of the deviation, planning action, reviewing after action has been taken (all these to be done involving the concerned employees), and finally, accountability of the individuals of the team.

Emphasis on quality is the management mantra everywhere. Quality improvement would require involvement of the employees, and joint action on maintaining and improving quality. The employees should have a high concern for quality. Quality consciousness can be increased through quality circle, zero-defect approach, and so on. The following steps are involved.

a. Widespread concern for quality through top management talks, meetings, posters, and so on.
b. Formation of groups of employees to plan quality improvement and set individual and team goals.
c. Recognition of quality work through special rewards (to individuals and teams), ceremonies, and so on.
d. Diagnosis of problems and obstacles in raising quality standards.
e. Inviting suggestions from concerned employees.
f. Formation of special task forces to deal with specific problems, with time-bound goals.
g. Emphasising accountability of task forces by having their work reviewed by the top team, and recognising their contribution.

With the help of managerial control mechanism, the manager channelises the efforts of the employees and organisational resources in the desired direction for sustainable change.

9.8 COPING BEHAVIOUR OF A MANAGER

In our everyday life, we face disappointment or frustration quite often. The same applies to the human resources of an organisation, which reduces their productivity. Here, the manager plays a key role in helping employees emotional trauma cope with and improve their performance.

9.8.1 Managing Frustration and Stress

Managers are frequently required to deal with the frustration of their employees. The following steps are suggested for effective management of employee frustration.

a. Listen to the feelings of the staff The first step is taken by the manager to understand the feelings and point of view of the frustrated employee(s). This may be done by asking the employee(s) state the problem, his feelings, and perceptions. Instead of being defensive, when the employees express negative impressions, the manager must listen to them patiently.

b. Share own feeling of disappointment If a manager is able to level with his employees, he may be able to reach them. Most situations that produce frustration in employees, also disappoint the manager. If an employee is not rewarded, the supervisor is also disappointed. A manager can build rapport with the employees if he shares his own disappointment with them.

c. Share feelings of guilt (if any) Sometimes the manager may partly contribute to the disappointment of the employees. He may build high expectations, and the employees may feel frustrated because the expectations are not met. Or he may promise something to an employee who does not get it. In such situations, a manager must explain the situation to the employee.

d. Help the employees express their feelings The manager sharing his feelings and owning up may help employees express their own feelings of disappointment, anger, and so on. This may help in taking the next constructive steps.

e. Help the employees to accept and confront reality The first step in constructive action is to acknowledge reality and be ready to deal with it. Clearing the feelings may help the employee-supervisor team to move forward, and not get fixated at feelings.

f. Help the employees assess damage by frustration Frustration causes some damage in terms of physical effects (sleeplessness, tension, loss of appetite), social effects (on personal relationships, reduced social contacts, lack of enjoying life together), effects on work (neglect of work, errors, fall in quality), absenteeism, and so on. It may be useful to help the employee reflect upon and assess the damage frustration is doing to them. Even if the work in the organisation suffers, the main damage is done to the employee. The employee needs to understand and realise this.

g. Develop alternatives to solve problems The final step is to involve the frustrated employees in generating alternatives to deal with the problem, and take constructive steps. While employees generate the alternatives, the supervisors may suggest some possibilities.

9.9 CONSULTANT SUPPORT DURING CHANGE

(Coaching for Change)

Once the ability to manage transition is tied to the realities of an actual manager in an actual situation, mutual trust between adviser and manager is essential. Only then can managers be honest enough to bring their fears and concerns to the surface quickly, hear what the situation is really "saying" rather than focusing on a programme that a consultant is trying to sell, and gain the personal insight and awareness of the transition process that can be carried into the future. Because this transition management relationship is a close and ongoing one, the adviser gets to know the manager's situation well and follows it as it changes. Understanding the dynamics of transition is far removed from the kind of leadership training most organisations provide. Traditional trainers and consultants seldom possess such intimate knowledge of their client. Whatever personal coaching they provide is usually subsumed to the teaching of a generic skill or body of knowledge. And because the relationship is time-bound, there is a natural pressure to produce quick, clear results.

However, because transition advisers work within the context of the situation at hand, their focus is not on how to "be a manger (leader)" or even how to "change an organisation" but on how to provide the particular kind of leadership that an organisation in transition demands. For that reason, the results of the relationship are very specific: the development of new skills and behaviours geared to the needs of the unique time and circumstances in which the person leads.

Though the details of a transition management plan are unique to each situation, the adviser must help a leader with the following essential steps.

a. Learn to describe the change and why it must happen, and do so succinctly—in one minute or less. It is amazing how many leaders cannot do that.
b. Be sure that the details of the change are planned carefully and that someone is responsible for each detail; that timelines for all the changes are established; and that a communications plan explaining the change is in place.
c. Understand (with the assistance of others closer to the change) just who is going to have to let go of—what is ending (and what is not) in people's work lives and careers—and what people (including the leader) should let go of.
d. Make sure that steps are taken to help people respectfully let go of the past. These may include "boundary" actions (events that demonstrate that change has come), a constant stream of information, and understanding and acceptance of the symptoms of grieving, as well as efforts to protect people's interests while they are giving up the status quo.
e. Help people through the neutral zone with communication (rather than simple information) that emphasises connections with and concern for the followers. Keep reiterating the "4 Ps" of transition communications (Fig. 9.6):
   The *purpose* Why we have to do this?
   The *picture* What it will look and feel like when we reach our goal?
   The *plan* Step-by-step, how we will get there?
   The *part* What you can (and need to) do to help us move forward?

Fig. 9.6 The 4 Ps of effective managerial communication during change

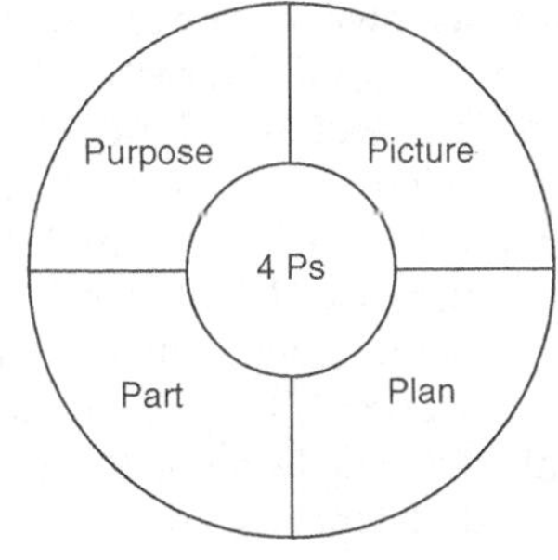

f. Create temporary solutions to the temporary problems and the high levels of uncertainty found in the neutral zone. For example, one high-tech manufacturer, when announcing the closing of a plant, made interim changes in its usual reassignment procedures, bonus compensation plans, and employee communications processes to make sure that displaced employees suffered as little as possible, both financially and psychologically. Such efforts should include transition monitoring teams that can alert the leader to unforeseen problems—and disband when the process is done.

Help people launch the new beginning by articulating the new attitudes and behaviours needed to make the change work—and then modelling, providing practice in, and rewarding those behaviours and attitudes. For example, rather than announcing the grandiose goal of building a "world-class workforce", leaders of transition must define the skills and attitudes that such a workforce must have, and provide the necessary training and resources to develop them.

9.10 MANAGER AND GROUP DYNAMICS

Small groups have existed since the time of the first human family. Only recently, however, have people started to study scientifically the processes by which small groups work. Some of the questions to be answered are: What is the role of a "leader" in a small group? Does the role vary with different objectives? Does a group have different kinds of leaders operating concurrently? In what ways and under what conditions are groups better than individuals? These questions still remain partly unanswered.

The social process by which people interact face to face in small groups is called group dynamics. The word "dynamics" comes from the Greek word meaning "force"; hence, "group dynamics" refers to the study of forces operating within a group. Mayo showed that workers tend to establish informal groups that affect job satisfaction and effectiveness. Curt Lewin showed that different kinds of leadership attitudes produced different responses in groups.

Groups have properties of their own that are different from the properties of the individuals who make up the group. This is similar to the physical situation in which a molecule of salt (sodium chloride) has different properties from the sodium and chlorine elements that form a "group" to make it. The special properties of groups are illustrated by a simple lesson in mathematics. Let us say, "One plus one equals three." In the world of mathematics that is a logical error, and a rather elementary one at that. But in the world of group dynamics, it is entirely rational to say, "One and one equals three." In a group there is no such thing as only two people, for no two people can be conceived without their relationship, and that makes three.

9.10.1 Three Uses of Groups in Idea Generation

Groups may be used by the manager in a number of ways for improvement. Three important ways are brainstorming, nominal groups, and Delphi decision-making as depicted in Fig. 9.7.

Fig. 9.7 Major uses of group dynamics

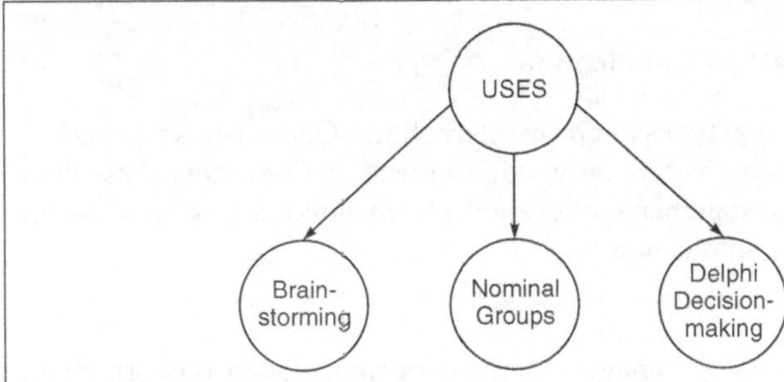

a. Brainstorming This is a popular method of encouraging creative thinking. Its main advantage is deferred judgement, by which all ideas—even unusual and impractical ones—are encouraged without criticism or evaluation. Ideas are recorded as fast as they can be suggested; they are evaluated for usefulness later. The purpose of deferred judgement is to encourage people to propose bold, unique ideas without worrying about what others think of them. This approach typically produces more ideas than the conventional approach of thinking and judging concurrently. Brainstorming sessions last from ten minutes to one hour and require no preparation other than general knowledge of the subject.

Other advantages of brainstorming are enthusiasm, broader participation, greater task orientation, building upon ideas exchanged, and the feeling that the final product is a team solution, which helps managers in execution.

b. Nominal groups Here individuals are presented with a problem, and each develops solutions independently. Then their ideas are shared with others in a structured format and their suggestions are discussed for clarification. Finally, group members choose the best alternatives by secret ballot. The process is called "nominal" since the members are, on the whole, part of a group in name only. Advantages include the opportunity for equal participation by all members, the non-dominance of discussion by any one member, and the tight control of time that the process allows.

c. Delphi decision-making Here, members do not meet face to face. All communication typically is in writing. Members are selected because they are experts or have relevant information to share. They are asked to share their assessment of a problem or predict a future state of affairs. Explanations of their conclusions can also be shared. Replies are gathered from all participants, summarised, and fed back to the members for their review. Then they are asked to make another decision based on the new information.

The process may be repeated several times until the responses converge satisfactorily.

The success of the Delphi process depends on adequate time, participant expertise, communication skill, and the motivation of members to immerse themselves in the task.

9.10.2 Managerial Communication

There are two principal types of group interactions. One exists when people are discussing ideas and is generally called a meeting. The other exists when people perform tasks together and is called a team. Following is a discussion of each type of group interaction.

Meetings

Meetings are convened by managers for many purposes, such as information, advice, decision-making, negotiation, co-ordination, and creative thinking. A committee is a specific type of meeting. This means that if a supervisor and a worker serve as members of the same committee, both usually have equal committee roles.

Operation of Meetings

Groups tend to require not one but two types of leadership roles of the manager: task leader and social leader. The task leader works towards the achievement of the task, but the difficulty arises because in playing this role he may irritate people and affect the unity of the group.

It is the social leader's role to restore and maintain group unity and satisfaction so that the task can be accomplished. Although one person can fill both the task and social roles, often they are separate.

When they are separate, it is important for the task manager to recognise the social leader and try to form a coalition of the two leaders for improved effectiveness.

Group Process The task manager's job in a meeting is to help the group maintain group process, which means to help the group keep functioning properly so that it may accomplish its objectives. The manager encourages open communication so that all members can participate equally. Essentially the leader plays a supportive role to help the group develop.

Superordinate Goals A major responsibility of the manager is to try to keep the meeting on track towards its task. When discussion drifts to side issues that do not seem to contribute to the meeting, the leader can raise questions about the usefulness of these side discussions. The idea is to help members recognise and explore a superordinate goal, which is a higher goal towards which all can work. For example, in a hospital meeting the leader said, "We are all here to help the patient. Can we think of today's problem in those terms?" When the superordinate goal was recognised, several minor internal conflicts were resolved.

Emotions Managers who are the leaders of meetings try to maintain an even emotional tone so that emotional conflicts or outbursts do not disrupt meeting. At all times the leader needs to be sensitive to feelings of members so that they can be dealt with before they become magnified into major difficulties.

One leader, for example, learned from experience that a committee member typically showed excitement by squirming in his chair and tapping his fingers on the table. When another member answered with a direct "yes," it meant she agreed; but when she said, "I guess so, " it meant she had doubts and was not sold on the idea being discussed. The leader used these cues as signals to guide meetings with these people.

Agendas

Meetings work simultaneously at two different levels. One level is the official task of the group, known as the surface agenda. The other level involves members' private emotions and motives, which they have brought with them but keep hidden under the conference table. These are the hidden agendas of the meeting. Frequently when a group reaches a crisis in its surface agenda, these hidden agendas come to life to complicate the situation. Conversely, sometimes a group seems to be making no progress and then suddenly everything is settled. What may have happened is that a hidden agenda finally was solved (even though members did not known they were working on it), making it easy to settle the surface agenda.

Support for Decisions

Probably the most important by-product of meetings is that people who participate in making a decision feel more strongly motivated to accept it and carry it out. In many instances, this is more than a by-product—it is the primary purpose of the meeting. Meetings undoubtedly are one of the best means available to commit people to carry out a course of action. A person who has helped make a decision is more interested in seeing it work.

Group decisions also carry more weight with those who are not group members. Associates, subordinates, and even superiors are more likely to accept group decisions. They feel that decisions of this type are more free from individual prejudice because they are based on a combination of many viewpoints. Further, the combined social pressure of the entire group stands behind the decision.

Teamwork

When groups perform operating tasks, they act as a team and seek to develop a co-operative state called teamwork. If it is necessary to distinguish two types of teams the company-wide one is an institutional team and the small one is a task team or an operations team. The latter is defined as a small co-operative group in regular contact that is engaged in co-ordinated action and whose members contribute responsibly and enthusiastically to the task. This kind of genuine teamwork makes the job easier and generally improves job satisfaction.

A group is able to work together as a team only after all the people in the group know the roles of the others with whom they will be interacting. All members also must be reasonably qualified to perform their jobs and want to co-operate. When this level of understanding is reached, members can act immediately as a team based upon the requirements of that situation, without waiting for someone to give an order. In other words, team members respond voluntarily to the job and take appropriate action to further teamwork goals.

An example is a hospital surgical team all of whose members respond to a crisis during an operation. Their mutual recognition of the crisis alerts them to the need for simultaneous action and co-ordinated response. The result is a highly efficient level of co-operation characteristic of a team. If one member of a surgical team fails to perform in the right way at the right time, a person's life may be endangered. In more ordinary work situations, a life may not be in danger but product quality and team effectiveness can be weakened by the failure of one member. Further, lowered product quality can later lead to consumer injury or loss. In any case, society is the loser because lower group effectiveness wastes society's resources. All the members are needed for effective teamwork.

Need for a Supportive Environment

Teamwork is most likely to develop when management builds a supportive environment for it. Supportive measures help the group take the first necessary steps toward teamwork. These steps become the basis for further growth towards co-operation, trust, and compatibility, so supervisors need to develop an organisational climate that builds these conditions.

Weaknesses of Group Communication

The group approach also has weaknesses. As a result, some have developed the attitude "You go to the meeting and I'll tend the store," meaning that meeting is unproductive labour and someone has to keep the production humming. Some meetings are unproductive, but a single case does not prove the generality. Meetings and teams are an essential and productive part of work organisations. Part of our trouble is that we expect too much of them and when they do not meet our expectations, we criticise them. But we will get nowhere criticising a tennis court because it is a poor football field.

Properly conducted meetings and team building can contribute to organisational progress by providing participation, integrating interests, improving decision-making, committing and motivating members to carry out a course of action, encouraging creative thinking, broadening perspectives, and changing attitudes. To use them, one must know their weaknesses, which fall into three major categories: slowness and expensiveness, leveling effect, and divided responsibility (Fig. 9.8).

Fig. 9.8 Major weaknesses of group dynamics

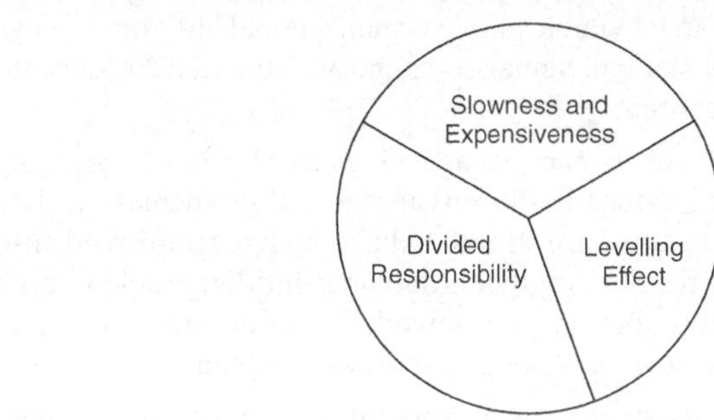

Slowness and Expensiveness As one manager observed, "Committees keep minutes and waste hours!" Meetings of all types are a slow way of getting things done. On occasion, delay is desirable. There is more time for thinking, for objective review of an idea, and for the suggestion of alternatives. But when quick, decisive action is necessary, a sure way to reach confusion is to hold a meeting. A manager, for example, does not call a committee meeting to decide whether to tell the fire department that the building is on fire!

Levelling Effect The tendency of a group to bring individual thinking in line with the average quality of the group's thinking is called the leveling effect or "group-think". One of the most convincing criticisms is that this often leads to conformity and compromise. A person begins to think less individually about a problem and adapts to the desires of other members. The result can be that the ideas of the most dominant person, rather than the better ideas, are accepted.

Levelling is not wholly undesirable, however. But it is a group tendency that must be held in check by a constant focus on careful analysis.

Divided Eesponsibility Management literature has always recognised that divided responsibility is a problem whenever group decisions are made. It is often said that "actions which are several bodies' responsibility are nobody's responsibility." Group decisions undoubtedly do dilute and thin out responsibility. They also give individual members a chance to shirk responsibility, using justifications such as "Why should I bother with this problem? I didn't support it in the meeting."

Many of the disadvantages of group performance can be overcome readily. The preceding discussion suggested that proper group structures must be selected, that group size is an important factor, and that various leadership roles must be played by the manager to achieve positive group dynamics.

Conflict as a Major Weakness of a Group

As people with different backgrounds, points of view, values, needs, and personalities interact, a variety of conflicts often develop. Organisational change also contributes to conflict, because it realigns relationships among people. The result is that conflict is an inevitable part of organisational life. Sometimes the amount of conflict is substantial. Managers spend an estimated 20 per cent of their time dealing with conflict.

Conflict is not all bad. It has its benefits as well as its disadvantages; the manager's goal is to try to reduce the disadvantages while increasing the benefits. One benefit is that people are stimulated to search for improved approaches that lead to better results. Another is that once-hidden problems are brought to the surface where they may be solved. Out of all this ferment a deeper understanding may develop among the parties involved.

There also are possible disadvantages. Co-operation and teamwork may deteriorate. Distrust grows among people who need to co-operate. Some people may feel defeated, have a poorer self-image, and lose their motivation.

Interpersonal Conflict Such conflicts are a serious problem for many people because they deeply affect a person's emotions. There is a need to protect one's self-image and self-esteem from damage by others. When these self-concepts are threatened, serious upsets occur. Among the common causes of conflict are personality clashes, such as those arising from differences in temperament. In other instances, conflicts develop from failure of communication or differences in perception.

An office employee was upset by a conflict with another employee in a different department. It seemed to the first employee that there was no way to resolve the conflict. However, when a counsellor explained the different organisational roles of the two employees as seen from the whole organisation's point of view, the first employee's perceptions changed and the conflict vanished.

Inter-group Conflict Such conflicts between different departments also cause problems. On a minor scale these conflicts are like the wars between juvenile gangs. Each group sets out to undermine the other, gain power, and improve its image.

Conflicts arise from such causes as different viewpoints, group loyalties, and competition for resources. Resources are limited in any organisation. Most groups feel that they need more than they can secure, so the seeds of inter-group conflict exist wherever there are limited resources. For example, the production department may want new and more efficient machinery while the sales department wants to expand its sales force, but there are only enough resources to supply the needs of one group.

Conflict Outcomes Conflict situations may be divided into four depending on the perspectives of the people involved. Fig. 9.9 indicates the different outcomes. The first situation is lose-lose, where one person wants the conflict to

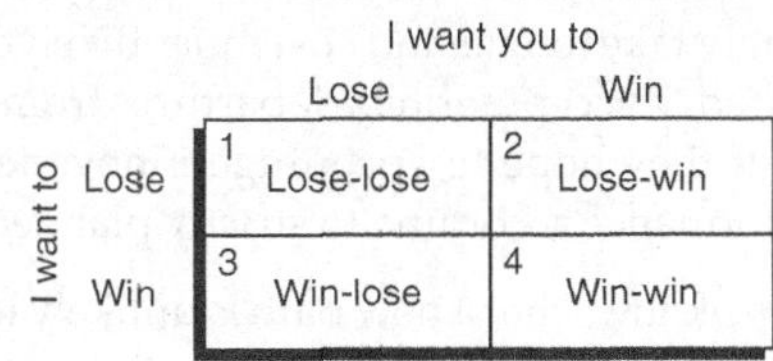

Fig. 9.9 A matrix of conflict outcomes

deteriorate to the point where both parties are worse off than before. (A murder-suicide is an extreme example of this.) The second quadrant (lose-win) portrays a situation where one person sees the benefits of being defeated on this issue. This perspective may emerge because of the preponderance of evidence or because the person hopes that the other party will reciprocate in the future.

The win-lose strategy often seems to dominate emotional conflicts. Here, one individual acts so as to become the victor through defeat of the other. These conflicts are the product of a "fixed-pie syndrome", wherein each party believes that it can gain only at the expense of the other.

A fourth alternative is the win-win approach. In this situation, creative solutions are sought that provide benefit to both parties. Many labour-management councils have been established with this objective in mind. A manager must strive to get to the "win-win" situation.

9.11 OBSTACLES IN THE MIDDLE OF CHANGE AND HOW TO OVERCOME THEM

Every idea, especially if it is new or different, runs into trouble before it reaches fruition. However, it is important for change leaders to help teams overcome four predictable—but potentially fatal—roadblocks to change.

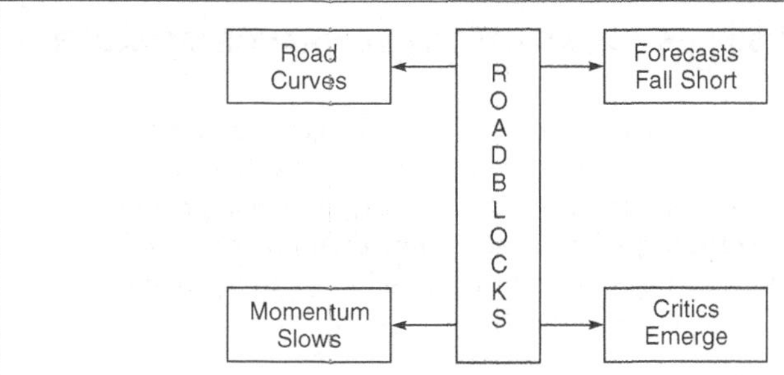

Fig. 9.10 Major obstacles during change

Forecasts fall short You have to have a plan—but if you are doing something new and different, you should not expect it to hold. Plans are based on experience and assumptions. When attempting to innovate, it is difficult to predict how long something will take or how much it will cost (you can predict, however, that it will probably take longer and cost more than you think). Change leaders must be prepared to accept serious departures from plans. They must also understand that if they hope to encourage innovation, it is foolish to measure people's performance according to strictly planned delivery.

Road curves Everyone knows that a new path is unlikely to run straight and true, but when we actually encounter those twists and turns we often panic. Especially when attempting to make changes in a system, diversions are likely, and unwelcome. It is a mistake to simply stop in your tracks. Every change brings unanticipated consequences, and teams must be prepared to respond, to troubleshoot, to make adjustments, and to make their case. Scenario planning can help; the real message is to expect the unexpected.

Momentum slows After the excitement and anticipation of a project launch, reality sinks in. You do not have solutions to the problems you face; the multiple demands of your job are piling up; the people you have asked for information or assistance are not returning your calls. The team is discouraged and enmeshed in conflict. It is important to revisit the team's mission, to recognise what has been accomplished and what remains, and to remember that the differences in outlook, background, and perspective that now may divide you will ultimately provide solutions.

Critics emerge Even if you have built a coalition and involved key stakeholders, the critics, sceptics, and cynics will challenge you—and they will be strongest not at the beginning but in the middle of your efforts. It is only then that the possible impact of the change becomes clear, and those who feel threatened can formulate their objections.

This is when change managers—often with the help of coalition members, outside partners, or acknowledged experts—can respond to criticism, remove obstacles, and push forward the process of change. Tangible progress of change process will produce more believers than doubters.

9.12 CLASSIC SKILLS FOR AN EFFECTIVE CHANGE MANAGER

The most important things a manager can bring to a changing organisation are passion, conviction, and confidence in others. Too often executives announce a plan, launch a task force, and then simply hope that people find the answers—instead of offering a dream, stretching their horizons, and encouraging people to do the same. That is why it is said. "Leaders (managers) go first."

However, given passion, conviction, and confidence, managers can use several techniques to take charge of change rather than simply react to it. The following classic skills are equally useful to CEOs, senior executives, or middle managers who want to move an idea forward (Fig. 9.11).

Fig. 9.11 Classic skills required to become an effective change manager

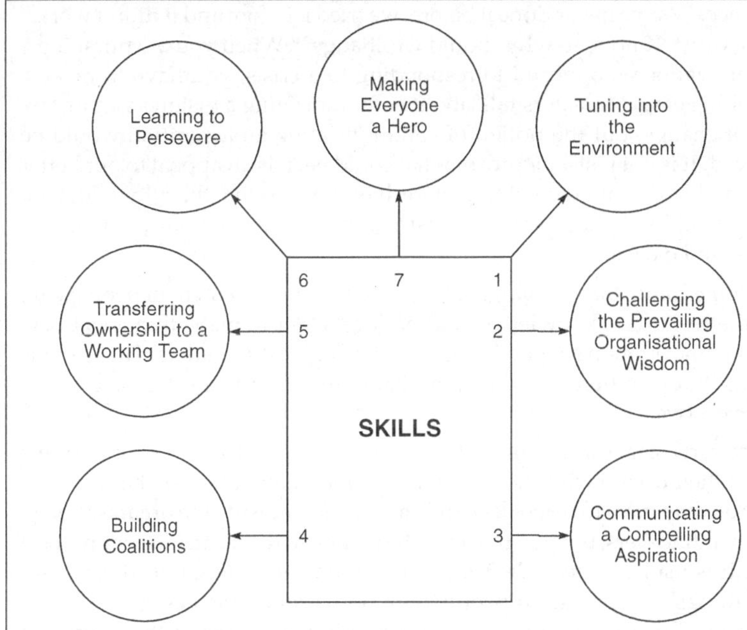

a. Tuning into the environment As a manager you cannot possibly know enough, or be in enough places, to understand everything happening inside—and more importantly outside—your organisation. But you can actively collect information that suggests new approaches.

b. Challenging the prevailing organisational wisdom Managers need to develop what is called kaleidoscope thinking—a way of constructing patterns from the fragments of data available, and then manipulating them to form different patterns. They must question the assumptions about how pieces of the organisation, marketplace, or community fit together. Change leaders know that there are many solutions to a problem and that by looking through a different lens, somebody is going to invent, for instance, a new way to deliver health care.

There are lots of ways to promote kaleidoscopic thinking. Send people outside the company—not just on field trips, but "far afield trips." Go outside your industry and return with fresh ideas. Rotate job assignments and create interdisciplinary project teams to give people fresh ideas and opportunities to test their assumptions. For instance, one innovative department of a U.S. oil company regularly invites people from many different departments to attend large brainstorming sessions. These allow interested outsiders to ask questions, make suggestions, and trigger new ideas.

c. Communicating a compelling aspiration You cannot sell change, or anything else, without genuine conviction, because there are so many sources of resistance. "We've never done it before; we tried it before and it didn't work." "Things are OK now, so why should we change?" When you are pursuing a true innovation as opposed to responding to a crisis, you have to make a compelling case. Managers talk about communicating a vision as an instrument of change, but the notion of communicating an aspiration would be preferred. It is not just a picture of what could be; it is an appeal to our better selves, a call to become something more. It reminds us that the future does not just descend like a stage set; we construct the future from our own history, desires, and decisions.

d. Building coalitions Change leaders need the involvement of people who have the resources, knowledge, and political clout to make things happen. You want the opinion shapers, experts in the field, value leaders. That sounds obvious, but coalition building is probably the most neglected step in the change process.

In the early stages of planning change, leaders must identify key supporters and sell their dream with the same passion and deliberation as the entrepreneur. You may have to reach deep into, across, and outside the organisation to find key influencers, but you must first be willing to reveal an idea or proposal before it is ready. Secrecy denies you the opportunity to get feedback, and when things are sprung on people with no warning, the easiest answer is always no. Coalition building requires an understanding of the politics of change, and in any organisation those politics are formidable.

When building coalitions, however, it is a mistake to try to recruit everybody at once. Think of innovation as a venture. You want the minimum number of investors necessary to launch a new venture, and to champion it when you need help later.

e. Transferring ownership to a working team Once a coalition is in place, you can enlist others in implementation. You must remain involved—the leader's job is to support the team, provide coaching and resources, and patrol the boundaries within which the team can freely operate. But you cannot simply ask managers to execute a fully formed change agenda; you might instead develop a broad outline, informed by your environmental scan and lots of good questions, from which people can conduct a series of small experiments. That approach not only confers team ownership, but allows people to explore new possibilities in ways that do not bet the company or your budget.

In addition, managers as a leaders can allow teams to forge their own identity, build a sense of membership, and enjoy the protection they need to implement changes. One of the temptations leaders must resist is to simply pile responsibility on team members. While it is fashionable to have people wear many hats, people must be given the responsibility—and the time—to focus on the tasks of change.

f. Learning to persevere One of the mistakes leaders make in change processes is to launch them and leave them. There are many ways a change initiative can get derailed. But stop it too soon and, by definition, it will be a failure; stay with it through its initial hurdles and good things may happen. Of course, if a change process takes long, you have to return to the beginning—monitor the environment again, recheck your assumptions, reconsider whether the proposed change is still the right one. Abdicating your role undermines the effort because, unlike bold strokes, long marches need ongoing leadership. Most people get excited about things in the beginning, and everybody loves endings, especially happy endings. It is the hard work in between that demands the attention and effort of savvy leaders.

g. Making everyone a hero Remembering to recognise, reward, and celebrate accomplishment is a critical leadership skill. And it is probably the most underutilised motivational tool in organisations. There is no limit to how much recognition you can provide, and it is often free. Recognition brings the change cycle to its logical conclusion; it also motivates people to attempt change again. So many people get involved in and contribute to changing the way an organisation does things that it is important to share the credit. Change is an ongoing issue, and you cannot afford to lose the talents, skills, or energies of those who can help make it happen.

SUMMARY

- Manager is a person who plans, organises, co-ordinates, and controls the resources for their effective utilisation.
- For the effective management of changes, the concept of developmental supervision is required.
- For the execution of managerial tasks, a manager has certain responsibilities. These are appraisal, training carrier, work culture, self-renewal, organisational learning, stress management, and research system.
- A motivated manager is the key to effective change in the organisation. Such a change can be achieved by the proper application of the role efficacy concept.
- A manager channelises the performance of the organisation with the help of the powers available to him. These are powers reflective authority, coercive, emotional, reinforcing, charismatic, expert, and referrent powers.
- Managerial control is possible by establishing norms, monitoring performance, and corrective actions.
- To help employess cope with the problem of frustration and stress, a manager has to listen, share, and guide their feelings.
- The advice of the consultant is very important for the manager for guidelines to work and improve his execution style.

- A manager is a pivot functionary in group dynamics. He utilises these dynamics for idea generation, effective communication, and for teamwork. He manages the conflict situation in the group.
- Finally, a manager needs some classic skills for the proper formulation and execution of the change programme. The efficiency of the manager determines the success of the organisation-wide change programme.

Case Study: "Genesis" A National Scientific Laboratory

History

A research division of a major, long-established national scientific laboratory "Genesis", had a project team that was suffering from issues of disaffection, poor morale, and lack of internal cohesion. The divisional director appointed a new project leader, and wanted these issues to be addressed as part of the transition.

Task

Develop and facilitate an off-site retreat for 30 scientists, engineers, technicians, and support staff to bring organisational issues to the surface. Develop action strategies for developing a more integrated, cohesive, and empowered team.

Intervention

Through interviews with key players, the project leader carried out a pre-retreat assessment of issues and change readiness, designed a customised retreat process geared to the research culture of the participants, facilitated the retreat, and provided consultation to the other members on follow-up implementation.

Result

The project team emerged from the retreat experience with a number of practical teamwork tools, concrete action items to address long-standing problems, desire to collaborate better as a team, and trust in their new leader's commitment to team empowerment.

Key Disciplines

Organisational Development, Communication, Resistance, Retreat Facilitation, Team Building.

Review Questions

1. How do you define the concept of developmental supervision in light of effective management of change?
2. What are the responsibilities of a manager?

3. How do you define motivation? How can the organisation work for the enhancement of motivation level in a manager?
4. How does a manager manage the power and control mechanism in the organisation?
5. Write a brief note on each of the following.
   (i) Group dynamics and the role of a manager as a change agent
   (ii) Coping with frustration and stress by the manager during change
6. What are the qualities required in a manager to become an effective change programme manager?

EXERCISE 1

This activity encourages team members to think about and set personal aims, and commit to them in a memorable and meaningful way. The exercise also enables positive encouragement and mutual support among the team members towards meeting each person's aims.

First, ask everyone in the group to set themselves a personal, achievable, short-term goal. The aims can be to do with higher performance, quality standards, problem-solving, or any other challenges in their work or life. Supply the team some coloured paper, marker pens, glitter, scissors, stickers, and (optionally) directions/instructions for paper airplane models.

When all team members have decided on their short-term goal(s), ask them to choose a paper airplane design and make the plane. Ask them to write their goal, with a few points or steps as to how they will achieve it, on the inside of the paper plane (which enables people to keep their goals private). Then, as the facilitator, tutor, or team leader, write a positive encouraging comment on the outside of every person's plane—the emphasis should be on encouraging comments, for example, "I believe you can do this," or "I know this is something you can achieve," and so on. Optionally, you can involve the group as well in writing positive, inspiring comments on the outside of each other's planes. Allow the group to continue finishing the decoration of the outside of their planes.

The exercise enables each team member to take pleasure in visualising their own aims, and to give and receive lots of positive encouragement. Finally, the activity provides the opportunity to go outside as a team and fly the planes, and maybe win a few prizes for the longest flight, best design, best trick, and so on.

EXERCISE 2

This is flexible and physical role-playing for big groups of 30 or more. It helps to understand the concepts of group dynamics, leadership, and teamwork.

You will need plenty of space. If necessary, ask the delegates to move all the chairs to the side of the room (they can easily move them back again, which also helps the warm-up process).

Ask the group to sort itself into teams according to a set of categories that you call out. A simple example is for people to sort themselves into teams according to the month of the year they were born. This would obviously create twelve teams, assuming the group is large enough to produce representatives from each month. If the group size is smaller, choose a category set with fewer divisions, for example, the number of creases on the middle knuckle of the dominant hand (which causes people to think in an unusual and fun way, and is therefore enjoyable and interesting—it is a great "leveller" too).

When formed, give the teams a competitive task or tasks, for example, decide a motto which reflects them as people, which they then shout as a war cry at the other groups (creative and energising). Or ask the teams to find a "champion" or "expert"—someone in the team who excels at something or is remarkable in a particular field outside of working life. Each team then announces their "champion" in turn, at which everyone can applaud and cheer the champion's (hitherto unknown) achievements (great for recognition). You can devise all sorts of other team challenges, perhaps even quick contests or quizzes between teams.

It creates more purpose if you can award winners "tokens" or "cards." These could be anything suitable—paper slips, counters, play money, wrapped sweets, whatever is easy to obtain or produce for the facilitator.

You can give people tight timescales for each team-sorting activity, team challenges and tasks, to focus them on quick team-working, decision-making, communications, and so on. The exercises can also be used to illustrate many aspects of team-building, chaos, forming and working in virtual teams, working under pressure, team-working, risk-taking, role of the champion (manager), anticipation, decisiveness, taking responsibility, communications, especially if you are less than precise about some of the category descriptions, for example, eye colour (that is, if you don't tell the group whether green is equal to hazel or is a different colour, then they have to decide for themselves....).

It is important to have a strong facilitator who can see (ideally from a good vantage point, the top of a table, for example, what is going on, and who can make quick arbitrary decisions (in the style of "the judge's decision is final and absolute...")

You could offer tokens to the winning teams in each round according to speed, motto, champion, and so on (decide by quick cheer-based votes from all teams), and then see which individuals accumulate the most tokens at the end of all the exercises to identify overall winners.

You can take tokens away from people, or teams, who are indecisive, or who fail to help stragglers and those who waver.

Ideas for team categories into which the group could sort itself (each one is a separate activity, without without a time limit—you decide)

- Month of birth (this would create up to 12 teams depending on the total group size)
- Creases on a given knuckle of a finger, or number of rings on the hands
- Favourite colour (depends on category description, if given—you could leave it to the group to interpret and decide)
- Sweet, sour, bitter, salt (four teams; the way they interpret this is interesting, that is, description of a person or taste in food)
- Signs of the zodiac
- Eye colour

- Hair colour
- Think what is and do what is, think what could be and do what is; think what is and do what could be, think what could be and do what could be (an interpretation of the four temperaments, a very interesting exercise in its own right)
- Favourite food
- Days of the week that exercise is done
- Car colours

For a short energiser exercise, you can use just one category. Extend and make the activity more challenging and sophisticated by using several team-sorting sessions, plus team challenges.

If you are leaving it to the group to decide, you can tell them this, or not. It depends how much freedom, chaos, and responsibility you seek to create and assess.

The type of category by which teams sort themselves should obviously relate to the total group size, number of teams, and number of members in the team that you might wish to create for any particular team activity. Think about how many teams a particular category is likely to produce and ensure it fits your purpose.

Chapter

Learning Organisation: The Ultimate Objective of Management of Change

Chapter Outline

- Introduction
- Nature of Learing Enterprises
- Building a Learning Organisation
- Features of a Learning Organisation
- Total Quality Management and Learning Organisation
- Blueprint of a Learning Organisation
- Managing and Sustaining Change in a Learning Organisation
- Basis of Learning Approach in an Organisation
- Summary
- Case Study
- Review Questions
- Exercises

"Anyone who stops learning is old, whether at twenty or eighty. Anyone who keeps learning stays young. The greatest thing in life is to keep your mind young."

—Henry Ford

10.1 INTRODUCTION

Improvement depends on learning. Without learning, there is no improvement. In the absence of learning an organisation can only repeat old practices. Rapid technological change and exponential growth in knowledge require that individuals continue to learn at a fast pace.

Organisations whose members commonly and continuously acquire, learn, share, store, distribute, and use knowledge for their effective collective action, are defined as learning organisations.

10.1.1 What is a Learning Organisation?

A learning organisation is one that has developed the continuous capacity to adapt and change. Just as individuals learn, so do organisations.

Most organisations engage in what has been called single-loop learning. When errors are detected, the correction process relies on past routines and present policies. In contrast, learning organisations use double-loop learning. When an error is detected, it is corrected in ways that involve the modification of the organisation's objectives, policies, and standard routines. Like second-order change, double-loop learning challenges are deep-rooted assumptions and norms within an organisation. In this way, it provides opportunities for radically different solutions to problems and dramatic jumps in improvement.

Table 10.1 summarises the five basic characteristics of a learning organisation. It is an organisation where people put aside their old way of thinking, learning to be open with each other, understand how their organisation really works, form a plan or vision that everyone can agree on, and then work together to achieve that vision.

Learning organisations adopt TQM's commitment to continuous improvement. Learning organisations are also characterised by a specific culture that values risk taking, openness, and growth. It seeks "boundarylessness" through

Table 10.1 Characteristics of a learning organisation

a. There exists a shared vision that everyone agrees on. b. People discard their old ways of thinking and the standard routines they used for solving problems or doing their jobs. c. Members think of all organisational processes, activities, functions, and interactions with the environment as part of a system of interrelationships. d. People openly communicate with each other (across vertical and horizontal boundaries) without fear of criticism or punishment. e. People sublimate their personal self-interest and fragmented departmental interests to work together to achieve the organisation's shared vision.

breaking down barriers created by hierarchical levels and fragmented departmentation. A learning organisation supports the importance of disagreements, constructive criticism, and other forms of functional conflict. Transformational leadership is needed in a learning organisation to implement the shared vision.

Thus organisations with the capability of adapting to change with minimum resistance, aware about their environment, and proactive in nature are known as learning organisations.

10.2 NATURE OF LEARNING ENTERPRISES

Learning organisations are "knowledge-creating companies." They are places where "inventing new knowledge is not a specialised activity...it is a way of behaving, indeed, a way of being, in which everyone is a knowledge worker."

Learning organisations are effective not only in creating and/or acquiring new knowledge, but also in applying that knowledge to their tasks and activities. Rapid realisation of new technology into products is a core competency of a learning enterprise.

In a learning organisation, the nature of one's job at any time is defined by problems and challenges facing the organisation as a whole. Every member of such an organisation is involved in discovering problems and suggesting solutions.

10.2.1 Adaptive and Generative Learning

Learning organisations also need to differentiate between adaptive and generative learning. Adaptive learning is concerned with adapting to environmental changes and improving the organisation's capacity to achieve known objectives in a reactive manner.

Generative learning goes beyond just adapting to change in a reactive mode. It involves creativity and innovation, anticipation of change, staying ahead of competition, and change in a proactive mode. Generative learning involves a creative reframing of an organisation's problems and experiences. It involves formulation of and experimentation with novel approaches to problem-solving and decision-making, and learning from those processes. It involves openness and flexibility of mind, and a willingness to take manageable risks.

10.2.2 Knowledge-intensive Organisation

Such an enterprise is significantly networked with other organisations. Its material focus is not on functions but on processes. Its authority does not lie merely in hierarchical position, or command and control systems; it resides in professional influence, communication, and collegiality based on shared beliefs and values. Controls of work and work outcomes within it are not vested in the supervisory process, or with the central management. They vest in the individuals, and are negotiated between supervisors and groups of knowledge workers.

10.2.3 Levels of Knowledge-creation Process

The process of knowledge creation occurs across three organisational levels—the individual, group, and firm. Each of these levels differs from the others in critical characteristics that, however, contribute to the overall process.

a. The individual level is characterised by action and reflection. Individuals combine action and thought, and engage in experimentation in terms of their autonomy. The interplay between their thoughts and action expands their base of tacit knowledge, and enhances their intuitive approaches to problem-solving.
b. The group level facilitates the drawing out of the tacit knowledge of individuals through discussion, dialogue, and interaction. Ideas are made concrete when group members try out various interpretations and meanings.
c. The nature and extent of inter-group relationships, and the autonomy available to individuals characterise the firm level. The firm's structure also serves as a regulating mechanism in competitive resource allocation.

10.3 BUILDING A LEARNING ORGANISATION

Changing an organisation into a laboratory for learning requires sustained, purposive effort. It needs to be designed, created, maintained, and strengthened continuously through communication of values and vision; the checking of policies, structure, methods, and procedures for congruence and consistency; and, above all, the adoption of holistic systems thinking.

It involves careful and sustained efforts the results of which may unfold slowly over time. A useful beginning in this direction can, however, be made through the following three steps (Garvin, ibid);

a. Fostering an open, supportive environment conducive to learning by providing employees time and facilities for reflection and analysis, training in and cultivation of problem-solving skills, participation in and autonomy of work team/group.
b. Stimulating the exchange of ideas, ensuring fresh flow of ideas, and providing opportunities for consideration of competing perspectives. This would necessitate the loosening and removal of internal organisational boundaries which inhibit the flow of information. It would also involve creation of horizontal structures for communication and sharing of ideas across the organisation.
c. Creating "learning forums," that is, programmes and events designed with explicit learning goals in view. These programmes and events can take a variety of forms. Strategic review which examine the changing competitive environment and the company's product for learning.

Going forward towards building a learning organisation is, however, an exercise in personal commitment and community building. This, in turn, requires a basic change in individual world views and personal transformation.

10.4 FEATURES OF A LEARNING ORGANISATION

Broad and basic features that distinguish a learning organisation are listed below.

a. Individual and collective knowledge of its members provides the base and cutting edge of the organisation's competitiveness.
b. Members of the organisation can access any information they need. Everyone is viewed as a possible source of important insights and ideas.
c. Employees close to a problem often have the most useful ideas regarding how to solve it. Empowerment is, therefore, facilitated throughout the organisational structure.
d. Learning and knowledge flow up, down, and across the company, so that organisation as a whole benefits from its collective knowledge resource.
e. New ideas and insights are deemed important. Individuals and teams are encouraged and rewarded for their contribution to the organisation's knowledge base. Formulation and implementation of ideas take place at all levels of the enterprise. The world is seen as too

complex and dynamic to be understood fully by a few persons at the top of a hierarchy.

f. Errors and failures in the pursuit of new initiatives, experiments, and opportunities are viewed as useful learning experiences.
g. Managers are receptive to new ideas and perspectives. They do not exercise close control over operations.
h. Learning organisations teach their people to break the constraints of conventional thinking and look at things differently. They encourage experiments, facilitate exploration, and promote enhancement and improvement of every business experience.
i. Learning process is promoted through development of systemic thinking among organisation members. Systemic thinking involves the ability to perceive relationships between issues, events, situations, and information in a holistic manner.
j. People are taught to identify the source of conflict they may have with other persons, units, sections, and departments. They are enjoined and encouraged to direct their attention and energy towards the substance of disagreements rather than towards clash of egos or political manipulations. People are expected to repair strained relationships quickly through dialogue, refraining from blame or criticism, problem-solving, empathy, and the maintenance of mutual respect and trust.
k. Creativity and innovation by individuals and teams are actively promoted and recognised.
l. Shared vision emerges from a collective endeavour, but its nurturing is the responsibility of top management.
m. Employees understand well their own jobs, work, and responsibilities. They also understand how their work affects the work of others, and related to organisational goals and performance.
n. Creation of knowledge involves an integration of learning and doing. Human capacities and capabilities are enhanced through testing of creative insights and ideas. Creation of knowledge can occur or emerge from any part of the company. However, without individuals' emotional commitment and intellectual ability to learn, there cannot be a learning organisation.
o. Learning organisations continuously acquire process, interpret, and disseminate through the organisation knowledge about markets, products, technologies, and business processes.
p. Members of a learning organisation question and examine regularly their long-held assumptions and beliefs regarding their business and business environment.
q. Knowledge acquisition sources include experience; experimentation; information from customers, suppliers, competition and business partners; employees; and external stakeholders.

r. Through communication, co-ordination, and conflict resolution processes, learning organisations reach a shared interpretation of information. Such a shared interpretation, in turn, enables them to act in time and decisively to exploit opportunities and defuse problems.

s. Learning organisations are highly developed in their ability to anticipate and act on opportunities in turbulent environments and fragmented markets.

t. The role of managerial leadership is to build a shared vision, empower people, serve as exemplars, create trust, generate commitment, promote teamwork, facilitate collaborative problem-solving, and strengthen a culture of continuous learning, besides steering the enterprise in pursuit of its values and vision.

u. Learning companies possess a strong culture of knowledge and imbibing. An ethos or spirit of excitement, of questioning and experiment, of exploration and adventure, of innovation and invention characterises this culture. Such a culture cannot be imposed. It can be sustained only when people like, respect, and trust each other, and the organisation is seen as actively promoting and caring for such values.

10.5 TOTAL QUALITY MANAGEMENT AND LEARNING ORGANISATION

Total quality management (TQM) is both a philosophy and a set of guiding principles that represent the foundation of a continuously improving organisation or a learning organisation. TQM is the application of quantitative methods and human resources to improve the materials and services supplied to an organisation, all the processes within an organisation, and the degree to which the needs of customers are met, now and in future. TQM integrates fundamental management techniques, existing improvement efforts, and technical tools under a disciplined approach focused on continuous improvement.

Definitions could differ but essentially total quality management comprises the following elements (Fig. 10.1). They are the building blocks of a learning organisation and required for its success.

Top management's commitment
Customer focus
Process focus and improvement
Measurement
Continuous improvement
Supplier teaming
Teams

Fig. 10.1 TQM in learing organisation

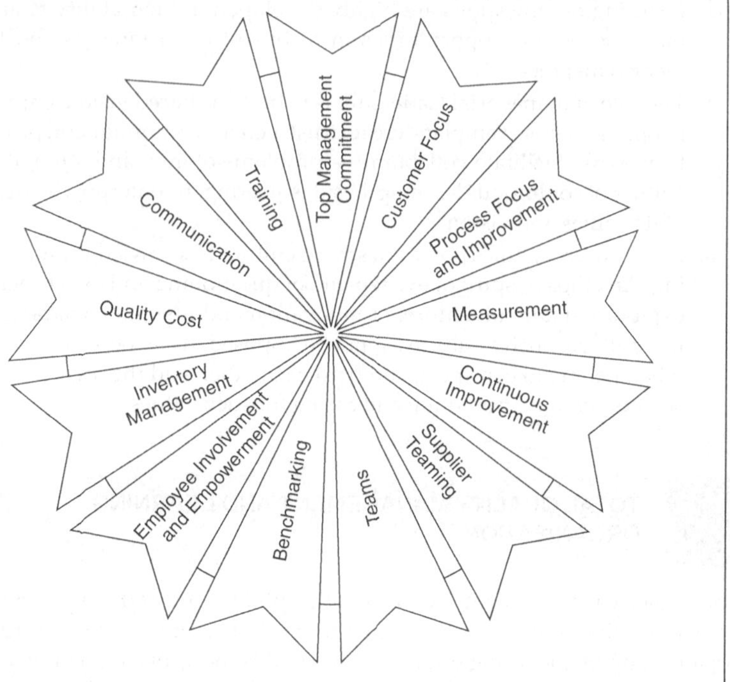

Benchmarking
Employee involvement and empowerment
Inventory management
Quality costs
Communication
Training

10.5.1 Top Management's Commitment

The culture of an organisation is the reflection of the training of top management. It is useless to embark on a quality journey without the top management's commitment to quality.

The leader plays a vital role in the development of the culture of an organisation. Culture is the pattern of shared beliefs and values that provides the members of an organisation rules of behaviour or accepted norms for operations. It is the philosophies, ideologies, values, assumptions, beliefs, expectation, attitude, and norms that knit an organisation together and are shared by employees. Institutionalising a strategy requires a culture that supports the strategy. Total quality requires a quantum change in the way people think and act in an organisation. This is possible when the initiative is from the top.

Top management should be unwavering in its commitment to quality. There might be countless opportunities which may invite compromises but the leader should not waver. The leader's commitment should be demonstrated and be visible in all actions. Do not forget, people do not listen to a leader but always watch him.

Quality is not possible without the participation of the leader. People make quality but the leader makes it happen. The leader is a very powerful role model. He is watched and talked about by people. His activities count more than his words. Every action must reinforce the quality commitment. As already mentioned, a successful quality transition must start from the top and progress down in a controlled way.

A quality leader should start learning about total quality like any other person in the organisation. He should work exhaustively with other colleagues to draft a comprehensive framework of a mission statement, values, and quality policy, which will be debated later by others in the company. He must constantly evaluate himself and his behaviour and should improve upon them.

A basic requirement of a quality leader is that he should listen to people and understand their behaviour. He should present his views and help people see the strategic direction. He should invite feedback and comments. And he should be positive.

Thus, a quality leader/top management should be a role model who is both a visionary and missionary, is able to empower the leader below him, and constantly improve himself.

10.5.2 Customer Focus

In a learning organisation, quality begins and ends with customers (internal as well as external). Gone are the days when organisations and customers were treated as two different entities. The marketplace has become very competitive, and it is no longer possible to run a business without a very strong focus on the customer.

Who Is a "Customer"

The Webster Dictionary defines a customer as "one that purchases a commodity or service." This definition talks of an interface between the seller and the customer who are two different entities. Here customers are beyond the bounds of an organisation.

By the TQM perspective, a customer is anyone (organisation) who receives and uses what an organisation or individual provides. This definition provides an important dimension that customers are no longer just beyond the organisation. Instead of being outside the organisation supplying goods and services, customers are also within the organisation doing the supply. Selling is not always required for this type of customer/supplier relation. What TQM tries to point out is that everybody in any organised endeavour has a customer. So customers could be internal as well as external.

A doctor's customers are his patients. A teacher's customers are students. A planning manager's customer is the production manager.

It is imperative that within an organisation all internal customers are satisfied to ensure complete satisfaction of the external customers. If one of the customers is dissatisfied he can create havoc in the business process. Proactively unearthing and fulfilling the demands of internal customers is one of the basic requirements of TQM.

Fig. 10.2 Customer focus

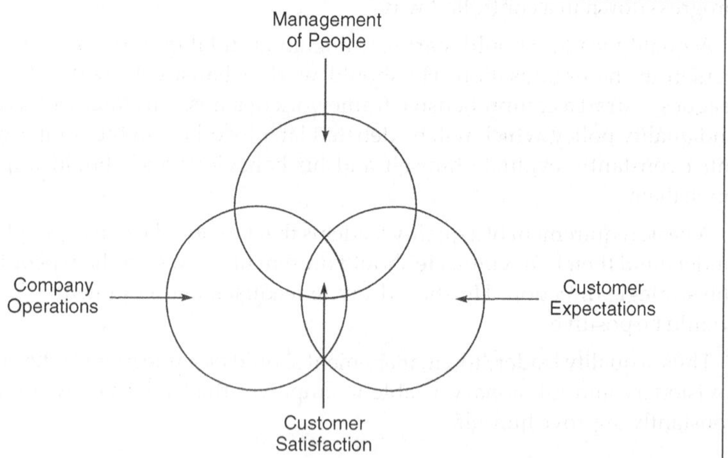

From a company's viewpoint, customer satisfaction is a result of the following (Fig. 10.1).

a. Company process (operations)
b. Company employees who deliver the product and service
c. Customer expectations

The extent to which customer satisfaction is achieved is based on the success of the above three. Customer satisfaction should not be treated as a mere slogan. The ultimate target of all businesses is to effectively invest resources to satisfy customers through empowered people in the face of market competition, so as to realise a profitable return on investment. Customer satisfaction leads to customer loyalty, which drives up market growth and share.

The following eight steps help place an organisation ahead of its competitors and help in customer retention.

a. Top management commitment to the concept of customer focus
b. Know your customers and what they like or dislike about you
c. Develop standards of quality service and performance
d. Recruit, train, and reward good staff
e. Always stay in touch with the customer
f. Work towards continuous improvement of customer service and retention
g. Reward service accomplishments by your staff
h. Process analysis and consulting

Traditionally, any product which had originality and was excellent in quality and function, captured the market share consistently. However, in today's world, product life is short, and new products are being launched regularly. Thus it may not be possible to obtain profit from the previously launched product. The need of the day, therefore, is to create distinction in "process."

Process means work arrangement or method of doing work. This is typical of an organisation and is associated with its culture. Thus, not allowing any rival company to copy the entire product easily due to established culture and customs.

Every production process (of goods or services) must be continuously updated, and altered customer preference constantly incorporated. The organisation culture should be such that everyone, from the shop floor to the board of directors, has an obligation to be constantly on the lookout for opportunities for improvement.

Aspect of process reforms is parallel processing of jobs. This results in a major reduction of process time. The reduction of cycle time is becoming more and more important from the viewpoint of creating distinction on the basis of time. For achieving this, the work is made to flow smoothly through rigorous exchange of information between different processes and at the same time all those jobs which can be carried out beforehand are executed simultaneously before the work comes from the previous process. This not only reduces cycle time but also enhances productivity. This is the production-oriented attitude of the organisation.

10.5.3 Measurement

Measurement is an integral part of the quality process. If an organisation cannot measure its progress, it is useless for it to go on a quality journey. Measurement is the propellant that fuels improvement. Without measurement, improvement fades away. To keep improving, people need to know where they are and where they want to tread. Without measurement, embarking on the road to TQM is like driving a car bereft of gauges. So if your organisation wants quality, it has to measure all factors at all levels.

Measure is the qualification of progress towards a goal. The aim with quality is to find appropriate measures which guide improvement actions at all levels and render a competitive advantage.

Why Measurement is Required

a. Quality is a measurable characteristic.
b. Quality measurement should be based on quantity and cost of non-conformance.
c. Quality is based on a product's compliance with expectations.
d. Poor quality raises costs unnecessarily.
e. Value and quality can be efficiently improved by measuring non-conformance in terms of quantity and costs, and systematically attacking the dominant non-conformance.

Every organisation must have a corporate measurement system that integrates a series of strategic and operational measures with the corporate vision. This linkage provides a clear picture of how key measures throughout the operation support broad corporate direction.

It is suggested that before developing appropriate measurements, the eleven Ws must be answered.

a. Why should you measure?
b. Where should you measure?
c. What should you measure?
d. When should you measure?
e. Who should be measured in the system?
f. Who should do the measuring?
g. Who should provide feedback in each system?
h. Who should provide performance audits?
i. Who should set business targets/standards in each system?
j. Who should set challenge targets in each system?
k. What should be done to locate, solve, and prevent problems in each system?

The following quality measurement presentations are recommended in any quality system.

a. Summaries of non-conformance quantities and costs
b. Summaries of scrap, rework, and costs
c. Summaries of supplier performance
d. Summaries of products' reliability
e. Summary of what quality is costing the organisation

10.5.4 Continuous Improvement

This refers to constant refinement and improvement of products, services, and organisational systems to yield improved value to consumers. The term "continuous improvement" is derived from the Japanese term "Kaizen" meaning small but continuous improvement.

Continuous improvement is at the heart of the TQM process.

The flow chart below outlines the steps towards implementing continuous improvement. It begins by defining the organisation's current quality status. This could be in any perspective such as defects, customer satisfaction levels, and so on.

Define current status
Define improvement objectives
Select specific improvement projects
Make teams
Define the process
Assess the reason for variability
Develop improvement plans
Take pilot runs
Modify/upgrade as required
Implement pilot process results
Measure results
Implement fully

Just using tools and techniques may not be sufficient to implement the theme of improvement. What is required is disciplined improvement that can hold the gains made through quality orientation.

There are many tools and techniques available to channel more discipline into improvement but the leader should ensure that his quality process makes the best use of those acceptable across functions. The six main drivers for improvement in organisations are strategy, leadership, customers, processes, people, and discipline.

10.5.5 Supplier Teaming

Supplier and vendors play a significant role in the TQM process. Organisations have realised that vendors are no more external entities but a part of their business process. Company-wide efforts, no matter how intensive, may not be enough for quality improvement if the suppliers are not involved.

The traditional relationship between the buyer and the supplier has been adversarial with the customer and supplier having different objectives. The focus has been on negative issues and is characterised by uncertainty.

But in a TQM company, suppliers and vendors are treated as partners who, the company realises, contribute to creating quality. So the organisation undertakes to work closely with them. Now this sort of relationship cannot be developed overnight and requires considerable changes in behaviour and attitude of both parties.

Suppliers need some surety that the money they are investing yields returns after a reasonable period of time. All TQM companies have very few suppliers, developed through vendor quality programmes designed to foster quality concepts and practices. They aim at a win-win situation wherein both meet their expectations, are satisfied, and make profits.

Did You Know?

Barriers to effective supplier-purchaser relationship

a. Poor communication
b. Complacency of the supplier about customer satisfaction.
c. Divergent objectives of both parties
d. Lack of trust
e. Lack of purchasing organisation's credibility on commitment to quality in the eyes of the supplier
f. Big brotherly attitude of the purchaser

What is Keiretsu?

It is a Japanese concept that emphasises long-term relationship with a few key suppliers over short-term relationship with many suppliers.

10.5.6 Teams

Teams are an important element of the TQM process. All companies treading the path to total quality know that team activity is one answer to quality issues. It is one of the essential TQM tools that can keep the wheel of quality moving.

The elements of this philosophy are as follows.

- The team should have an objective to develop the team member's individual abilities.
- The team should have an objective to make improvements for the organisation's benefit.
- During the problem-solving process, team members should evolve a team spirit and encourage every member to learn from each other.
- No single person should be allowed to dominate.
- Criticism should be avoided and creativity should be encouraged.

- Employees should not be forced to be part of the team; it should come from within.
- Management involvement is imperative in providing time, resources, and guidance.
- Management should not feel insecure that the credit for problem-solving is going to the teams.

Two prevalent types of teams are: (a) quality circle and (b) focus teams.

Quality circles are small groups of employees doing similar or related work who meet regularly to identify, analyse, and solve product, quality, and production problems and to improve general operations. This team originated in Japan under the tutelage of Kaoru Ishikawa. The basic objective of these teams are shifting of problem-solving responsibility to those on factory floor, who are close to the problems (Fig. 10.3).

Fig. 10.3 Quality circle (effective team)

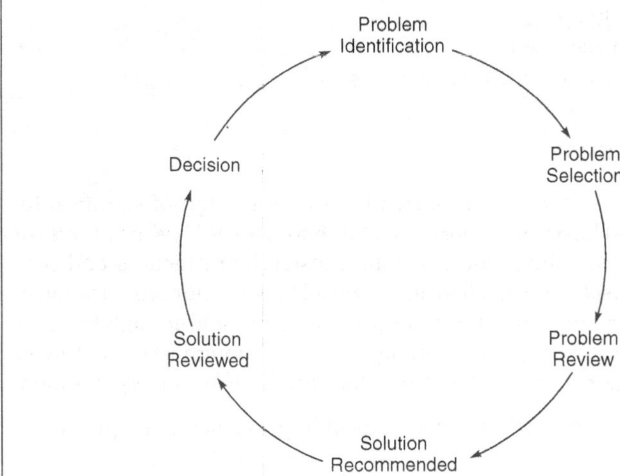

Quality circles comprise five to six people at the work centre and are led by the work centre supervisor. They are trained in quality assurance techniques and meet regularly during a stipulated time of the day when there is less work. The meetings are loosely structured and begin with a brainstorming session. Then they turn to solving of problems identified by the members.

The biggest disadvantage of quality circles has been lack of focus. They may not have the required expertise to solve specific problems. Also, the selected problem may not have any real consequence.

As a result focus teams were born. These teams were born in the USA and are essentially similar to the quality circles except that

- Management provides input to the focus teams to identify which problems it considers significant.

- Individuals from other disciplines within the organisation with requisite skills to solve problems are included in the focus team.
- Teams are normally abandoned once the problem in solved.

Thus focus teams are multi-disciplinary teams charted to focus on specific problems on continuous improvement objectives.

It becomes vital for management to establish the basic rules that can provide the right milieu for team activity. Thus, it is imperative for management to understand the following.

a. Types of teams
b. When and where different teams are to be used
c. Training requirements of the teams
d. Time required for the teams
e. Number of teams required
f. Tools teams use
g. Reasons why team fail
h. Management's role in team operations

10.5.7 Benchmarking

Benchmarking is the continuous search for an application of significantly better practices that lead to superior competitive advantage. It is the process of identifying, understanding, and adopting outstanding practices and processes from organisations anywhere in the world to help your organisation to improve its performance. It is the practice of being humble enough to admit that someone else is better at something, and wise enough to learn how to match, and even surpass them at it. This is the core of a learning organisation.

a. It enables organisations to effect radical improvements not just incremental ones.
b. It exposes managers to practices that they would have never developed on their own
c. It accelerates change and an awareness of world-class status.
d. It provides a goal that is attainable.
e. It helps to improve the organisation's performance.
f. It help the organisation to jump into global quality league.

Steps to Benchmarking

Planning	Identify what is to be benchmarked
	Identify comparative companies
	Determine data collection method and collect data (Fig. 10.4)

Analysis	Determine current performance gap
	Project future performance levels
Integration	Communicate benchmark findings to gain acceptance
	Establish functional goals
Action	Leadership position attained
	Practices fully integrated into process

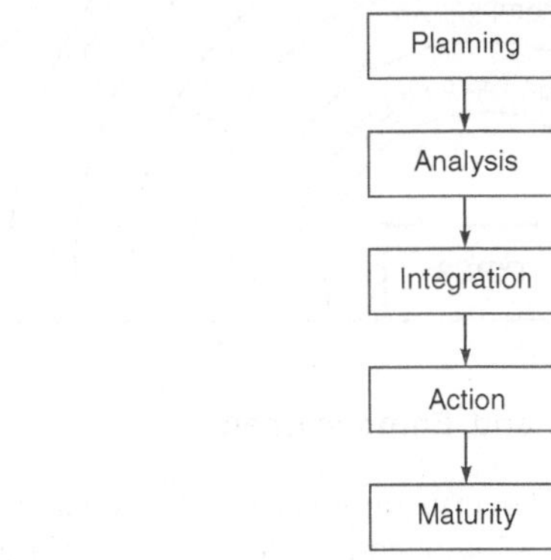

Fig. 10.4 Steps to benchmarking

Types of Benchmarking

First Generation Reverse Engineering This involves evaluation of a number of organisations similar to your organisation, analysis of the features of these organisations, sometimes analysing all these organisations looking at their performance, examining their design, studying all details of the competitor's organisation, and determining where your organisation stands with respect to the competitor's organisation.

Competitive Benchmarking This benchmarking is restricted to competitors.

Process Benchmarking This benchmarking focuses on the processes with the intention to learn how a business process is carried out—irrespective of whether it is a competitor's or anybody else's.

Strategic Benchmarking This is of interest to top management who want to know how strategic business processes are carried out in some other organisations compared to their own.

Global Benchmarking This involves benchmarking with world-class products/services cutting across your country's border. This is very important for organisations who want to set up global operations.

Fig. 10.5 Types of benchmarking

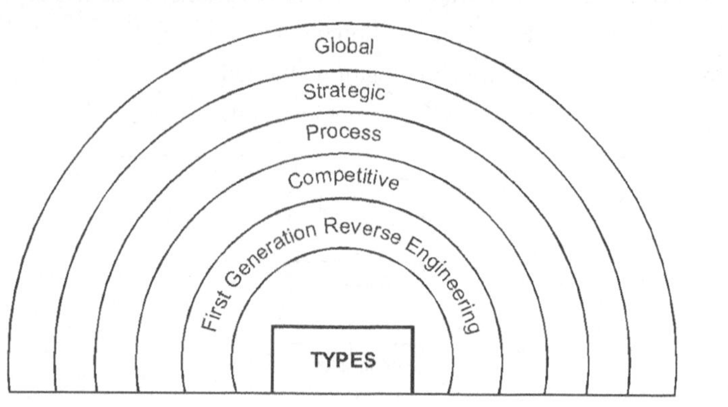

10.5.8 Employee Involvement and Empowerment

Employee involvement means that every employee is regarded as a unique human being, and each employee is involved in helping the organisation to meet its goals.

Employee empowerment means sharing with non-managerial employees the power and authority to make and implement decisions.

Some benefits of employee involvement are given below.

a. Involvement may result in better decisions. Workers may often have information that is of relevance to the business and management.
b. If decisions are made by groups, reaction of changing environment may be particularly slow.
c. Employees are more keen to implement decisions that they have been part of.
d. The mere process of participation may satisfy such non-pecuniary needs as creativity, achievement, and social approval.
e. Involvement improves communication and co-operation.
f. Involved workmen supervise themselves, thus reducing the need for supervisors.
g. Participation increases people's sense of power and dignity. It reduces the need to show one's power through fighting with management and restricting production.
h. Involvement increases loyalty and identification with organisation especially if the group's suggestion is implemented.

i. Participation frequently results in the setting of goals. There is considerable evidence that goal-setting is an effective motivational technique.
j. Involvement teaches workmen new skills and helps to train and identify leaders.

Now let us talk about empowerment. There are two steps to empowerment. One is to arm people to be successful through coaching, guidance, and training. The second is delegation, letting people work by themselves.

Some principles for empowering people are listed below (Fig. 10.6).

a. Tell people what their responsibilities are
b. Give authority that is commensurate with responsibility
c. Set standards for excellence
d. Render training
e. Provide knowledge and information
f. Trust them
g. Allow them to fail
h. Treat them with dignity and respect

Fig. 10.6 Some principles for empowering people

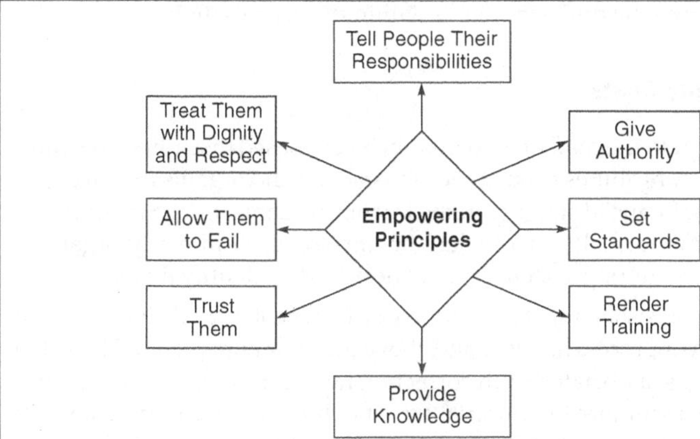

A key dimension to empowerment is alignment. All employees need to know the organisation's mission, visions, values, policies, objectives, and methodologies.

Another dimension of empowerment is capability. Employees must have the ability, skills, and knowledge needed to do their job as well as the willingness to co-operate to build a learning organisation.

10.5.9 Inventory Management

Traditionally, organisations have been following the concept of economic ordering quantity (EOQ) for effective inventory management.

The presence of excess inventory increases the risk of obsolescence and deterioration, increases the need for warehouse and shop-floor space, and by "pushing" parts through the assembly process encourages a number of wasteful practices.

Just in Time (JIT) inventory management embraces the philosophy of zero inventory in which elimination of waste is the central goal. JIT is a manufacturing system the goal of which is to optimise process and procedures by continuously pursuing waste reduction.

The benefits of JIT are as follows.

a. Elimination of extraneous activities
b. Less requirement of floor space per unit of output
c. Less requirement of direct and indirect labour
d. Lessening of set-up time and schedule delays
e. Lessening of lead times due to small lot size
f. Judicious utilisation of men, machine, and material
g. Improvement in supplier relationship
h. Quality gets ingrained in the process
i. Brings down the functional-silos within the organisation

10.5.10 Quality Costs

A key ingredient to the road of total quality is cost-based discipline. A sound quality system contributes to customer satisfaction and organisational objectives, including financial stability in the learning organisation. Significantly, quality costs are normally overlooked or unrecognised in many organisations because accounting systems are not designed to identify them.

Quality cost, or cost of quality, is defined as the cost of those activities which an organisation or process has over and above the minimum required to do the job well. Any cost associated with correcting failure or waste go into quality costs, as do any assurance or approval activities built in to cushion customers from the effects of such failures. A further set of activities are those in which we attempt to prevent such failures occuring at all, such as effective design, market research, and training.

Essentially, quality costs are defined as the total costs incurred by a) investing in the prevention of non-conformance to requirements, b) appraisal of a product of service for conformance to requirement, and c) failure to meet requirements.

10.5.11 Communication

One of the essential elements of TQM is "internal communication". It is useless to embark on a quality journey without an effective management of "internal communication." While communication is central to success, many organisations think it is peripheral.

Like any other element of TQM, the drive for communication must emanate from the top. It should be treated as a key business strategy and there must be a tremendous sense of purpose to keep it going.

Internal communication should give a clear picture of how each employee fits into the company. They should be shown how their individual work contributes to the success of their department, and how the work of their department affects the work of the other departments, and how this ultimately impacts the customer.

Employees want to know what is in it for them both on the upside and on the downside. The more specific and personally relevant this is, the better people will respond. Communication should make employees feel that they are important, involved, and not just robots dancing to the tune of the bosses.

Quality is people and if an institution is really people-oriented, it needs plenty of words to describe the way people ought to treat one another. One way, which many American companies have adopted, is the usage of phrases that upgrade the status of individual employees. They are called "hosts", "associates", "partners", "crewmembers", and so on.

The leader will need to emphasise that a total quality organisation can only achieve its desired "state of being" when there is active collaboration among all, aimed at moving in unison towards the goal.

A striking characteristic of many excellent companies is the apparent absence of rigidly followed chain of command. Of course, the chain of command exists for big decisions, not for day-to-day communication. For information exchange, informality is the norm. Top management use the technique known as MBWA, or Management By Wandering About. They wander around and are in regular contact with employees at lower levels. They interact with them not as curious supervisors but as long-lost friends.

Listening is the most valuable part of communication. It is essential to be a good listener on the job in order to provide customers with superior services and products. Poor listening not only creates a poor impression, it can also cause mistakes.

For successful communication, a flat organisational structure is desirable. Often the hierarchy mindset acts as a major hurdle.

Finally, leadership and communication go hand in hand as best described by the statement "leadership is communication." People put their best foot forward when they believe the person who has inspired them to do something.

10.5.12 Training

"Quality control begins with education and ends with education," said Kaoru Ishikawa in his book *What Is Quality Control*.

It is true that implementation of total quality initiative is synonymous with employee training and education. They are vehicles for quality deployment and are the basic requirements for a quality journey of a learning organisation.

Why Is Training So Important?

Management for quality means focusing on people, training them, and providing leadership. As a result, training cannot be an ancillary activity. It has to be given top priority with maximum impetus.

Before we go ahead, let us distinguish between "training" and "education." The difference between the two is that they are each for a definite purpose. While training is specific, targeted at the skills required for the job; education is general in nature. Its aim is to improve employees' general knowledge. A management seminar on TQM is an example of general education, while an instruction on the usage of quality tools is an example of training for learning.

Process improvement integrates three sets of skills comprising job knowledge, team skills, and process analysis. The content of each of these depends on the current capabilities and the level of proficiency expected.

Quality education and training should begin with top management and should flow down through middle management and staff. Being a long-term process, their delivery in the top-down manner should go on until everyone is equipped with the necessary philosophies, attitudes, and tools. Thus, continuing education and training at all levels must become a part of corporate culture.

Training and education should be viewed as a powerful strategic tool. It should liberate the forces of creativity and initiative of the individual.

In a learning organisation, the objective of training should be clear, performance-oriented, and quantitatively measured. The true goal of good quality training is not to teach the use of quality tools but to equip employees with tools that they will comfortably use for process improvement opportunities.

10.6 BLUEPRINT OF A LEARNING ORGANISATION

What is or should be the structure of a learning organisation? How should it be designed? What are its dimensions? These questions are perceptively addressed by Pedlar et al. (1991). They not only specify the dimensions of design, but have also developed a blueprint of its organisational format or pattern. The blueprint of a learning organisation consists of eleven dimensions organised into four core clusters as shown in Fig. 10.7.

The enabling structures represent the central point of the learning organisation since they are designed to create opportunities for business and individual development. For instance, rules and procedures are frequently

Fig. 10.7 Blueprint of a learning organisation

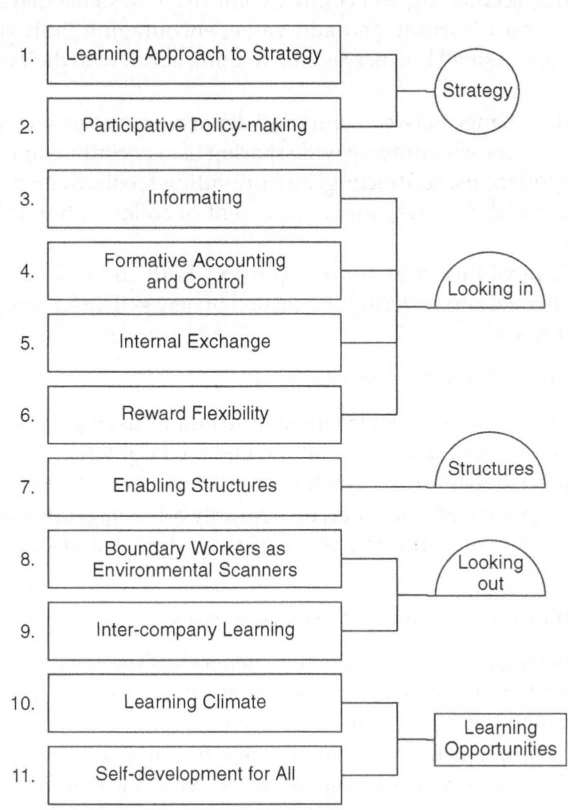

reviewed and changed, if necessary; and appraisals are geared to learning and development rather than to reward and punishment.

The two clusters above "Structures" in the blueprint of a learning company are mirrored by the two below. The "Strategy" cluster consists of

a. A learning approach whereby the company policy and strategy formation, together with implementation, evaluation, and improvement, are consciously structured as a learning process enabling continuous improvement through flexibility; and
b. Participative policy making which involves all stakeholders (including customers, suppliers, and owners) in the strategy-forming processes with commitment to discuss and work through conflicts.

The "Looking in" cluster covers four dimensions.

a. Informating, which means that information technology is used to inform and empower people, encouraging wide access to information and more "open" systems;
b. Formative accounting and control, comprising systems that are structured to assist learning and add value, encouraging individuals and units to act as small businesses, and to think about who their customers are;
c. Internal exchange between units and departments as mutual suppliers and customers, encouraging wide sharing of expectations and information, negotiations, contracting, and providing feedback on goods/services received, fostering an environment of collaboration rather than competition; and
d. Reward flexibility towards recognising both individual and team achievements, and fostering acquisition of new skills and competencies by employees

The "Looking out" cluster consists of

a. Boundary workers as environmental scanners, asking for, respecting, and using the experiences of all members who interact with external customers to feedback information on customer needs; and
b. Inter-company learning whereby neutrally advantageous learning activities such as joint-trading, sharing in investment, and job exchanges, are initiated.

The "Learning Opportunities" cluster comprises

a. The fostering of a learning climate, a general attitude of continuous improvement, the positive valuing of difference (age, gender, colour, and so on), learning lessons from mistakes, and so on.
b. Self-development for all, whereby facilities and resources are made available to all members, employees at all levels, and external stakeholders.

The blueprint of a learning organisation proposed by Pedlar is not a finished product. It is, rather, a creative exercise in organisational design which pulls together and synthesises a number of relevant insights and inferences. As such, it breaks new ground in advancing our understanding of the learning organisation.

10.7 MANAGING AND SUSTAINING CHANGE IN A LEARNING ORGANISATION

Building a learning organisation involves a major process of change and transformation in both the mindset and the working of the organisation. Such a process needs to be managed and sustained if a learning organisation is to be created. This, in turn, means, that the members of an organisation must understand the need for such a change, and feel motivated towards implementing it. Managing change may then be seen to involve the following dimensions.

a. Creating motivation for change in the light of the present or impending, and potential crisis facing the company; and its very survival being at stake owing to unprecedented competitive pressures
b. Creating motivation for change by providing a vision of what the enterprise will look like after the change
c. Educating and coaching employees about what to change, why, and how, by describing the changes needed
d. Inspiring employees through success stories of organisational transformation in other companies
e. Identifying skills and behaviours necessary to support change, and providing training and tools to employees for implementing change
f. Providing employees with role model behaviours and examples of change agents
g. Accelerating the process of change by identifying and employing best practices for managing change
h. Designing and creating effective reward and recognition systems for supporting the new knowledge culture
i. Designing and creating appropriate organisational structures that best support the new knowledge-based culture.

According to them, when you need to communicate a major change, stop communicating values, communicate face-to-face, and spend most of your time, money, and effort on frontline supervisors. Frontline employees do not want to find out about change by watching a video. Nor do they want to read about it in a company publication which they distrust. Large meetings and slogans do not motivate them. Frontline employees prefer to receive information from their superior—the person to whom they are closest. Frontline supervisors are the real opinion leaders in any company. Senior managers must discuss change face-to-face with supervisors, who will pass information along to their subordinates. Communication between frontline supervisors and employees counts the most towards changed behaviour where it matters the most—at the frontline.

10.7.1 The Change Imperative

Confronted with the relentless pressures of uncertainty and fast-paced change, there may perhaps be no single best approach, or way of coping with a turbulent business environment. Business enterprises today operate in a highly complex, increasingly uncertain, and rapidly changing environment of global economy, trade, and industry. Coping with continuous change is not an option for them, it is an imperative compulsion. They can cope with change in a proactive and anticipatory manner, or in a reactive crisis-oriented mode. But they need to be prepared for facing the emergent and emerging, anticipated and unexpected, ordinary and extraordinary change situations, in a rapid, flexible, knowledgeable, and competent manner.

Organisations today have no choice but to try to be competent in capabilities that are appropriate for coping with environmental turbulence, complexity, ambiguity, and uncertainty in a continuing manner. Organisations have to acknowledge and accept high levels of volatility and uncertainty. They should learn to live with the stress of unstable and unclear situations. They have to accept errors, and use them as learning opportunities. They have to learn to anticipate and visualise the future, and map it against their desired vision.

Today, knowledge, technology, and managerial practices that provide competitive edge are becoming more short-lived. The techno-scientific, geo-political, and socio-economic trends and forces affecting organisations are increasing. The rate of change is consequently intensifying. How organisa-tions respond to fast-paced change will largely determine their survival and success.

An organisation, therefore, needs to build its internal capacity to respond to fires, in terms of multi-dimensional, co-ordinated, and proactive approach to prevent, or put them out quickly and effectively. Such an approach can, however, be fashioned only in terms of knowledge and information, capabilities and skills, all of which require learning. Change needs to be viewed and managed for new advantages, not merely reacted to for minimising loss and danger.

The architecture of change involves the design and construction of new patterns, or the reconceptualisation of old ones, to make new and hopefully more productive action possible. Crystallisation of new action possibilities and design and construction of a new pattern of productive actions can, however, only be based on relevant insights, knowledge, capabilities, and skills. The latter cannot, however, be sustained or used effectively over time, without being supported by continuous learning.

For coping with continuous change, an enterprise must constantly engage in both exploitation and exploration of knowledge. Exploitation focuses on refinement, fine-tuning, productivity, improvement, efficiency, selection, implementation, and execution. Exploration, on the other hand, focuses on search, experimentation, risk taking, flexibility, discovery, and innovation.

Learning has to be not only continuous, but also match and exceed the pace of change in a business environment. In case of failure to do so, an enterprise cannot really practise a proactive and anticipatory approach towards managing change. The learning effort, therefore, needs to be both purposive and fast-paced, in order to be proactive and anticipatory, foresighted and flexible.

10.8 BASIS OF LEARNING APPROACH IN AN ORGANISATION

Purposive, fast-paced, and continuous learning provides the overarching approach of a learning organisation for coping with change. Within the framework of this approach, certain salient elements or bases of the approach may, however, be distinguished. These elements, or bases, serve to elucidate the relatively distinctive nature and rationale of a learning organisation's approach towards facing and coping with change. These elements are not objects, or activities. They are primarily mental orientations, or cognitive anchors, defining the mindset of the members of a learning enterprise. They may be listed (in a non-ordered manner) as follows (Fig. 10.8).

a. Unlearning
    i. Replacing a fragmented perspective
    ii. Discarding entrenched untested assumptions
b. Openness to new ideas
c. Creativity and innovation
d. Receptivity to uncertainty
e. Strategic viewpoint
f. Vision and values

These elements/bases provide directional guidelines, or mental anchors, for their thinking and behaviour to the members of a firm's knowledge-creating crew. They are equally valid and binding for frontline employees and staff, specialists, middle managers, and top management personnel. The latter, however, have the further and more important responsibility for fostering and nurturing them across the enterprise as catalysts for organisational renewal.

Fig. 10.8 The basic elements of learning approach in an organisation

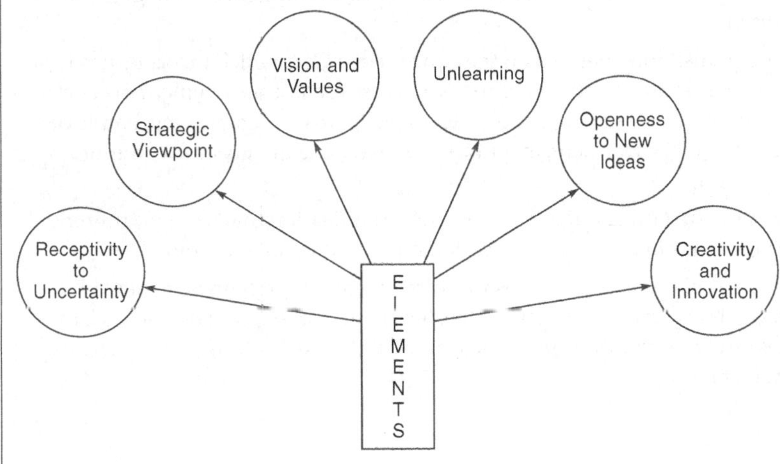

10.8.1 Creativity and Innovation

Creativity provides the cutting edge of organisational excellence. It is reflected in the organisation's ability to achieve improvement after improvement, and innovate both incrementally and radically, in its continuing quest for competitive advantage(s).

World-class organisations develop and use creativity through structural mechanisms like quality circles, employees' suggestion schemes, creative team and task forces, and appropriate systems of reward and recognition.

10.8.2 The Ultimate Requirement

The people must, therefore, also correlatively hold that for mastering change, they must continually engage in the learning and use of knowledge; in generating value through creativity and skills; in developing technological and manufacturing competencies; in operating and managing fast and flexible structures; in collaborating with other organisations for mutual benefit; in accelerating their decisions, actions, work processes, and co-ordination through IT; and in critically examining their assumptions concerning changes in and relationship with the external environment.

SUMMARY

- A learning organisation is one with flexibility in its structure, operations and performance which gives it the strength to adapt itself to its changing environment.
- A learning organisation is a "knowledge creating company." Every member in the organisation is involved in adaptive and generative learning. In building a learning organisation, a well-designed, maintained, and strengthened managerial system is required.
- A learning organisation operates on the concept of TQM, which incorporates top management commitment, customer focus, process focus, improvement measurement, continuous improvement, supplier teaming, teams, benchmarking, employee involvement and empowerment, inventory management, quality cost, communications, and training.
- To manage and sustain change in a learning organisation, motivation, training, reward, proper communication, and leadership qualities are required.
- Finally, the basis of a learning organisation are unlearning, openness to new ideas, creativity, and innovation. Receptivity to uncertainty, strategic viewpoint, vision, and values are the foundation stones on which the building of a learning organisation stands.

 Case Study: A Software Development Company

History

A young software development company delivering media management solutions to large media companies was on a rapid growth trajectory. This involved bringing in large numbers of new, and very diverse, managers and employees. Every newcomer arrived with different experiences and expectations of how performance evaluation should be done. The older informal ways of evaluating employee performance were no longer adequate.

Task

Work with the HR director to create a state-of-the-art standardised performance evaluation process. Develop and deliver a customised performance evaluation training programme for all managers and supervisors in the company.

Intervention

The OD Practitioner interviewed the CEO and HR director to determine what the company's philosophy of performance management was and then recommended revisions to the performance evaluation process, timeline, forms, and instructions. Three trainings were developed and delivered to all the company's managers and supervisors: (a) writing and delivering performance appraisals; (b) Objectives, tracking, feedback, and ongoing mentoring; and (c) Performance evaluation across cultures. This was followed by small-group coaching sessions.

Result

Dramatic improvement in the quality of employee goal-setting and performance evaluation by managers and supervisors, as well as general communication within the company about performance.

Key Disciplines

Learning Organisation, Human Resource Strategy, Performance Management, Performance Evaluation, Management Training, Training Programme Development.

Review Questions

1. Define a learning organisation and explain its nature and characteristics in detail.
2. How can an organisation be transformed into a learning organisation?
3. What is TQM and how is it applied in the concept of a learning organisation?
4. What must an organisation do to manage sustainable learning?

EXERCISE 1

Gather the team around a large sheet of paper—the bigger the group the bigger the paper. Four sheets of flip-chart paper joined together makes a good work area for a team of four to ten people.

Participants can play as individuals or in pairs. Using felt-tip marker pens, team members begin by drawing their own section of coastline for one whole team island, with whatever features are desired, so that sections are connected with those of adjacent colleagues to create one big island.

Next, team members can mark out the territory, working inland from their own sections of coastline, with whatever features are desired—residential, industrial, transport, geographical, and countryside. Try to agree to a suitable scale before this commences, although the facilitator can deliberately leave this vague to demonstrate the challenges of scaling, interpretation, and compatibility as the activity unfolds.

As team members begin to meet the intentions and drawn features of their neighbours, they will encounter a variety of issues and situations that need discussing, negotiating, agreeing, and so on, just like those of any growing community or organisation.

These will commonly involve issues about boundaries, roads, communications, resources, culture, environment, co-operation, dispute, factions, and decision-making. Many parallels will be observed between the game and the actual team's work issues and dynamics and life.

This exercise can be used as a stand-alone activity, or at the beginning of a long programme and then repeated at the end to identify the change in communication and understanding that has occurred as a result of the programme or session. For larger groups, the activity can be extended to involve the development of a number of islands—one per team—which when completed can then begin to engage with the other teams' islands—visit, trade, explore, learn from, attack, build alliances, and so on.

EXERCISE 2

A perfect balance between the practices of the past, present, and future is the core of a learning organisation. This exercise explains the above mentioned in a more practical and on a personal experience basis.

Ask each team member to put his briefcase or personal organiser on the table in front of his. Then ask each to think about the unnecessary material in it that he has been too lazy to throw away or delete.

Then ask each person to actually remove the useless items, screw them up, and put them into a pile in the middle of the table along with everyone else's. Where individual team members are reluctant to admit to holding on to any obsolete, useless material, ask them to identify the three oldest pieces of material they are still keeping, and to justify why they are keeping them.

The act of throwing everyone's collective junk into a bin can be used to symbolise the "look-ahead" theme, and to reinforce a commitment to de-clutter, to welcome and make the most of change, and not to dwell on the past, to complain about past issues, or regret past mistakes.

You can extend or change the exercise by asking people to produce and scrutinise their own bunch of keys, or contents of handbags (be mindful of sensitivities), or wallets, or even the address books of mobile phones, to illustrate how we all keep unnecessary baggage, which holds us back, weighs us down, and hinders our ability to stay fresh and welcome change. Getting rid of clutter is a vital aspect of staying fresh, looking forward, and positively embracing change.

Control the baggage from your past, and you control your future.

Chapter

Some Models of Organisational Change

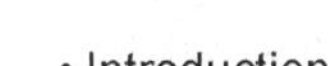

Chapter Outline

"Vision without action is a daydream,
Action without vision is a nightmare."

—Japanese Proverb

11.1 INTRODUCTION

There are several models of organisational change. A model is an integrated way of explaining why and how change takes place, based on a known and acceptable basic explanation (theory) of relationships of several aspects involved. It is obvious that there are different ways of explaining change, depending on what theory we follow or use.

Two contrasting models of change are the "trickle down" model and "identity search" model. The first is also termed in sociology as Sanskritisation, that is, following the example of an elite group.

Trickle down model According to this model, organisational change occurs because top management takes a decision and adopts some new ways (technology, systems, structure, and so on) and others follow it.

Identity search model This model believes that the urge to develop one's own uniqueness and identity will make the group or individuals accept change.

Another way is to look at the external or internal forces as determinants of changes.

Adaptation model It emphasises the role of external factors (a new government policy, competitive environment) in producing change in organisations (more emphasis on quality, restructuring, and so on).

Projection model According to this model, the explanation comes from within the organisation (the decision of the organisation to set an example, to be a leader, anticipate the future) and act and change itself in response to such an internal urge.

Yet another explanation of organisational change may lie in emphasis on the structure or the process.

Structure model Successful change, according to this model, would require preparing the necessary structural details (technology, design of the organisation, systems) and introducing them systematically. People will also change according to the process and model them systematically. People will also plan by helping people to develop process competencies (ways of planning, decision-making, problem-solving, collaborating, communicating, and so on), and then people will find new ways of organising and so on.

A more comprehensive way is to look at the main emphasis on producing change in individuals, roles, teams, or organisations. They are the core models, to make the process of change more lucid; accessory models are also applied in the management of change.

We shall use this way of looking at some models of organisational change.

11.2 INDIVIDUALISTIC MODEL

According to this model of change, the individual is the prime force in organisational change. Individuals can promote or resist change. If individuals get motivated, change is easy. How do individuals get motivated? We shall consider three explanations in this context.

a. Individuals change when they learn new and more desirable ways of doing things.
b. Individuals change when they get non-threatening feedback.
c. Individuals change when their motives change.

11.2.1 Adoption Diffusion Model

Change as a Learning Process

The adoption diffusion model of change, so popular in agriculture, is based on the theory of change being the process of learning. Learning takes places when one is dissatisfied with the present state, wants a change, sees new alternatives, debates mentally about the pay off of the new alternative, checks with others, tries the new alternative, assesses its advantages over the old ways, and finally adopts it.

This model has been discussed in detail in the chapter "Strategic Management of Change." Two main elements of this model are that change is regarded as a sequential process, and the rate of change varies from one individual or group to another.

As already discussed, there are eight stages in the process of change in an individual): initiation, motivation, diagnosis, information collection, action proposal, deliberation, implementation, and stabilisation.

Individuals do not respond to change at the same rate. Those who accept change have been classified into five groups: innovators (about 2.5%), early adopters (about 13.5%), early majority to adopt change (about 34%), late majority (about 34%), and laggards (about 16%).

A large number of studies have been made, and extension practices developed to help people go through the sequential process faster, and to help "late majority" and "laggards" learn to quicken their pace of change. One popular method of help is "demonstration" of the new alternative, by taking people to a place where it has been successfully used.

11.2.2 Feedback Model

Change through Feedback

Another model of change is based on the assumption that individuals change if they get feedback on their behaviour, and also have a theoretical framework which shows that the current behaviour is dysfunctional. The feedback needs to be objective and non-threatening.

A good example of this model is the work done in schools on changing teaching style, using Flanker's theory of teacher's classroom interaction behaviour. The teachers learn how to score objectively a teacher's behaviour while teaching. The teacher's behaviour is scored every third second during the period of teaching. A scoring reliability of 98 percent (agreement between two scores) has to be established before scoring a teacher's behaviour on "direct influence" (behaviour which restricts initiative and freedom of the student, like lecturing, criticising, reprimanding, ordering, asking questions with one known answer) and "indirect influence" (behaviour which encourages students' initiative and autonomy, like student talk, recognising students' contribution, building on students' ideas, recognising feelings, asking questions with multiple answers). Then i/d (indirect divided by direct) influence behaviour is worked out and feedback given to the teacher concerned.

The teachers learn the theory and research results showing that direct influence behaviour results in dependency, lack of initiative, low activity level, lower interpersonal trust, and low adjustment of students, while indirect influence behaviour results in the opposite effect. Such feedback alone leads to a change in a teacher's style of teaching and a change of the school climate.

11.2.3 Motivation Model

This is the most important model to facilitate the process of change in the organisation.

The work of David McClelland on changing larger systems by changing basic motives of individuals is quite well-known, and has been widely used in India in the development of entrepreneurship.

The basic explanation is that individuals engage in certain activities because of their dominant motive or psychological need. A person with affiliation motive (the need to establish and enjoy close personal relations) will socialise more and enjoy meeting and being with people. Similarly, a person with achievement motive (the need to excel and do something unique) will be engaged in competitive activities, and is likely to spend more time in work (business, selling, competitive games, and so on). If we can change the main motive of a person, for example, from affiliation to motivation, the patterns of activities can be changed from "club-like" behaviour to work-related excellence.

Successful attempts have been made to change motivation patterns of individuals, and produce large change.

McClelland has suggested the following 12 propositions for designing intervention to help adults acquire motives which they desire to have.

Proposition 1 The more an individual believes in advance that he can, will, or should develop a motive, the more likely he is to succeed in the educational attempts designed to develop that motive.

Proposition 2 The more an individual perceives that developing a motive is consistent with the demands of reality (and reason), the more likely is the success of educational attempts designed to develop that motive.

Proposition 3 The more thoroughly an individual develops and clearly conceptualises the associative network defining the motive, the more likely he is to develop the motive.

Proposition 4 The more an individual can link the newly developed network to related actions, the more likely it is to occur and endure in thought and action.

Proposition 5 The more an individual can link the newly conceptualised association-action complex (or motive) to events in his everyday life, the more likely the motive is to influence his thoughts and actions in situations outside the training experience.

Proposition 6 The more an individual can perceive and experience the newly conceptualised motive as an improvement in self-image, the more the motive is likely to influence his future thoughts and actions.

Proposition 7 The more an individual can perceive and experience the newly conceptualised motive as an improvement on prevailing cultural values, the more the motive is likely to influence his future thoughts and actions.

Proposition 8 The more an individual commits himself to achieving concrete goals in life related to the newly formed motive, the more likely the motive is to influence his future thoughts and actions.

Proposition 9 The more an individual keeps a record of his progress toward achieving goals to which he is committed, the more the newly formed motive is likely to influence his future thoughts and actions.

Proposition 10 Changes in motives are more likely to occur in an interpersonal atmosphere in which the individual feels warmly but honestly supported and respected by others as a person capable of guiding and directing his own future behaviour.

Proposition 11 Changes in motives are more likely to occur if the setting dramatises the importance of self-study and lifts it out of the routine of everyday life.

Proposition 12 Changes in motives are more likely to occur and persist if the new motive is a sign of membership in a new reference group.

This core model is based on the individual as a major factor of change.

11.3 ROLE-ORIENTED MODEL

Changing organisational roles can bring about organisational change. It has been argued that individual change is too expensive in terms of time and effort, and may not necessarily lead to organisational change. If organisational roles can be modified, these will, on the one hand, increase individuals' involvement, and, on the other, increase organisational effectiveness.

One approach used for organisational change is that of role efficacy. Role efficacy has been already explained in the chapter "Manager as a Change Catalyst."

Organisational roles are analysed for role efficacy (potential effectiveness) in terms of the following 10 dimensions (Fig. 11.1). The more these dimensions are present in a role, the higher the efficacy of that role is likely to be.

a. Centrality vs Peripherality The dimension of centrality measures the role occupant's perception of the significance of his role. The more people feel their

Fig. 11.1 Role-oriented model

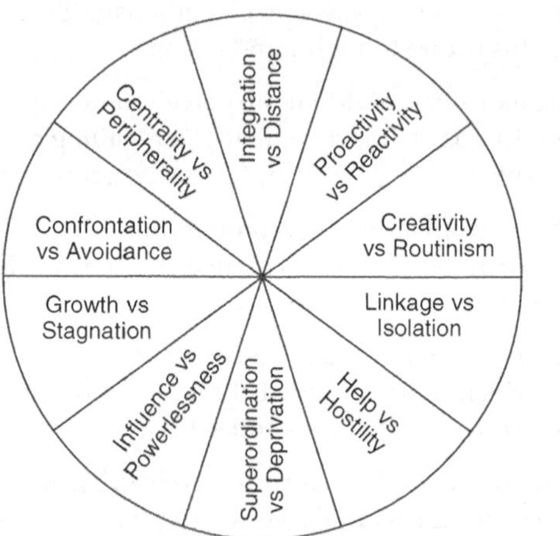

roles are central in the organisation, the higher will be their role efficacy. For example, "I am a production manager, and my role is very important."

*b. **Integration vs Distance*** Integration between the self and the role contributes to role efficacy, and self-role distance diminishes efficacy. For example, "I am able to use my knowledge very well here."

*c. **Proactivity vs Reactivity*** When a role occupant takes the initiative and does something independently, that person is exhibiting proactive behaviour. On the other hand, if he merely responds to what others expect, the behaviour is reactive. For example, "I prepare the budget for discussion" versus "I prepare the budget according to the guidance given by my boss."

*d. **Creativity vs Routinism*** When role occupants perceive that they do something new or unique in their roles, their efficacy is high. The perception that they do only routine tasks lowers role efficacy.

*e. **Linkage vs Isolation*** Inter-role linkage contributes to role efficacy. If role occupants perceive interdependence with others, their efficacy will be high. Isolation of the role reduces efficacy. For example, "I work in close liaison with the production manager."

*f. **Help vs Hostility*** One important aspect of efficacy is the individual's perception that he gives and receives help. A perception of hostility decreases efficacy. For example, "Whenever I have a problem, others help me," instead of "People here are indifferent to others."

*g. **Superordination vs Deprivation*** One dimension of role efficacy is the perception that the role occupant contributes to some "larger" entity. Example, "What I do is likely to benefit other organisations also."

*h. **Influence vs Powerlessness*** A feeling by role occupants that they are able to exercise influence in their roles increases their role efficacy. The influence may be in terms of decision-making, implementation, advice, or problem solving. For example, "My advice on industrial relations is accepted by top management." "I am able to influence the general policy of marketing."

*i. **Growth vs Stagnation*** When a role occupant has opportunities—and perceives them as such—to develop in his role through learning new things, role efficacy is likely to be high. Similarly, if the individual perceives his role as lacking in opportunities for growth, his role efficacy will be low.

*j. **Confrontation vs Avoidance*** When problems arise, either they can be confronted and attempts made to find solutions for them, or they can be avoided. Confronting problems to find solutions contributes to efficacy, while avoidance reduces efficacy. An example of confrontation could be, "If a subordinate brings a problem to me, I help to work out the solution." "I dislike being bothered with interpersonal conflict," is a statement indicating avoidance.

11.4 GROUP (TEAM)-ORIENTED MODEL

Some models of organisational change are based on effective group dynamics as the medium of change. Organisation Development (OD) emphasises team development. Work design is also based on making work groups more effective. While OD mainly emphasises organisational processes, work designing focuses on distribution of power in the organisation.

11.4.1 Organisation Development

The OD model of change is based on the assumption that effective organisational change would require a change in the basic values or ethos of the organisation, strong teams, and involvement of organisational members in the different stages of planning of change (problem identification, diagnosis, searching for alternative interventions, using an intervention, that is, action and evaluation). A change would be effective if the entire organisation (including top management) is actively involved in designing and implementing change with an external process expert.

OD emphasises both team building and development of values—OCTAPACE (openness, confrontation, trust, authenticity, production, autonomy, collaboration, and experimenting) values. Team building is both the objective and an important medium of change. Members of the organisation work in teams at different levels of change. Enough experience on OD is available, although not much research has been done. Experience has shown that OD is a useful model of change if internal facilitators can be developed to sustain change. Both research competence and process competency is needed in OD.

11.4.2 Process Consultation Model

Process consultation is a specific approach. It is the help given to a client group in understanding and developing the methodology of working in general and understanding and managing the effects of work methodology on involvement, alienation, collaboration, conflict, consensus, and such other group processes which affect decision-making and the members' commitment to the decisions made (Fig. 11.2).

Edgar. H. Schein suggests three main characteristics of, or steps in the process consultation model.

a. Joint diagnosis of the process with the client
b. Helping the client learn diagnostic skills
c. Active involvement of the client in searching for a solution

Fig. 11.2 Process consultation model

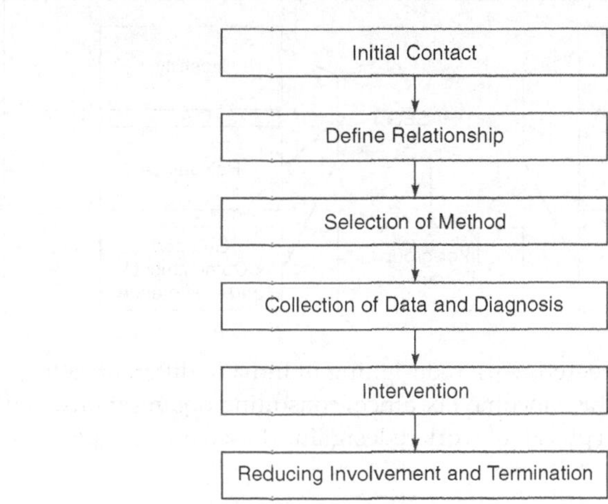

A consultant helps a client group by giving feedback on their ways of working, in examining data, and in planning improvement in the process of working and decision-making. The process consultant helps the client group move from dependence to interdependence and independence in diagnosis and action planning. As the term suggests, consultation is on the process of working and not on the content.

11.4.3 Work Redesigning Model for Group

Work redesigning focuses on distribution of power of decision-making in work-related matters to the group, which is responsible for results. It is a radical model, emphasising integration of intellectual (managerial-supervisory) and physical work (production). Work redesigning is done by training members of a team in multiple skills, and giving complete autonomy to the team to plan, supervise, and produce products or services. The role of the supervisors then changes; they plan boundary management (getting resources needed by the team, solving their external problems) and educational roles (helping the team when needed on new information, training, and so on).

Work redesigning emphasises the use of responsible autonomy, adaptability, variety, and participation. It uses the socio-technical systems and open systems approaches, suggesting that technical systems need to be integrated with the social systems, and should be open to feedback and change. Self-regulation is greatly emphasised (Fig. 11.3).

Fig. 11.3 Work redesign model

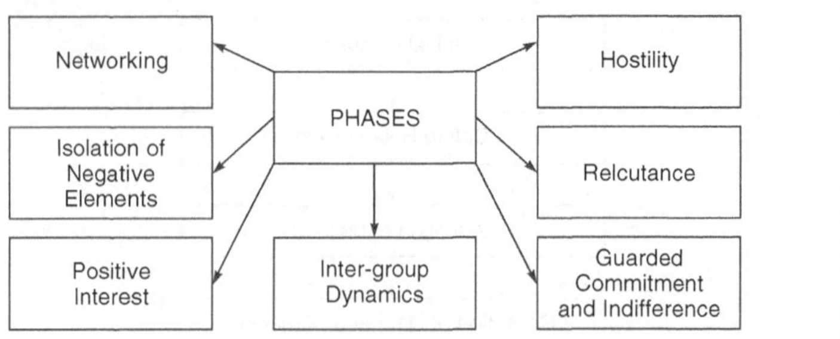

Nitish De, who pioneered work redesigning in India in different settings (industry, post office, LIC, income tax office, consulting organisations, and banks) proposed seven phases of work redesigning, based on his experience in India.

a. Hostility Despite preliminary explorations, discussions, and clarifications sought and offered, there is a feeling amongst employees, irrespective of their positions and roles, that the experiment is a motivated one, conditioned by management's desire to gain and researcher's desire to conduct the research in order to publish. Internal consultants are seen as motivated by career considerations. Depending on the dynamics of the situation in most Indian organisations, this phase has been operating covertly. Overt expression of hostility has often come from isolated individuals.

b. Reluctance Though some degree of curiosity develops amongst the members, there is no visible symbol of commitment. However, a few persons involved in the experiment feel that something is possible and that some changes for the better can be effected. Positive leaders among the experimental groups do play an important role in this as well as in the earlier phase.

c. Guarded commitment and indifference A substantial number show interest in what is happening, seeking data, taking initiative in group discussion, and offering suggestions, while the majority still remain indifferent. Indifference is more passive compared to the two earlier stages.

d. Inter-group dynamics Something of a Hawthorne effect is produced in terms of attention received. On the one hand, an in-group feeling gets created at the experimental site and, on the other, a feeling of jealousy and some amount of hostility is often expressed by way of jokes and caustic comments by the other groups.

e. Positive interest On the one hand, an in-group feeling brings some degree of stability to the experimental group and on the other, some internal dynamics takes place in terms of power struggle regarding the experimental scheme.

At times it is aggravated by caste and regional considerations, factional in-fighting between sub-groups with negative and positive attitudes and others who are in between. The positive groups, however, acquire more visibility because they now take more active interest and gradually take over the control functions in the autonomous groups.

f. Isolation of negative elements The majority are already committed to the experiment having experienced some positive gains on some of the key criteria such as variety of job, meaning, social support, challenge, autonomy, and evolving norms for the group.

The isolated are the negative elements who, depending on how the majority treat them, either indicate withdrawal of a passive kind or personal hostility. By and large, however, the group settles down to work out the operational details of the scheme.

g. Networking An experimental group takes the initiative in looking outwards and seeks to compare notes and experiences with other similar groups. This phase becomes a potential force for the diffusion process.

11.5 ORGANISATION-ORIENTED MODEL

Structural change models have been extensively used for organisational change. The emphasis is on developing a new structure of the organisation in response to the changing environment or the changing priorities of the organisation, and on designing relevant systems (budgetary and information systems). The changes introduced demand new ways of working, and individuals respond to such demands. Some good examples are available of such changes. Some turnaround work done is also in this category.

Management by objectives (MBO) is a specific example of structural change, using a structured way of helping on organisation plan its time-bound objectives at all levels, and working to achieve the objectives set. Specific ways are adopted to monitor the working of groups and individuals on these objectives.

While various models have been suggested in this unit, it should be emphasised that these do not work in isolation, and in practice many approaches are combinations.

Experience has shown that structural changes, for example, cannot be sustained without relevant process support. Similarly, process facilitation must be followed by relevant structural changes so that the processes can be institutionalised and sustained.

Framework of Work Redesign in an Organisation

Three brief accounts of the steps taken in work redesigning in three settings are given. The work redesigning was done in L&T India.

a. Organisation
   i. *Selection* of Groups
   ii. *Meeting* of all the workers, supervisors, officers connected with the group, to explain the philosophy of the scheme and fully involve them in decision-making
   iii. *Reorganisation* of the working group—all members divided into two groups, with each responsible for a single task
   iv. *Formation* of a task force—from the members of both groups a task force consisting of permanent members/temporary members was formed. The temporary members were replaced by other group members every month to give everybody a chance.

b. Role of the Task Force
   i. *Receive* overall target from management
   ii. *Breaking* this into sub-targets
   iii. *Plan* the requirement of materials, tools, equipment
   iv. Use of job rotation and multi-skilling

c. Training
   i. Training needs to be identified to settle issues and review progress
   ii. Emergence of "self-managing" work teams
   iii. Change of job from elemental job to work task

With the introduction of this scheme, employees had an improved feeling of ownership of work and enjoyed an improved quality of worklife, and were thus committed towards their work productivity.

11.6 LEWIN'S THREE-STEP MODEL

Kurt Lewin, the father of change processes, identified three phases in initiating and establishing any change—unfreezing, changing or moving, and refreezing. Kurt Lewin argued that successful change in organisations should follow these three steps: unfreezing the status quo, movement to a new state, and refreezing the new change to make it permanent (Fig. 11.4). The status quo can be considered to be a state of equilibrium. To move from this equilibrium—to overcome the pressures of both individual resistance and group conformity—unfreezing is necessary. It can be achieved in one of three ways (Fig. 11.4).

Driving forces, which direct behaviour away from the status quo, can be increased. Restraining forces, which hinder movement from the existing equi-

Fig. 11.4 Lewin's three-step model

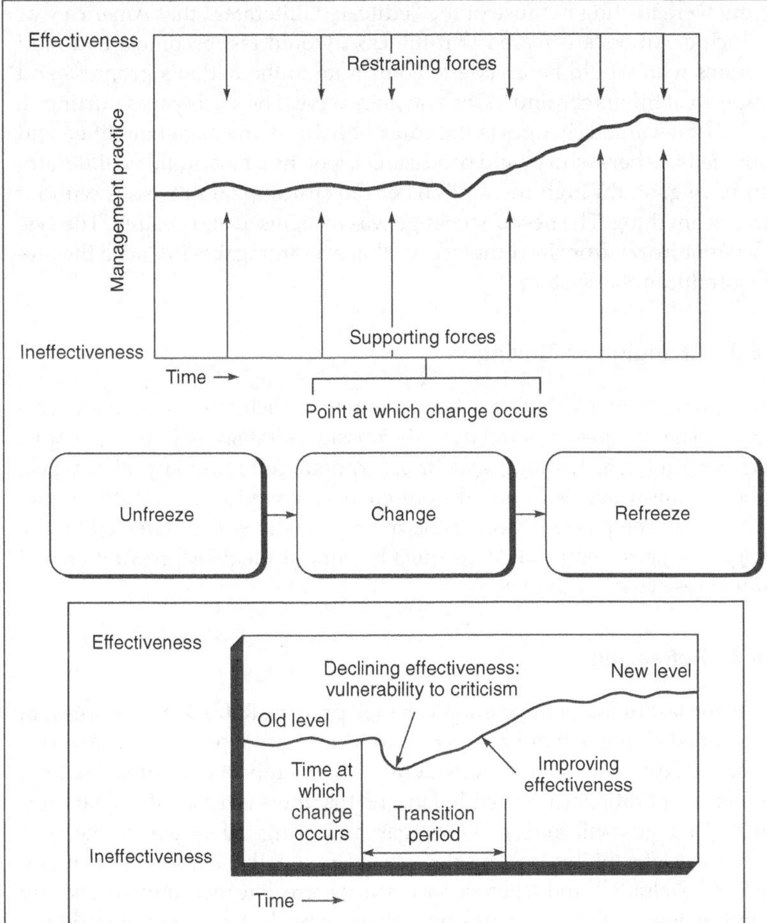

librium, can be decreased. A third alternative is to combine the first two approaches.

11.6.1 Unfreezing

Unfreezing is actually the process of preparing the system for change through discontinuation of the old practices, attitudes, tendencies, or behaviours. This is the initial phase where those involved in the change experience a need for something different and a sense of restlessness with the status quo. In essence, everyone feels that the system is hurting itself badly and desperately requires a change if it is to survive.

An excellent example of this is the recent hue and cry in the USA that the elementary, secondary, and high school education in the country desperately needed to be improved. Here, parents, educators, students, job market, and society were hurting because of the "educated illiterates" that America was producing. Americans feared that the USA would fast become a nation of illiterates who would be unable to contribute to the nation's progress and prosperity if things continued the way they were. The society was hurting so much that it wanted changes in the educational system—better qualified and motivated teachers who would produce competent scholars and no illiterates who have gone through the motions of the educational processes without learning anything. The need for change was recognised and desired. The system was unfrozen from its complacency that everything was fine with the pre-college educational system.

11.6.2 Changing or Moving

In this phase changes, that have been planned are actually initiated and carried out. The changes could relate to the mission, strategy, objectives, people, tasks, work roles, technology, structure, corporate culture, or any other aspect of the organisation. Well-thought-out changes have to be carefully implemented with the participation of the members who will be affected by the change. Changes incorporated too quickly without adequate preparation will result in resistance to change.

11.6.3 Refreezing

This is the last phase of the planned change process. Refreezing ensures that the planned changes that have been introduced are working satisfactorily, that any modifications, extra considerations, or support needed for making the change operational are attended to; and that there is reasonable guarantee that the changes will indeed fill the gap and bring the system to the new, desired state of equilibrium. This necessarily implies that the results are monitored and evaluated, and wherever necessary, corrective measures are taken to reach the new goal. If the refreezing phase is neglected or not attended to properly, the desired results will not ensue and the change may even be a total disaster.

This model suggests a systematic approach towards the proper introduction of change in a business organisation.

We have studied the core models for effective change in organisations. Apart from these core models some accessory models are also used to facilitate the process of change. These are mainly related to organisational performance, communication and interpersonal skills, leadership styles, motivation, and so on. Some of the important models are described below.

11.7 EQUATION MODEL OF ORGANISATIONAL BEHAVIOUR AND PERFORMANCE

In this model, the place that organisational behaviour occupies in a work system is illustrated by a set of equations (Fig. 11.5).

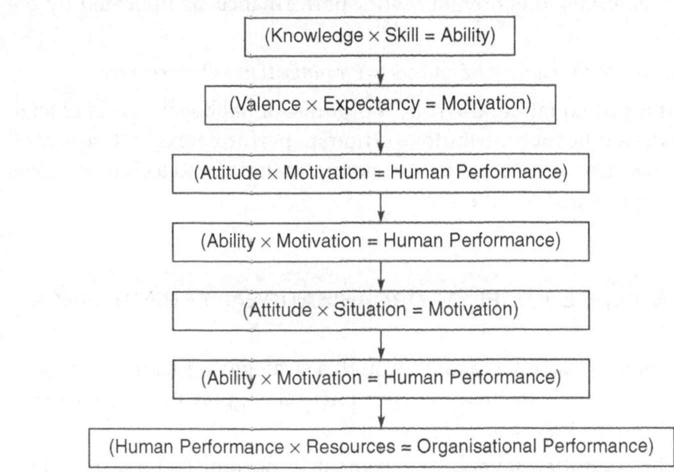

Fig. 11.5 Equation model

Let us look first at a worker's ability. It is generally accepted that knowledge and one's skill in applying it constitute the human trait called "ability." This is represented by the equation

$$\textit{Knowledge} \times \textit{Skill} = \textit{Ability}$$

Motivation results from a person's reactions in a specific situation. Technically, this is represented by the equation

$$\textit{Valence} \times \textit{Expectancy} = \textit{Motivation}$$

More operationally it is

$$\textit{Attitude} \times \textit{Motivation} = \textit{Human Performance}$$

Motivation and ability together determine a person's performance in any activity.

$$\textit{Ability} \times \textit{Motivation} = \textit{Human Performance}$$

We now have a series of equations (Fig. 11.5).

The scope of organisational behaviour is represented by the equation

$$(\textit{Attitude} \times \textit{Situation} = \textit{Motivation}).$$

The importance of organisational behaviour is shown by the equation

$$(\textit{Ability} \times \textit{Motivation} = \textit{Human Performance})$$

Organisational behaviour, as represented by the term "motivation," is one of two factors in the equation. Further, organisational behaviour has played a part in motivating workers to acquire the other factor, ability. Thus, organisational behaviour is part and parcel of the whole equation of human performance.

Human performance has to be combined with resources such as tools, power, and materials to get overall work performance, as indicated by the equation

$$Human\ performance \times Resources = Organisational\ Performance$$

Even in this last equation, the role of organisational behaviour is crucial, because it is a significant contributor to "human performance." "Resources," on the other hand, relate primarily to economic, material, and technical factors in organisational transformation.

11.8 SATELLITE MODEL OF ORGANISATIONAL PERFORMANCE

We need to remind ourselves again through a strategic model that organisational performance and effective management of change are products of many factors, as shown in Fig. 11.6.

This model identifies several of the most important factors, including organisational structure, knowledge, non-human resources, strategic positioning, and human process.

A strategy is a broad, integrated plan of action to accomplish organisational goals; in our frame of reference, the goal of improving human productivity. Because a strategy is an integrated plan, you will note that all the factors or variables are interrelated. You should also note that all the factors contribute to performance, which is defined in the model as achieving or surpassing business and social objectives and responsibilities from the perspective of the judging party. But integration is not only essential to meeting current business and social needs but as Fig. 11.6 suggests, also to the change process necessary to meet future business and social needs of the organisation.

11.9 ACHIEVE MODEL OF PERFORMANCE

Paul Hersey and Goldsmith isolated seven variables related to effective performance management during the process of change. They are: (a) motivation, (b) ability, (c) understanding, (d) organisational support, (e) environmental fit, (f) feedback, and (g) validity. Next they put these factors together in a manner that managers could easily remember and use. One technique for making items on a list easy to remember is to make their first letter form a word, called an

Fig. 11.6 Satellite model of organisational performance

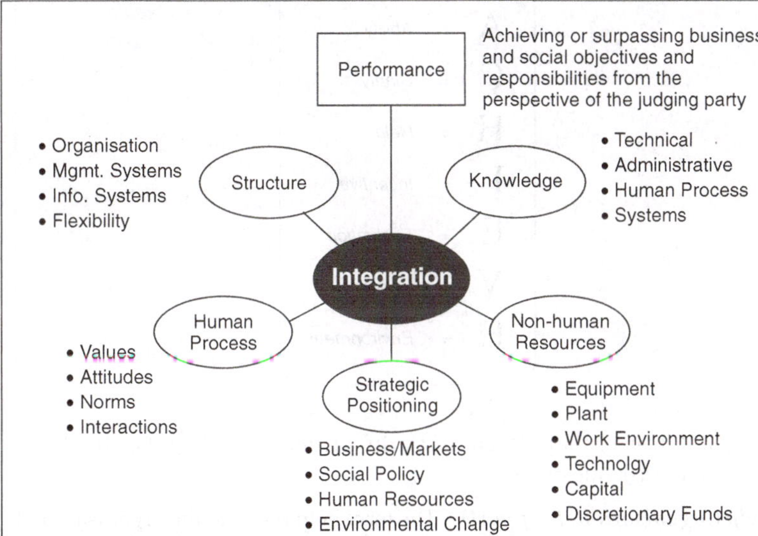

acronym. A seven-letter word that is synonymous with "to perform" is "achieve". By substituting incentive for motivation; clarity for understanding: help for organisational support; and evaluation for feedback, the ACHIEVE model was developed. The seven factors in the model are listed as follows (Fig. 11.7).

A-Ability (knowledge and skills) In the ACHIEVE model, the term ability refers to the follower's knowledge and skills, the ability to complete specific tasks successfully. It is important to remember that individuals are not universally competent. Key components of ability include task-relevant education, task relevant experience, and task-relevant aptitudes.

If a person has an ability problem, solutions may include specific training, coaching, formal educational courses, or reassignment of specific duties or responsibilities. These alternatives should be considered from the viewpoint of cost effectiveness.

C-Clarity (understanding or role perception) Clarity refers to an understanding and acceptance of what to do, when to do it, and how to do it. To have a thorough understanding of the job, the follower needs to be clear on the major goals and objectives, how these goals and objectives should be accomplished, and the priority of goals and objectives.

Fig. 11.7 ACHIEVE Model

A	=	*Ability*
C	=	*Clarity*
H	=	*Help*
I	=	*Incentive*
E	=	*Evaluation*
V	=	*Validity*
E	=	*Environment*

If the follower has a problem in clarity or understanding, he should be encouraged to ask questions.

H-Help (organisational support) The term help refers to the organisational help, or support, that the follow effective task completion. Some organisational support factors might include adequate budget, equipment, and facilities that are suitable for task completion, necessary support from other departments, product availability and quality, and an adequate supply of human resources.

If there is a lack of help or organisational support, managers should clearly identify where the problem exists. If the problem is lack of money, human resources, equipment, or facilities, the manager should see whether the necessary resources can be acquired in a cost-effective manner.

I-Incentive (motivation or willingness) The term incentive refers to the follower's task-relevant incentive—the motivation to complete the specific task under analysis in a successful manner.

If the follower has an incentive problem, the first step is to check the use of rewards and punishments. The follower should clearly understand that performance on this task is related to pay, promotion, recognition, and job security. People have a natural tendency to pursue tasks that are rewarded and to avoid tasks that are not.

E-Evaluation (coaching and performance feedback) Evaluation refers to informal day-to-day performance feedback as well as formal periodic reviews. An effective feedback process lets followers know how well they are doing the job on a regular basis. If there is an evaluation problem, it may be caused by the lack of day-to-day feedback on both effective and ineffective performance.

Many managers tend to focus on the bad news and forget to recognise good performance.

V-Validity (valid and legal personnel practices) The term validity refers to the appropriateness and legality of human resources decisions made by the manager. Managers need to make sure that decisions about people are appropriate in the light of laws, court decisions, and company policies.

If there is a validity problem, the manager should know that the trend of the law in management is clear: personnel decisions need to be documented and justified on the basis of performance-oriented criteria.

E-Environment (environmental fit) Environment refers to the external factors that can influence performance even if the individual has all the ability, clarity, help, and incentive needed to do the job. Key elements of the environmental factors include competition, changing market conditions, government regulations, suppliers, and so on.

If there is an environmental problem beyond their control, followers should not be rewarded or reprimanded for performance. In short, followers should be expected to perform at a level consistent with the limitations of their environment.

Functions of Performance Management

Performance management during change includes three major functions.

a. *Performance planning*—setting objectives and directions for followers at the beginning of a planning period and developing plans for achieving these objectives.
b. *Coaching*—day-to-day feedback and development activities aimed at the enhancement of performance plans.
c. *Performance review*—overall evaluation of performance for a specific planning period.

The situational approach to performance management enables managers to individualise performance planning, coaching, and review by choosing managerial techniques.

11.10 JOHARI'S WINDOW MODEL

In developing effective managerial skills to effect openness and interpersonal trust during the enforcement of change, a conceptual device established by Joseph Luft and Harry Ingham provides the basis for understanding the basic process involved.

As indicated in Fig. 11.8, the model consists of portraying the varying degrees of information held in common between two people, as well as the methods that can be utilised in increasing the size of one's "window."

Fig. 11.8 Johari's window model for effective communication during change

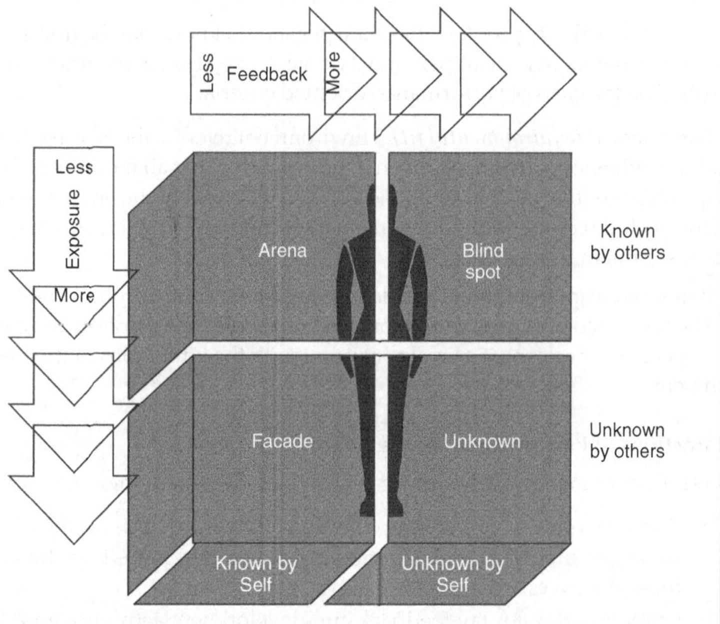

Cell 1 of the figures denotes the "arena" of communication, that is, information held in common and known simultaneously by oneself and others.

Cell 2, labelled the "blind spot", is information known by others but not by oneself. One of the purposes of sensitivity training is to reduce the size of the blind spot by providing increased honest feedback from others about one's personal style. The old phrase, "Even your best friend will not tell you," is indicative of the existence of such a class of information.

Cell 3, termed the "facade," is a class of information known to ourselves but not to others. It is the protective front that all people find necessary to some degree in order to defend the self.

Cell 4, the final cell, is that information which exists but is unknown to all. Hall suggests that this is indicative of a hidden potential, the unconscious, or the "database of creativity".

Communication will be enhanced if Cell 1 is increased in size. This can be effected through two processes: (a) exposure of self to others and (b) soliciting feedback from others. Exposure requires an open, candid, and trusting approach where one "lets it all hang out." Feedback requires an active solicitation of feelings, opinions, and values from others. For these processes to be fully developed, reciprocity is required. An attempt to use one to the exclusion of the other often generates resistance from associates in the long run.

In a research conducted by Hall, it was discovered that interpersonal styles of exposure/feedback correlated with types of leadership styles as depicted on the management grid. In a study of 200 managers, classified into the five leadership styles: deserter (1,1), autocrat (9,1), missionary (1,9), compromiser (5,5), and problem-solving integrator (9,9), measurements were taken of the size of their reported "arenas" in Johari's window. The greater bulk of 1,1 managers possessed a relatively small "arena", managers had the largest "arena", involving a balanced and heavy use of both exposure and feedback processes. The 5,5 manager also exhibited a balanced utilisation (as did 1,1), but the size of the "arena" was intermediate, lying between 1,1 and 9,9. Autocratic managers, (9,1), tended to over expose, resulting in the creation of a large blind spot. They did not solicit feedback from subordinates and colleagues as much as they were willing to convey their own opinions, orders, and values. The missionary style, (1,9), tended to emphasise feedback to the detriment of exposure, with the "façade" assuming greater importance.

Attempts have been made to develop a means of auditing a manager's communication style. In one study, six independent dimensions of style were identified: (a) careful transmitter, (b) open, two-way communicator, (c) frank, (d) careful listener, (e) wordy, and (f) informal. When combined with assessment of the manager's credibility, it is contended that these dimensions are related to job satisfaction, role clarity, and effectiveness.

11.11 MANAGERIAL GRID/9:9 GRID MODEL

The managerial grid, or 9:9 grid model, is based on Ohio and Michigan university studies. Robert R. Blake and Jane S. Mouton developed this grid. The full model consists of six phases, although not every organisation may go through all of them.

Phase 1 is the presentation of a framework called the managerial grid, as shown in Fig. 11.9.

The grid is based on the management style dimensions of *"concern for people"* and *"concern for production"*, which essentially represent the dimensions of consideration and structure. The grid clarifies how the two dimensions are related and establishes a uniform language and framework for communication about behavioural issues. "1,9 managers" are high in concern for people but so low in concern for production that output is low. They are *"country-club managers."* "9,1 managers" are overly concerned with production and tend to be authoritarian bosses.

Fig. 11.9 Managerial grid

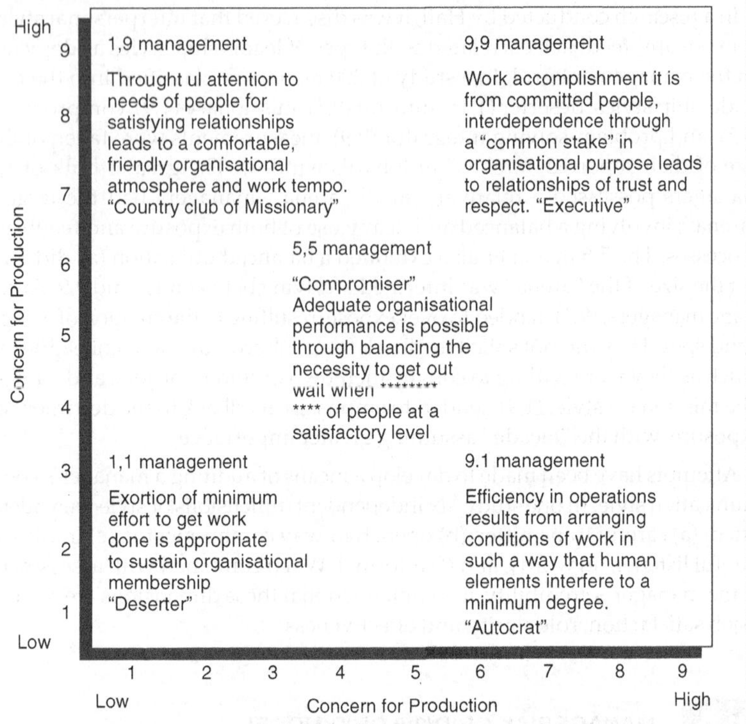

A more desirable balance of the two dimensions is from "5,5" to "9,9." Using the grid, the entire managerial job can be discussed, such as the "back-up style" of managers. Back-up style is the one managers tend to use when their normal style does not get results. It tends to be more autocratic and concerned with production.

Phase 2 of the model is concerned with team development, using the grid as a framework for discussion. The focus is upon a single team and the manager to whom it directly reports. Phase 3 is concerned with inter-group development to reduce conflict among groups. This phase tries to reduce the win-lose power struggles among groups by showing how co-operation can benefit all parties. Phase 4 develops an ideal organisational model, phase 5 seeks to apply the model, and phase 6 provides evaluation of the programme.

An OD framework using four systems of management has been developed by Rensis Likert. The systems are as follows.

- *System 1* Exploitative-authoritative
- *System 2* Benevolent-authoritative
- *System 3* Consultative
- *System 4* Participative

System 1 is the most autocratic and System 4 is the most participative. The object of the OD programme is to move an organisation as far as possible towards the participative system, which is considered the best one. The OD consultant in the Likert programme administers a written climate survey to find out about the system now used in the organisation. The consultant also surveys participants to determine their view of the ideal system that the organisation should have.

The difference between the present system and the desired system represents a realistic area of improvement for the OD programme to seek. The complete System 4 remains an ultimate goal, but Likert believes that a firm should move towards it gradually. The Likert approach is also known as the survey feedback method because of its heavy use of feedback based on surveys.

In order to analyse the present system and move towards a better one, the Likert programme uses a model of an organisation with three types of variables—causal, intervening, and end-result variables—as shown in Fig. 11.10. The causal variables are the significant ones, because they affect both intervening and end-result variables. Causal variables are the ones the management should try to change; they include organisational structure, controls, policies, and leadership behaviour. Intervening variables are those that are affected subsequently by the causal variables. They include employee attitudes, motivation, and perceptions. End-result variables represent the objectives sought by management. They usually include improved productivity, lower costs, and higher earnings. They represent the reason the OD programme was initiated.

11.12 3-D MODEL OF LEADERSHIP FOR CHANGE

William J. Reddin, has an OD programme called 3-D management. This programme, like the managerial grid, is organised around consideration and structure; however, it also is stated that these two orientations can be used in combination or can be ignored by a manager, giving a choice of four styles. Since any of these four styles can be effective or ineffective, there are eight managerial style options available. The 3-D programme is built around a study of these eight style options. When they are assembled into a chart, the result is a three-dimensional structure, hence, the origin of the term "3-D management." (Fig. 11.10).

Fig. 11.10 3D model

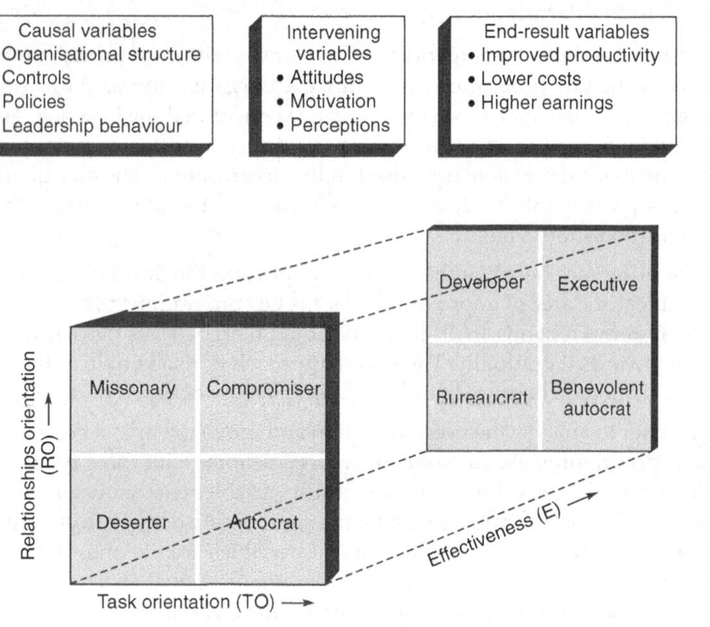

The 3-D system is materially different from the other two systems mentioned because it assumes that there are four effective styles, while the other systems focus on only one, the considerate, participative approach. This system is more realistic in terms of contingency concepts. It carefully emphasises that no one style is effective by itself. A style's effectiveness depends on the situation in which it is used. This gives a wider outlook of the communication and leadership styles during change.

11.13 S. P. S. T. MODEL OF ORGANISATIONAL CULTURE

Management working for change in a culture needs to pay attention to four aspects: structural elements, process, strategy of change, and tactics to be employed. Eventually cultural change must be built into the system so that the new culture becomes a part of the organisation. This S. P. S. T. (structure-process-strategy-tactics) four-fold model can help to develop culture-changing management (Fig. 11.11).

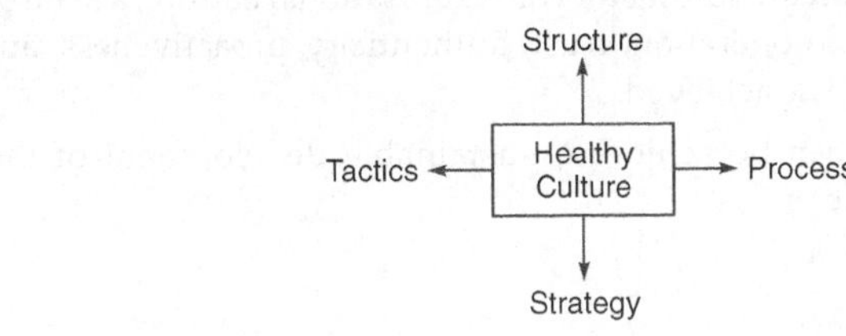

Fig. 11.11 S.P.S.T. model for healthy organisational culture

S. STRUCTURAL ELEMENTS

a. Stable structure
b. Temporary systems
c. Linkage-building mechanisms
d. Information system
e. Rewards
f. Regular budget
g. Guidelines

P. PROCESS

a. Incremental planning
b. Action research approach
c. Modelling
d. Mentoring
e. Process awareness and orientation
f. Counselling
g. Organisational norms

S. STRATEGY

a. Anchoring in and using strengths
b. Sensitivity to stone walls
c. Competency building
d. Critical concentration
e. Developing key institutions
f. Sanction and support
g. System ownership

T. TACTICS

a. Prepare in advance
b. One step at a time
c. Prepare for the journey (resources)

d. Go together
e. Stop and review progress
f. Keep up the spirit (reinforcement)
g. Keep going (perseverance)

By paying due attention to these factors of organisational culture, a state of OCTAPAC—openness, co-operation, trust, authenticity, proactiveness, authority, confrontation can be achieved.

If these core values can be achieved, sustainable development of the organisation is inevitable.

11.14 ROVER'S LEARNING PROCESS MODEL

The company's R&D unit has developed a learning process model consisting of 13 key elements (Fig. 11.12).

a. ***Business opportunity*** Learning activities and efforts should contribute directly to bottomline business performance. This, in turn, depends on creating and utilising business opportunities in terms of new and important projects, as well as substantive improvement in the performance of existing activities and areas of business.
b. ***Champion*** The person who identifies with the goals of a new project, or strategic initiative, and brings together and co-ordinates the relevant persons, expertise, and resources. A Rover board director will normally be a champion for a major strategic project or change initiative.

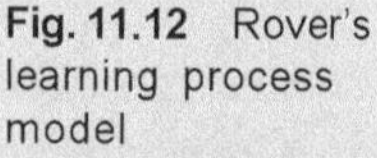
Fig. 11.12 Rover's learning process model

c. ***Key players and expert group*** These include all individuals whose role and co-operation are deemed to be crucial for the success of new project(s) and/or strategic initiative(s) in the context of a perceived business opportunity.
d. ***Developing specification*** This includes an elaboration of the business opportunity, goals and objectives, learning process and methods, time horizon, infrastructural requirements, and methods for appraising progress.
e. ***Design of change process and plan*** These include a detailed scheme for the planning, programming, and budgeting of various steps, stages, and phases of the implementing change project(s)/programme(s).
f. ***Preparing coaches and learners*** Individuals in [c] and other relevant employees are familiarised with and involved in the project towards preparing and motivating them for carrying out the organisational learning process. They will serve as change agents.
g. ***Creating learning material*** High-quality material in the form of videos, audios, books, articles, write-ups, models, training kits, instructional packages, graphical displays, and so on are developed and assembled in a timely manner as part of the project/programme implementation efforts.
h. ***Preparing change/learning environment*** Learning infrastructure close to, and aligned with the workplace, is organised and put in place.
i. ***Implementing change*** This involves the execution and co-ordination of a spectrum of activities of both learners and coaches to capture learning both off and on the job.
j. ***Measurement*** The effect of the learning and change process, and the bottomline benefits achieved, are measured and assessed against prespecified objectives.
k. ***Recording experience*** The contents and results of learning are recorded in a computer system for the company and in the personal development files of the learners.
l. ***Developing learning/change material*** Lessons from, and for learning, are drawn from (i) to (k), and developed for future use of the organisation.
m. ***New best practice*** The best practice standard is revised, and the gains from new learning experience are shared throughout the organisation. The new experience and lessons are cycled back.

SUMMARY

- A conceptual framework for effective management of change has been given in the form of models. These models are classified into two categories: (a) core and (b) accessory models. Core models are those which are directly related to the process of change and accessory models are those which support the process of change.
- Core models include the individualistic model which encompasses the adoption diffusion model, feedback model, and motivational model.
- In the role-oriented models, the different roles performed by the individual and group are manifested.
- In-group or team-oriented model, organisational development model, process consultation model, and work redesigning model are discussed.
- In organisation-oriented models, MBO and Levins three step models are discussed.
- In accessory models for successful change, equation model of organisational behaviour and performance, satellite model of organisational performance, and ACHIEVE model of organisational performance are given.
- In Johari's window model, the importance of communication process during the process of change is given.
- In the managerial grid model, the style of managerial supervision is systematised.
- In the 3-D model of leadership, the leadership orientation for change in management is illustrated.
- In the SPST model of organisational culture, change-friendly organisational culture building factors are given.
- In Rover's learning process model, key elements for building a learning organisation are given.
- The basic prerequisites for effective management of change are explained in terms of a model for a better understanding of different managerial concepts and applications.

REVIEW QUESTIONS

1. What do you understand by models? Differentiate between core and accessory models of change.
2. Explain the individualistic model with suitable examples.
3. Discuss role-oriented models.
4. Write a brief note on each of the following.
   (i) Lewin's three-step model
   (ii) Equation model of organisational performance
   (iii) Satellite model of organisational performance

5. Explain the ACHIEVE model of performance with suitable examples.
6. What do you understand by Johari's window model, managerial grid, and 3-D model of leadership for change and what is the correlation among these three models?
7. Draw the framework of Rover's learning process model.

EXERCISE 1

One of the best activities (particularly to develop problem-solving/analytical skills) is to actually set the group the task of designing activities or games themselves. You can mix it up any way you want, for example, split the group into teams of threes and give them different games or activities to design (communications, team-building, problem-solving, and so on), which all teams will then participate in.

Ensure everyone understands the criteria for designing development activities. Brainstorming to establish a clear understanding of the aims and parameters with the group is a good starting point. The main criteria can then serve as assessment criteria for each team to assess the activity designs of their peers.

To add extra interest and fun, you can give each of the groups some props such as paper, scissors, string, dice, building blocks, newspapers and magazines, cotton-reels, a bucket or two of water, blindfolds, foreign language dictionary, and video cameras, and limit their designs to using the props. Introduce other rules and constraints such as the activity must be held outdoors/indoors, must be a ten-minute exercise, and so on.

EXERCISE 2

This is a simple activity, or can be used as an exercise to provoke discussion about self-image and mutual perceptions within teams as per the understanding of the different models in this chapter.

When introducing themselves in turn to the group, participants must play their mobile phone ring tones, and (here is the important bit) explain the reason for their choice of the ring tone (or lack of interest in a "personal" ring tone), and offer some comment as to what it might suggest about their personality and style.

The extent to which discussion and feedback among the group is encouraged is left to the discretion of the facilitator, depending on the group composition and whether the activity is used simply as an ice-breaker, or for more involved discussion, which could easily be linked with the other concepts of change.

Chapter

Case Study: "21-Milestone"

CHAPTER OUTLINE

- It smells like money
- Nainital Crises
- Organising the President's Administration
- Samarth Rao and His "Alcoa" Project
- The Performance Rating
- Magic Kingdom
- The High-priced OD Consultant
- Scenarios for Dealing with Change
- Mr Krishna Rao's Confusion
- India in Diagnosis
- Is it Work Load or Motivation
- Training Programme in Hindustan
- Doing My Own Thing
- Bad Brakes
- Rama and His Changing Plan
- The Case against Vision
- A Combat Zone
- Love it or Leave it
- Rama Swami and the Rumour
- Seeing the Forest and the Trees

> "I read, I study, I examine, I listen,
> I reflect and out of all this,
> I try to form an idea, in which I can put,
> as much common sense as I can."
>
> —Sherlock Holmes

CASE 1 IT SMELLS LIKE MONEY

For more than thirty-five years, the Perfect Paper Mill had produced fine papers at its New India Mill. The mill was located in a small town of Gujarat. It employed about two hundred local workers. It was the only industry in the town. Most of the workers had spent their entire careers in the mill, and there was practically no hope of their getting good jobs elsewhere.

The mill heavily polluted the air around it with materials that had a distinctive, obnoxious odour. However, the town people never complained, claiming that after a couple of months one got used to the odour and did not even notice it. Besides, they said, "It smells like money."

With the standards of permissible levels of air pollution becoming increasingly restrictive over the years, the mill had been given notice two years ago to reduce its air pollution to permissible levels. It was given a time period of two years to do so. The grace period had recently expired. On the final day, the mill permanently ceased its operations. As President Bhargva said, "There never was any hope that we could meet the standards. We simply can't afford to install the equipment that would be required to bring us within standards."

Questions

1. Explain how a change in the environment of the mill destroyed its viability. What happened to the firm's ecological niche?
2. Suppose the townspeople were able to bring enough political pressure to change the standards so that the mill could continue operations. Explain this development in organisation–environment ecological terms.
3. With the benefit of hindsight, what changes in policy, if any, do you think the management of the mill should have made through the years? Under the essentially unchanged policies that were followed, was the mill doomed to eventual extinction? Why?

CASE 2 NAINITAL CRISIS

Shobhit owned a gas station with departmental store at one end of Mall Road in Nainital. The station had always been associated with one of the major oil companies. A co-operative relationship between Shobhit and his supplier had developed over the years such that Shobhit had no desire to change brands.

The gas station had always experienced the highly seasonal sales associated with any tourist area. Peak sales had traditionally been reached during the months of March through September. Since the sales volume regularly followed the pattern year after year, Shobhit had been able to adjust his supply ordering with a fair amount of accuracy in the past. Since the high school and college students in the area were eager to work during the summer, Shobhit had never had any trouble adjusting his "labour force" to meet the seasonal demand problem.

The Nainital area was dependent largely on the Kumaon Air Force Base for its year-round business support. In 2001, Kumaon cut back its base personnel to comply with the national goal of defence and armed service reductions. The entire Nainital business community, Shobhit included, experienced a severe slowdown in the latter part of 2001 and 2002. The permanent residents of Nainital thought that tourist trade would take up the slack created by the pullout of the Air Force personnel.

The energy crisis, which began in 2000, however, intensified the economic slowdown in Nainital. Shobhit's problems were compounded. Not only did he face a drop in sales, but also because of the slowdown in 2001 and 2002 and because fuel was being rationed by his distributor on the basis of the prior year's consumption, Shobhit had turn away even regular customers and even eventually face a close down.

Questions

1. Identify the major environmental changes challenging Shobhit.
2. How might these environmental changes affect Shobhit's organisation?
3. Are the environmental changes faced by Shobhit conflicting? If so, how should Shobhit deal with the conflicts?

CASE 3 ORGANISING THE PRESIDENT'S ADMINISTRATION

Richard, a former president's aide, and political analyst, thinks the newly elected president's office is wrongly organised. According to Richard, the structure the previous president and his people had chosen, promoted new ideas, but it also wasted time, sapped morale, and invited disaster.

The present administration has organised itself as an adhocracy—an organic structure that minimises reliance on regularised and systematic patterns of providing advice and instead relies heavily on the president to distribute assignments and select whom he listens to and when. Richard claims that an adhocracy has six drawbacks. (1) It tends to discourage debate and dissent. Important meetings—where sensitive information is discussed and decisions made—may include only those people the powers-to-be want. Adhocracy, thus discourages truthfulness, for people fear being left out. (2) It leads to inconsistency because no one is given full responsibility for a policy. (3) Adhocracy undermines morale. Those with titles but no power feel slighted. (4) This structural form is error-prone. The lack of standardised procedures increases the likelihood of mistakes. (5) The lack of standardisation also increases the probability of scandals. The emphasis on personal relationships leads individuals to think too much about protecting the boss; the absence of formal procedures lets them get away with it. (6) Finally, adhocracy ends up misallocating the president's time. The president becomes his own chief of staff, taking time away from his primary task of providing leadership for the country.

Richard notes that the president's kitchen cabinet of old friends, consultants, and favoured appointees have created "government by inner circle," which favours people over positions. The president listens to this favoured group more than those in formal positions. And because president and his senior advisers neither trust nor respect standing bureaucracies, they rely heavily on task forces (run by presidential intimates) to handle issues like health care or welfare.

Richard argues that many of the president's problems can be attributed to this adhocratic structure. Foreign policy, according to Richard, suffers from a lack of direction. Relations with Congress falter due to inconsistent directives from the administration.

Questions

1. Richard dwells on the drawbacks of adhocracy. What do you think its strengths are? Is their any need for change?
2. A dynamic environment demands flexibility and adhocracy is flexible. Why, then, is this structure not an ideal mechanism for managing government?
3. "The structure of an administration should compensate for weaknesses in the president." Do you agree or disagree with this statement? What would the implications of this statement be for the president's administration?
4. Contrast the president's role in leading a country with the CEO's job at a multibillion–dollar corporation. Is the president merely implementing a "boundaryless organisation" in government the way, say, Jack Welch is at General Electric?

CASE 4 SAMARTH RAO AND HIS "ALCOA" PROJECT

On a recent summer day in Hyderabad, CEO Samarth Rao unveiled his plans for Aluminum Co. of Andhra (Alcoa), the basic materials giant. What he presented was nothing short of a complete overhaul of a corporation that employed more than 30,000 people across 22 countries. He proposed a new structure that would focus on Alcoa customers and business units—"not Hyderabad, not the vice-presidents who service them, not the chairman—but business units." Pooled corporate resources would exist for the sole purpose of linking and supporting the company's 22 business units.

Corporate structure was not the only thing about to change. By way of introducing the company's new strategy, Rao challenged the popular notion of continuous improvement. That approach would work for companies that we are market leaders, he asserted, but "It is a terrible idea if you are lagging the world leadership benchmark. It is probably a disastrous idea if you are far behind the world standard."

In Alcoa's case, they seemed to be laggards. Rao argued that the company needed rapid quantum leaps in improvement, rather than slow, incremental changes. Rao's challenge to his people was this: Close the gap between current practices and world benchmarks by a minimum of 80 percent in two years.

"Waiting until outside events force change is at best reactive administration and, at worst, management cowardice," he told his team. Leadership has nothing to do with "Change that is forced on an organisation by performance that is so pitiful that shareholders have to think for change."

Questions

1. What do you think of Samarth Rao's approach to implementing change?
2. Is Rao suggesting that continuous improvement, a basic tenet of TQM, is mismatched for dynamic times?
3. Do you agree or disagree with Rao's perspective on leadership? Support your view.

CASE 5 THE PERFORMANCE RATING

Madhav was employed as a training assistant in the state civil service for twelve years. His supervisor for the last nine years has been Maya, a woman young enough to be his daughter. Although civil service regulations require that employees be given a performance report once a year, they are not well enforced. Madhav received only one report of "satisfactory" in his second year as training assistant.

Madhav is a mild and quiet person without an outgoing personality but he feels he has performed effectively as a trainer because he has held the job for twelve years and has never received either oral or written comment that his work is less than satisfactory. On three occasions he took the required examination for those seeking promotion to Training Officer I. In each case he passed the written test but failed the interview by a state personnel office panel. He assumed he failed because of a lack of an outgoing personality, but he received no feedback about the reasons for his failure.

Recently, the State Personnel Board decided to abolish the title of Training Assistant and give assistants the title of Training Officer I, since they were performing training work equal to that job. Madhav believed his change in title would be automatic, but the Personnel Board decided that, since a pay increase of over 15 percent was involved, assistants must take the test for promotion. Madhav assumed this procedure would be routine, since he had performed satisfactorily for 12 years and his duties would not change the new title. He passed the written test but failed the oral test again.

At this point Madhav was frustrated and angry. He approached his supervisor with determination "to get to the bottom of his problem, even if I have to go the State Personnel Board." After a heated exchange with Maya, Madhav learned that he had failed the oral tests because Maya had given the interview panel a negative recommendation about him. Her recommendation stated that Madhav had not developed sufficiently to merit promotion to Training Officer I. All this was unknown to Madhav. He had received no feedback from Maya or the Personnel Board. Although a mild person, Madhav exploded after learning this new fact. In a stormy session with Maya he stated that he had a right to get feedback about his performance and Maya had an obligation to help him develop if she felt he was not developing adequately.

Later Madhav requested to examine his personnel file and was allowed to see it. The personnel file had no negative reports on performance, reprimands, refusal to take development opportunities, or other negative information. There was one satisfactory performance rating ten years old. Also there were no commendations, records of training taken, or other positive information.

Since the title of Training Assistant was abolished, Madhav is now working as a Staff Services Analyst performing the same training services that he formerly did. His salary remains the same. His self-image has declined, and it is evident that he is less motivated. Other conditions remain the same.

Questions

1. Analyse some of the organisational behaviour issues raised in this series of events.
2. If you were Madhav, what changes in behaviour would you try to make, if any?
3. If you were Maya, what changes would you try to make, if any? Use specific organisational behaviour models, frameworks, and ideas to explain why you would attempt these changes in behaviour, if any.

4. Assume you are a member of the State Personnel Board and know about this situation because of a grievance filed by Madhav. The board has the authority to decide Madhav's grievance.
   a. What ideas and recommendations would you present in the board's discussion of Madhav's grievance? Present the organisational behaviour reasons behind your statements.
   b. At an appropriate time later, what ideas and recommendations, if any, would you present to the board regarding policy changes in the area of Madhav's grievance? Present the organisational behaviour models and ideas behind your recommendations.

CASE 6 MAGIC KINGDOM

One of the most popular tourist attractions in the USA is Disney World at Orlando, Florida. It is a theme park with numerous attractions and a visit to the USA is not considered complete without a visit to Disney World. Prior to the opening of Disney World at Orlando, there was a similar theme park near Los Angeles in the state of California, known as Disneyland. Disneyland was the creation of Walt Disney, a famous family moviemaker, who had produced such movie hits as *Fantasia* and *Snow White*. Disneyland is a family entertainment phenomenon and is also known as the Magic Kingdom.

Following Walt Disney's death, Magic Kingdom hit a downward trend. The management rested on the laurels of its success and the organisation stagnated. It shunned innovation and stayed in its ivory tower, away from the pulse of the audience. It became fearful of change and, by all accounts, it was not fully utilising its potential or its resources and considering the demand for its products and services, it was undercharging for its licensing of cartoon characters and admission to its theme parks.

Michael Eisner, the head of Disney organisation, felt that he had to become more like Walt Disney, an innovator and a risk taker who encouraged creativity and had built the Disney empire. After analysing the situation carefully, he devised a plan that would encourage openness to change, and a culture of strong creativity, which had always been a hallmark of Disney's success.

Eisner himself came up with a number of new and creative ideas including new health food restaurants. He encouraged and induced creativity among others and creativity became one of his top priorities. His idea of creating a Euro Disneyland in Paris came into high focus. He met with 12 of the world's most respected architects in a widely creative session to bring out as best a design for the theme park as possible. He encouraged and rewarded new ideas, opened the channels of communication, and took the members into confidence by sharing with them his strategic plans and ambitious growth strategies.

One change that came into being was the renovation and expansion of Disney's hotel chain. Eisner ordered an ambitious $ 1.0 billion hotel expansion plan which doubled its room capacity to 20,000 and came at par with the well-known Ritz Carlton chain of hotels.

The movie business which had practically come to a standstill and was hardly reaching break-even point, got a boost of creativity. By tightening budget without sacrificing quality and working with adventurous scripts and unknown but talented actors, it became a dominant force in the American movie industry and produced such hit films as *Beauty and the Beast, Pretty Woman*, and *Ruthless People*.

Michael Eisner's creativity, openness, innovation, and team spirit was not without its rewards. From 1984 to 1990, Disney's sales increased from $ 1.7 billion to almost $ 6.00 billion. Disney expanded its family entertainment business to include book publishing and records and opened a theme park in Japan.

Michael Eisner made a dramatic turn around of Disney fortune in the 1980s. He is even more ambitious during the 1990s and called it the Disney Decade. He surrounded himself with ambitious, energetic, and creative staff and he expected a period of extensive growth for Disney operations around the globe. With the fall of closed societies and advent of instant communications and emphasis on internationalisation, Eisner has been very optimistic that Disney will become a household name around the world, as it became in the USA.

Questions

1. Why do you think that the Disney organisation, once a highly successful and growing organisation, became stagnant after the death of its founder Walt Disney? Describe as many reasons as possible.
2. How important is Michael Eisner's role in the process of turn around of the company fortunes? Does it mean that the success of the entire organisation depends upon the philosophy of its chief operating officer? Give reasons.
3. List and explain the internal and external forces that necessitated the change in the outlook of Disney operations.
4. Can you identify the change agents that were at work in changing the behaviour of the organisational members?
5. If you were hired as a consultant to the organisation, what changes would you suggest, if any, to bring Disney organisation into the global limelight?

CASE 7 THE HIGH-PRICED OD CONSULTANT

The corporate human resources office told the middle managers of a large bank in India that a group of consultants from the UK would be calling on them later in the week. The purpose of the consultants' visit was to analyse inter-functional relations throughout the firm. The consultants had been very effective in using an OD intervention called team building. Their particular approach used six steps. When their approach was explained to the managers, a great deal of tension was relieved. The managers had initially thought that team building was a lot of hocus-pocus, like sensitivity training, where people attack each other and let out their aggressions by heaping abuse on those they dislike. By the same token, the managers generally felt that perhaps the consultants were not needed. One of them put it this way: "Now that we understand what is involved in team building, we can go ahead and conduct the sessions ourselves. All we have to do is to choose a manager who is liked by everyone and put him or her in the role of the change agent/consultant. After all, you really don't need a high-priced consultant to do this team-building stuff. You just have to have a good feel for human nature." The other managers generally agreed. However, the corporate human resources director turned down their suggestion. He hired the OD consultants to do the team building.

Questions

1. What is a team-building approach to organisational development? Do you think the managers had an accurate view of this OD technique?
2. Do you think the managers had an accurate view of the role of the external consultant? Do you agree or disagree with the corporate human resources director's decision to turn down their suggestion? Why?

CASE 8 SCENARIOS FOR DEALING WITH CHANGE

Over the last decade, there have been dramatic changes in many industries; firms that used to be the leaders have now disappeared or fallen behind while new companies, often unheard of until recently, now lead the way. In the airline business, Eastern Airlines is gone; in computers, IBM is scurrying to catch up; and in retailing, K mart has been pummelled by the competition. What went wrong? One problem is that senior-level management was not prepared for the new challenges. A change in top management was needed. A second, and accompanying, reason is that many companies did not know what to expect, so they forecast that the future would be similar to the past. And they were wrong. A third, and supplemental, reason is that instead of leading change, too many companies chose to wait and then respond. For example, when things were going well, they continued their current actions. When things began to turn sour, they started looking for changes to make. However, as some of the brightest and best thinkers on management have long pointed out, the time to begin planning for new developments is when everything is going well. This is when companies have to start vigorously training their people to learn new skills and methods. Then when the industry changes, the personnel are prepared to change with it. One way in which some astute firms have managed to avoid slumps in their business is by using scenario forecasting to predict what is likely to happen and to start preparing for the upcoming and inevitable changes.

In carrying out scenario forecasts, organisations typically undertake five steps. The first is that the management team will meet and identify a host of external factors that are likely to influence the company's future. Quite often the list entails as many as 100 to 150 factors that are essentially outside of management's control. Next, these factors are clustered into dimensions or groups for the purpose of analysis. Here is an example:

A dimension into which a number of [external environmental] drivers might logically fall would be: Developing Countries' Economic Situations. Within each dimension [managers] push things to extremes to define sharply different conditions. For example, in the case of the developing countries, (they) might well imagine the emergence of a largely industrialised, democratic Third World, the ongoing creation of sweat-shop nations, the increasing improvement of underdeveloped countries leading to ruthless exploitation of natural resources, natural disasters that produce famine, mass migration and political instability, and so on.

When all the dimensions such as in the above example are assembled, the result is a unique set of characteristics comprising a "world." Typically, there will be no more than three or four worlds, and managers will then create four scenarios for each. These scenarios often encompass the best case, worst case, most likely case, and least likely case. Finally, strategy is developed for dealing with each, and early indicators are identified so that the organisation knows if one of the scenarios is coming to fruition and can get a head start on dealing with this new, emerging environment.

Scenario forecasting cannot guarantee that an organisation will not be caught flat footed by changes. But it can help reduce the likelihood of surprises and being unprepared. This is why so many business today are beginning to incorporate scenario forecasting into the planning process.

Questions

1. Why is it difficult to predict the types of organisational changes that need to be implemented?
2. In what way does scenario planning help deal with the problem of predicting needed organisational changes?
3. How can organisations get their personnel to accept and respond to new conditions that are often viewed as threatening to the status quo?

CASE 9 MR KRISHNA RAO'S CONFUSION

Mr Krishna Rao was utterly baffled. He took over the office four months ago and has since initiated several changes, all of which are good. His main intentions in making the changes were that the office should look more professional and employees should be facilitated to become productive without making them work too hard.

The office now indeed looks more spacious with the new layout, and in fact, his colleagues from the other departments who pass by, comment on how nice and professional the office looks. Mr Rao put the secretaries' desks close to their bosses' cabins so that they did not have to walk up and down all the time. Previously, they were huddled together in the secretaries' pool, and whenever they had to take dictation—which was several times a day—they had to walk quite a bit. He also purchased new calculating machines for the department which are quick, efficient, and accurate, so that the assistants now do their calculations without making mistakes. In fact, he had just placed an order for a high-speed computer which would take away the boredom and monotony of all the laborious human calculations and would be a boon to all. Actually, once the computer is installed, the managers will not have to be dependent on the lower level staff. Whatever statistics or information the managers need, the computer will generate that in no time at all. And the computer manufacturer was going to offer free programming sessions for all those who wanted to attend them. Manuals will also be made available to all the staff. It was the best of all possible worlds for the entire department but Mr Rao could not understand why the staff were not enthusiastic and some actually seemed rather unhappy.

Questions

1. Discuss why the changes did not produce the desired results in this situation.
2. Suggest ways to help Mr Rao solve his problems.

CASE 10 INDIA IN DIAGNOSIS

Consider the following information about India: (a) The population is over 550 million and is increasing rapidly. (b) Parents seek to have a large number of children, in part because they see children as being an important way of having some economic security in old age. (c) Several hundred million cattle roam freely, eating much of the crops. The cattle are considered by many to be sacred. (d) Each year many Indians starve to death.

Questions

1. Describe the problems of this case using a multi-level analysis.
2. What are your solutions? Explain the advantages and limitation of your solutions.
3. Why have traditional methods of solving such problems been of limited effectiveness?
4. What changes do you suggest in the Indian social, economic, and political system that will help in solving these problems?

CASE 11 IS IT WORKLOAD OR MOTIVATION?

Rohit was the first repair manager to be hired at Mahajan's Electronics. He was a field repairman for another company before he took his present position. In the past, the repair department had operated without a manager; the repairmen, Nitin and Manav, simply divided the work between themselves in whatever manner they wanted. There was always a backlog of work, but it was finished on time.

When Rohit joined, he decided to divide the work load into repairs for company and individual accounts and to assign certain types of repairs to each man. He had to check all repairs before they were returned to the customer, and he wanted all problems discussed with him before action was taken on them. He started holding meetings with the repairmen to discuss problems the section was facing. At first, meetings were held during working hours, then after work, and finally on Saturdays. During these meetings, the increasing number of problems was discussed, but no solutions were ever offered. In the meantime, the work load kept increasing, and some of the work was not being finished on time. It seemed that Nitin and Manav were spending most of their time getting Rohit's approval on their work so they could have it shipped back to the customer. Rohit then decided that the repair department should start working overtime.

Questions

1. Discuss this case in terms of role efficacy through job enrichment.
2. Is anyone to blame for the increased work load, or could it be just an increase in business?
3. Do you believe that the repairmen should be motivated to increase their productivity because they now have their own manager?
4. Discuss morale in terms of the relationship of satisfaction to productivity.

CASE 12 TRAINING PROGRAMME IN HINDUSTAN

Somnath Mazumder and Javed Khan, both consultants with Malhotra and Company, had just finished teaching an all-day management development session for the Research and Development Division of the Hindustan Engine Company, one of the nation's largest manufacturers of diesel engines. Participating in this particular day's programme were upper- and middle-level managers from the division, as well as Prashad, the division head, and Ed Pinter, the personnel manager.

In the morning, Somnath and Javed had conducted some formal training. In the afternoon, the upper- and middle-level managers were separated into two groups to discuss the implications of practising what they had learned that day and how their relationship with the other group of managers could be improved. By the end of the afternoon, the two groups of managers, together, decided on policy and procedure change for the division.

Somnath, who worked with other consultants on the project, planned the whole change effort. It was designed to respond to a survey of all managers and professionals that Somnath had done months earlier. The survey had identified a number of problems in this division. There was high stress among the managers and professionals due in part to the considerable ambiguity about each individual's major responsibilities and because of a lack of sufficient structure in the organisation. The training programme design involved the development of materials that focused on the causes of the organisation's problems as revealed by the survey. This material was first used in working with the top management group. These managers were asked to determine how they could change the practices and how they could change their own behaviour to solve these problems. A good deal of time was spent on developing the acceptance and commitment to these changes by the top group. Then they worked on developing a new set of relationships with the lower-levels of management. A similar process would occur for each lower management level, until all organisational levels were trained and had worked out its relationship with the next lower level.

Questions

1. Evaluate the effectiveness of the change programme according to the above discussion.
2. Can the training programme be designed to reduce stress and ambiguity identified in the survey?

CASE 13 DOING MY OWN THING

Rita Lowe has worked for the same boss for eleven years. Over coffee one day, her friend, Sara, asked her, "What is it like to work for old Charlie?"

Rita replied, "Oh, I guess it's okay. He pretty much leaves me alone. I more or less do my own thing."

Then Sara said, "Well, you've been at that same job for eleven years. How are you doing in it? Does it look like your will ever be promoted? If you don't mind me saying so, I can't for the life of me see that what you do has anything to do with the operation."

Rita replied, "Well, first of all, I really don't have any idea of how I am doing. Charlie never tells me. But I've always taken the attitude that no news is good news. Charlie mumbled something when I started the job about being important to the operation, but that was it. We really don't communicate very well."

Questions

1. Analyse Rita's last statement: "We really don't communicate very well." What is the status of the manager-subordinate communication in this work relationship?
2. It was said that communication is a dynamic, personal process. Does the situation described verify this contention? Be specific in your answer.
3. How do such communication processes develop the resistance to change in the organisation during the introduction of change?
4. Are there any implications in this situation for upward communication and for interactive communication? How could feedback be used more effectively?

CASE 14 BAD BRAKES

Sukhvinder Singh is the maintenance supervisor of a large taxicab company. He had been very concerned because the cab drivers were not reporting potential mechanical problems. Several months ago, he implemented a preventive maintenance programme. This programme depended upon the driver's filling out the number of occasions a cab left the garage with major problems that the previous driver was aware of but had not reported. Calling out the field repairs teams to fix the breakdowns was not only costing the company much time and trouble but also was very unsafe in some cases and created a high degree of customer ill will. The drivers themselves suffered from a loss of fares and tips, and in some cases their lives were endangered by these mechanical failures. After many oral and written threats and admonishments, Sukhvinder decided to try a new approach. He would respond directly to each report of a potential mechanical problem sent in by a driver with a return memo indicating what the maintenance crew had found wrong with the cab and what had been done to take care of the problem. In addition, the personal memo thanked the driver for reporting the problem and encouraged reporting any further problems with the cabs. In less than a month the number of field repair calls had decreased by half, and the number of turned-in potential problem reports had tripled.

Questions

1. In communication terms, how do you explain the success of Sukhvinder singh's follow-up memos to the drivers?
2. Explain and give examples of the three communication processes in this company (that is, downward, upward, and interactive) and how they are involved in the change process.

CASE 15 RAMA AND HIS CHANGING PLAN

The federal government, to write a new regulation governing the management of maintenance on air bases, retained a group of four private consultants. Rama, a GS-16 in the Civil Service, heard of this effort and telephoned the group inviting them to look at a new maintenance setup that he had installed at an Indiana air base. He said that he had left the base some four weeks earlier, but would fly to Indiana from Louisiana to meet the team. Rama personally escorted the four to the base, and proceeded to outline the procedures involved in setting up a maintenance repair project. After explaining the route sheet, he led them into the next room where an airman was sitting at a desk. Rama gestured towards a huge chart covering two walls in the room. He said, "Now, let's take the project listed on the second line. You see that it begins with its identifying number, followed by the proposed scheduled time for starting it.... Wait a minute! That doesn't make sense! Airman, what's going on with this control board?"

The airman replied, "Oh, Mr. Rama, we stopped using this chart over three weeks ago."

Questions

1. Why did the military personnel stop using the chart immediately after the departure of Rama?
2. What methods of change introduction could Rama have used to insure that the change will continue to be implemented?

CASE 16 THE CASE AGAINST "VISION"

Robert J. Eaton had big shoes to fill. In July 1993, he took the post of chairman at Chrysler Corp. that had previously been held by "Mr. Charisma" Lee Iacocca. Iacocca had taken over the top spot at Chrysler in 1980, when the company was on the verge of bankruptcy. In only a few short years, Iacocca had turned Chrysler into a money-making machine.

Iacocca's style was bold and visionary. He developed several grand strategies for Chrysler. To get the company immediately profitable, he created a basic compact model—the K car—and used its platform to create a host of new cars including the incredibly successful minivan. To fill the need for subcompacts, he began importing cars from Japan and putting Chrysler Corp. nameplates on them.

But that was then and this is now. Robert Eaton has joined an impressive group of chief executives who no longer buy the notion that leaders need to provide grand visions or long-term strategies for their companies. In its place, they are emphasising the short-term bottom line.

"Internally, we don't use the word vision," says Eaton. "I believe in quantifiable short-term results—things we can all relate to—as opposed to some esoteric thing no one can quantify."

The view is also being articulated by CEOs at Apple Computer, IBM, Aetna Life and Casualty, and General Motors. When asked for his recipe for an IBM comeback, the recently appointed Chairman, Louis V. Gerstner, said, "The last thing IBM needs right now is a vision."

It appears that, at least among some leaders, grand visions are out of fashion. They are concentrating on the nuts and bolts of running their businesses.

Questions

1. Is this short-term focus not likely to hurt their companies in the longer term? Will they be the hurdles in the process of change in future?
2. What is the purpose of a grand vision? What takes its place if a company's leader does not provide it?
3. Do organisations not need radical new ideas to win in the marketplace?
4. Eaton says his goal for Chrysler is "getting a little bit better every single day." Is that a viable goal for a real "leader"?

CASE 17 A COMBAT ZONE

Karan Singh has been mid-level manager in the production department for about six months. Just prior to joining Hindustan Manufacturing, Karan retired from the army after serving his last "hitch" as a company commander in a combat zone. Morale in Karan's department has been low since he joined the company. Some of his employees act dissatisfied and aggressive.

At lunch one day Karan asked Mr Mahoney, the head of the finance department, if he knew anything about the low morale in the production department. Mr Mahoney replied that he had heard through the grapevine that Karan's employees were unhappy with him for making all the decisions for the department. Karan was noticeably surprised. "In the army," he said, "I made all of the decisions for my company, and my men expected me to."

Questions

1. What leadership style has Karan Singh been using? What are its characteristics, advantages, and disadvantages?
2. What will the consequences be if Karan cannot change his leadership style?

CASE 18 LOVE IT OR LEAVE IT

After September 11, 2001 (attack on World Trade Centre), the slogan, "America—Love It Or Leave It," has appeared on many automobile bumpers.

Some people have agreed with the slogan, some have strongly disagreed, and others have been indifferent to it. Diagnose the reasons for the different point of views.

Questions

1. How do you explain the different reactions?
2. What communication problems does this slogan cause?
3. How might this slogan be improved?

CASE 19 RAMA SWAMI AND THE RUMOUR

Rama Swami had been with the Balaji Corporation for several years, during which time he had worked his way up from the bottom to a position of foreman. He was proud of what he had accomplished, and he liked his work at Balaji. He had recently bought a house, and his wife and children were delighted with their new neighbours.

In recent months, the Balaji Corporation had lost two good accounts and as a result had been forced to lay off some employees. They had, for the most part, laid off employees with the least seniority, although this was not required. Now, there was a rumour circulating that they were going to lose another account.

As Rama Swami considered the situation, he realised he now had the least seniority of the foremen in his division. Thus, he concluded that the company was losing more business and owing to his lack of seniority, he was going to be laid off. As a result of this conclusion, Rama Swami became extremely despondent. His interest in his job deteriorated and he began to have a hard time getting along with his co-workers.

Actually, the rumour circulating in the company was incorrect. Instead of losing business, the Balaji Corporation was anticipating some new accounts. Further, management was very pleased with Rama Swami as an employee and had no intention of letting him go.

Questions

1. In what ways, if any, has poor communication caused this problem?
2. How might this situation be improved?
3. What is the basis for Rama Swami's anxiety?

CASE 20 SEEING THE FOREST AND THE TREES

The changing face of competition, both domestic and global, was looking directly into the window of the headquarters of the Forest Products Company (FPC) of the Wood India Corporation, Mumbai. It was a face that reflected the trend away from the large-firm, commodity lumber business and towards the small mills that tailor-made products to meet the demands of their customers. Interestingly, these small mills owed their existence, in large part to the sale of machinery by the larger firms when they were faced with the depressed housing market in the early 1980s. As a consequence of being able to buy this machinery at depressed prices, these small, non-union, owner-operated, entrepreneurial, customer-oriented mills were able to not only be the most market-oriented but also the lowest cost operations.

Deciding that going out of business was not an alternative, Sujeet Kumar, the CEO of FPC, suggested that something needed to be done, preferably sooner than later. Together, the top dozen managers decided that a massive reorganisation was called for, accompanied by a radical change in strategy. According to Sujeet Kumar, the change in strategy went something like this:

Approximately 80 percent of our sales in 1982 represented products sold on commodities. By 1995 we resolved that we must reverse the proportions.

The massive reorganisation mirrored that being done by the headquarters. The headquarters decided to decentralise dramatically. The three operating units, of which FPC was one, were given free reign on how to do their business. Given this scenario, Sujeet Kumar and his top team decided they needed to create an organisation capable of acting and responding just like their competitors. Thus, they created 50 profit centres with each centre being largely responsible for its own bottom line.

This restructuring soon proved to be only a step in the right direction. The ability of the organisation to implement its new strategy was being undermined by the pervasive poor morale. In addition, many middle managers, those that needed to actually carry out the change, were pessimistic about the possibility of sustained future success. Silently, they even questioned their own ability to operate the profit centres.

With insights from Shrikant, director of executive development at FPC, the rest of the top team came to realise that there would have to be a total transformation of the organisation: the corporate culture, knowledge base, skill levels, style of leadership, and team orientation would all have to change, for all employees. With 6,000 employees across India, Shrikant was not sure where to start. The others said they would help, but Horace had to tell them what to do. Shrikant, of course, is waiting to hear what you have to tell him.

Questions

1. What are the business objectives that Shrikant must use here to focus his activities?
2. What are his new management and executive development objectives?
3. How should he go about addressing the implications of these objectives for management and executive development?
4. In addition to management and executive development, what other organisational changes are needed to support this transformation?

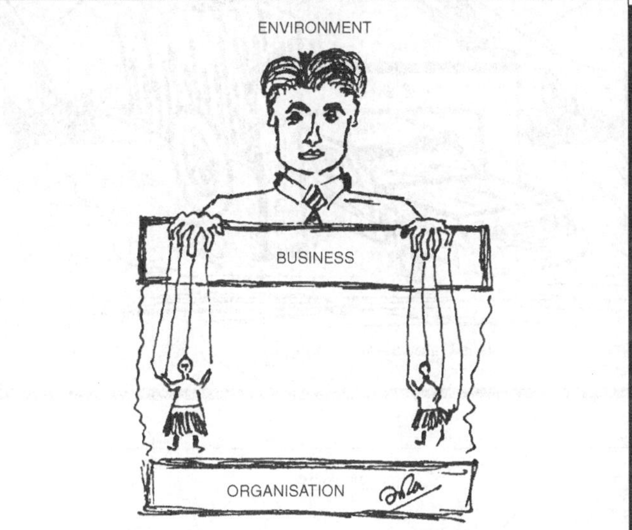

Ladies and Gentlemen! "This puppet show (business) is directed by Mr. Environment."

I know I get rotten advice all the time, but I cannot sack my advisers! They are my aunt, son-in-law, cousin, nephew...!

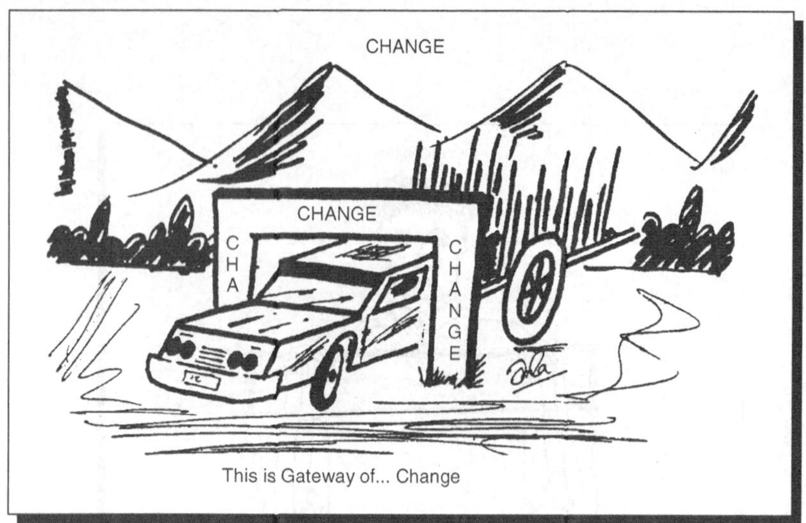
CHANGE
CHANGE
CHA
CHANGE
This is Gateway of... Change

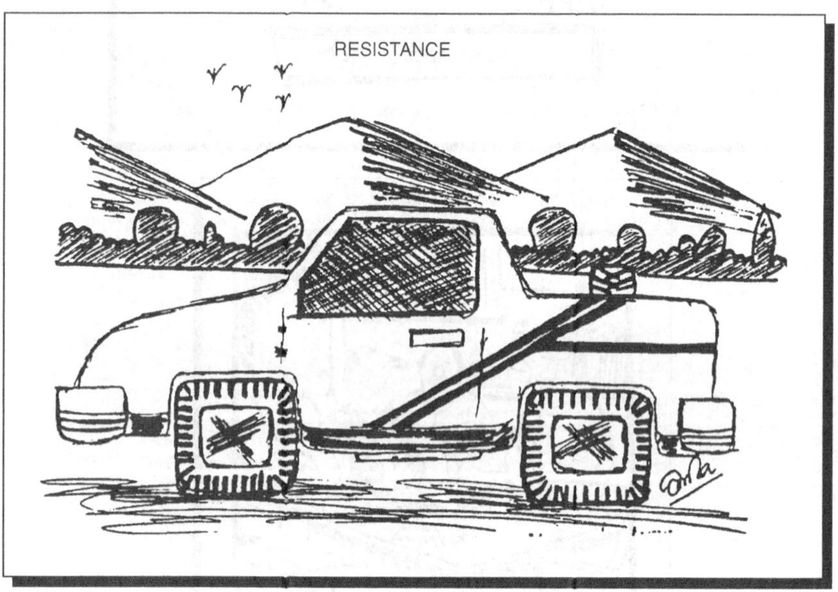
RESISTANCE

CONSULTANT

My new consultant is extremely good, no doubt. But I don't like everyone coming to visit me going straight to him.

STRATEGY

Further up. Up, a little to the right and up-that's it!-And now let us set out to achieve it!

My, my, what has happened? Your career line was clear and straight only yesterday! Today it looks thin and wobbly?

I got it done, Sir. The idea, I understand, is to give a cheerful new look to the whole place!

Manager managing the organisational traffic

What is similar between a Python and Learning Organisation?
Both of them are flexible.

MODAL

True, gentalmen, the model has become popular-what about the soap?

CASE STUDY

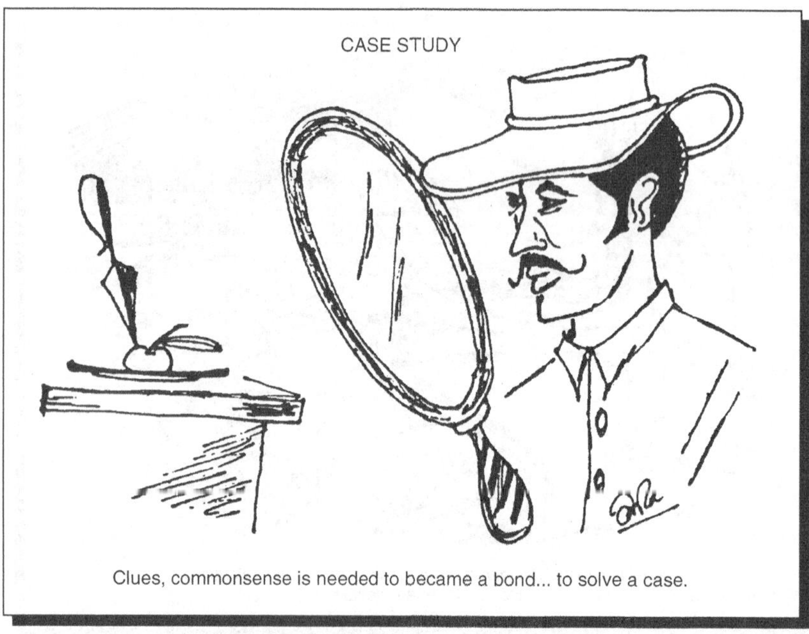

Clues, commonsense is needed to became a bond... to solve a case.

REFERENCES AND SELECTED BIBLIOGRAPHY

1. Likert, Rensis (1961). *New Patterns Of Management*. New York: Mc Graw Hill, pp. 102–103.
2. Harrison, Frank (1974). "The Management of Scientist: Determinants of Perceived Role Performance", *Academy of Management Journal*, June, pp. 234–241.
3. The Davis Keith, (1986). "Human Relations, Industrial Humanism, and Organizational Behaviour", presentation to the Southern Division of the Academy of Management, November 13.
4. Ford, Robert C. and Frank McLaughlin (1995). "Questions and Answers about Telecommuting Programs", *Business Horizons*, May-June, pp. 66–71.
5. Edward C. Baig (1995). "Welcome to the Wireless Office", *Business Week*, June 26, pp. 104–106.
6. Davenport, Thomas H. and Keri Pearson (1998). "Two Cheers for the Virtual Office", *Sloan Management Review, Summer*, pp. 51–65; Michael Adams (1995). "Remote Control", *Performance*, 1995, pp. 44–48; and David Stamps (1994). "The Virtual Office", *Training*, February, pp. 17–18.
7. Davis, Keith (1953). "Management Communication and the Grapevine", *Harvard Business Review*, September–October, p. 44.
8. Newstrom, John W., Robert M. Monczka, and William E. Reif (1974). "Perceptions of the Grapevine: Its Value and Influence", *Journal of Business Communication*, Spring, pp. 12–20.
9. Wilson, Meena (1995). "The Intercultural Values Questionnaire", *Issues and Observations*, Center for Creative Leadership, vol. 15, no. 1, pp. 10–11.
10. Kahn, Robert L. et al. (1964). *Organisational Stress: Studies in Role Conflict and Ambiguity*. New York: John Wiley & Sons, pp. 56, 99–124.
11. Schein, Edgar H. (1999). *The Corporate Culture Survival Guide: Sense and Nonsense about Cultural Change*, San Francisco: Jossey- Bass.
12. Daniel Denison, (1996). "What is the difference between organizational culture and organizational climate? A Native's Point of View on a Decade of Paradigm Wars", *Academy of Management Review*, July, pp. 619–654.

INDEX